D1593631

Huichol Mythology

Huichol Mythology

by Robert M. Zingg

edited by Jay C. Fikes, Phil C. Weigand,
and Acelia García de Weigand

The University of Arizona Press   *Tucson*

The University of Arizona Press
© 2004 The Arizona Board of Regents
Originally published in Spanish as *La mitología de los Huicholes*
(El Colegio de Michoacán, Zamora, Michoacán; El Colegio de Jalisco,
Guadalajara, Jalisco, 1998; Secretaría de Cultura de Jalisco)
First English-Language Printing 2004

♾ This book is printed on acid-free, archival-quality paper.
Manufactured in the United States of America

09   08   07   06   05   04   6   5   4   3   2   1

Library of Congress Cataloging-in-Publication Data
Zingg, Robert M. (Robert Mowry), 1900–1957.
[Mitología de los huicholes. English]
Huichol mythology / by Robert M. Zingg ; edited by Jay C. Fikes,
Phil C. Weigand, and Acelia García de Weigand.
p. cm.
"Originally published in Spanish as La mitología de los
Huicholes"—Verso t.p.
Includes bibliographical references.
ISBN 0-8165-2317-7 (cloth : alk. paper)
1. Huichol mythology—Mexico—Tuxpan de Bolaños. 2. Huichol
Indians—Mexico—Tuxpan de Bolaños—Portraits. 3. Huichol
Indians—Mexico—Tuxpan de Bolaños—Rites and ceremonies.
4. Legends—Mexico—Tuxpan de Bolaños. 5. Tuxpan de Bolaños
(Mexico)—Social life and customs. I. Fikes, Jay C. (Jay Courtney),
1951– II. Weigand, Phil C. III. García de Weigand, Celia, 1933–
IV. Title.
F1221.H9Z48 2004
299.7′84544013—dc22
2004002746

Publication of this book is made possible in part by the proceeds
of a permanent endowment created with the assistance of a Challenge
Grant from the National Endowment for the Humanities, a federal
agency.

Contents

Editor's Preface

Robert Zingg's orthography, the correspondence between sounds and letters that represent them, will undoubtedly be revised by linguistically oriented researchers in Tuxpan. I am not fluent enough in Tuxpan's dialect of Huichol to feel comfortable correcting Zingg. I can say that Zingg's use of a barred l (e.g., in Tewiali) probably indicates that he heard it as a soft r sound. I usually heard a soft r in such words pronounced in Santa Catarina (but spelled it as if it were an ordinary sounding r).

Robert Zingg used lowercase letters for all Huichol ancestors (who are alternatively called gods or deities). To make his corpus of Huichol myths consistent with other publications about Huichol religion, we capitalized the names of all ancestors (gods or deities). Except for capitalizing Huichol ancestors' names, Zingg's transcriptions of Huichol words were not corrected.

Other minor editorial changes included renumbering footnotes and making the chapter titles and all subtitles consistent with University of Arizona Press style. In his manuscript Zingg had placed footnotes at the bottom of each page, starting the numbering sequence again on each page where a footnote appeared. We put all footnotes for each myth (or chapter) together at the end of the book. This was done to make the book more readable, uncluttering the text for nonspecialist readers while retaining the footnotes for Huichol specialists. Zingg underlined all foreign words and proper names. We did not underline proper names. Foreign words were only underlined the first time they were mentioned in each chapter.

Robert Zingg consistently misspelled certain words. To improve readability we silently corrected such errors (e.g., anoint, baptize, center, and spittle).

Any other variation from Zingg's original manuscript was placed inside square brackets. Such editor's corrections, comments, or additions were made only when I had complete confidence that a correction was accurate or an addition justified (e.g., deer horns [antlers]).

Jay C. Fikes

Acknowledgments

We are grateful to Robert M. Zingg's widow, Emma K. Zingg, and her lawyers for their cooperation in selling us the publication rights to Robert Zingg's *Huichol Mythology*. Her interviews with Jay Fikes clarified many misunderstood aspects of her husband's life, including the fact that he died as the result of a massive heart attack. We also appreciate the efforts of Robert Zingg's son, Robert Zingg Jr., who provided Fikes with many interesting insights into his father's life as well as two photographs of his father that appear in this book.

A Spanish edition of Zingg's *Huichol Mythology* was published in 1998 by the Colegio de Michoacán. That publication included 204 original photographs from Zingg's research in Tuxpan and was co-sponsored by the Colegio de Jalisco and the Secretaría de Cultura del Estado de Jalisco. We are grateful to the Colegio de Michoacán for their collaboration in presenting Zingg's *Huichol Mythology* for the first time in English.

We want to acknowledge Professor J. Charles Kelley for locating Zingg's enormous Huichol photo collection and then entrusting it to the Amerind Foundation for safekeeping. We appreciate the confidence Charles DiPeso, Director of the Amerind Foundation, placed in the Weigands by giving them all of Zingg's photos, which are now preserved as a research collection at the Colegio de Michoacán.

Mark Hoffman, editor of the journal *Entheos*, did the difficult job of preparing the manuscript for publication with great dedication and enthusiasm. We are much obliged to him for all his fine work.

We are especially pleased with the work done by Dr. Christine Szuter and Dr. Yvonne Reineke at the University of Arizona Press. Nancy Arora's meticulous editing of this book was inspirational. We are grateful to the manuscript reviewers, all of whom recognized the extraordinary value of Zingg's landmark study of Huichol mythology.

We remain indebted to the Huichol people, especially those living in Tuxpan, for their willingness to share their homes, their culture, and their memories of Robert Zingg. Last and most important, we dedicate this book to the memories of Juan Real and Robert Zingg, whose collaboration in preserving these myths should finally bring them the recognition they have always deserved.

Introduction

This book is the most authentic and comprehensive work on Huichol my-thology ever published. We have little firsthand experience recording myths and observing rituals specific to Tuxpan, the Huichol community where in 1934 Robert Zingg transcribed the myths we have edited for this volume. Our Huichol research has focused on Santa Catarina (Fikes) and San Sebastián (the Weigands). For this reason, and because no other anthropologist has matched the volume of myths collected by Zingg from a single Huichol informant, we believe that it is premature to attempt an extensive analysis of his collection of myths. Accordingly, in this introduction we will summarize Huichol ethno-history, a topic we feel well qualified to address and one that has been relatively neglected in most recent studies on the Huichol. This introduction is intended to give nonspecialist readers the historical and cultural background necessary to appreciate the richness of Huichol culture and to enable future researchers in Tuxpan to assess more precisely the value of Zingg's monumental work on mythology.

In 2000, from ten to fifteen thousand Huichol Indians inhabited some 4,107 square kilometers of rugged mountain and canyon country, largely drained by the Chapalagana River, located in the Mexican states of Jalisco and Nayarit. The Huichol settlement of Tuxpan de Bolaños, where Robert Zingg collected the myths presented here, is about two hundred kilometers north of Guada-lajara. Five distinct micro-environments described by Weigand (1972, 1992a) have provided Huichols with a variety of plants, animals, and land for growing crops. Traditionally, the Huichol system of slash-and-burn horticulture sup-plied maize, beans, and squash. These and other crops (e.g., amaranth, chile, *jitomate*) were supplemented by deer and rabbit hunting, fishing, small-scale cattle herding, and gathering of wild plants such as prickly pear cactus, maguey, and mesquite.

Contemporary Huichols have a division of labor based on gender and age. They reside in a dispersed settlement pattern wherein bilateral lineages cluster around ceremonial centers and villages (ranchos). Although Huichols have a system of bilateral kinship and inheritance, they prefer to select firstborn sons of the first wife as rancho leaders.

Carl Lumholtz, the first explorer to write books about the Chapalagana Hui-chol, discovered nineteen or twenty Huichol temples, the central structure in ceremonial centers called *tukipa* (Lumholtz 1900: 9–10, [1902] 1973: 27). Most ranchos and ceremonial centers are concentrated in a habitation zone about fifteen hundred meters above sea level (Fikes 1985; Weigand 1972, 1992a). In

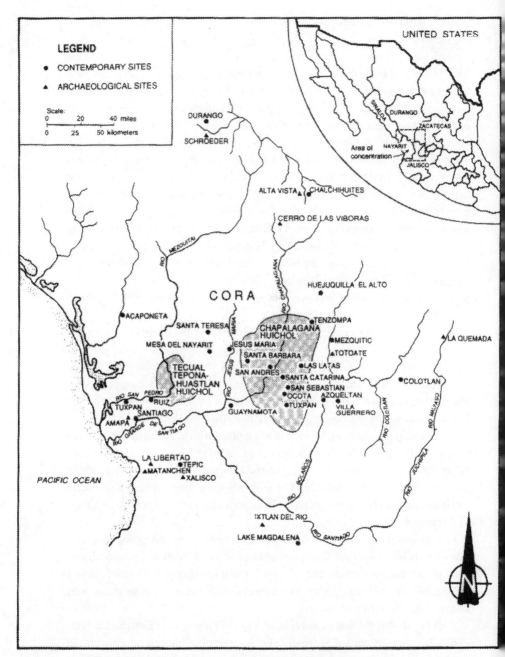

Contemporary Chapalagana Huichol territory in Nayarit and Jalisco showing Mexican centers, drainages, and major archaeological sites (adapted from Weigand 1969a: 2).

actively functioning ceremonial centers, about twenty-six Huichol temple officers are recruited from numerous ranchos surrounding the closest ceremonial center.[1] They are expected to perform an annual ritual cycle for five consecutive years before selecting their replacements (Fikes 1985, 1993a, 1993b). The annual cycle of temple rituals is performed to honor and feed deified ancestors whose aid is essential to Huichol subsistence. The famous peyote hunt is one of several subsistence-oriented rituals held at Huichol ceremonial centers.

Huichols believe that the fundamental structure of the environment they inhabit was originally established by deified ancestors such as Great Grandmother Germination, Grandfather Fire, Father Sun, and Kaoyomari, their tutelary spirit and world organizer. Their ancestors generally personify natural phenomena and are, in effect, embodied by Huichol temple officers. Each officer represents and serves a specific ancestor. During their five years of service, these officers call each other by the names of the ancestors they represent. At Santa Catarina, nine out of twenty-six temple officers serve Rain Mothers, a clue suggesting how crucial rain symbolism and ritual are to Huichol agriculture (Fikes 1985).

Performing temple rituals maintains and pleases these ancestors, who control the ecological order that sustains Huichol survival. Huichol temple officers must collect peyote, bring back sacred water from shrines of various Rain Mothers, fish, hunt deer, provide cattle to be sacrificed, and give away food to Huichols attending the rituals they are entrusted with performing. By replicating in ritual the world-organizing precedents their ancestors set, temple officers dispose them to protect human health and provide abundant subsistence for all Huichols. Fikes's research in the late 1970s at Santa Catarina demonstrated that the Huichol annual ritual cycle once encompassed deer and rabbit hunting, fishing, and maize agriculture (Fikes 1985). The aboriginal temple ritual cycle at Tuxpan de Bolaños was being revived when Zingg studied it in 1934.

Evidence reviewed by Weigand (1978, 1985), Weigand and Foster (1985), and Fikes (1985) suggests that Huichol culture, with its distinctive circular temples maintained by ranchos widely dispersed around them, has existed in the Chapalagana River basin of the Sierra Madre Occidental since about 200 A.D. Huichol circular temples are about twelve meters in diameter (Fikes 1985: 71) and are ultimately derived from circular temples belonging to the "Teuchitlán Tradition, which focused upon the highland lakes of western Jalisco in the Volcán de Tequila region" (Weigand 1985: 156, 1993).

The Huichol language belongs to the Uto-Aztecan family and most closely resembles the language spoken by their western neighbors, the Coras of Nayarit. The Cora and Huichol languages are relatively distant from Nahuatl (Aztec), belonging to a western branch of Uto-Aztecan, which includes Totorame and

Tecual. Valiñas has demonstrated that these languages should be classified within the Sonorese branch of southern Uto-Aztecan (1994). Similarities in social organization and religion between Cora and Huichol are profound and pervasive (Fikes 1985: 85–87). The antecedents to the Cora and Huichol cultures were involved in a vast system of regional trade and common ceremony well before Spanish conquest (Weigand 1992a; Weigand and Weigand 2000). Until Spaniards disrupted it, the Huichol ritual cycle regulated trade of sacred items such as peyote, conch shells, feathers, and perhaps silver (Fikes 1998; Weigand 1985: 142) with Coras to the west and with Tepecano Indians, who formerly lived east of the Huichol.

In addition to regulating subsistence activities and trade of sacred items, the temple ritual cycle was an institution providing an opportunity for education and prestige. Among conservative Huichols, such as those singers studied by Fikes (1985), the quality and quantity of community service an individual provided was a mark of prestige. To qualify as a healer, five years of service, that is, serving one term as an aboriginal temple officer, is required. To qualify as a singer, or ritual leader, ten years (two terms as a temple officer) is required. Elders whose expertise in ritual is highly valued are called *kawitéros*.

Spaniards eventually recognized that Coras, Huichols, and Tepecanos were all followers of the Cora ancestor whose oracle or mummy was venerated at the Mesa del Nayarit. Spaniards called all Indians who paid allegiance to this Cora oracle "Nayaritas." They were military allies and trading partners in an east to west exchange system predating Spanish conquest (Fikes 1998; Weigand and Weigand 1996a, 2000).

Until Spaniards conquered the Cora capital located on the Mesa del Nayarit in 1722, Coras and Huichols actively consulted mummified ancestors at the shrine there. Nayarita independence ended in 1722, but Huichols residing in the *comunidades indígenas* (administrative units created by colonial Spaniards to control Huichols) of Santa Catarina Cuexcomatitlán, San Andrés Cohamiata, and San Sebastián Teponahuaxtlán had already been partially assimilated. By 1650, almost all Huichols had been brought under colonial control (Rojas 1993: 71; Weigand 1985, 1992a). By 1750, Huichols had completely assimilated the Spanish political system (of *gobernancias*) and religious system (of *mayordomos*).

Seeking Silver, Pacifying Pagans

Few scholars realize how drastically silver mining in Mexico and throughout the Americas altered the course of world history. A brief summary of that crucial chapter in world history, based on the data presented by Philip Powell (1975, 1977) and Jack Weatherford (1988), will enable readers to appreciate the objectives and strategy by which Huichols were incorporated into the Spanish colonial world. As we shall see, the traumatic effect silver mining had on the Huichols is vividly illustrated by the Christian myths that Robert Zingg transcribed from his Tuxpan Huichol informant, Juan Real.

By 1546, when the La Bufa silver mine opened in Zacatecas, the amount of silver and gold circulating in Europe had increased by about 300 percent from what it had been when the Americas were "discovered." By 1600, the supply had increased another 500 percent as mines all over Mexico began yielding silver. More than any other precious metal, it was silver that superseded land as the basis for wealth, power, and prestige in Europe. The inflationary effect exerted by all this new silver soon spread far beyond Europe. By 1584, the *akce* silver coin, whose circulation sustained the vast Ottoman Empire, had lost 50 percent of its value. It never regained its former value. Silver extracted from the Americas probably did more than anything else to undermine Islamic power for the next five hundred years. The enormous volume of silver flowing from the Americas paved the way for a world economy in which Asia was soon involved. The slave trade boomed in Africa, thereby supplying laborers to mine precious metals in the Americas. The natives of the Americas, whose silver had helped launch the greatest economic transformation in world history, were forced to labor in mines controlled by colonists. These Native Americans were also stripped of their lands whenever silver deposits were discovered on them (Weatherford 1988: 14–18).

As the richly endowed La Bufa mine at Zacatecas began producing quantities of silver in about 1550, it became imperative to guard the convoys carrying silver from Zacatecas from Indian raiders (Powell 1975; Rojas 1993: 46–47). To make the colonial world safe for shipping silver back to Spain, presidios and colonial towns such as Jerez, Fresnillo, and Aguascalientes were quickly established. Between 1550 and 1590, Spanish colonists in north central Mexico were occupied with the Chichimec War. This conflict included the Tepecano Indians, who were then living just east of the aboriginal Huichol homeland. The Chichimec War imperiled the shipment of silver from Zacatecas and obstructed new mining. Although the mine at Tepec (north of the town of Bolaños) was discovered in 1550, it was not exploited until after the Tepecanos residing nearby were subdued. Bolaños and the nearby Tepec mines came under colonial control after 1590 with the formation of a special new jurisdiction whose administrative center was Colotlán (Weigand 1985: 158–60; Rojas 1993: 29).

Colotlán was founded in 1591 to administer activities necessary for pacifying and colonizing Tepecanos, Huichols, and, eventually, Coras. The vast new jurisdiction headquartered at Colotlán was independent of Nueva Galicia, and its governor was appointed directly by the Viceroy (Rojas 1992: 14). To aid the Spaniards in colonizing aboriginal peoples in the district of Colotlán, Tlaxcaltecan families were imported from central Mexico. Natives residing within Colotlán's purview were exempted from payment of tribute and granted the right of owning three times more land than was permitted for natives in central Mexico. In return, they were obligated to provide military service in proportion to their populations (Rojas 1992: 14; Velázquez 1961). Such a lenient policy toward indigenous inhabitants of Colotlán indicates that the colonists' primary goal was accumulating wealth. To achieve that purpose it would be sufficient to pacify the natives.

The Spanish Crown was entitled to one fifth of all bullion extracted from every mine it licensed. The Crown insured that its mines in Mexico remained productive by preventing true ownership of them, by a decree specifying that whenever a particular mine was not worked "at least four months a year by at least four workers," another person could "denounce the mine and register it in his own name" (Sheridan and Naylor 1979: 86, 100). To provide mine "owners" (and owners of ranches and haciendas) with dependent workers, the Spanish Crown mandated various laws in 1614. The purpose of those regulations was to protect native populations from despoilment while permitting operation of the *repartimiento* (forced labor) system. One of the "laws of the Indies" stipulated that no more than 4 percent of Indians could be taken for forced labor, but it was seldom enforced because doing so might have interfered with ambitious colonists attempting to amass their fortunes (Sheridan and Naylor 1979: 82, 87, 89–90).

Unless further archival research discloses that the repartimiento system was applied to Colotlán's aboriginal inhabitants, we may conclude that they were shielded from this coercive institution endemic to New Spain. Because such protection was rarely extended to native Mexicans, the Cora and Huichol frontier became more attractive as a region of refuge. Weigand concluded (1985: 147) that the Huichol homeland first became a region of refuge immediately after the Mixton War of 1541–1542, if not before. Its appeal to native Mexicans seeking relief from violence or oppression was increased by Colotlán's relative leniency toward indigenous people.

Within the district of Colotlán, silver mining and missionization were integrally connected. After 1580, Franciscans began working to convert natives living near Tepec. In 1591 Franciscan missionaries established a mission at Chimaltitán, a Tepecano village near Bolaños (Rojas 1993: 29, 60–61), placed just south of Tepec, where natives could be converted and prepared for entry into the colonial economy. By 1605, the natives of Tepec were working in nearby mines and even going as far as Valparaiso (Rojas 1993: 58–59). Similarly, the Franciscan convent completed in 1620 at Amatlán de Jora supported workers at a silver mine located about fifteen miles to the south (Rojas 1993: 62).

By 1700, mines at Bolaños were becoming a Mecca for fortune seekers. Those seeking silver were joined by those whose livelihood was gained by serving the miners. As a result, the colonial population of Bolaños and Colotlán started increasing dramatically (Rojas 1992: 16). It is probably no coincidence that the most notable Huichol-Tepecano uprising erupted in 1702, when Indians throughout the district of Colotlán began stealing cattle. They asserted that their thievery was necessary because they were left without sufficient food after several Spanish families stole their lands. Some 1,500 warriors, including Huichols recruited from numerous villages, entered Colotlán and killed Captain Mateo de Silva, evidently because he had failed to protect their lands.

Their assassination of Captain de Silva was quickly forgiven once they reaffirmed their loyalty to the Spanish crown and promised to return all cattle stolen from colonists of Colotlán. The rebels seem to have been easily reabsorbed into Colotlán's colonial orbit. Documents written after the rebellion subsided reveal that some livestock stolen by Huichols was returned. After the rebellion, a judge from Guadalajara was sent to inspect title to lands in that section of the frontier in order to prevent future conflicts (Rojas 1992: 43–49). Little is known about the measurements made or conclusions reached by that Guadalajara judge, Don Juan de Somosa (Rojas 1993: 92–93).

The 1702 rebellion was intended to reassert native ownership of lands whose title should already have been recognized by the Spanish Crown. Several letters written in 1702 or shortly thereafter (Rojas 1992: 50–60) indicate that Huichols regarded themselves as loyal and faithful vassals of the King of Spain. They also prove that Huichols had already accepted Spanish colonial offices, including governor, *alcalde* (mayor), *alguacil* (sheriff), and Capitán de Guerra (War Captain). These political positions have retained their original functions until recently (Weigand 1978: 101–15).[2]

Conquering Coras

Colotlán's indigenous inhabitants felt their 1702 rebellion was justified because colonial officials charged with defending Indian land had failed to do their duty.[3] Colotlán's colonial leaders overlooked the fact that rapid and substantial immigration into their district was a catalyst contributing to the rebellion.

Spaniards seemed concerned only that migration into Colotlán was becoming attractive to non-Spaniards living in districts other than Colotlán. They were alarmed because Colotlán was becoming a region of refuge for mulattos, ex-slaves, and Indians fleeing from other jurisdictions wherein they were obliged to pay tribute. Accordingly, in 1705, the Captain General of Colotlán ordered all Indian officials within his jurisdiction to deport any strangers entering their communities. He also asked them to prevent any Indians from changing their place of residence (Rojas 1993: 93). Colotlán officials probably suspected that refugees entering their district were likely to become allies of the unconquered Cora, or of Colotlán's renegades. Their tougher posture against immigrants to the district of Colotlán may also be linked to the discovery of veins of silver some Indians from Chimaltitán had just made. They knew that insuring the safe transport of silver from the mine near Chimaltitán (opened in 1709) would make it imperative to pacify the Coras.

The King of Spain wanted the Coras to be brought under missionary control as early as 1686, when he proposed that Coras be exempted from paying tribute for twenty years and be freed from having to do obligatory work in mines and haciendas, if only they would submit to Spanish control (Rojas 1993: 72). After the 1702 rebellion and the silver strike at Chimaltitán, a priest was appointed to tranquilize the indomitable Coras by converting them to Catholicism (Velázquez 1961: 9). That particular Franciscan priest, Antonio Margil de Jesus, had worked for thirty years as a missionary. In 1711 he attempted, with the aid of two Huichol interpreters, to convert the Coras (Rojas 1993: 94–95). Only his two Huichol interpreters were allowed to meet with the Cora leaders. They were told by the Cora leaders that they could not accept Christ because their chief, whose mummified cadaver they revered, had not authorized it (Rojas 1992: 62). After Margil failed, several other efforts to subdue the Coras by peaceful means met with disappointment; the Spaniards soon realized that they would be conquered only by force (Rojas 1993: 97).

What little evidence there is suggests that some Huichols remained faithful allies of the Coras, even while Coras were under attack by Spaniards in 1721. Other Huichols sided with the Spaniards against the Coras (Rojas 1992: 61–71, 100; 1993: 99).

Rojas (1993: 72) implies that most authorities at Colotlán expected to receive minimal aid from the Huichol and Tepecano in conquering the Coras because if the Coras were conquered, their former allies would lose the privileges they had been enjoying. Ten years after the Coras lost their independence, the Colotlán colonists tightened their control over Huichols and the Franciscans established a convent to begin missionary work in San Sebastián Teponahuastlán.

Evangelizing Indians

San Sebastián became a Catholic *doctrina* (mission) in 1733 under the authority of the bishop of Guadalajara. *Visitas* were soon established at San Andrés and Santa Catarina (Rojas 1992: 127–29). Franciscans baptized and married some Huichols, but most aboriginal Huichol rituals were still performed. Veneration of distinguished ancestors, whose cadavers were elegantly dressed and protected in shrines, horrified Franciscans. Despite the destruction of these cadavers by the Franciscans (Rojas 1992: 73–75), Huichol adoration of them continued covertly (Diguet 1992: 112) and continues today (at least in San Sebastián).

After Jesuit priests were officially expelled from Cora Indian territory in August of 1767, Franciscans tried to take over their work (Hers 1977: 19). Replacing the Jesuit missionaries diluted the Franciscan efforts to evangelize the Huichols, which had been ineffective at best anyway. In 1783 the Magistrate of Bolaños declared that Huichols still did not comprehend Catholic sacraments and ceremonies, did not attend mass, nor marry under the auspices of the church. Even worse, they still practiced aboriginal rituals (Velázquez 1961: 34). By 1798, only a dozen Franciscan missionaries were active among both Coras and Huichols (Franz 1977: 17).

In 1811, the doctrina at San Sebastián had to be abandoned because of the chaos caused by Mexico's fight for independence from Spain. Thirty years passed before Franciscans resumed evangelization (Rojas 1993: 129). When they returned, after having finished a century of missionary work among Huichols, it was obvious that they had failed to persuade the Huichols to abandon their ancestral ways (although the system of gobernancias and mayordomos had been accepted). In 1839 Friar Buenaventura was appalled to witness the Huichol of San Andrés Cohamiata worshiping idols and invoking Christ and Catholic saints to bless their cattle. He lamented that they could not make the sign of the cross, never confessed their sins, and did not know how to recite prayers. He refused to celebrate mass in their church because he thought it was desecrated. He had destroyed so many "idols" he feared that some Huichols wanted to kill him (Rojas 1992: 124–25).

Buenaventura was one of many Franciscans doing his utmost to compensate for those thirty years in which Huichols were free. From 1843 to 1861, aboriginal Huichol temples and shrines were destroyed, a band of homeless Huichols was congregated at Guadalupe Ocotán under the supervision of a priest who directed them to build a new church there, and another was built over the ruins of the church at Santa Catarina (Rojas 1992: 139–85). Despite all this, priests complained that they were losing the battle to save Huichol souls, primarily because Huichols were too occupied with subsistence activities, and the non-Christian ceremonies connected with them, to pay attention to Catholic teachings. To remedy this problem, they proposed that the government compel Huichol parents to send their children to mission boarding schools that would feed those children and equip them with a religious education (Rojas 1992: 167), a system that, in modified form, continues today with the INI (Instituto Nacional Indigenista, Mexico's equivalent to the Bureau of Indian Affairs).

Missionary efforts to evangelize Huichols were halted again after legal reforms enacted in the Benito Juárez administration closed all convents and missions in Mexico (Weigand 1979: 168). Such federal reform laws curbing the power of the Catholic church were not extended to the Huichol until several years later; it was not until 1861 that the last Franciscan left San Sebastián (Rojas 1993: 142). The Franciscan missions soon came under the control of a secular clergy led by Father Marentes. In 1869 Marentes wrote a letter to the chief administrator at Colotlán requesting his permission to outlaw aboriginal temple rituals and destroy the ceremonial centers at which Huichols performed what he regarded as perverse rituals (Rojas 1992: 186).

Missionization in San Sebastián continued to be hampered by the Huichol commitment to performing aboriginal ceremonies that sanctified and sustained their subsistence practices. Their participation in the rebellion led by Manuel Lozada (1854–1873) distracted their attention from Franciscan teaching. By about 1914, Huichol participation in the Mexican Revolution had crested and Franciscans were evicted from San Sebastián (Weigand 1979: 169).

When Zingg arrived in 1934, the Huichols of Tuxpan had scarcely returned from twenty years of exile in Bolaños. The Christian influences Zingg observed at Tuxpan (in ceremonies such as the Cambio de las Varas, Carnival, and Semana Santa, and in the Christian myths he recorded) prove that Huichols had made their intellectual adaptation to colonial life some two hundred years before his arrival.

Franciscans were unable to implement the policy of *reducción*, which had proven so effective in evangelizing natives elsewhere (Spicer 1962: 463–64, 570–71). Efforts to eradicate Huichol religion and replace it with Catholicism failed primarily because Huichols were never removed from their ranchos and concentrated in compact towns where priests could have them under continual scrutiny. Despite Franciscan pressure, older Huichol subsistence and settlement patterns persisted. For centuries Huichol life had depended on ranchos being dispersed throughout the rugged mountain and canyon country drained by the Chapalagana River. Given the limitations of the environment, dispersed ranchos were the only practical way to exploit natural resources.

The dispersal of Huichol ranchos had sustained their adaptation to a rudimentary form of maize cultivation (whose output depended mostly on slash-and-burn strategies), which was restricted by the scarcity of level, arable land. Even after Huichols were incorporated into the colonial economy, their subsistence pursuits continued to be supported by cooperative labor groups organized largely by extended families residing in ranchos (Weigand 1972, 1992a). Priests were never able to concentrate large numbers of Huichols in new mission communities because they could not substitute new sources of subsistence for the aboriginal Huichol strategy that combined hunting, fishing, maize cultivation, and the collection of wild plants. Aboriginal ceremonies remained of vital concern because Huichol settlement patterns and subsistence practices were altered only slightly rather than completely replaced. Accordingly, at both ceremonial centers and ranchos, Huichol religion flourished despite the best efforts of Franciscans. Huichols simply integrated Catholic creed and customs into their aboriginal myths and annual ritual cycle.

Exiled from Ostoc, Vindicated at Tuxpan

Citing Peter Gerhard, Rojas (1992: 12) concludes that the southern boundary of aboriginal Huichol territory contained all lands between Huajimic and Amatlán de Jora. Colonial documents of de Barrios and Arias y Saavedra analyzed by the Weigands (1996a, 2000) support this contention. Ostoc was one of several Huichol settlements located within that southern Huichol region. Until 1790, Ostoc was the home of those Huichols who were studied by Robert Zingg at Tuxpan in 1934.[4]

Communication between Spaniards and Ostoc Huichols commenced by 1624. The doctrina of Camotlán, which included Ostoc as a visita (place sometimes visited by priests), was founded in 1624 (Velázquez 1961: 12). Ostoc may have had some contact with Spaniards even earlier inasmuch as missions and convents were established nearby at Huajimic in 1610 and at Amatlán de Jora in 1620 (Rojas 1992: 13). During the early years of Spanish colonial rule, Huichols at Ostoc, like other natives within Colotlán's purview, were exempted from payment of tribute and accorded other dispensations. Colotlán's policy of pacification and indulgence toward its aboriginal inhabitants was gradually replaced by exploitation, especially in the late 1700s as the colonial era ended.

After the Coras were conquered and systematically exposed to Catholicism, the demand for labor at the Bolaños mines and for workers needed to supply goods and services to the miners gradually increased. By 1752, natives and native lands bordering Bolaños were in danger of being seized. Miners wanted natives to work in their mines. Other colonists coveted native lands for the trees they offered and for the crops and cattle they could supply to feed miners. Several Huichol villages had to answer to colonial authorities after Bolaños miners complained that Huichols had refused to rent their forests and pastures (Rojas 1993: 109). One of the Huichol settlements whose existence was imperiled was Ostoc.

In 1770 a portion of the communal lands occupied by Ostoc Huichols was awarded to a Spaniard named Antonio Peres de Contreras (Rojas 1993: 109–10). That ruling, favoring the invading colonist, was the beginning of the end for Ostoc. By 1790, Ostoc was deserted because of its conflict with don Miguel Maximiliano de Santiago, a wealthy mine owner from Bolaños (Rojas 1993: 111–12). Colonel Felix Calleja reported to Colotlán officials that in 1790 he observed that Ostoc was abandoned. Calleja stated that Ostoc was empty because of the "ravages of scorpions," adding that all ornaments and bells from Ostoc's church had been relocated to the church at Camotlán (Rojas 1992: 102–3).

Don Miguel de Santiago, the Bolaños miner who had harassed the Huichols of Ostoc, also invaded land surrounding Tuxpan, even though it still belonged to the comunidad indígena of San Sebastián. Santiago was finally expelled from Tuxpan in 1788. By 1790, a group of Huichols from Ostoc had installed themselves at Tuxpan de Bolaños, in the southern part of the comunidad indígena of San Sebastián. The Huichols of San Sebastián evidently permitted Huichols from Ostoc to occupy lands recently vacated by Santiago.[5]

By 1810, when Mexico declared its independence from Spain, the Huichol had lost control of the southern portion of their territory. In 1814 the Cura de Bolaños reported that both Camotlán and Huajimic were deserted and their churches completely ruined (Rojas 1992: 114). The only benefit Huichols received from the turmoil caused by Mexico's struggle against Spain was a period of relief from overzealous missionaries.

Well before then they had also been expelled from the northeastern settlements located around Huejuquilla (Weigand 1992a). In addition, during the nineteenth century, the Huichols were effectively expelled from their small settlements in the Bolaños valley.

The rebellion led by Manuel Lozada, which lasted from 1854 to 1873, had a positive aspect for Huichols. Lozada, with French support, declared the existence of the "República del Occidente," that is, an independent country, which would have an overwhelming indigenous flavor. This declaration explains in part the fierceness of the Juárez repression of Lozada, as well as his demonization in subsequent official histories. The fighting between Lozada's rebels and government forces brought a postponement in implementing laws connected with the reforms of Benito Juárez. One such reform authorized allotment of communal lands. This measure would have devastated Huichol culture (Weigand 1992a).

Reform laws authorizing partitioning of Huichol communal lands in order to grant title to individual landowners were not applied until after 1882. Huichols resisted efforts to allot their land (Rojas 1993: 144). Nevertheless, in 1893 and 1901 Santa Catarina was stripped of some of its communal lands (Rojas 1993: 156–57, 159–60). Weigand suggests (1979) that during this period, much of this comunidad indígena was incorporated into the Torres's estancia-hacienda system, based in Monte Escobedo (Zacatecas). Fortunately, all other Huichol communities managed to preserve their communal lands intact (Rojas 1992: 19). Huichols at Ostoc seemed to fare even better.

In 1885 four hundred Huichols who had originally inhabited Ostoc were granted possession of land at Tuxpan (Rojas 1992: 198–99, 1993: 148). Perhaps these Huichols had heard the news that allotment of communal land could not proceed if litigation clouded title to any communal land ready to be partitioned. However it happened, the Huichols of Ostoc were able to solicit land at Tuxpan to compensate them for land stolen from them at Ostoc.

Regaining land at Tuxpan facilitated retaining their identity as Huichols of Ostoc, a group whose history differed somewhat from that of San Sebastián. In 1892 Tuxpan's governor requested and was given instructions on the duties and powers vested in political offices that Tuxpan had recently activated as a result of their newly acquired status as a Huichol community (Rojas 1992: 226–27). However, since Tuxpan remained an annex of San Sebastián, its real status was a gobernancia (Weigand 1972, 1992a).

Tuxpan's lands were soon threatened by surveyors, who had included it within the boundaries of Camotlán. Letters written by two Tuxpan governors, in 1908 and 1909, testify to their fear that their new land would be taken from them, just as Ostoc had been (Rojas 1992: 236–38, 1993: 158). They perceived that measuring their land was the prologue to stealing it. This menace evaporated with the outbreak of the Mexican Revolution.

Revolution, Counterrevolution, Chaos, and Exile

More than one million people died in the violence brought by the Mexican Revolution (1910–1917). The years of violence after 1913 unleashed by that revolution tore apart Huichol communities and caused a massive exodus of Huichols from their homeland on both sides of the Chapalagana River (Rojas 1992:

20). Some Huichols fled to take up permanent residence in the coastal hamlets of Nayarit (Fikes 1993a; Weigand 1985, 1992a). Other Huichols became temporary refugees. Zingg reported that to escape the Mexican Revolution, Huichols from Tuxpan had endured twenty years in exile among "Mexicans of the barranca of Bolaños," where they worked "as peons in herding and agriculture" (1938: xlv, 34, 219).

During the Mexican Revolution, Chapalagana Huichol communities were disunited among themselves and divided from their eastern neighbors, who were no longer Indian but mestizo. The Huichols of San Sebastián and mestizos from Huejuquilla were antigovernment during the revolution (Rojas 1993: 164). The Huichols of San Andrés and mestizos of Mezquitic remained loyal to the government. For Huichols of Santa Catarina, the revolution provided an opportunity to expel the Torres family and other Mexican settlers who had recently invaded their land (Meyer 1992: 262; Weigand 1979: 168).

When the revolution ended in 1917, San Sebastián emerged stronger, wealthier, and more antigovernment than any other Huichol community. As a result, San Sebastián was targeted for destabilization and acculturation (Meyer 1992: 262; Weigand 1979: 170). With the complicity of the government, Mexicans soon began invading Huichol land, planting crops and grazing their cattle on it. The federal government's attack on the Catholic Church in 1926 helped unite Cristeros with Huichols who had already identified the government as their enemy. For many Mexicans, the Cristero Rebellion was welcomed as a positive response to the Mexican government's cancellation of all religious activities in 1926. Most of the Huichols of San Sebastián became Cristeros in order to continue their resistance to a government they perceived as hostile or indifferent to their welfare. Although some pro-Cristero Huichols came from other Huichol communities, those communities remained either neutral (Santa Catarina) or pro-government (San Andrés and Tuxpan). Only San Sebastián was overwhelmingly pro-Cristero. The brutality of the conflict between government forces and Christian militants prompted another massive exodus of Huichols (Fikes 1993a; Meyer 1992: 262–63; Rojas 1993: 168–69; Weigand 1979: 171).

From 1927 to 1938 the Cristeros of San Sebastián fought against the federal government. Their leader, Juan Bautista, was an ambitious and intelligent Huichol (Rojas 1993: 173; Weigand 1979). The Huichols of San Sebastián were deeply hostile toward Huichols of Tuxpan because the latter had not become pro-Cristero (Rojas 1993: 170). Some Huichols from San Sebastián attacked Tuxpan during the Mexican Revolution and the Cristero Rebellion (Zingg 1938: xlv, 740). Juan Bautista's assassination in 1935 was accomplished by Tuxpan Huichols paid for their "services" by Mexicans (Meyer 1992: 263; Weigand 1979: 171). The brutality of the government revenge in San Sebastián is still a central theme in their oral and cultural history, and is referred to on almost every occasion when government agencies present themselves as working on their behalf.

Robert Zingg's research documents the enmity between Tuxpan and San Sebastián (1938: 37) but leaves readers to speculate about the ways in which their antagonism may have modified his fieldwork. When Zingg first arrived in Tuxpan in January of 1934, the Huichols had just returned from twenty years in exile. At the end of 1934, when he accompanied Tuxpan officials to Mexico City, they had still not secured final title to their communal lands (Zingg 1938: 67–68).[6] Tuxpan's political future remains insecure.

Alienated Labor, Silver, and Christ's Betrayal

Shortly after the colonial period started, silver mining began at the southern and eastern boundaries of Huichol territory. Some Huichols were induced to work in mines, probably from a very early period. Others were illegally forced to labor in mines. The Huichols from Ostoc were pushed into exile. They fled to avoid being absorbed by the turmoil caused by silver mining and its auxiliary industries (e.g., crop and cattle production, timber harvesting). The Huichols of Ostoc were disturbed or traumatized, but not devastated, by colonial economic enterprises and evangelization. They were able to alter and reformulate Franciscan doctrines to fit their needs, thereby maintaining their cultural core. Their ability to accept useful innovations introduced by Spaniards illustrates Spicer's "incorporative model" of cultural change whereby elements brought by Spaniards were integrated "in such a way that they conform to the meaningful and functional relations" of Huichol culture without it being "disrupted or changed in fundamental type" (Spicer 1961: 530).

Huichols from Ostoc have survived much adversity, enduring a century of exile before acquiring land at Tuxpan. They protected their unique ethnic identity by adopting an "incorporative model," thereby making an accommodation to some colonial innovations, including Catholicism, while hardening their resistance to full acculturation. Zingg's *Huichol Mythology* reveals how Tuxpan Huichols accepted certain colonial changes while discarding few of their aboriginal customs. Tuxpan's version of Catholicism contains a penetrating but implicit critique of how Jesus Christ and the Spanish colonists who brought him were incorporated into Tuxpan's annual ceremonial cycle. Although Catholic influences were added, Tuxpan's mythology supported an aboriginal ceremonial cycle in which subsistence activities, including maize horticulture, deer hunting, and fishing, remained connected to the world-organizing exploits of their deified ancestors.

There is a fundamentally Huichol response to all momentous events, both pre-Hispanic and colonial. Momentous events (i.e., those that significantly alter subsistence, settlement patterns, or political organization) are sanctified by mythical explanation and repeated perpetually in ceremony. In the Huichol universe, history as we know it has been held in abeyance by performing ceremonies dedicated to honoring ancestors endowed with eternal life. Linear time and its concomitant historical perspective had not yet intruded on Tuxpan Huichols in 1934 and was only beginning to be accepted during the 1960s, when the first INI schools were established in the area. Very few Huichols were literate when Zingg transcribed the narratives his informant dictated to him. Huichols had never written their history nor described details of their struggle to resist being engulfed by Spanish colonization. Instead, they performed rituals and recited myths that embodied their feelings and thoughts on how Huichols should adjust to changes stimulated by Spaniards. Tuxpan's understanding of history is buried in their oral history, most of which is contained in Zingg's *Huichol Mythology*, and recited in those ceremonies associated with that mythology. It is a reflective history embodied in ritual and myth rather than a recitation of events or a chronicle in the strict sense of the word. Nevertheless, some important events and leaders, especially those from the nineteenth and twentieth centuries, are remembered in a chronicle format. The Cristero Rebellion is the best example of an event described in a chronicle rather than a ceremonial format.

In Huichol songs and ritual speeches, which together comprise their "mythology," certain deeds accomplished by Huichol ancestors are recognized as having set precedents that reorganized their world, thereby creating the reality in which Huichols presently exist. Maintaining the world they inherited from their "mythical" ancestors means that Huichols must perform ceremonies in which myths explaining the origins of elements vital to insure survival in their world are recited. The myth describing the origin of maize cultivation consecrates maize, the central component of Huichol subsistence for centuries before Spanish conquest, and typifies the Huichol covenant to recreate the world established by sacrifices made by their ancestors.

The Huichols of Santa Catarina assert that after surviving a deluge, their ancestor Huatácame had to atone for the insult his mother gave to the maize maidens he had married. The method Huatácame used to atone for his mother's mistake set the precedent that still obligates Huichols to offer deer and/or cattle

blood to divine ancestors honored in their first fruits ritual, Tatei Neixa. Huatácame's sacrifices furnish the model Huichols use to exalt the blood offerings
they must make to insure that maize will continue to be plentiful (Fikes 1985:
173–74, 232–34, 288–97; 1993a: 225–32). The maize myth transcribed by Zingg
(1938: 256; see also section II.D., The Corn Myth, this volume) is essentially
identical.

The same logic—that certain sacrifices transformed the world and obligate
Huichols to renew that world annually—illuminates the economic alteration
that the Huichols of Tuxpan attribute to Christ's betrayal. For them the sacrifice of Jesus Christ established this world's economy in which silver money
circulates as a medium of exchange. In 1934 Tuxpan Huichols viewed Christ's
betrayal for thirty pieces of silver as a crucial event, one which initiated capitalism. The chronicle of Christ's betrayal, crucifixion, and resurrection was recited
during Tuxpan's Semana Santa (Holy Week) ceremony. This Christian myth
and ceremony rationalized Huichol participation in the silver-based economic
order that the Spaniards gradually imposed on them. The Weigands observed
the same symbolism during the 1960s in San Sebastián.

Some non-Indians may be tempted to ridicule Tuxpan's version of Christianity because it equates the origin of capitalism with the crucifixion of Christ.
Yet consider the statement made in 1730 by a priest to the Tarahumara: "If there
were no Tarahumaras, there would be no silver; if there were no silver, there
would be no royal fifths (i.e., twenty percent royalties due to the Crown on all
silver) or other tax income, nor any trade. . . . these poor Tarahumara Indians
should be cared for with special charity because . . . their souls were redeemed
with the blood of Jesus Christ, . . . they are necessary and useful to the Crown"
(Sheridan and Naylor 1979: 74).

It is likely that a similar rationale, one acknowledging that Christ and silver
were the two items most indispensable for Indians and the Crown, was em-
ployed when the bishop of Zacatecas arranged for an Anglo-American company to exploit mines located on Huichol lands without first obtaining Huichol
approval. Fortunately for the Huichols, the Mexican Revolution erupted before the unauthorized mining could begin (Rojas 1993: 159). If Catholics have
behaved as if their interests are identical with those of miners, then it should
not be too surprising that the Huichols of Tuxpan perceived that silver mining and Christ were part and parcel of the same colonial system. They simply
associated seeking silver and saving souls in a cause and effect manner that
orthodox Catholics would reject as historically inaccurate. The Weigands observed something similar in San Sebastián, where the Huichols are intensely
anticlerical, although sympathetic to many Christian ideas and practices.

Tuxpan's Christian mythology contains a kernel of existential truth: together,

Spanish missionaries and miners created the new regime to which Huichols had to conform. Tuxpan's interpretation of Christianity is no more enigmatic than the cargo cults that proliferated in New Guinea, the baptism of money common among certain rural Colombians (Taussig 1977), or other attempts that people from noncapitalist economies have made to cope with the drastic upheavals triggered by European colonization. It would be unreasonable to expect the Huichols of Tuxpan to construct a Marxist critique of how alienated labor is a concomitant of capitalist relations of production. In 1934 that type of historical analysis was foreign to Huichols.[7]

Robert Zingg's pious informant "felt like crying" as he spoke of the ordeal connected with Christ's crucifixion. Zingg had to pay this informant thirty pesos, an "enormous sum for this story," because "thirty pesos were paid for the betrayal of Santo Cristo" (Zingg 1938: 370). To appreciate how Zingg managed to record the narratives that comprise *Huichol Mythology*, Zingg's life and fieldwork strategy are briefly summarized.

Robert Zingg's Principal Ethnographic Achievements

Robert Zingg was born in Colorado in 1900 but grew up in northern New Mexico, where his father was the superintendent of a boarding school for American Indians. His mother, Bernice, was "deeply religious." Zingg's lifelong fascination with American Indians developed during his childhood in New Mexico (Emma Zingg 1996). Zingg completed his doctorate in anthropology at the University of Chicago. He did considerable ethnographic fieldwork in 1930–1931 among the Tarahumara Indians of northwestern Mexico with Wendell Bennett (Bennett and Zingg [1935] 1976). Zingg did ethnographic research among the Huichols of Tuxpan in 1934, following his Tarahumara fieldwork. Zingg was subsequently engaged as a professor of anthropology at the University of Denver. During World War II he worked for the Red Cross. His first marriage produced three children before it ended in divorce. In 1957, in his tenth year of marriage to his second wife, Emma Zingg, he died suddenly of a heart attack at their home in El Paso, Texas (Emma Zingg 1996). A persistent rumor of suicide is not supported by interviews with his heirs.

Robert Zingg's investigation at Tuxpan de Bolaños, located near the southeastern boundary of Huichol territory, yielded an enormous book, *The Huichols: Primitive Artists* (the assortment of stories presented here as *Huichol Mythology*), a museum collection of more than six hundred artifacts, more than five hundred still photographs (some of which are included in this book), and approximately fifty minutes of unedited motion picture film footage. Zingg's

Huichol research represents the type of anthropology advocated by Franz Boas, and rests on his commitment to document and survey the full range of native activities, from material culture to myth and ritual. The weakest sections of his study involve social organization, although he provides extensive data on this topic.

Zingg's activities had a profound impact on the Huichols of Tuxpan. He sold them candles, small round mirrors, and other merchandise (1938: 638–39, 702). He bought several hundred artifacts and vaccinated them against smallpox. Because the first vaccine was ineffective, he vaccinated them a second time during Holy (Easter) Week (1938: lviii, 151). He wrote to Mexican officials to defend Huichol rights and later accompanied a delegation of Tuxpan officials to Mexico City. Once Zingg's offer to take Tuxpan's officials to Mexico City was accepted, his key informant consented to allow him to record their myths (1938: liii). Tuxpan officials were favorably impressed with Zingg's political advocacy on their behalf. They invited him to "wear a Huichol costume and cane and sit with them on the 'bench of the mighty'" (1938: lviii, 16). He also promoted Huichol crafts.

Zingg's attitude toward the Huichol was romantic, a feeling widespread among North American anthropologists of his generation. "Were the choice mine to be born a Huichol or an American, I might prefer the former, though there are few primitive cultures I would choose" (1938: 746).

Zingg's admiration for the Huichols seems to have been matched by their fondness for him. Introducing the reprint edition (1976) of Bennett and Zingg's 1935 book on the Tarahumara, Thomas Hinton declared that Zingg "is remembered by the Tuxpan Huichols today as a good friend."

One traveler relates how, upon meeting a group of Huichols on a mountain trail, he produced a photograph of Zingg and asked the Indians if they knew the man in the picture. They responded by kissing the photo and calling him by name (Bennett and Zingg [1935] 1976: 26).

Zingg's ethnographic research still stands as a landmark study of Huichol culture. It is comprehensive in scope and includes profound insights into Huichol religious beliefs and practices. Zingg's insights were achieved not only because he built upon data collected by two of his predecessors, Carl Lumholtz and Konrad Preuss, but also because he remained in one Huichol community, Tuxpan de Bolaños, for a full year. He was the first professional anthropologist and the first North American to study the Huichols. While Lumholtz's study is better known, Zingg's research was truly anthropological. His focus on a specific Huichol community has been followed by most anthropologists who have worked among Chapalagana Huichols. Such studies have revealed that significant variations exist among Huichol comunidades indígenas.

Zingg recognized that the kawitéro (premier ritual specialist) played a key role in the aboriginal temple ritual cycle, a cycle Zingg identified as belonging to a sphere of social organization beyond that of individual ranchos. He observed that kawitéros directed both the aboriginal ceremonial cycle and the civil and religious cargo system imposed by the Spaniards. He remarked that the Huichols considered their aboriginal ritual cycle to be "an integral part of the technology for the control of nature." In fact, they ranked performance of ritual ahead of material techniques in securing subsistence and simultaneously maintaining health (Zingg 1938: 744). Zingg learned that vital elements in the Huichol natural environment were the focus of ritual, that the "gods" which dominated Huichol culture were essentially "personifications of natural phenomena" (Zingg 1938: 746). Weigand (1985: 150) and Fikes (1985, 1993a, 1993c) have applauded Zingg for his thorough understanding of how the alternation between the wet and dry seasons furnishes a foundation that pervades and structures Huichol subsistence activities and ceremonies, and to a great degree defines their deified ancestors. This basic and highly important analysis is fundamental in cross-cultural studies comparing the Huichol with other Mesoamerican natives, both ancient and contemporary.

In addition to his prolific data gathering, Zingg's interpretations of Huichol ritual are generally accurate and free from theoretical manipulation. His theoretical perspective on Huichol religion was, by today's standards, rather underdeveloped, being derived largely from Durkheim and Levy-Bruhl. His juxtaposition of mystic participation (epitomized by sincere participation in their world-maintaining rituals) and rational economic calculation (an individualistic attitude typical of modern Europeans) has considerable explanatory power but has been undervalued by professional anthropologists.

Zingg's predilection was to examine historical processes. He reconstructed Uto-Aztecan cultural history (1937) and hinted at how the Huichols of Tuxpan were responding to political, religious, and economic elements introduced by Spaniards. Zingg's meticulous research documented the fact that Huichols were never isolated from the outside world, an observation that was largely ignored by New Age studies that began in the 1960s. Zingg noted how money, firearms, cattle, and other items of European origin were modifying Tuxpan Huichol society and providing the stimulus for development of Tuxpan's interpretation of Christianity. His research on Tuxpan's version of Christian myth and ritual is exceptionally valuable, not only because of its wealth of detail and accuracy, but also because this topic has been treated as if it were trivial by some anthropologists.

Zingg's research revealed that concepts and ceremonies originally introduced by Franciscan missionaries were heavily filtered through, and well integrated into, ancient Huichol patterns. The governmental offices and Catholic religious cargos imposed on Huichols of San Andrés, San Sebastián, Santa Catarina, and Tuxpan were obviously grafted onto an ancient cargo system of political and ceremonial obligations. Fikes's fieldwork in Santa Catarina and the work by the Weigands in San Sebastián confirmed Zingg's conclusion that the Catholic Church "organizations are imitated from the pagan temple officers" (Zingg 1938: 174). However it may have happened, the colonial government and religious cargo system introduced by the Franciscans were adjusted to be compatible with the Huichol cultural core.

Obtaining reliable information about what the ceremonies Zingg witnessed meant to the Huichols was challenging because of the strict "tribal sanction against divulging tribal secrets to foreigners" (1938: 411). Zingg finally got his key informant "after months of patient kindness" and political advocacy (1938: liii, 411). It was only after Zingg's primary informant, Juan Real, dictated the mythology that Zingg attained the perspective indispensable to interpret accurately the ritual activities he had observed. Juan Real feared that revealing the mythology would make him a target of sorcerers, despite his importance in Tuxpan's ceremonial life.[8] As Zingg departed from Tuxpan, Juan Real felt worried, "maybe someone will work sorcery against me for having told you these 'delicate' things" (1938: liii).

A few precautions about *Huichol Mythology* may be useful. Because Juan Real dictated the myths during the final four months of Zingg's fieldwork, he had limited opportunity to independently confirm Real's data with myths provided by other Tuxpan informants. Moreover, Real's myths were dictated and transcribed in Spanish (Zingg 1938: xxii).[9] Fikes has noted certain anomalies in Zingg's myths and suggested that some of these may best be explained as a result of regional variation, while others may be attributable to acculturation and Tuxpan's combination of Catholic and aboriginal personalities (1985: 36–40).[10] Despite such acculturation and syncretism, Zingg's myths reveal that an unmistakably Huichol perspective on life still prospered in 1934.

Tuxpan de Bolaños in 1934

In 1934 Zingg noticed only the foundations of an unfinished Catholic church at Tuxpan (Zingg 1938: 8–10). Construction of Tuxpan's church was undoubtedly halted by one of this region's many political disturbances. Franciscan priests introduced Tuxpan Huichols to punishments for misbehavior including public whipping, confinement in the stocks, and fines (Zingg 1938: 31–32, 140), and taught them the beliefs and practices from which Tuxpan's Christian myths and rituals were fashioned. In 1934 the Franciscans had abandoned the Huichols of Tuxpan, whose accommodation to Christianity was incomplete, if not superficial.

The Huichols of Tuxpan performed both Catholic and aboriginal ceremonies at Tuxpan's Casa Real, which was serving functions that other Huichols normally apportioned to three separate structures: a building for official government business, a church for Catholic ceremonies, and a ceremonial center for aboriginal temple rituals. Tuxpan's fusion of these three functions was matched by its merging or combining of certain indigenous, colonial Spanish, and Catholic elements. However, at San Sebastián, where the three realms are performed in three separate complexes, the same basic fusion and symbiosis of Catholic and indigenous ritual has occurred.

Tuxpan was a fascinating hybrid culture in 1934, less Catholic than San Sebastián and less native than Ratontita. When the first *capilla* (chapel) was built at San Sebastián in 1733, it became the Franciscan doctrina or "focal point for the introduction of the Spanish governmental-religious cargo system" (Weigand 1981: 13).

Because it served as the Franciscan doctrina, San Sebastián was at first subjected to more intensive evangelization than other Huichol areas. Extensive exposure to Franciscan teaching during the nineteenth century probably contributed to San Sebastián's support of the Cristero Rebellion. Lumholtz asserted ([1902] 1973: 258) that San Sebastián was the only Huichol settlement where aboriginal Huichol and Catholic beliefs had been blended (an observation that is not completely accurate). Zingg detected definite signs of syncretism in the Tuxpan Huichol myths presented here, yet he also realized (1938: 12, 18) that San Sebastián was more completely Catholic than Tuxpan. Perhaps this was because Franciscan missionaries based at San Sebastián could only have made short visits to Tuxpan, somewhat like the brief loans of portraits and wooden replicas of Catholic saints, which Tuxpan obtains from the church at San Sebastián today.

Tuxpan had abandoned more of its native culture than had Ratontita and other less accessible ceremonial centers in Huichol territory. Unlike Ratontita, Tuxpan had no tukipa or ceremonial center (Zingg 1938: xxxiv, 174). Zingg's sketch of how economic rationalism was replacing mystic participation implied that enthusiastic involvement in indigenous ceremonies was wavering at Tuxpan. In 1934 Tuxpan's indigenous temple officers found only three persons to replace themselves (Zingg 1938: 342, 478). Peyote pilgrimages organized by Tuxpan temple officers had been suspended since at least 1931 (Fikes 1985: 37) and may have been terminated immediately after Tuxpan Huichols went into exile, around 1914. One indigenous ritual seen by Lumholtz may have disappeared entirely from Tuxpan by 1900 (Zingg 1938: 658–60). One of Real's myths indicates how the Huichols of Tuxpan had preserved the foundation of older native culture while simultaneously supplementing it with Christian concepts. This illustrates the essence of symbiosis.

Zingg's observation that Huichols regard wind as "unusually sacred," and a "favorite form of messenger of the gods" (1938: 245) has been verified by the Weigands and Fikes.[11] One of Zingg's most intriguing myths features a contest between Kaoyomari, the world organizer and messenger of the ancestors, and his rival, Hortimán, a Wind-devil and deceiver. Zingg's Kauymáli is distinguished as Elder Brother Wolf, while Hortimán is closely connected with coyotes, an animal often depicted as unreliable in North American Indian myths. Hortimán is portrayed as an unethical trickster who manages to deceive Kauymáli several times. As a result of his dishonesty, Hortimán becomes wealthy. Kauymáli is injured after being bucked off the horse Hortimán sells him. The accident cripples Kauymáli and makes him realize that Hortimán is a charlatan, but Kauymáli gets revenge; Hortimán soon loses his illicitly gained wealth and becomes a whirlwind, forced to live in holes in the ground and rocks and to wander restlessly over the world. Tacutzi Nacahue cursed Hortimán and "commanded that he always remain a devil. Thus the Huichols believe that whirlwinds cause sickness and death" (see "Kauymáli Is Outsmarted by Hortimán, the Wind-devil," this volume).

This myth suggests that whirlwinds symbolize an uncontrollable element in nature and in ourselves—they are a residue of Hortimán and the disorder that his deceit left within our world. Huichols fear whirlwinds because they cannot be controlled through ceremony. Zingg saw that Huichols were so fearful of whirlwinds that they would "scurry away at their approach, making the sign of the cross" (see "Kauymáli, the Wolf-Man, Is Outsmarted but Gets Revenge," note 16). This Christian gesture must have been a last recourse against an evil for which there was no remedy in their indigenous world. Their fear of whirlwinds reminds us that the Huichols inhabited a universe in which virtually everything had been, or could be, arranged in a beneficial manner. This myth is an obvious exception to the secure world established by the Huichol ancestors, though chaos is recognized in sorcery and other realms of Huichol life (Fikes 1993c; Weigand 1992a).

The primary purpose of the Huichol ceremonial cycle, and the myths intrinsic to it, is to maintain positive relationships with ancestors who control nature and its processes. As long as the Huichols properly perform the rituals that perpetuate the world their ancestors organized, they are convinced that they will be blessed with good health and abundant subsistence. Proper recitation of myths and performance of ritual holds disorder in abeyance and insures the Huichols that they have little reason to fear sickness or starvation.

Jay C. Fikes, Phil C. Weigand, Acelia García de Weigand

I Myths of the Dry Season Cycle

The Birth of Tatevalí (Grandfather Fire) and the Contest of Fire and Water (Nakawé)

Tatevalí was born in the first times. Before then the people had no fire.

Tatevalí was born as a very small spark on a round rock near the point of the sea. In those times it was quite dark, because there was neither fire nor sun. The people wondered how they might remedy this darkness.

When fire came out of the rock, it half flew (like a will-o'-the wisp?). The god-people did not know what it was. The next night the fire came out again. The people did not approach the rock because they thought the fire was very ugly. Fire came from the rock four times, and flew to each of the four points. The fifth time it flew past the god-people like the firefly, *taweami*,[1] and encircled them. They did not recognize it, however.

So for another five days Fire flew to the different directions. This time it was larger, and looked like a mirror[2] flashing in the sun. It was glowing also, like a firefly, and was looking for a house where it might be able to live.

Someone said, "This must be one of the great gods who has just been born. Ask what it is. Perhaps it is an animal."

So they went and asked Kauymáli. Kauymáli told them that what they saw was fire, and that it would serve the people's use because it would give both heat and light. He advised them to await calmly and patiently [to see] what would happen.

The following five days Fire flew to the five points.[3] This time it was as big as a *teapáli*,[4] and was burning brightly.[5] A young boy and a young girl who had never had sexual intercourse were told to go and watch it. It was too "delicate" for older people.[6]

So the boy and the girl went to the rock where the fire was coming from. The fire was issuing from a hole in the rock, because Grandfather Fire lived inside. The sight of the flame stupefied them and they no longer remembered their errand.[7]

While they were drunk, Grandfather Fire spoke to them, saying, "I am talking to you because I like you and your people. I have talked to all the other great gods. We wish you to make me five little teapáli. They must be well carved and well arranged. Leave them right here at this hole. Then we will see how I come out. Make me also five arrows of [b]razil-wood with feathers of *güakamaya*.[8] I wish, too, [for] five votive-bowls, ornamented with beads, and five very large, thick candles. Furthermore, you must pray and bring me five shaman's baskets *(takuátci).* Remember what I have said and tell your people. Come back with your offerings in five days and see what you find. My name is *tai* (fire).[9]

The boy and girl recovered from their drunken stupor.[10] They returned home and told the people what Tatevalí had said to them. For five days they were busy, preparing the things that had been requested of them. The shaman's baskets were filled with the feathers belonging to birds of this god. The people were very anxious to complete the orders satisfactorily, since they needed fire badly. In these times they had to eat their corn and meat raw. And the great gods did not like them to eat as if they were animals.

Then Grandfather Fire charged the boy and the girl to take care of him.[11] He wished them to be his masters ("dueños"). They had to take the valuable offerings to the shrines dedicated to the Sun.

After five days they went [back] again. Grandfather Fire said, "I am very 'delicate.' I cannot leave here or I should set the world on[12] fire. You must, therefore, bring me a censer, a pouch, and a gourd bowl. Furthermore, when you come, wet your hands with water. And bring me also five little rocks on which I may sit as live coals."

The boy and the girl went and told the people what Grandfather Fire had said.

They brought the censer (*pútsi*, H.).[13] When this was brought, five little coals jumped out of the hole in the rock and sat in the censer. The coals were burning so hotly that they burned through the censer. So five more jumped out and sat in the shaman's basket. This, too, was burned. In a similar fashion was the pouch burned. Then the girl held out the corner of her handkerchief. This was immediately burned through, and the coals fell back into the hole. Five coals then jumped on to the wet hands of the boy. But they burned him, and he had to drop them.

This made Grandfather Fire exclaim, "I am indeed the most 'delicate' of all the gods. I cannot move. I burn everything in sight. Take, rather, my feathers to the gods of the five points. There place them on my five teapáli, which you have brought. Pray to them."

The boy and the girl did this, and the feathers took fire. Thus the people had fire whenever they wished.[14]

The boy and the girl now became the *mayordomos* [custodians] of the Fire-god and took care of his paraphernalia, including his teapáli(s), which are his heart.[15]

Now that there was fire, however, the whole world began to burn up, because Fire was so "delicate." This was very serious. The people hurriedly made an oven[16] in which to save the paraphernalia of the Fire-god. Those things that belonged to him were put in the earth-oven. The flames approached this place, causing the people great consternation. They thought, "What shall we do?" The circle of flames rose up and approached. The people threw rocks at the fire, but even they [the rocks] were consumed. They threw wood at the fire. This was burned also.

Then on top of the oven they placed a teapáli, and on the teapáli they set a little fire in hopes of attracting the clouds. As they did this, they prayed to Nakawé and the great gods of the sea (water).

Nakawé heard the prayers. She loosened her hair-net *(wipí)*,[17] thereby releasing much rain[,] which fell heavily. It rained for five days and nights. The fire was put out completely, except for that on the teapáli on top of the earth-oven. Thus was the fire conquered.[18]

The little fire on the teapáli on top of the earth-oven then told the people to make it a little house[,] as well as fields. All the people were called for the work. Thus could Grandfather Fire repay them by serving them all.

In his house the people put a *nealíka*.[19] From the rafters they hung a bunch of feathers called *haíci*, to sound at night at the approach of the gods. At the altar they put the feathers belonging to Grandfather Fire, with which they themselves could make fire, and also his votive-bowls.[20] All this was made and done according to the command of Grandfather Fire.[21]

The girl then was asked to make a votive-bowl.[22] The boy in the meantime put up five deer-lassos. While the girl guarded the sacred paraphernalia of Grandfather Fire, the boy set his traps to see if he could catch a deer. With the blood of the deer he wished to anoint the new votive-bowl.[23]

Meanwhile all the people made votive-bowls (*"jicaras"* [jícaras, Sp.]) for Grandfather Fire, and placed arrows on his altar. This done, a singer sang all night. During the night[,] Grandfather Fire told the singer that the next day the boy would kill three male and two female deer.

This came to pass, and thus was established the custom for the Huichols to offer deer-blood to Grandfather Fire.[24]

From the deer the blood was taken, and with it all the ceremonial paraphernalia was anointed. Grandfather Fire revealed to the boy that this was the custom to be followed by the Huichols for all time. And the custom has been followed by the Huichols ever since, according to the wishes of the great gods of the sea. Thus the Huichols became the family of Grandfather Fire.

The custom was established when the first people blessed the ceremonial paraphernalia with the sign of the four points in deer's blood. When this was done, Grandfather Fire was tamed, and was no longer "delicate."[25] Thus the Huichols could have fire at will.

The people then brought wood to the house where Grandfather Fire had to be "watched," as he could not go out in all parts as yet. This watching was done for five nights for fear that Grandfather Fire would escape or that bad people would steal it.[26] The people remained awake to prevent this, and were very watchful.

Four nights passed in peace. The watchers were certain that nothing would happen. The great gods, however, knew better. That night a little animal, *iáusu tewíałi* (takuátci *[tlacuache]*, Sp., opossum), decided to try to steal the fire while the foolish watchers were asleep. He approached very quietly and with much care, deliberately leaving a track to see if the watchers would recognize it. When he came very near the fire, a spark leapt out from fear. But the watchers did not notice, because they were asleep.

The next night the animal again approached and circled the watchers, who were again asleep. He decided to try to steal the fire.

The fourth night Kauymáli was called by the great gods of the sea. He was told that if the watchers did not take better care[,] they would lose Grandfather Fire. But Kauymáli was "half-bad." He went and asked only if there were any signs of intruders. The people replied that there were none. The same night the animal [opossum] came again. The watchers, however, were asleep and did not recognize him. One watcher dreamed poorly and awoke. But nothing had happened.

The fifth night the animal [opossum] decided to steal the fire. He opened his breast and hid the fire in his heart. Then he closed his breast and went away to a rock that has five holes in it. Here he buried the fire.

The people did not know immediately. The great gods, however, knew of the theft.

The next night the possum returned and stole some more of the Fire-god. This was done three times. The great gods sent someone to find out about it, but the watchers denied that any of the fire was gone.

The fourth night the great gods warned the people to be especially careful lest they awake and find no fire at all.

The fifth night they awoke to see the animal [opossum] running away with the fire. He was climbing the hill with the fire burning in his heart. They ran to overtake him. But he got into his hole[,] and they could not get at him.

As a consequence of these repeated thefts[,] the fire was left very small. Darkness almost overpowered the people. The great gods were angry. The people were warned that if they lost the little bit of fire that remained[,] it would be the end of the Huichols (who are the children of the Fire-god), because the animal put out the fire that he stole.

That night, however, they fell asleep again. The animal [opossum] succeeded in stealing the last of the fire. The watchers had extreme difficulty in following it in the dark. But they finally caught the animal, killed it, and took out its heart of fire.

But as soon as the people left, the animal [opossum] collected itself together, and ran away, no worse for its misadventure. The people again caught it, knocked it to pieces, and hung it up by the tail. The animal composed itself again, however, and went back to its house. It was reborn within the hole where its heart had been. From this hole also its young were born. Its teats were on the inside.[27]

Now it was ordered that this was an animal whose fat would be good to serve as medicine. Although it had been killed twice, and even knocked to pieces, still it had collected itself together. The great gods ordered that its fat would make a good remedy when used as an ointment.[28] They also ordered the animal [opossum] not to leave its own fields very far. It was permitted to maintain itself from the corn of the Huichols, however, because of the injuries they had given it.

B The Sun Myth

The family of the Sun were many. They had been born in the underworld during five days. They were pushed out at the sea where the great gods of the sea were sitting in their shaman's chairs near their votive-bowls. The great gods of the sea did not know what these new creatures were, since they came out of the sea as green-blue spray. The next time some came out as yellow spray. Finally others came out as red foam. This was their hearts.

From this spray emerged a small fly. It flew to the arrows of the great gods of the sea. Then it returned to its father, the Sun.

The [Sun F]ather said, "Spread your wings."

The sound of the wings went to the five corners of the world. At the sea the great gods did not know what this sound could possibly mean. They thought that the water was angry.

The second time the heart changed into a little sea-bug. It bathed the votive-bowls of the great gods with water thrown from its wings.

The [Sun F]ather sent the little sea-bug to find out if he would "fit" (if there was a place for him). If the heart — that is, the small sea-bug — fit, then there would also be a place for Father Sun.

The great gods of the sea were puzzled by the offering of water on their votive-bowls. This was because they had not seen anyone do it. Kauymáli was there. The great gods asked him if he knew what caused this.

The heart returned into the earth, carrying to its father (Sun) the measure of the world to test whether or not he could be born. Its father told it to fly like the bird, *taukúkui [taukukúi]* (heart-of-the-sun).[1] It was supposed to fly in the wind to the point of the sea. So it went, measuring the world (like a measuring-worm), until it arrived at the point of the sea, which became very red. Here the bird placed an upright cross so that his children could climb to the sky.[2]

The little heart-animal stopped at the top of the cross.[3] Then, singing, it flew to the sky. After this it returned to a tree of the great gods of the sea, the *lápa* (*matareal*, Sp.).

Then the [Sun F]ather changed the heart into a bug[,] which was able to sound its wings. This bug is called *tauwélika* (and lives in the arroyos of the Huichol country). In this form the heart flew to "this side." Here it sounded its wings. Kauymáli watched, as he had been commanded to by the great gods of the sea.

In these times there was only the light of the moon. The Sun had not yet been born.

The bug went to all of the world regions. The fifth time he went on "that side." Here Kauymáli made a ladder, *imúmui*, on which the Sun could climb out of the underworld.[4]

Father Sun emerged without any clothes on. He spit in the sea, and another animal came out. This was the small woodpecker, *tsimakai*. This bird flew to "that side." Here he sat on an arrow, which he pecked. Then he sat on the votive-bowls. Kauymáli continued to watch.

Then Father Sun sat down in a shaman's chair. He spat again. This time the long-beaked bird, *hotái*,[5] came out.

Again Father Sun spat. A macaw came out and sat on the cross.[6] There it was changed into a painting on a votive-bowl.[7] Ten of its feathers fell out. Kauymáli got them and put them in a votive-bowl. In five days these were placed on votive-arrows made of brazil-wood. Father Sun had created these also by spitting. Thus the macaw is very much an animal of the Sun, and good for ceremonial arrows, which the Sun made.[8]

The macaw sat on the limbs of the matareal [lápa] and beat his wings. Small parrots came from the wings and flew to the five points.[9] Thus there are parrots everywhere. Their feathers serve for the arrows of the Sun, according to his command.

The Sun was still very "delicate"[10] and could not go about. Kauymáli watched him closely, remembering everything in his heart. The Sun spit again. From the foam came the great royal eagle.[11] Spreading its magnificent wings[,] it flew to the cross. Then it flew to the shaman's chair of Father Sun. This bird belonged to him.[12]

Again the Sun spit. This time a hawk[13] came out. The hawk left its image on the door, and then [it] went to the mountains. Here it remained to guard the Sun, because it belonged very much to him. The black hawk, *kuawáme*,[14] emerged also at the Sun's spitting and sat on the Sun's chair.

The Sun said, "You must take care of me. Otherwise the sea-gods will harm me. Let us see who will win."[15]

The hawk then went into the earth to the place where the Sun had been born.

Again the Sun spit. The rattlesnake, *saiye*,[16] came out. Kauymáli wondered what it was for. The snake climbed over the chair of Father Sun and rested at his feet. Thus the Sun watched, surrounded on all sides by many protectors. Kauymáli also watched, and noted everything. The Sun said, "Here I will arrange all my animals."

A sea-animal, *tigre del mar* ("tiger of the sea," *hatúwi*; a shark, possibly?)[,]

came out of the sea when the Sun spit. It cast off its body and left the water. When the Sun turned his head, he saw the animal on a cliff just above his head. Then he told all his animals to defend him always against his enemies.[17]

A fearful cry was heard from the sea, and from the foam a jaguar emerged. The Sun recognized the yellow color of its body. He had the jaguar guard him from the great gods of the sea.

Kauymáli remembered everything he saw so that he might inform the great gods of the sea. He went to them and told them. They, however, did not think that all these precautions the Sun had taken would amount to much.

The Sun ordered that his body be painted and then embroidered and carved on ceremonial paraphernalia.[18] Kauymáli was able to do all this. The Sun also wished [for] a sacred wand[19] so that the others would know him (as a god?). Thus reeds were commanded to grow, and Kauymáli carved the Sun fifty ceremonial wands. They were beautifully painted red, blue, and green.[20]

The Sun spit, and many feathers emerged from the sea. Kauymáli picked them up and from them made many shaman's plumes *(movieli)*.[21] Then he took the reeds and feathers to the four points in order that these materials for shaman's plumes should be found everywhere. He also took the seeds of the plant *tsikalótci* (*chikalóta*, Sp.). These were to [be] put inside the ceremonial wands so that the wands would sound like the Sun's animal, the rattlesnake.[22] Thus people would be able to hear the Sun,[23] and therefore serve him in all of the world regions.

A green bird came out of the sea. It was the very blue-and-green parrot, *kakámame*,[24] which lives in the sierra. It cast off its feathers. These, Kauymáli picked up and took everywhere. He did this so that the Sun would not lack feathers for his paraphernalia, including the boar *tawíkame*.[25] Thus considerable paraphernalia of all kinds was arranged.

Now the great gods of the sea were jealous of this paraphernalia. They covered the Sun with water. This, however, did not harm the Sun[,] but the paraphernalia was blessed with sacred water.[26] Kauymáli cut the wattle of a turkey, and bathed the votive-bowls in the blood.[27]

Kauymáli then copied on the votive-bowls the forms of all the animals of the Sun. He also made *nealíka*, etc. These were taken to "this side[,]" not to "that side," which was closed. He worked like a peon [tirelessly] in making all these things for Father Sun.[28] They were also painted with oxen, horses, jaguars, tigres-del-mar, hawks, the eagle, and snakes, all of which the Sun had created. Had Kauymáli failed in making all this paraphernalia, the Sun would not have come out.[29]

At this time the moon was not very well arranged and did not give much light. It was therefore important that the Sun come out. If Kauymáli had failed in his work, the world would have remained as dark as a cave.

While Kauymáli was doing these things, the Sun had to sit in his shaman's chair guarded by his animals. He ordered Kauymáli to make him a house.

The Sun communicated with the great gods of the sea through a parrot that flew to the underworld as well as the other four regions. The great gods of the sea heard the cries of the parrot as the Sun had commanded. They said, "This is not [a] god which is crying. Let us kill it with our arrows."

But the Sun's rays were so strong that the great gods of the sea could not aim their arrows. The parrot called five times, saying that the Sun was born. Thus the information was given out.[30]

The screeching of the parrot was also a command for everyone to make all kinds of ceremonial paraphernalia. Thus would the Sun be able to leave his chair[31] and climb to the sky to shine. He was very "delicate" and had to be "gentled" [tamed].[32]

The fifty great gods of the sea wagered as to who could find a name for the Sun. They thought that the Sun was an animal, not a god. The Sun therefore ordered his votive-bowls bathed in sacred water so that the great gods of the sea would know him.[33]

In the contest to guess the name of the Sun[,] the turkey was ordered to stand behind. Those animals that knew how to dream[34] were placed in front. Kauymáli won the contest, because he knew how to dream everything. When the moon went down into the sea, it became quite dark and many night animals came out. This lasted for five hours.

Then the Sun asked, "What is my name?"

The great gods of the sea were afraid of the night animals that prowled about. But the sea took on another "aspect" (nealíka)[35] and became green and blue. The animals retired a little, remaining at some distance from the great gods of the sea. Thus the Sun worked the first miracle of light.[36]

Then the Sun arose from his chair. He ordered his animals to the four points to guard and protect him from anyone who might try to kill him. After this[,] he climbed the cross at the side of the sea.[37] Then he went to the four points, slaying the darkness on all sides with heavy blows.[38]

None of the great gods of the sea could give the Sun a name.[39] Thus they were worried lest the Sun should win over them. If they lost to him and could not think of his name, he would break their votive-bowls. Still, none of them could think of his name.

Finally Kauymáli asked, "Doesn't anyone know what to call the Sun? If you don't soon guess, the animals will come in the dark."

These words frightened the great gods. They set their ceremonial parapher-nalia on an altar and prayed. But the Sun's name was not revealed to them in their dreams.

Then a macaw flew up calling, and sat on one side of the altar. The great gods listened to their arrows, trying to hear what the macaw was saying. Time was passing, and they were feverishly anxious to learn the name of the Sun. In the meantime the Sun was climbing away.

Just then the turkey, which was standing behind the great gods, gobbled, "*Tau! Tau! Tau!*" Thus he named the Sun.[40] The great gods were angry with the turkey because it had won the contest of naming the Sun.

The Sun climbed to the top of the sky. In the afternoon he had to descend into the sea. This was very dangerous for him because he was still "tender,"[41] and because the snakes (that is, water) in the sea would try to kill him.

The Sun then named all his animals,[42] after which he told them to go and make ceremonial paraphernalia. This would enable him to win his battle with the serpents. The Sun's animals are so fierce that the Huichols still fear to sleep in the high sierra at night.

At the end of five days[,] the Sun, although still "tender," fell into the sea.[43] The world became dark, and the night animals were emboldened by the dark-ness. The people (great gods of the sea) were again afraid of the animals. They tried to keep the beasts away by making a great noise all night.

For five days it remained dark, because the Sun was very "tender" and not as strong as he is now. But at the end of this time[,] he again climbed to the sky and there shone in the full splendor of the finest Huichol man's costume.[44]

The great gods wondered why the Sun had been away so long. Kauymáli told them that the Sun lacked a shaman's chair[45] in the sky. None of the great gods knew how to make one. They said to Kauymáli, "You are a cunning devil *(muy maldito)*, so you make it."[46]

Kauymáli replied that he would do what they requested, though it took five days. Not only did he do this, but he made *teapáli*[47] and all other ceremonial paraphernalia for the Sun in the sixth world region (above).

Then he asked María Santigissima Nakawé[48] how this was done.

She replied, "Put flowers in the votive-bowls and nothing will happen to cause the Sun to drop back into the sea." She also ordered a cross and an arch covered with flowers,[49] saying, "This is also good that people may have chil-dren."

All this paraphernalia was taken to the five great cliffs in the Middle Region. Here there were many jaguars and other bad animals. (Therefore the Huichols still take paraphernalia there for the Sun so that he will not disappear from the sky.)[50]

Here were placed five candles, five votive-bowls having paintings of deer with horns [antlers], teapáli, arrows, nealíka, etc. At noon the candles were lighted to strengthen the Sun.[51]

Tatevalí (Grandfather Fire), the great myth-shaman and one of the first to be born, sat down on the patio of the temple in the chair of the Sun. This chair was also very "delicate."[52] He told the people to listen to the song that the Sun was about to reveal to him. By this song they would be able to tame the Sun. Tatevalí said that he would sing and tell the myths for five nights. These myths would explain how everything in the world had been arranged.[53]

Now if the great gods of the sea could understand and remember these songs, the Sun would be gentled. Further, the great gods who had charge of the temple had to become "sacred" (*delicado*, Sp.) for five years, according to the command of the Sun.

During the five days of this work (that is, singing) there was sickness among the people. All remedies failed of their purpose. But the people still took their places around the fire (Tatevalí) so that they might listen to the myth telling.

Five days passed while the people went without sleep and "worked" at myth telling.[54] Then the shaman, Tatevalí, said, "Now we are approaching the end. A child must sing tonight according to the command of the Sun."

The child, Kauymáli *mara'ákame* (singing-shaman, H.), was ashamed before the old man, Tatevalí (Grandfather Fire). He was not even big enough to fill the shaman's chair.

But the child-shaman tried to find out why the remedies did not work. He took his shaman's basket and from the plumes[55] learned that offerings would have to be made to the Sun. Thus the Sun revealed what must be done for the sickness.

The child-shaman then took his bow, arrows, and shaman's basket. As he left, he passed the old man, who was working. Tatevalí thought that the myth telling had not been very good. So they talked in the ancient language of the first times.

The child-shaman placed his bow and arrows at the door of the temple. He took off his hat and began to talk. Meanwhile his shaman's basket had been taken by the women and placed on the altar. They prayed with the basket. The child-shaman first placed his shaman's chair in the middle of the dancing-patio. The other myth-tellers were silent to listen to this boy.

He said, "I did not come because I wished to. I was ordered to come."

The "keepers of the votive-bowls" of the temple told him what was the matter. As soon as they were finished, food was brought to him. Since he could not eat all of the food himself, he gave much to the others.

The boy-shaman told them that he hardly knew how to dream[,] since he was only a child. He was only fit for play, and the only gods he knew were the Sun and the Fire. Indeed, Grandfather Fire had to sit beside him so that the others would not say he was a fool and his myth telling wrong.

At dusk the boy-singer began to narrate this myth of the Sun, for the people were dying from the disease with no relief whatsoever. Then he began to sing. His shaman's plumes had been placed on a little sack at his feet. They had been placed there by each of the "keepers of the votive-bowls."[56] Some of these plumes had rattlesnake rattles attached to them. The sound of these frightened the people, and they knew now that the boy-singer was of great worth.[57]

The great gods sat in shaman's chairs on all sides of the child-shaman. He, however, sat in a god's-chair.[58] On each side of him was an old chanter to assist him.

By midnight they were tired listening to all the Sun would communicate to the Huichols.[59] The child told them to cut down a small pine-tree *(hokó)* and bring it at dawn. This was revealed as the body and heart of the Sun.[60]

They were also to prepare a small bird as an effigy of the heart of the Sun (taukukúi).[61] This effigy was to be placed in a votive-bowl with nealíka on all sides of it. To do this would surely cause the sickness to leave.

So without eating and drinking (except at noon) they went to work until all these things[,] along with the ordinary paraphernalia of the Sun[,] were prepared. The work continued for five days, when, according to the command of the Sun, the boy-singer should sing again. The older ones took his words, because they knew he was better than they.

So they fasted and performed the work that the boy-singer had said would gain the favor of the Sun. During the five days that the work was going on[,] they had to kill a deer. They could not, however, use the lasso-trap. This had to be done by following the signs, since the deer had to be caught alive and brought to the boy-singer.[62]

After a night's sleepless vigil, *tetukuewiwa*[63] went to catch the deer. He directed the work of the others. Soon they found a deer and surrounded it. When this was done, a huge deer sprang up, just as some of the hunters were preparing an altar.

The boy-singer carried chocolate, bread, candles, grape-wine, and two large candles, as well as a votive-bowl. The candles were to be tied to the horns [antlers] of the deer.

The boy-shaman caught the deer by the horns [antlers]. On the horns [antlers] he stuck lighted candles. Then he offered the contents of the votive-bowls to the deer. Five paper flowers were placed on the deer's horns [antlers]. A ribbon also was tied to the horns [antlers].

From the tail of the deer the boy-shaman took five cents. From the horns [antlers] he took five grains of corn. Then from the heart of the deer he took out the dust, *uSra* (peyote-paint).[64]

Thus the boy-singer was successful. Surely now the sickness would leave. He cut the ear of the deer slightly.[65] Much blood streamed out. With this blood he bathed the votive-bowls. The deer, which was not hurt very much, was set free again, because he belonged to Father Sun.[66]

The singer was extremely pleased to see that his orders had been well carried out. He ordered the blood to be taken to the sea. With this blood the great gods of the sea could bathe their ceremonial paraphernalia.

Now that everything was ready, the child-singer, Kauymáli, began to sing. In the meantime the pilgrims were on their way to the sea.

While Kauymáli sang, deer-lassos were put up. As soon as the pilgrims returned, these were bathed in the sacred water from the sea. Also the old men told the myths of the first times and thus explained the owners and significances of everything.[67]

When all the paraphernalia was finished, and the myths and songs chanted, an offering was made to Father Sun. This was so he would retire the sickness that was plaguing the people.

First, however, five blocks of stone, *Sauwáta*, had to be made for Tatevalí, because Grandfather Fire could not move of his own accord[,] since he was so very "delicate" (sacred or dangerous, as fire is). A hole was carved in a block of stone. In this hole was to be placed a small votive-bowl. An eagle and several snakes were painted on the stone.[68]

For Nakawé the people wove a shirt of ixtle (fiber of *Agave*, sp.) as a decoration for an image of this goddess, and also to offer [to] her as a garment. She was also offered a ball of wool and five balls of twigs *(ipulí)*.

Then a wig of white cotton was placed on the head, and thus the idol was made. The idol was taken with wild sweet-potatoes *(iéle)*, "candles of Nakawé," as an offering to this goddess. Furthermore, a bunch of grass was used to decorate her votive-bowls. This had to be taken to her cave, along with the leaves of trees (*maSáwi*, H., "deer-grass") [that were] suitable to her.

A special stone was also made for Nakawé by sticking beads together with a sort of glue. This is still used by the Huichols as an offering in cases of sickness.[69]

All these offerings, together with the idol of Nakawé, were put in the sacred cavity of the temple so that the singers there could communicate with the gods.[70] Other offerings were taken to the sea. These were given by the Huichols as a payment to Nakawé so that they might have children.[71]

When this was done, deer were again killed. The first deer was hung up to dry without first being roasted (as the Huichols do with all their deer now). It was dried in the sun, as was commanded by Father Sun.[72]

This dried meat was very "delicate" (sacred). None might eat of it. Even the dogs might not touch a drop of the dried blood of this first deer or they would die.[73] It had to be well cared for (guarded). The other meat could be cooked, offered to the gods, and then eaten as soup.

The Sun ordered the Huichol "keepers of the votive-bowls" to attend his wishes and commands. They were ordered to bring the usual Huichol offerings of chocolate, wine, sotol, bread, candles, and the like. These were to be placed in the sacred cavity of the temple, together with the blood-filled sections of the intestines of the deer.[74] *Tesgüino* [corn beer] could be made only by those who had followed the orders of the Sun.[75] These orders were communicated to them by the boy-shaman, Kauymáli.

Then the Sun ordered that the candles should be turned over to him by being offered lighted as he arose.[76] An effigy of a jaguar, shining from being covered with tin-foil, was made and placed on the altar.[77]

Kauymáli, the boy-singer, had sung five times while all these preparations were going on. He told the old men the amount of the payment that should be made to him for his singing. But he could not collect all that his singing was really worth, because he had saved the lives of all the people. As a token for his services, however, they should pay him fifty dollars. This value the old men gathered up in cash, as well as in a pile of Huichol effects.[78]

Now that the sickness was gone[,] the people could make a feast of deer-soup.

1. Sub-story: The Jimson-weed Myth

But things had been in order for no more than ten days when the bad shaman, *kieli tewíali* (a personification of *Datura*, sp., "Jimson-weed man"), pretended to sing again to find out the will of the Sun. Kauymáli, although sleeping, heard the singing. He recognized it as false and done to deceive the people and cause harm.[79] For this false singing[,] Jimson-weed collected a large fee—namely, three bulls, two cows, ten sheep, and forty dollars in cash.

In the crackle of the fire Tatevalí told Kauymáli that the singing of the other was pure deception and would produce great harm. He also told Kauymáli that it would be necessary for him to sing again.

The next day the people were sick once more. So Kauymáli prepared to sing. He sang all night. The people became better somewhat. But they could not pay Kauymáli because they had given all their money to Jimson-weed, the bad shaman. The Sun knew of this, since he had heard the song of the child-singer, Kauymáli.

Then Tatevalí communicated with Kauymáli. He ordered him to come quickly to him. When Kauymáli came, he found that the Sun had commanded all of the people to come together again, bringing their animals. This was because sickness was once more passing through the world.

Within five days Kauymáli went where he had been before. He told the people that sickness was visiting them because of the false singing of kieli tewíałi, Jimson-weed.

Kauymáli could not sit in the shaman's chair of the other because Jimson-weed had polluted it. He changed to another chair. Then he began to sing to see what the trouble was.[80]

When Kauymáli began his singing, he shook his shaman's plume that had the rattlesnake rattles on the feathers. By means of this he picked up a small stone, *teáka* (a "very delicate" stone that makes people sick). This was thrown into the fire.[81] After the night's singing[,] the sick animals were cleaned with grass. The grass was then burned.[82]

Then Kauymáli ordered his companions to see if they had "vision" strong enough to kill one of the animals. But none of them had such strong vision. So they had to fast for five days. While they fasted they wept[,] because the disease had returned among them.

But Kauymáli was not afraid. On the contrary[,] his courage was high. He knew that Jimson-weed had made an "arrow of sickness" (*ulú túweli*, which Huichol sorcerers make for use in black-magic). He had stuck the arrow into the animals and into the corn.[83] Also the hair of deer had been used on the animals and the corn.[84] Jimson-weed, furthermore, had taken the pollen of the flowers of *Datura*, sp., and offered it on his plumes to the four points.[85]

Kauymáli had to take away this curse. He could do this by pleasing the Sun, so that the curse would go.[86] So bravely he set out to catch Jimson-weed. He intended to cut Jimson-weed's ear and also his large toe to get his blood as a punishment for his sorcery. He was successful. Not only did he get the sorcerer's blood, but he tied him up and brought him to the fire in the temple.[87]

The Sun and the great gods of the sea said, "Now by our orders you must burn this bad shaman and bury his ashes far away in a hole."[88]

This was done. From the heart of the body came a rock. This rock is still seen in the peyote country.[89]

When the stone came from the heart of the Jimson-weed's burned body, Jimson-weed asked the Sun to bless him so that he would be less bad.[90]

The Sun replied, "I can do it if you wish. In front of your face is a rock. On this rock you can live. Give me your sandal and arrow so that I can communicate with you. I may need your assistance, because there are others who are trying to harm me. I wish you to present yourself to the great gods of the sea."[91]

So with his bow, arrow, and his staff[,] Jimson-weed went to the great gods of the sea. He was playing his violin, and walked like a drunken man.[92] He had to go carefully, because he was very "delicate."[93]

He presented himself to the great gods of the sea. Then he gave his arrows to them. The great gods recognized these as belonging to the Sun. By means of these arrows they communicated with the Sun. In the meantime they told Jimson-weed to stay still and not go away, because for all they knew[,] he might have been on a harmful errand.

The Sun answered the great gods. He told them that as a favor to Jimson-weed he had made him less harmful than he had been.

Thus the rain-gods knew that, although Jimson-weed was half-bad, the Sun was helping him. The Sun informed them that the nealíka of Jimson-weed would be green and yellow, because he was changing him.[94] Thus as Jimson-weed's "face" (aspect) was changing, so the Sun was changing his heart. The Sun asked the great gods of the sea to help him change Jimson-weed.[95]

The great gods of the sea told Jimson-weed that they would give him a water-hole. In this he was to bathe in order to see if he would not change his color (nature?).[96]

Jimson-weed made five jumps to the water-hole. In it he bathed. Then he climbed on top of five high rocks where he could fit. This was ordered by the great gods of the sea.

Jimson-weed climbed the five rocks in order to be tamed and made less bad. On these rocks also he could defend himself if he were attacked. Thus he would have courage.

As he climbed and reached the top, the rock broke open. This happened because he was so "delicate." From the broken rock there were sticks and stones that fell into the sea. This was the heart,[97] and it fell into the sea.

When this happened, Jimson-weed went to a palisade of fifty cliffs. These cliffs were to be his *ranchería* where he could work and live. Here he put his ceremonial paraphernalia. For five days he had to remain awake and communicate with the great gods to learn their orders. They were to inform him if they needed him. Thus he stayed on the rocks that were assigned to him.

Where Jimson-weed lived[,] a small plant (*Datura*, sp.) grew up. He ate this, and thus did not need peyote. His custom was different because he ate jimson-weed.[98] He got drunk on a small bit of the leaf. Then he sang for five nights with his paraphernalia arranged as for a Huichol ceremony.

The great gods sent a woman to his ranchería to find out what he was doing.

Her name was *suyé* (the armadillo).[99] She brought flowers, five bottles of sotol, and her violin on which to play music. She left a *batea*[100] as well.

As Jimson-weed sang, the cliffs listened and chanted the replies. The wind made the violin play, and the batea sounded like a drum. Jimson-weed noticed this, and knew that the batea had been sent to him. He searched carefully and found the armadillo. She was weaving him a shirt. When she heard the music, she hurried to finish the shirt for the feast.

Jimson-weed ordered that the batea should serve as an eating-trough for his dogs. His tobacco-gourds were changed into acorns.[101] The sound of the wind through the acorns and the oak-leaves was the music of the flute, called *tuapúSa* (acorns).

When Jimson-weed heard his music replied to by the rocks, trees, flowers, and batea, he knew that it was well and that it meant the great gods were taming[102] him.

The flowers that sang were the *tatélepots* (some lichen, probably). They live on the rocks in the sierra.

Although Jimson-weed had sung for five days, there had been no dancing. This was because there were no people. So the rocks danced, because Jimson-weed lives near the rocks.[103]

Then the armadillo came out. She dug around where Jimson-weed was seated. Among the roots of his field she found a squash, *súsi [sutsi]*, and the wild squash, *ará*. She ate the seeds of the latter, and passed these seeds as she went abroad. Thus the seeds of the wild squash were distributed to all parts of the world. It is because of its digging that the armadillo is very harmful to the squashes of the Huichols.[104]

Since Jimson-weed was still half-bad, and since the female armadillo had lived with him, she was changed from a great sea-goddess and had to assume her shell. She had to burrow into the ground for her home, and she was ordered to eat grubs when there were no squashes obtainable.[105]

Kauymáli noted all this. He ordered the [sacred] clowns to carry the armadillo in their custom.[106] Then the Jimson-weed singer finished his feast as the Huichols still do for black-magic.

2. Sub-story: Kauymáli Counteracts the Black-Magic of Jimson-weed with Peyote

Now Kauymáli had great courage. He sang again to remove the curse of the false singing of the Jimson-weed singer. Since Kauymáli had been paid once for his work, the "keepers of the votive-bowls" asked him not to collect again.[107]

By means of his sandals[,][108] Kauymáli communicated with the Sun. He wished to find out how to get rid of the ill-effects of Jimson-weed's body, which had been burned. The body had given rise to the wolves, [mountain] lions, rattlesnakes, jaguars, and other animals that threaten the Huichols. The Sun replied that they would have to follow his orders, because these animals belonged to him.[109]

The "keepers of the votive-bowls" asked Kauymáli how much they must pay him to protect them from the attacks of the animals of the Sun. He told them to get tesgüino and offer it at the altar of his (Kauymáli's) god-house.[110] Kauymáli had dreamed[111] all this. He would help to protect the people from the animals, according to the Sun's commands.

The bowls for the tesgüino, as well as ten strings of peyote,[112] were placed on the altar of the god-house of Kauymáli. The peyote had been miraculously placed upon the altar by the Sun. This was pure good [a blessing], and by this sign the Huichols knew that the animals of the Sun would go. The people ground up the peyote and distributed it among the gourds of tesgüino. When they consumed this, the peyote made them drunk, and they sang and danced.[113]

Kauymáli was afraid they would all go crazy, since they acted so strange and wild. There was one peyote-button left. This he ordered brought, since he had not touched it. It was peeled and cut into pieces. Then he spit on it, as Huichol shamans do in curing, and thus prepared it as a remedy for the drunken people.[114]

A bit of this was given to the people so that they would be calm and listen to what Kauymáli was singing. They had to be serious, as all Huichols are in their ceremonies while the singing is going on. Before this[,] even the women were drunk like the men, and tore off their clothes. Kauymáli also sprinkled them with sacred water to make them sober.[115]

Kauymáli learned in his singing that, as a payment to placate the Sun, ceremonial paraphernalia would have to be taken to the peyote country in Real [de] Catorce, San Luis Potosí. So he ordered the people to dance the peyote dance, *Híkuli Neiáli*. He told them to dress in their best clothes. So that the Sun could hear, he had them dance with the carved wand.[116] Then, in order that the great gods of the sea might hear, the people were told to use notched deer-bones, *kaSatcíki vokaki kumukáme [kumúkame]*, for *kumukáeme*. The dancing had to be done to the four points to permit all the gods to see.[117]

This work had to be done by the Huichols every day for five days without rest or food.[118] This was what the Sun desired.

So the people who did not have new clothes borrowed from those who had them, just as the Huichols still do.

3. Sub-story: Kauymáli Vaccinates the People and Brings the Sun Back to the Sky by His Ceremony and Singing

When the Sun was thus far tamed, he went into the sky with all his animals. The Sun was dressed in all the splendor of the Huichol man's costume. He bore many mirrors representing the blaze of the sun in the sky. These mirrors were worn around his shoulders. Around his waist were many little woven pouches.[119]

In this regalia the Sun made a trip across the sky. He was so splendidly dressed, and the mirrors were shining so brightly, that no one could look at him.[120] None could bear the sight of him.

The Sun then changed himself into a small child to go and see the great gods of the sea.[121] He passed so close to the earth-people that he was like fire. The water-holes dried up. The grass burned. The animals and people began to die. The water of the rivers boiled in the face of the Sun, which is so "delicate."[122] Even the rocks melted.[123]

The people could not live under such conditions. There remained only five each of cattle, sheep, deer, etc. In the intense heat of the Sun the people went sweating to Kauymáli. He saved the remaining water and the bodies and blood of the burned animals.

The people implored Kauymáli to save the world from this new danger of the Sun, who was not yet completely tamed but still rather too "delicate."[124] The Sun had disappeared in the sea for fifteen days, leaving the people without water. Kauymáli, therefore, had to do something quickly.

He ordered the people to make five large arrows of brazil-wood. With these they were to communicate with the Sun.[125] Then the bodies of the dead animals were brought. The people were very sad. But Kauymáli told them not to be afraid but to sit before him and listen to his words.

Then the blood from the burned animals was brought to the altar. It was to be used as a preventative for these ills and the greater one of small-pox. Kauymáli was to sing for five nights. He would learn what punishment the people would have to suffer before the Sun could be tamed and made less "delicate."[126]

The small-pox is the brand of the Sun-god [Sun Father] for the Huichols, since people (unlike cattle) do not need to be branded.[127] To prevent small-pox Kauymáli was going to vaccinate *(tcetcieNe)* the people. Pus, taken from an ill man, was scratched in the form of a cross on the shoulders, foreheads, and chests of those who were well.

At the end of the fifth day, after they had gone without eating salt, fifteen people gathered around Kauymáli. Each of them paid ten centavos as a payment to the Sun (to buy candles). One of the women gave Kauymáli a thorn of "wishache." But the Sun said that the thorn was not good enough. So fifteen thorns were placed in a votive-bowl full of sacred water, where they remained all night.[128]

All night Kauymáli talked to Tatevalí, Grandfather Fire (the fire in the center of the circle). He told the people to confess their sins to the fire and to be ashamed of them. The people were then cleaned of their sins by grass, which was afterwards burned.[129] The next day Kauymáli continued his fast to help the Huichols.

After the thorns had been in the sacred water all night[,] they were brought to be used in vaccinating the people. Drops of pus from the sores of those sick with small-pox were also brought. Kauymáli told the people to wait and see what would happen. The pox would remain as a "sign" or brand of the Sun.[130]

In ten days the words of Kauymáli were fulfilled and all the children got well. No more people died. When all got well[,] they had to gather five grains of colored corn and five candles as a payment to the Sun. The corn was ground into flour to make *atole* (mush) for the Sun.[131]

This was done promptly, and everything turned out well. Indeed, it was just as if the small-pox had never occurred, except that many of the people had pox. The man whose pus was used died, however, because the "bad" was taken from him to infect the others.[132]

Each of the fifteen people had to pay six pesos for male children and three pesos for female children. This payment was taken by Kauymáli.[133]

Thus Kauymáli was paid the shaman's fee, although it was difficult for the people to raise the money. He came back in five days when the money had been collected. He had such a bowlful of money that it filled his large pouch.[134]

This vaccination had been done in the middle world region. So Kauymáli repeated it in all the other four regions. This work occupied time throughout all of the dry season. (This is the time of the Sun. Vaccination cannot be done during the wet season, says the informant. Then it would be too "delicate.")[135]

Had the vaccination not been successful, there would be no Huichols today.

Kauymáli instructed the people in the commands and customs of the Sun. Some of the people did not have good hearts. They smoked and laughed while he was instructing them by telling the myths.

Kauymáli told the people that the Sun wanted the blood of a deer. Nakawé, on her part, desired the blood of a peccary and the blood of a goat.[136] The last had to be offered in the sacred cavity[137] so that there would be many children to replace those who had died.[138]

Kauymáli instructed the *compadres* [biological parents allied with ceremonial parents of a baptized child] to help one another as is done among the Mexicans, who belong to the Catholic Church.

The Sun wished the Huichols to be well dressed.[139] So the women were commanded to make many beautiful things for the Huichol costume. Thus the Sun would help the Huichols and protect them from danger.[140]

The final orders of the Sun were received by Kauymáli. Kauymáli told the people it would be necessary to observe these orders to keep the Sun tame. They must get the animals of the Sun, such as [the] brightly colored quail *(súau)*, and another, *kucílaSu*, and the mountain blue-jay, *mainoáiva*, and another small bird which has a very loud cry, *kokaimúeli* (*cireal*, Sp.).[141]

There was a rock where the animals were placed so that their cries would cause the Sun to rise.[142] There also was placed a violin, and there Kauymáli stood beside the paraphernalia that had been set out for the Sun. He played the violin, adding its music to the songs of the birds in order to please the Sun.

All the paraphernalia sounded; the wolves howled; the [mountain] lions roared; and the eagles screamed. Their father (the Sun) heard their song and was pleased.

Then all rose and climbed into the air to approach closer to the Sun. They rose until they found a level where the Sun did not shine so brightly.[143] Here they sang for five hours and offered their burning candles[144] in the middle of the dry season.

This ceremony finally tamed the Sun. The Huichols continue to do it to keep the Sun tame. If this were not done, the Sun would remain in his cave and all the world would be dark. Or else he would be wild, and, coming too close to the earth, [he] would burn and dry up the world.[145]

Then they came down, and the animals and birds chose places on the earth that they wished for homes. The people had had hard work taming the Sun, but it was done.

The Sun ordered five gates to be made at the different directions[146] of the place where he had been born. It was here that the Sun had rested while the people were giving ceremonies to tame him. He had rested in his shaman's chair.

C First Peyote (Deer) Journey Brings the Sun to the Sky

Ceremonies During and After Journey

Nakawé is the mistress of the stars. When the earth was made and the rain fell on the sea, the stars emerged from the water as balls (or circles). Then they went up to the sky where they shine.[1]

In the water were many bad snakes — blue, red, brown(?), black, and striped.[2] They were everywhere, and people going to the sea for water had to look out for them. Nakawé asked the stars to help her, because when she went to the water[,] five snakes came out. So the stars fell on the snakes, killing them in the water.[3] Even so, the snakes always won, and came out five at a time.

Nakawé pleaded, "Don't take my people to the sea."

But the snakes took them in spite of her.

The stars, however, were tired of the battle, and so ten stars fought with fifteen snakes. Nakawé ordered that only fourteen of the snakes be killed. Four [of the] best stars fell and thundered into the waters of the sea. The snakes came out dead, falling to one side.

Still the snakes filled the water. Nakawé went to the one snake left and said, "I did not have you killed because you must have a family."

The snake that was saved had children; these, however, did not enter the water. They came out like balls of cotton (cloud symbol) or stones, but at the same time were snakes.

Nakawé named the first Teteoyéli, and told it, "You, child, you must remain here."

Then the snake had another child[,] which was like a drop of water (rain symbol) and which changed into a rock. Nakawé gave it the name of Na'aliwáme [Na'aliwaemi].[4]

Still another snake-child came out of the water, spinning around. Nakawé took it by the hand, held it close to her ear, and listened to it. Then she said, "Your name is Teteoyéli Sutuliuiákam (animal of cave-water)."

Another snake-child was born. Nakawé listened to it also, and asked its name. It said, "I am KaSíwali."

Nakawé ordered, "You stay there," and placed it with the others.

Another was born from the water. "I am named Mekíma," it said.

Another came out of the water and asked Nakawé, "Do you know me?"

Nakawé replied, "Of course. Your name is MoNíma (god of water). Stay with the others."

Still another was born, and Nakawé said, "I know your name. It is MáSama. Stand there."

(The story continues with the birth of the following under the same circumstances as the other female snake-goddesses:)

Halianáka	NauwSimá	Takaí Iúyami
Haliúwi [Haluwi]	Kuyuwáme	Otsimáwika
Hakaúwi	Mukwikwíełi	Tate Waínu
Haistuíma	Namákame	Tate HaíSama
HaiSinóra	Teakáyuwáweme	

Then Tatevalí said, "Another big one is being born, Nakawé. How will you call it?"

Nakawé called it Otuanáka.[5] She said, "You are the most important and will stay in the sea. The others will be your family. Your family will all sit around you. I tell you now there is going to be born another nation."

Then Nakawé commanded some male snake-gods to be born. These came out of the sea in the ancient times before the Sun lighted the world. Hitherto there had been only the light of the moon.[6] The following were born:

Kauymáli	Mataika Tewíałi
WáKuti	Hátsi Tewíałi
Tsakaímuka	Kutsimatimuwíałi
Komaiteámai	Kakaimutikasálika
Tatotsí[7]	S[t]uluwíakame[9]
MaSákwáSi[8]	Téawaikiaka
Kuaká'wa	Timaýweame
Awátsałi	Nealikáuła
Mo'ótami	USayuíta
Sisiótałi	Tuká Kamekwatsápa MukaSíła
Talíkwi	Iamúkwi
Mainákaúłi	Iáwi Tewíałi
TeawakonawSáłi	Tate [Our Mother] Ipu Tewíałi
Hułíakai	Ułáwe Tewíałi
Atákwe	Maye Tewíałi
Katsa Tewíałi	Káwi Tewíałi

Nakawé placed Kumúkame [father of the Wolf-people] at the head of these gods, and all prepared for a ceremony.[10]

Kumúkame announced, "I am going to sing." He made a drum at the edge of the sea.

Many people gathered to participate in the feast. All night the snake-gods served Kumúkame by running down deer, killing them only with arrows. In the meantime Kumúkame sang to his drum. Then the people went again; but though they shot many arrows, and though Kumúkame continued singing, they did not kill any deer. On learning this[,] Kumúkame tossed a glowing coal in the water,[11] and then tied a string around it and hung it from the middle of the house.

Towámo (the Rat) saw, however, that the singing was doing no good, and he said, "Let us cut down this hanging coal." At midnight, while Kumúkame was still singing and his people were out hunting the deer, he cut the string. The coal fell and burned the house together with all the ceremonial paraphernalia.

At the sight of the flames[,] Kumúkame cried out excitedly, "Who cut that string which has served me so well?"

All this happened while the others were away hunting, but when the house burned they knew of it. They thought at once of the lying Towámo, and swore he would never harm them a second time by cutting down hanging coals.

The Rat, however, got away, and the people were unable to find him. They followed his tracks away from the houses, but while they were gone the Rat returned and cut the string holding another hanging coal. From the burning house the Rat stole all the ceremonial paraphernalia. The hunters, seeing another house burning, left their search and rushed back. They could not save anything, however.

Then the people talked to Nakawé and Tatevalí. At the command of Tatevalí they constructed a new house and made new ceremonial paraphernalia. At night Kumúkame began to sing again, while the others went once more after deer, using only arrows. They hunted at a natural corral of stone (*mukuwáwi*, green[-]earth), but no deer ran in the corral.

The next night Kumúkame again began to sing, after telling the others to go to the sierra to a small break in the cliff (*ventana*[,] Sp.) called Suráwi (star) where deer could be shot in passing through. Near this break was sitting a turkey buzzard (*ualúku tewíali*).

Kumúkame said to *raínu tewíali* (a snake), "You go to one side where you may be able to kill a deer." On the other side he placed *topína tewíali* (the Humming-bird), who was the best shot of all of them. Behind, he sent *haiku tewíali* (another snake). He ordered *rai tewíali* (a rattle-snake) to go above. In the middle he placed *wisa tewíali* (eagle).

Then they went to their places, with dogs to follow the deer's tracks, and formed a large circle. The dogs barked at the place, mukuwáwi (green-earth), to frighten the deer.

Suráwe (Star), who saw the deer first, whistled five times like a dove. He signalled by beating his bow-string with an arrow. Then he beat his bow, and whistled like a quail.

The others heard. Suráwe (Star) said that he would shoot first. He crept to the place, mukuwáwi (green-earth), where he had seen five deer at the five points, took out an arrow and shot. But he missed the deer, which ran around in a circle and escaped below to the sea.

Suráwe asked another to shoot the next time. This one followed the deer's tracks five times. Finally he found one and shot at it, missing it, however. The deer ran back to the sea.

Another followed other deer tracks until he, too, saw a deer. He shot at it but was unable to hit it. This deer escaped to the sea as the others had done.

Then the people became angry with Star (Suráwe) and cried, "You said that you were a good shot, but three deer have escaped to the sea."

So Star hunted until he found another deer. He shot at it but missed, even though Kumúkame was singing all the while with his drum. This deer also escaped and ran away to the sea.

Finally, the fifth time, a very big deer was tracked to the middle of the place, mukuwáwi (green-earth). Suráwe had only one arrow. After going five times he saw the big deer. He took four more arrows out of his quiver. His first shot barely missed the animal's nose. The second shot went slightly to the left. The third went between the animal's horns [antlers]. The fourth passed very close to its tail.

The people now threatened to kill Suráwe if he missed with his last arrow. He took careful aim and hit the animal in the head. But the arrow broke, and the deer, who was so angry he shot clouds from his horns [antlers] and mouth,[12] ran off carrying between his horns [antlers] the arrow of Suráwe. The people shouted, "There he goes!"

Suráwe asked some of the others to chase the deer. Raínu (a snake) said, "Where is he going?" as he watched him disappear as a tiny cloud that looked like a bit of cotton.[13]

Even though the deer was at a great distance, Raínu shot at it, and the arrow went throught the animal's heart.

Kumúkame knew of this and sang, "Now they have killed a deer."

This deer did not escape. Suráwe shot it again from the other side. His arrow pierced the deer's side and entered its heart.

The people now chased the wounded deer and drew in close upon it, since it was slowing down from loss of blood.

But the turkey-buzzard, ualúku tewíałi, was witnessing all this from the heights (mountains). He cried to the deer, "Matsi ([Elder Brother] deer), come up here, come up here where the people cannot follow you."

Barely could the deer jump to the top because of the blood streaming from his wounds and his mouth. The people followed closely behind.

Kokáiwa (another name of the buzzard), however, was a master of deceit. He called to Raínu, "Give it a last shot and kill it immediately." But he drew the arrows from the deer and healed its wounds with *waSirá wa* (a little magic bead), which he placed in the holes. Thus the deer became well again.

Kokáiwa (the buzzard) then told the deer how to escape, first by jumping on bunches of grass to leave no tracks, then on to ice (hail), from there on to rocks, and finally on to the little white grass. "Go," he said, "to *hokowaiwelíka*[,] where there are five pine trees, and there rest in the shade of the trees. In five hours I will find you."

The deer obeyed him.

When the people got to the top of the mountain, they found the Buzzard playing innocently on his flute. They asked him where the deer was. He replied glibly, "He must be there, where there is so much blood." But the deer could not be found, since here the tracks ended. Buzzard sent them off again. The dogs tried to smell out the tracks, but they failed and could not follow.

Then the people called the gnats to aid them by taking up the scent of the deer. The gnats flew up to the sky and soon came to where the deer was lying. The people, however, could not follow. The gnats (or mosquitos) [maggots] covered the deer, which had died in the meantime.

Meanwhile the singer in his song told the people to force Buzzard to tell the truth.[14] Raínu found an arrow from the deer and recognized it for his by the smell. This was done five times. Thus it was discovered that Buzzard had pulled it out of the deer.

Buzzard became frightened at the sight of so many mad people.

In his song the singer ordered the people to make Buzzard a prisoner. This they did, tying him to a tree with his arms held out by means of bows. Then they stuck an arrow through his nose and left him in the mountains to die while they returned to mukuwáwi (green-earth). (That is why buzzards still have a hole in their noses.)[15] All this was done to Buzzard as a punishment for making the people foolish.

But when they had gone, Buzzard released himself and pulled the arrow out of his nose. Then he said disdainfully, "These people don't know anything except the very little that goes on down there below. I, however, know everything. I can see through the sky as far as the sea. Thus I can make fools of them." Then he called five times, and said, "I will go and find the deer."

The people heard his cry and saw that he had freed himself. They shouted, "Buzzard has got away and gone."

Buzzard was garbed in the full ceremonial array of the Huichols. Now his smell was much keener than that of the people, and he was able to follow the scent of the deer. He went to the five pines[,] which were in the mountains (suggestion that by mountains here is meant the sky), searched around each tree, and at the fifth found the dead deer covered by maggots from the mosquitos. He frightened the mosquitos [flies] away with his hat, and then cleaned the carcass by eating all the maggots with his tongue.[16]

Then Buzzard took an arrow and tapped the deer's feet. But he received no response. He then tapped at the deer's heart and horns [antlers], saying, "Deer, get up."

The deer sprang up. "My[,] I was frightened by all those people," he said, "[b]ut I came a long distance and have slept well despite my arrow-wounds."

Buzzard replied, "You did not sleep. You were dead. The people would surely have cooked and eaten you had I not saved you."

The deer replied gratefully, "It is good that you gave me life."

"Your fathers and your ancestors, Tatotsí and Nakawé," Buzzard continued, "did not wish you to die down there on the earth. You are safer here in the sierra. But leave here, because the people will not delay to hunt you even in the sierra. The singer, Kumúkame, will help them by his singing.[17] Pálikata will hunt you. So go to your father and mother to see them. Go."

"Yes," the deer said, "it is better that I go."

Then Buzzard said, "Go this way. Jump blue, yellow, white, black, and at the little-earth *(maya nuítsi)*. There you will find your parents waiting at their house." (This is in the peyote country.) Buzzard also told him, "There you will find your father the Sun, Tau.[18] Now when you get there attend to what they say."

The deer went, although he was covered with blood. His mother, S[t]uluwía-kame, was waiting for her son. When she saw his condition, she said to him, "What has happened to you?"

The deer replied, "Buzzard told me to come."

The Sun, Tau, soon arrived with Kauymáli, a singer, and Pálikata, the elder brother. To them the deer told his story.

Pálikata said, "Kauymáli, you must sing."

The rat, Towámo, was there also, with all the things he had stolen from the burning house. The Sun, Tau, asked for them. "I must have the plumes, the tobacco pouch, and everything else," he said.

Thus they arranged a Huichol altar, placing the paraphernalia in the usual manner, in order to celebrate their victory over the rain-god people below.

The Sun, Tau, then brought forth people [in his image] by breathing from his heart.[19] Topína (Humming-bird), the father of the Sun, said, "I will await you here, when all is arranged for the feast. Use what was stolen from the burning house by the Rat."[20]

Motioning to Kauymáli, who was going to sing, the Sun ordered, "You sing here. And here we shall place the altar with the paraphernalia."

Meanwhile Pálikata had ordered a house to be built so that he could live there as well.

The Sun, Tau, then invited all the great gods to the feast, and he accompanied them. The great gods are:[21]

1. Tatevalí (Grandfather Fire)
2. Tatotsí (Grandfather [Great-grandfather] Deer-tail)
3. TsipuSáwe
4. Tsakaímuka [Tsakaimúka]
5. MaSákwáSi (Deer-tail)
6. Takaláo Iwamáleame

To his companions the Sun said, "Let us go and see the mother of the deer."

Because the Sun still lived in the sea, they had to go by the light of the moon in the sky, sleeping five nights and fasting before arriving. On the fourth night they arrived at *kakaimutine* (beyond Zacatecas).

The fifth night many animals gathered near the camp, since the gods did not have any fire. Takaláo slept a little, while the others guarded him.

The Sun said, "We lack fire. The moon does not give us enough light."

During the night[,] the wind carried away all their clothes.

When they finally awakened, one asked, "Who dreamed what will happen to us?"

"No one dreamed," he was answered.

Takaláo then said, "I dreamed that these animals that have gathered near us will kill us before [within] five days. We must go back and talk to Tatevalí."

So they returned in four days and asked Tatevalí for favors to help them in their trip. Takaláo shot an arrow to attract the attention of Nakawé.[22]

Tatevalí got the arrow, listened to it, and heard it say, "Someone is coming to see you on business."

Three more arrows were shot, and Tatevalí listened to them also. The third and fourth passed very near to him, and the fifth came very close. Tatevalí listened again, and the arrow said, "The people are drawing near. They were going to see their mother, but have returned to ask you a favor."

Then the people came up close, stopping a short distance from Tatevalí. They told him their troubles. Takaláo informed him of his dream, and said, "The moon does not give us enough light for our journey."

Tatevalí answered, "I will send animals to lead you back."

"I have made all my ceremonial paraphernalia — face-painting things, tobacco gourd, hat, shaman's plumes, and shaman's baskets," replied Takaláo. All these I will give you for frightening the animals that have frightened us."

"Go for five nights," Tatevalí ordered, "and nothing will happen to you. When the animals come around you, have your people gather much wood. Here, I give you a teapáli (god-disc)[,][23] which is my heart. I myself cannot go."

They returned on their journey, and on the third night they collected wood and dried grass for kindling in order to test the virtue of the teapáli. Then they opened the shaman's basket, and all took hold of the teapáli and placed it on the ground, after which they set plumes on it. Then they began to say a prayer, and when they had finished[,] the plumes lighted. Thus they were able to build a fire.[24] They heated their food in the coals.

When the rooster crowed, they started off again in order to arrive on the fifth day. Tatevalí had told them their journey would be gruelling [*sic*], and that, if they did not wish to imperil themselves, they must punish themselves by neither eating nor drinking.[25] If they were successful, they would find candles, bread, and meat at the home of the deer.

On the fourth day each made arrows in order to insure their arriving on the morrow.

Only one of them, *maim[á]li tewíali*, was crying from hunger and thirst, saying, "I cannot bear the suffering of this trip." From a cactus (nopal) he stole fruit and refreshed his heart.

When the others learned he had broken the fast, they would not let him go with them.[26] "You remain here near the cactus," they told him, "and eat its fruit always." And here he remained, as a rat.

They continued their journey, and on the fifth day arrived at the house of their mother, S[t]uluwíakame,[27] where there was food and water. Here also was all the ceremonial paraphernalia. As they drew near, the mother and all the women brought paraphernalia, and greeted them (in the Huichol fashion to pilgrims arriving at a feast).[28]

The people had stopped where there were five streams of water. In crossing, each had to step in the footprints of the one ahead. They all sat down in the temple, where they were given food. After praying, a gourd (or wooden bowl, *piliwáli*, a very old word) was brought, and with a white flower the guests were blessed and baptized in Huichol fashion.[29]

In order to find the house of the deer, the people were not allowed to drink water but must content themselves with the baptism.[30]

The mother told them, "Within five days you will come to the house of the deer (i.e., peyote).["]

Then they journeyed for five more days in order to arrive at the upper world, *niwatáli*,[31] where they looked for the tracks of the deer, their father (Peyote). Taking five arrows from their quivers for their bows, they climbed up a little mesa. There they saw the deer alone by the nawatáli (probably niwatáli).

This was the deer hidden by the Buzzard. Others soon saw him. Then, slowly, in a long line they began to encircle the deer. Every track the deer made resulted in a peyote. These they shot as they climbed, and each was shot four times. When they had finished [shooting] their arrows, they left their tobacco gourds, sandals, hats, feathers, and pouches. Then each helped to enclose the circle, according to the command of Tatevalí. In the middle a spray of foam sprang up. This was the deer, which was an enormous peyote. One side was green, one white, one red, another black, and another yellow.[32] By means of these colors from peyote each of the hunters painted his face. These colors are the life.[33] The peyote was left clean.

Then those who carried the paraphernalia arranged an altar around the peyote (deer), and here they prayed. Tatevalí ordered them to put tobacco in their mouths and swallow the juice.[34] This, combined with their fatigue and the effects of their fast and thirst, made them extremely sick, and they fell down and prayed, leaving their paraphernalia.[35]

Then they returned to the edge of the mesa where they had left their possessions, and dug out all the peyote they had shot on climbing the mesa. Taking their belongings and their arrows they returned to the house of the deer's mother, S[t]uluwíakame.[36] Only one stayed behind. He had to go to look for two peyotes for his life.

Now they lighted many candles in the midst of the peyote. The color put on their faces went to their hearts and made them curers.[37] Then they got grass and cleaned the peyote, cutting off the skin to get the pure heart[,] which was cut up. Even the husk of the peyotes was brought back. A pile twelve inches high was made of the peyote, and Tatevalí gave a bit to each person. The peyotes were finally ready to be placed in newly washed gourds, while the men prayed to the deer.

Now they could eat of the peyote. It caused green spittle in the mouth. What was left they put in their pouches to carry back to their homes. Having now eaten the peyote, they could drink water.

Then Tatevalí said, "Fill your gourds with water, and drink your fill. Also eat your tortillas. Thus you may have life for a long time to come."[38]

Palikata then said, "Let us each eat half of the large peyote."

This they did, and Tatevalí said, "In five years you will know how to sing, cure, and be a shaman."[39]

They went on for one more day to where there is peyote. (This is near Del Torro.) By this time they were drunk from eating so much peyote, and thus some had to help the others. Here, where the ground is covered with peyote, they waited.

"Do not remember your home or your mother," cautioned Tatevalí, "but work hard."

From fire which they carried[,] they made a fire, and at night, while Tatevalí sang, they gathered around it.

At midnight, at the house, the mother said, "The men can be given food." So she sent ten women with tamales, tortillas, and such, as their reward for having brought here the ceremonial paraphernalia. "Food will take away their peyote drunk," she said.

So they were given bitter, black atole [corn mush].

In the morning Tatevalí asked Kauymáli to lend him one of his deer-horns [antlers] (peyote). Kauymáli complied. One bit of the deer-horn was broken off and ground with a teapáli as a sacrifice to the deer. Soon there were three baskets of deer. Then the small bowls were given to all. Tatevalí took up the magic deer-horn food, and all the leaders blessed it by dropping a bit of it into the fire.[40] Then the deer-meat was given to all. This magic deer-horn food is very strong and must be eaten only by very strong men. Others it would make crazy. To prevent their going crazy, S[t]uluwíakame put sacred water into the bowls. This was used on the people also.[41]

Meanwhile Kumúkame in the underworld was singing to the rain-gods. At the same time, Tatevalí was singing to the fire-people above. Those in the underworld heard the singing of Tatevalí. Tatevalí said, "Those people are coming, and they think that we are crazy. But let them come."

The Rain-people from below arrived but stayed to one side. They said, "We are [have] come to find the deer, and at dawn we are going to hunt."

Kumúkame himself did not fear the magic liquor [sacred drink] of the deer-horn (peyote). He was given two bowls of the liquid, but it only made him drunk. Nor did it harm the party of Tatevalí. The others, however, were driven crazy and staggered away. Thus in the morning only the men of Tatevalí were fit to hunt the deer (peyote). The other party remained in a drunken stupor from the deer-horn.

At dawn, the Sun, Tau, came out to replace the moonlight, for once deer (peyote) had been killed[,] the Sun could come out.[42]

When the others went out to hunt the deer, Topína and Raínu remained behind[,] hidden in the center to kill the deer. Topína shot one, and Raínu, using two arrows, another.[43]

The altar in the house of the mother was already set up, and the deer-blood finally obtained for the dedication of her ceremonial paraphernalia. The rain-god hunters, who were still drunk from partaking of so much peyote, were getting a little better. Tatevalí then asked, "Who will win in telling me in advance the name of the killer of the deer?"

One of the men who were still peyote-drunk said, "I know who it is. It is Waokúakua." But he was wrong.

Another gave another name, but he was not right either, and so did not win the wager of Tatevalí.

Then they brought the dead deer so that they could see who had killed it. Kauymáli said, "He who brings the deer is Wápakame."

Meanwhile the altar of the mother had been prepared with all the paraphernalia. The rain-god party of peyote-hunters, still drunk, approached the feast. One of them, Pálikata, recognized his arrows among those things stolen by the Rat. He became violently angry, and, taking his arrows from the altar, offered to do battle. There were fifty arrows, and one he gave to each of the fifty men in his party. Then the battle began. Of Pálikata's group, only the Wolf died from his wounds. The wounded ones of the other party were forced to fly before Pálikata's arrows.

When those of the Sun's party came back with the deer, there were many people waiting to feast. Tatevalí ordered that arrows of brazil-wood be made so that prayers could be passed to the Sun.[44] Then Tatevalí said, "Who is that coming out? Let us see who can tell the name of the Sun."

The Sun was truly coming out for the first time because of the success of the deer-hunt. Indeed Tatevalí had left his votive[-]bowls upon the killing of the deer and become the Sun.

But the people of below, accustomed only to the light of the moon, could not tell the name of the Sun.

One said, "It is the Fire." But none of them could win.

Then the others from the sea shot arrows toward the Sun. One arrow approached close but fell back and hit the shooter in the eyes, making them white. Thus some animals (albinos?) always have white eyes. But none was able to shoot an arrow as high as the Sun, and thus the Sun could say, "I have more worth than any of them."

Then the Fire said, "No one has yet told the name of the Sun."

Some small animals even after five attempts still had chances of success, but they did not succeed. All failed because they had no thought (or ability).[45]

The people in the meantime had formed five circles and were praying for aid in telling the name of the Sun. The greatest gods had come up from behind to find out who, if anybody, had won. Off to one side they heard someone playing. It was the Turkey, and he let out his neck. The Fire asked him if he knew.

Now although the Turkey could not talk, he could make sounds. He strutted arrogantly about and beat the earth many times with his wings. His neck grew longer and longer and trembled. Finally he cried, "*Tau! Tau! Tau!*"

The sea people lost, and the Turkey won.

Thus it was in the olden times, as given down by the ancients.[46]

When it was noon, the Sun came back to where he had started from. He cried, "You, down there! Some of you must dream." He said this because he was still pagan *(cimarrón)*, or wild, since he had just emerged from the sea.

The people sounded with machetes, pieces of gourds, and bells (as when swarming bees are tamed). The Rooster and the Turkey made their cries. And the Sun came out in pleasure with greater light. He lacked votive[-]bowls and arrows, so the people made them for him in order to tame him.[47]

When the Sun went down again, many animals collected as before.

The people decided that for protection against the animals they would have to tame the Sun. They said, "To tame the Sun, and to make him come out, let us dream; and then he will drive away the wild animals."

The Fire dreamed that they should make ceremonial arrows, nealika [nea-líka], shaman's chairs, teapáli, and the like.[48] He dreamed also that the Sun wished to sit in a chair, and that he would not come up until the chair was finished and the teapáli painted.

When the people were at last ready to leave for their homes, they dressed in deer-skin with horns [antlers] and hoofs and went to the house of Pálikata.[49] All the festal tamales were piled on an altar. Then small, god's-sized tamales were offered to the Fire with a prayer. At dawn, these were changed into peyote,[50] and were in turn collected so that the people could go.

Then five *akastes* (Mexican Indian crates)[51] were brought. They were filled only with peyote. Some, however, were given to Tatevalí, who told the hunters that he would watch the peyote on the return trip. Then the people gathered their own peyote, as well as that of Tatevalí, and returned to their homes.

On the way they finished the tortillas they had brought for food, so [they] were forced to live on peyotes. They said, "Let us see if we can arrive back at our homes in fifteen days."

Meanwhile their families had placed [tended] the fire in the temple, awaiting the return of the peyoteros.

The pilgrims got very weak and needed aid. Fire said to them, "I will give you burros to carry the peyote." He also gave them saddle-blankets, pack-saddles, and the like. Tatevalí went first with five burros loaded with akastes of peyote.[52]

The pilgrims shortly reached a place where they could take their first ceremonial bath.[53] Tatevalí told them to thank their mother for their safe return after so much fasting and "punishment," and then they could bathe and drink freely. When they lighted their candles, Mother S[t]uluwíakame blessed them and promised them long life and strength. Then she commanded them to return every year.[54]

At the end of another fifteen days they were not far from their homes. Ten days following this, Tatevalí ordered them to make a ceremonial wand to protect their return.

Meanwhile in the temple[,] the families of the hunters were informed in dreams that their men would return in five days. The women and the children prepared lighted candles as well as sacred water to prevent any harm [from] befalling the pilgrims. There were many dangers and many fierce animals to watch out for, but the great gods aided them.

When the pilgrims drew near, they tied all their pouches together to send twenty-five peyotes to their families. Tatevalí said, "I will go on ahead, and at midnight send an arrow to the temple and see if the arrows there hear it."[55]

The pilgrims themselves were happy with peyote drunkenness and fat from having eaten so much peyote.

Grandfather Fire put the peyote on his shoulder and went on ahead in order to arrive at the temple first. He said to himself, "I will fool those at the temple, and find out how our wives have been treating us. At sunset I will give them some peyote."[56]

Thus, while all the pilgrims remained behind drunk, Tatevalí approached the temple well-dressed and carefully painted, and surprised those who were waiting there. He had prepared an arrow stuck full of peyotes, so he disguised himself and entered. Within, he found the wives faithfully awaiting their husbands.[57]

Tatevalí motioned to a child, who was watching a votive[-]bowl, and to it and to all the others he gave a piece of peyote. Then he tossed them a peyote to see if they would pick it up. If these are picked up, the people die.[58]

Tekuamána was the chief guardian of all the women. He had entered in the meantime, but had said nothing.

At eight o'clock, in spite of his fire feathers, Tatevalí took a flint and steel and made a fire from wood the people had brought. When the women set before him all kinds of food, he remained grave and serious and refused to eat because his companions had not yet arrived. This was because he was still "delicate."[59] All the food and water he only sprinkled on his heart (chest).

Then Fire requested all to sit down in proper order. From Tekuamána he borrowed a blanket for an altar, and on it [he] placed one hundred and twenty-five peeled peyotes. Five were given to the women and children of the pilgrims. This made them drunk. Others were invited to take twenty-four. The women ate the peyote from the altar-blanket.

When the men came, all the peyote was eaten. The women were drunk and talking of everything that had happened while the pilgrims were gone. Thus had Fire fooled them to find out if they had been faithful.

To Tekuamána, Tatevalí said, "You should be ashamed that you are drunk from peyote. Your heart is hot from it."

The women then ate another cut-up peyote, and this quieted them. Tatevalí ordered them to prepare food for their men, even if they were drunk.

At dawn there were no sober women to meet the on-coming pilgrims (in Huichol ceremonial fashion). Though the men would arrive in a few hours, the women were still drunk.

Meanwhile the men ate tortillas and started out at noon carrying their burdens of peyote. They walked in a straight line.[60] On arriving they gave their things to the women. Then they made a ceremonial circuit of the temple and, entering carefully, placed their peyote on the altar. By this act they could enter their private houses again. In the afternoon all were again deceived by Fire, who gave them peyote to eat. This was done five different times.

The next day Fire ordered the men to clear the fields in order to fulfill a dream. As they worked they ate peyote. In the middle of the fields they placed a pile of peyotes. Four of the men made a circuit of the field, approached the altar, and prayed.

They worked until they had carried out Fire's order.[61] From the fields they carried wood for the night's fire. Returning, they made a circuit of the temple and dropped the wood as an offering for the fire.[62]

They were then commanded to change their language. They drank water and ate a little of the food brought, but very little, since they were still under a special fast. This fast lasted for three months[,] while the pilgrims were "delicate" and could not in consequence eat salt or sleep with their wives.[63] The leader always knew when the fast had been broken.

When the men had finished clearing the fields, deer were hunted. Then cattle, turkeys, sheep, and the like were killed so that the pilgrims might be brought out of their "delicate" condition.[64] Finally a feast [ceremony] with full ceremonial equipment was made, and all those who had heard about it came. Those who had brought sacred water back from the peyote-country carried that to the feast, and all the guests were baptized in it. Now, since their arrival, they could bathe for the first time. The following day the soup of the deer was consumed, and then [corn] beer was drunk.

The peyoteros now painted their faces so that they might live in the world and have life.[65] Then the singing started, and the peyoteros began their dance, which lasted for the best part of two days. Peyote was ground up and prepared in gourds, and on it the guests got drunk.

Then Tekuamána painted his face and hung several rattles on his belt to sound.[66] He talked to Tatevalí, and those around the two listened closely in order to hear about the bringing of the peyote. Tatevalí told Tekuamána that he had orders to invite others to the feast, and went an hour's journey distant to fulfill his mission.

These people started for the feast with all their paraphernalia, and Tekuamána came at their head. He took out his shaman's plumes to see what he could see.[67] Upon the arrival of the newcomers, the singer got up in full regalia and went among them, blessing them and baptizing them with the sacred water from the peyote country[,] which means long life.[68]

Then five boys within the temple danced very fast so that the people at the bottom of the sea could hear their sandals.[69] The peyote dancers in their dance did likewise.

Tekuamána was a bad spirit (a sort of devil), and he attempted to disperse the dancers. He forced apart those who were dancing together (arm over partner's shoulder, as Huichol women dance this dance).

As the Sun was going down, the singers made prayers of what the people wanted. The deer-tails used in the dance said they were thirsty. Accordingly[,] first the singers and then the dancers thrust the tails into water.[70]

Then after these ceremonies came the feast of parched corn (*esquite*) and soup, together with drinks of *tesgüino* [corn beer]. Following this feast[,] the women could sleep with their husbands.

The singer finally commanded husbands and wives to link arms and march around in a ceremonial circuit. Thus were they permitted at last to return to the customs and acts of marriage.[71]

The delicate tobacco taken on the peyote trip was fed to Grandfather Fire by being dropped in the fire.[72]

The food and drink was all consumed, and the feast ended.

D Myth of the Huichol Temple *(Túki)*

At the margin of the sea were people who had come to learn the will [of] the great gods of the sea. A message (arrow) fell at dawn from the Sun, who had just risen. The message said that the Sun commanded (was superior to, probably) the great gods of the sea. All the people came rushing out to see what it meant. They listened closely to the message.[1] It was a harsh command of [from] the Sun. It said, "If you disobey the Sun, he will finish [destroy] the world: the fields, the mountains — everything. If you do not respect his wishes, he will even kill all the children."

Now Kauymáli was nearby. He listened to what the arrow had to say. Then he suggested that they fast, and after this call the best singer-shaman. The singer-shaman could sing and thus learn the will of the gods.

So the people called the greatest singer, Tatevalí (Grandfather Fire). Tatevalí sang all night according to the command of the Sun.[2] He emerged from the fire, blazing in all his pomp of costume and feathers. Then he sat in a shaman's chair and drank sacred water. This calmed him.[3] After singing all night[,] he revealed what the gods had said to him as he sang.[4] "If you do not accept the command of Father Sun, your children, crops, animals, and everything will die."[5]

The people retorted, "This command is very harsh." They had to discuss it among themselves. They decided that they would have to accept the command of the Sun [F]ather. So they began to fulfill his desires.

They cleared a dancing-patio, and in this erected a dwelling for the Sun [F]ather and for Grandfather Fire. Then they gathered together twenty-five stools [shaman's chairs]. These were for the chief men of the people of Kauymáli to sit upon.

Kauymáli was asked if he could divine things. He said that he could. So the people asked him to take the feathers of Tatevalí. These were given to the child, Kauymáli. The people went with a child who wore a plume in his hair.[6] Then they dug and took out building-stone with which to make the walls of the temple. Others were sent to kill deer[7] and *javelíns*[8] [javelinas] (Sp. for the peccary). Still others, at the command of the Sun, had to offer sheep. Others had to collect twenty-eight votive-bowls. And others, twenty-eight ceremonial arrows, and front and back shields, etc., for hanging on the arrows. If this were not done, the Sun would kill all the children by small-pox; while the animals and plants would perish from drought.[9] All were commanded not to drink water for five days,[10] or taste salt, or touch their wives.[11]

The people busied themselves with these preparations. All had to be done within five days. The deer had to be killed within this same time. Many went after deer.

The first day they killed one. Thus they now had deer-blood with which to bathe the ceremonial paraphernalia. Further, after this they could drink and bathe.[12]

The second day they killed a female deer.

The third day, another.

The fourth day, another.

The fifth day, still one more.

Thus they were not liable for punishment; for indeed, had they not killed deer, everything in the world would have been finished.

On the sixth day the traps were taken down. The singer called the child (Kauymáli) to talk to him. One of the children was ill of small-pox. In order to save it they would have to kill a goat and bathe the ceremonial paraphernalia in the blood. The father agreed to do this under the circumstances. He promised to bring the goat within five days.

Then a woman was called. She was told what was going on, and was ordered to sit still by the fire. The others departed on their sacred business of hunting the wild pigs (javelíns). Whether or not the child would die was as yet unrevealed.

At the singer's command the people gathered. He sang to learn if the Sun was pleased with their work. He had been two months without salt and women, as had been the principal [sic] men.[13]

The Sun revealed that he desired one more sacrifice. The singer, in accordance with his revelation, gave the people a stick of bamboo. Then they had to go to the sierra, regardless of the snakes or other perils of the sierra that might threaten them. They were instructed to look for a hollow log. This had to be struck and listened to.

Thus the people went, testing the hollow logs. They found a thick log of sea-wood, called *yalí*. When they struck it, gave off a sound as of thunder.[14] They listened to the sound. It told them that this was the log they were looking for.

But they were still lacking the sixth sacrifice. This was the iguana (*kétse*, H.) needed by Nakawé. They searched until they found twenty-five of these. Then they brought them to the singer and laid them with their heads toward the sea.

The first was opened. Its blood was used to anoint the ceremonial parapher-nalia of Nakawé.[15] Four others were used similarly. The animals for sacrifice were then cooked in the oven.

Other people were chosen to give corn, while others gave a bull.

Then, having abstained from salt and sexual intercourse, the people fell to work. They built the walls and the roof of the temple. The work lasted for five months, for, despite the arduousness of their work, they were impelled by their desires to eat salt and have sexual relations.[16] Thus the temple was built in good order.

When the work was finished, the people gathered for a night's ceremonial singing. They wished to learn if the Sun was pleased with the work.[17] In this ceremony the Sun revealed that they should await his orders to learn who should be the "keepers of his votive-bowls." The shaman, however, was free to choose the "keepers of the votive-bowls" for the various other gods. The other gods were: TcipóSawi, MaSá KwáSi (Grandfather Deer[-]tail), Komatéame, Pálikata (Elder Brother),Wákali, Kauymáli,[18] Kuúami, Halian[á]ka, Meakíma, MáSama, Halamáli (goddess of the sea), Naléama, Muiníma, and Nakawé.[19] Thus many people had to be made "keepers of the votive-bowls."

The gods were delighted to be given so much paraphernalia.[20]

The singer said, "Now that you have received the votive-bowls, we must have a ceremonial singing. Otherwise misfortune may befall us."[21]

The work of the forthcoming ceremony was apportioned among the people according to the command of the Sun. All went to their *rancherías* to get corn. Some went to the sacred caves to get sacred water. This was taken to the temple.[22] Water of the sea was brought also. Thus were the preparations made for the feast.

When the sacred water had arrived, the animals were made ready for the sacrifice. This ceremony was done to prevent or counteract the small-pox that was beginning to come. After ten days of this work[,] the sun was slightly more pleased.

Then the shaman had a dream. This revealed why the small-pox had not completely disappeared when the temple was finished. It appeared in his dream that someone should be sent to the sea [the] next day. Although they had worked so hard, some of the paraphernalia was still lacking. Another was sent to a river from which some fish were taken.

At the margin [shore] of the sea would be found the heart of the Sun.[23] This was very necessary for the success of the ceremony and the prevention of small-pox. Those sent for it had to go while still fasting in order to be aided in their search. They took a child with a shaman's plume in its hair.[24]

They came across five hollow logs. The middle one was well rounded. From this they took out the three hearts the Sun had asked for. These were the brazil-wood, which the Sun and Fire gods needed for their arrows.[25] They were brought back and made into staffs (or prayer-arrows) and decorated with parrot, eagle, and hawk feathers.[26]

The Sun commanded that by the use of these prayer-arrows [staffs] the people would be able to pray to the great gods. Then their children and animals would live. Unusually large votive-bowls, also, were made, and after bathed in blood. Five other arrows of brazil-wood were made. Further, a cord was strung over the building to strengthen it so that the lightning would not strike it.[27] The long arrows, tipped with turkey feathers,[28] were ordered to be placed underneath the top of the roof. Then the "keepers of the votive-bowls" took out the ceremonial paraphernalia of all the gods.

Dancing-staffs[29] were made and paraded around the temple. Then the arrows were tossed to the people. These had to be caught in mid-air; for those who missed them would die. Little balls of *chual* (Sp.) (*tauli*, H.) were similarly thrown to be caught.[30]

One person, however, missed the balls. The great gods told the singer that for a punishment small-pox would come to all. But if they prayed and sacrificed properly, they would not die.

For five years small-pox came[,] but it only changed the faces of the people. Thus those who had sinned did not die but were left very ugly. Then Sun said that his commands would be fulfilled if they gave the feast with which to complete the custom for serving him.

Those in charge of the [votive-]bowls had to sing the sacred songs[,] since Sun was the most powerful god of all. These guardians of the votive[-]bowls had to serve with the fullest devotion. They had to place lasso-traps for catching deer. But they could not cook and eat the meat because the Sun wanted it raw. If they were so fortunate as to kill deer, they were instructed by the shaman to bring a certain cane (*otate[,]* Sp.) about a yard long. Until all this was done[,] they had to fast from water.[31]

Finally the deer and the cane reed were brought and placed at the temple. In five days there was going to be a change if the keepers of the votive[-]bowls had fulfilled these difficult commands of working five days without drinking water.

The first night they sang the sacred myths[,] and the Sun ordered the change of the keepers of the votive[-]bowls in charge of his paraphernalia. He ordered them to gather and grind the seeds of chual (*Amaranthus* sp., *wawé*[,] H.). This dough was shaped into the form of a rooster.[32] When this was finished, cooked[,] and cool[ed] again, feathers were put in the effigy. Thus they made a life-sized rooster[,] which was covered with feathers. When this was done[,] perhaps the small-pox would retire.

Meanwhile those in charge of the votive[-]bowls had to maintain their fast and sit by quietly while their wives feed [fed] other men and arranged their hair. If the keepers of the votive[-]bowls get jealous or angry[,] all is lost.[33]

On the last of the five days of this ceremony others go to look at the lasso-traps. This is not difficult since they have not been fasting. That night in the ceremony the people dance. Finally the men put on women's clothes.[34] One who has been lucky enough to find a deer in one of the traps comes running to the temple. He dashes to the altar[,] which has been prepared[,] carrying the intestine of the slain deer. This is filled with deer-blood so that the paraphernalia may be bathed (anointed) with blood while the deer is being brought.[35]

Then the effigy of the rooster is placed on a stone prepared at a great distance from the temple. The people go to this spot and make a ceremonial circuit.[36] Though it was dark[,] they went without light, walking very carefully in order not to fall. Several did fall[,] and they died from small-pox.[37] Then they brought the effigy of the rooster to the temple.

Before this had been done[,] all had contributed a handful of corn from which had been made a thick paste or dough. An earth oven has [had] been prepared[,] after which the people prayed. The dough was placed in the oven and cooked like a thick loaf of bread. When this was cooked[,] it was baptized with sacred water.[38] This water was not allowed to touch the ground, but was caught in votive[-]bowls. The loaf was called *tamíuwale* and was placed near the effigy of the rooster.[39]

At dawn they took the feathers from the rooster and it was broken up. The head was given to the child Teukúkue Wiwaámi. Other pieces were given to everyone present. Then the people gathered corn and danced. They shouted while a little boy, *teapú [teapúa]*, carried the drum [tepo]. His ears had been stuffed with cotton so they would not break from the sound of the drum.

Then, while the drum played all day, they feasted and drank tesgüino [corn beer]. Since 28 people had made the beer, there was plenty to drink. Then food was distributed to the people: soup, deer, javelín (wild pig), fish, meat of goat, and iguana (a large lizard). Thus the period of fasting was finished[,] and the people could drink water, eat salt, and lay [lie] with their wives. This was in the middle of the dry season.

Again[,] however[,] misfortune fell, and the people wondered why their ceremony had not served its purpose. It had to be repeated as soon as the (common?) [communal] field was cleared, because when the corn was planted and was ready to come up, the rains did not come. So they asked the singer what he had dreamed.[40]

He said, "We have given a ceremony to the Sun and the Fire. Now we must give one to the owners of the rain, the great gods of the sea. They wish another kind of a ceremony. Thus we must hasten to make other kinds of votive[-] bowls."

That day it rained a little[,] which showed that the shaman's dream was true.[41] So they knew that they must do as he said, else it would not rain enough for their crops.[42] The shaman said[,] "Hurry, we have important work to do. Who has a bull for sacrifice? Who bought candles? How many? Good." He told them to put sacred water brought from the caves into the votive[-]bowls.[43] This must be used to bless the candles[,] which are to be used at the altar. Then they could pray for health and happiness.[44] As the candles were bathed in the sacred water a five centavo piece fell together with corn from the sacred candle. Thus they knew that their prayer would be successful.[45]

The shaman told them that the gods ordered fifteen *topiles* and *tenanches* to sweep the temple. Then the candles could be lighted[,] and the sacrificial bull could be killed. The patio was swept while the [sacred] clown swept in mock fashion using the tail of the sacrificed bull.[46]

The gods were nearby and ordering everything. The altar was arranged. By the miracle of the singer's song[47] the blanket of the altar was magically changed into beautiful flowers of most fragrant odor.[48] When the sacrifice was finished[,] the ceremonial paraphernalia was "bathed" in blood and offered to the gods. No sooner was this finished than a rain[-]storm arose and water fell with much power. Rain fell all night, wetting the people and everything else. Thus by dawn everything had turned out very well.

Then the meat-soup and the [corn] beer were distributed and the feast began. It was ordered by the great gods that ten gourds of beer and a large gourd of the meat-broth as well as a leg of the animal should be given to the shaman.[49] These were set on his lap as is still done by the Huichols. Then his wife emptied all of the food and drink into her own receptacles.

Then the chanters who accompanied the singer in his song were given food. Then food was distributed to the heads of families, and finally the single people were given food.[50]

When the feast was finished[,] a scorpion stung one of the children. The people wondered what caused this misfortune. They decided that it was because Rapauwiemi [Rapawíemi, a rain mother whose shrine is located south of Huichol territory] had not been given a house, as the other rain goddesses had.[51] So one of the people made her a *nealíka* (ceremonial gable cap-stone) decorated with snakes, while another made a *haítsi* (the bunch of green leaves hung from the gable of the Huichol family god-house). They brought leaves for the roof of the house, and an altar was arranged with feathers of the hawk and parrot. The singer sang in a low voice by himself to bless the house.[52]

The altar was arranged with arrows and votive[-]bowls. The latter stood on *hawime itali* [itáli][53] (round boards). No one knew how to make the hawime itali [itáli], but a child asked to see one. From this for a model he began to work. After it was begun by the child (Kauymáli?) in a design with five circles, others tried to continue the work but failed. So the child was allowed to finish the task, which he did in a short time. It was very pretty and was decorated in many colors. As a reward for his effort Otuanáka promised to reward the boy with five young sheep from his pair.[54] Then for a long time the boy was well and prosperous.

In the temple there was no fire over the sacred hole,[55] which Otuanáka had asked to be made in the temple for her sacrifices. If this were not done[,] something unfortunate was sure to happen. Five small god cups and plates had to be made. Nakawé would help Otuanáka[,] who also needed a *comal, ticomate*, and *casuela* (pot). Votive[-]bowls had to be made and well decorated. All these things must be put in the sacred cavity. Five handfuls of corn had to be ground and made into five human effigies to be put in the sacred hole as well. Five other effigies had to be carved of the wood of the "fig-tree" ("salate[,]" Sp.[,] *Ficus* sp.). On these effigies white fiber was placed to represent the hair of Nakawé. Her sacred staves [staffs] were crossed across her body.[56]

On the top of the sacred cavity there was ordered to be placed a round carved stone (teapáli) on which was carved the animal of this goddess[,] i.e.[,] snakes. They were to be painted in blue, green, and yellow. Then the top of the god-disc must be further adorned by beads stuck in wax so that Otuanáka might bless the people with large prosperous families.[57]

The goddess, Otuanáka, ordered that holes [niches] should be put in the wall of the temple, so they could "listen" at the corners.[58] In these holes [niches] her nealíka[59] could be placed so they could look out on the world.

When all this was done[,] the "keepers of the votive[-]bowls" were chosen. When they were ready to serve, the singers were hastening so that by obeying the commands of the gods[,] the troubles of the people would be lessened. Anyone who did not wish to serve as a "keeper of the votive[-]bowls" or shamans who had already served and were tired were not made responsible for the paraphernalia of the gods nor their commands.[60] In a dream one of the shamans saw that the Sun knew that he did not wish to serve as "keeper of the votive[-]bowls." So he, as other officials who were tired of the duty, were changed.[61]

The "keepers of the votive[-]bowls" were appointed to sweep the dancing patio of the temple and to keep everything in order.[62] This task was to last for five years before he could be relieved of his responsibility.[63] All this time he must not have intercourse with any woman [who was] not his wife. The penalty was that the offender would go crazy.[64] If the votive arrows fell or the votive-bowls were broken, etc.[,] the families and animals, etc. of those responsible for the paraphernalia would die.[65]

The people were very sad because the shaman did not assure them that the misfortunes which assailed them would soon pass. So they went to the singer and asked him to come and sing in order to find out what that [*sic*] gods said as to the cause of these misfortunes. The shaman came not only to sing but also to cure.[66] But in his dreams[67] it was revealed that the people had failed in their duties as "keepers of the votive[-]bowls."

The shaman told them, "Now if this is true, did your spouses break the vow of sexual constancy? Tell the truth. If not[,] there will be no help for your children."[68]

One of the women did not wish to speak[,] because she preferred another man to her husband. She said, "So do not try to blame me."

The shaman told her, "If you are lying[,] your children will be worse within five days. If you speak the truth[,] they will be well."[69]

After five days the shaman came back, and the children were worse. So the woman had to confess. But she said that it was not her fault that she had broken the duty of constancy.

The shaman told her not to do it any more. But now that she had confessed to the "keepers of the votive[-]bowls," they would "clean" her with grass. This contaminated grass would then be burned[,] and her fault thus [was] taken from her.[70] The curer-shaman had to be paid six pesos for his work in curing the children.[71] The children were to be well within ten days.

The children then got better. The husband waited for the wife and said, "You did wrong and caused me to spend much money. I don't want anything more to do with you."

The husband sent a companion with his wife to see that she did not do wrong again. He continued to blame her and even beat her with a stick. Then he demanded that she should pay the fee of the shaman who had cured the sick children. She had no money[,] so he ordered her to go away and not come back.

The lover became angry because she would not leave her husband and join him. He offered her the money to pay her husband, but she refused. He said to her, "I will make you wings so that you can fly like a bird."

She replied, "No, I prefer to live here with my husband and family."

When she refused[,] the lover became ill from the thought and died within ten days.[72] He was buried because he had no force (or value), and could not bear up. The wife told her husband all of this[,] saying, "And now he died from his bad thoughts."[73]

The husband listened and then asked her what she wanted. Since she needed nothing she replied, "Nothing." She continued, "I only told you this because you punished and refused me even though we have worked very hard in our life together."

The husband replied, "Very well, I will say nothing more about it."

So they continued living together and continued their duties in the temple. At the end of their term as "keepers of the votive[-]bowls," they looked for someone to take over these duties because of the great expenses of that office. In order to earn money for these expenses they had had to work hard to make hats, *toache* [a tequila-like drink], and rope.

Thus the man turned over the paraphernalia to another "keeper of the votive[-]bowls" and was free. He was no longer "dangerous" (sacred). The *kawit[é]ro* told him that he could try other women if he wished to.[74]

The kawit[é]ro told the new "keepers of the votive[-]bowls," "You are like calves tied up in a pen because of the vows you have taken under your new duties. You must serve the gods who will cause it to rain on all of you." Thus the kawit[é]ro talked to them for two or three hours. He told the old officials that they might make toache to sell at the temple during the feasts in order to gain back the money they had losts [*sic*] while serving as "keepers of the votive[-]bowls."[75]

[1.] Sub-story: Myth of the Huichol God-House

Then the singer told the people that they should make god-houses for the paraphernalia of the various gods. First, however, they were to build a god-house for the Sun, a *taiopá ki [tauopá ki]*. This house was to be full of eagle plumes and arrows so that the gods could hear the prayers of the people. Inside the god-houses were to be built altars, neatáli,[76] on which to place the arrows. In the middle of each altar would have to be placed a god-chair filled with arrows bearing nealíka and *náma*. Also, as soon as the people had killed enough deer, fifty deer-tail plumes were to stand on the altar. This was the order of the Sun to the singer, who knew how to dream these things as he sang.

In the house had to be placed the decorated staffs for the peyote dance, *haká ítsu*. These sound like the Sun's animal, the rattlesnake. The Sun also commanded that there be a teapáli as a god-disc for the god-chair of the Sun.[77] The teapáli should be painted with male deer with horns [antlers] and female deer without horns [antlers]. In the middle of the teapáli a hole should be cut. The teapáli should be decorated with the forms [images] of the male and the female eagle.[73]

The Sun continued to instruct the singer [about] what to tell the people. He said, "Go now to the plain where there is soft volcanic rock. Sleep here, and I will tell you in your dreams where to find my stone."[79]

This was done. Then at midnight, while they slept, the people dreamed where to find the stone that was suitable for the teapáli of the Sun. It was cut round[,] and a small hole was drilled through it. This hole is for seeing, since the teapáli is the "vista" (Sp., sight or view) of the god. It must be there to permit him to see.[80]

The stone, therefore, was cut and carved with the designs requested by the Sun. Then the singer told one of the people to cut the wattle of a turkey and bathe the carved figures with its blood.[81]

The people then put a niche in the wall to hold some of the [sacred] paraphernalia. Above the door they put a nealíka so that the great gods of the sea could see the god-house[82] adorned with shaman's plumes. On a shelf above the altar were placed rattlesnake rattles. A bunch of leaves, *háici [haíci]*, were hung down from the middle of the beam on the inside to sound at night. By this sound the people would know that the Sun was helping them.[83] Two saplings of pine were also brought.

Then all the "keepers of the votive-bowls" contributed corn and hunted deer. These were used for corn-beer and deer-broth for the ceremony of the dedication of the god-house. The corn-beer was mixed with peyote. Thus half the people could drink ordinary beer, while the others drank beer mixed with peyote. The drinking could take place only after the god-house had been sprinkled ("bathed") with the liquors [sacred beverages].

Another god-house was ordered to be built for Pálikata, the patron of deer-hunting. Here the teapáli and nealíka had to be blue or green in color.[84] The small rattlesnake, Ráinu, had to be painted in blue on the teapáli. All the arrows in this god-house were to be made of hawk feathers. Pálikata also ordered that five deer horns [antlers] should be placed on his altar.[85]

Tesgüino (corn-beer) was not needed in the dedication of this house. This beer is used only for the houses of Father Sun. In the house of Pálikata the "keeper of the votive-bowls" kept the ceremonial paraphernalia corresponding to this god.

Then the god-house of Na'aliwaemi, the water-goddess, was commanded to be built and filled with paraphernalia. Here were to be placed five prayer-arrows decorated with parrot feathers. The shafts of the prayer-arrows had to be painted with blue, red, and green spirals to represent lightning.[86] They were to be hung with itáli similarly decorated.

The teapáli in this god-house had to show Háiku (the water-serpent), the child of Na'aliwaemi.[87] It should be painted green or black. Her votive-bowls must carry her "measure" to represent five corn-fields.[88] In her god's-chair five staffs of reed must be stuck. Na'aliwaemi also wished five arrows of a special sort. She would play with these and the lightning would not strike.[89]

It was ordered that *tévali* (rock-crystals) should be caught by the shaman while he was singing. These were rolled up in wool fabric (or Agave, Sp.) and hidden in votive-bowls.[90]

Then Na'aliwaemi told the singer to make a small god's-chair. This had to be decorated with green and red paper. It was not for the god-house, but was to be carried to the cave of this goddess.[91] The god-chair had to be bathed in the blood of a sheep. Votive-bowls for this goddess were ordered to be decorated with tin-foil. In the center a half-peso had to be placed with the eagle upwards. Cornfields are represented on the sides of her bowls.[92]

All was arranged thus according to the dreams of the shaman to gain the favor of this goddess. Her favor is especially powerful for children and for the un-married. For such favor[,] offerings like these must be taken to her cave. From the cave[,] water is brought for bathing the things in the god-house.

This water will also cure anyone who is sick. The cave of the goddess is full of offerings of this sort and for this purpose. Her votive-bowls must show many representations of parrots in wax and in beads. The beads must be green. In another votive-bowl a candle must be left standing upright.[93]

When the god-house of Na'aliwaemi was finished and all her commands ful-filled, the shaman instructed the people further from his dreams. Next they had to make the god-house of Otuanáka.

This had to be a large house, six meters long. It was to contain five altars (neatáli), one at each point. Each wall was to have niches in which were to be placed the paraphernalia of Otuanáka.

On the first altar are placed the prayer-arrows and votive-bowls. Here also is placed a *kuyé*, which is a small [wooden] disc, round in shape, and painted with five snakes. This [wooden] disc, the kuyé, is hemmed in with arrows standing stuck in the altar. From large arrows god-eyes are hung, since Otuanáka is a special patroness of children. Her animals, painted in all colors, are represented on her náma.

On her second altar must be five god-chairs, filled with votive-arrows. Her votive-bowls must have, at the center, money stuck in wax. All her votive-bowls must be painted in beads with snakes of all colors.

On the third altar, besides votive-bowls, must be the models of her animals: the crocodile, *háci*, and the *"tigre del agua"* [water jaguar], haluwi (axolotl?). They must be well carved, and painted in natural colors. Artificial flowers and large candles, as well as the ordinary small candles, must be offered to this goddess. A ladder, *imúmui*, "the road," must be placed on her altar so that the prayers of the people can go to her at the bottom of the sea.

A "candle," the wild sweet-potato, *iéli*, is sacred to Otuanáka. It must be carried to the cave of this goddess tied to the end of a stick. On the altar should be placed wooden models of the little bird of the sea, *tukáipu*.

The singer then ordered the people to make another god-house. This was for the rain goddess, Keamukáme. It was to have five teapáli, decorated with a cross to represent the "vista." By means of this "vista" (sight or view) the goddess can see the gods of the four points. Feathers must be stuck upright on the teapáli of this goddess.

Of these five teapáli it was ordered that two were to be taken to the sea. Two were to be taken to the sacred mesa of Nayarit. And one was to be taken to the peyote country.

The hunters for the peyote take with them arrows having cruciform decoration. These arrows are called *mayawápa*. The hunters carry these so they can easily find the peyote. The sacred water from the peyote country (and hence the association with this water-goddess) is brought to sprinkle the votive-bowls of this goddess, as well as the bowls of other goddesses.

E   Kauymáli Helps the Sun Win Over the Rain-Goddesses in First Getting Deer's Blood for the Sacred Paraphernalia

Kauymáli won over the gods by overhearing their conversation. Thus he could impose upon the singer who was instructing the people. So to fool the shaman and the people, Kauymáli told him that they should build him a god-house.

The shaman informed the people what Kauymáli had said. They went to work at once to make him a house. From his dreams the singer told them how to proceed. Kauymáli had also said to him, "For my part I should like my house to be in the middle part."

Kauymáli is very "delicate" (sacred). Not everyone was brave enough to work on his house, knowing that he was half-bad.[1] The people had to communicate with him through the shaman by means of a *nealíka* or a sandal. Kauymáli ordered that his house should contain green or blue *teapáli, náma,* prayer-arrows, sandals, a wrist guard,[2] a bow and arrows, and a shaman's basket.

Kauymáli communicated with the great gods of the sea. His arrow fell at the sea, just as the Sun was rising. Thus the great gods of the sea learned that he was up to one of his tricks again. They held a council to see what might be done. Finally they decided to send out five of their number to see for themselves just what he was up to. They went to each of the five points, sending their messages before them by thought.[3]

They also communicated with the Sun at the point where he comes up out of the sea. The Sun said, "Kauymáli cannot see as well as I because he is withered on one side. I have already fixed his position and place. I will change him to see if anyone can recognize him. Let us see what happens."

So Kauymáli had to follow the orders either of the great gods of the sea or the Sun.

Kauymáli came out of his place and was changed so that no one knew him. His hair was braided into two pleats. In five days he was changed into two large deer. The braids became the horns [antlers].

At the command of Father Sun the great gods of the sea came to see if they could tell what Kauymáli had been changed into. This was to find out if he belonged to them or not. Thus the Sun would see who won.

First the great gods of the sea went to "this side." In five jumps Kauymáli got there in the form of the two deer. He approached close to the great gods, and then went back. They did not recognize him at all. The great gods of the sea, at some distance, saw for the first time that he was there. Their arrows heard the deer.[4] They said, "Someone is fooling us again, and has come to see us and our sacred things." But nothing else happened.

Kauymáli, in his new form of two deer, then went to "that side." Here were the great gods of the sea. They did not recognize him, however. Thus Kauymáli found out the paraphernalia they had with them. He hid his sandals next to their paraphernalia; but they heard him only as he retired. Then they found his sandals and listened to them.

The sandals said, "Here there was one who was very well dressed."

Then Kauymáli, in the form of the two deer, went clear to the sea[,] although it was very "delicate" there.[5] The deer were without fear. They stopped at the very middle of the circle of the gods. Here the gods had piled all their ceremonial paraphernalia. Thus again did Kauymáli learn their secrets.

After he had learned the secrets of the great gods that were to be gained at the sea, he went to the "other side." He covered his tracks with damp earth so that the great gods of the sea would not be able to follow them.

The great gods were angry when they heard Kauymáli retreating. They did not know that he had been near them until he had already gone. They were so angry that the sea was stormy and roared.

The Sun then said, "Let us see if the great gods of the sea can figure out who was there." He told Kauymáli, "You are my very [own] son. I have determined this with my heart. Now I have given my bow and arrow to the great gods of the sea. Go to a great rock by the sea that is named TumuSáuwi Tsalíska. There you will find my bow and arrow, together with a god-chair, a nealíka, sandals, and a teapáli. Bring these to me. I will tell you what to do with them."

So Kauymáli went to that rock by the sea where the Sun had been born. In his present form of two deer he had horns [antlers] on his heads. If these horns [antlers] could see and hear as far as the great gods of the sea, all would turn out well.

The horns [antlers] succeeded in communicating that far. They caused the votive-bowls of the great gods to hear.[6] To the great gods this was a sign. They knew, therefore, that something was up. But none knew what it meant. So they had to search for five days to find out who was communicating with their votive-bowls.

Kauymáli went first to "this side" and then to "that side." Then he reported to the Sun that he had been successful in communicating with his horns [antlers] as far as the great gods of the sea. He had with him the [sacred] paraphernalia. This he had found at the rock that was the birthplace of the Sun. The Sun then gave the two deer permission to place their *ranchería* (Kauymáli's) at that rock.

The great gods of the sea noted the preparations going on at the rock. They waited five days to see what would happen. At the end of this time[,] Kauymáli, still in the guise of the two deer, went to the sea and jumped in. He came out as little stones. These are so sacred that any Huichol, in asking favors of them, may not eat salt for a month.

The little stones went to a cliff near Santa Catarina. Here they remained at the place where the paraphernalia from the birthplace of the Sun was deposited. With them were five rattlesnakes. Another companion of theirs was the hiss-adder.

The Sun told the little stones, which were Kauymáli, to gather the saliva of the snakes. Kauymáli anointed himself with this stuff.[7] There was also another rattlesnake, Táte Ipau [Taté Ipau] (like the peyote dancing staff). From this snake Kauymáli bit off the rattles, anointing himself with the blood.[8] He did this with all the snakes. Thus he became very sacred.[9]

He had to remain at this place for five months without eating salt because he had done such sacred things.[10] If he failed, he would lose his power.[11] So to follow the Sun's orders, he planned to stay there five months.

At the end of three months he was becoming stronger. At the end of four months he seemed to be almost well again. But he had to stay there until the end of five months. Otherwise he would be withered on one side,[12] because of his audacity to the great gods of the sea.

At the call of the great gods he presented himself at the sea, just at the rock where the Sun had been born. The Sun was still protecting him. But if he did anything wrong, the Sun would know of it. If he failed this last month, all his efforts would be wasted.

One of the sea-goddesses changed into the Moon, *metséle*, as a beautifully dressed woman. She met Kauymáli, and offered to be his wife. Kauymáli replied that he had to remain on his ranchería. Thus had the Sun commanded. He also said that he had to keep his vow of continence for five months.

Five days later, however, Kauymáli began to sing. The great gods heard the sound. They wondered where it came from. They said, "Let us see who can understand this singing."

The Moon-woman came again to Kauymáli. "Look," she said, "I can take good care of your things and make life very much easier for you."

But again Kauymáli remained firm.

Meanwhile the great gods of the sea were searching for the singer by means of their paraphernalia. They searched through half the world. Then the Moon-woman, metséle, decided to go under the sea and the land and come out just behind the chair where Kauymáli was sitting. When she had done this, she touched him, even though he had refused to go with her. The Sun told Kauymáli to be firm in his vows.

Kauymáli continued his sacred singing to learn the secrets of the great gods of the sea. The great gods heard this singing with their paraphernalia and their face-painting.[13] They wondered who was singing and what it was he wanted. They asked the Sun. But the Sun denied any knowledge of the matter. He told them that they would have to "dream" who it was,[14] in order to see if they could win. So they tried again, but without success. Only the best of them had any hopes of succeeding when they began to dream. The five months were almost over. They had to use new paraphernalia. Their old paraphernalia did not amount to much anymore.

Kauymáli continued to sing very well. But while he sang, he was bothered by dreams of the Moon-woman. These dreams in which metséle appeared were far from sacred. They were erotic and caused nocturnal emissions. Thus the Moon-woman won the first victory. It wasn't very important, however.[15]

The Sun cautioned Kauymáli to remain strong in his vows, else he would name him a sorcerer, *mara'ákame*. The Sun also ordered the Moon-woman to go back to the great gods of the sea and stop bothering Kauymáli.

The end of the period of Kauymáli's was very near. Then the great gods continued in their efforts to learn who was singing their songs. But they all failed again. There was, however, an indication of the singer in their votive-bowls. This was the tracks of someone who had passed.

The Sun liked the singing of Kauymáli. It was well and correctly done.

Wákuli and Pálikata asked permission to have their rancherías near that of Kauymáli. So they were ordered to bring their paraphernalia. They were also to bring the yellow peyote-root, *kíeli [kieli]* (which is the "vista" — that is, sight — of the singers), flowers, pollen, etc., for the votive-bowls.[16] These were very "delicate" and had to be kept for two months.[17] Kauymáli painted his face and wrists with this sacred material. Then Pálikata made nealíka and other sacred paraphernalia to hang on the prayer-arrows of Kauymáli.

Kauymáli also needed a shaman's basket for these arrows. It had to be made of materials taken from the top of the sierra and from the margin of the sea. Pálikata thus arranged a shaman's basket for Kauymáli. It had to be spread out open with its paraphernalia to see what it would be. At midnight five arrows were found among the paraphernalia. They were very "delicate." They could be touched only by Kauymáli. These he put in his pouch.

The next day Kauymáli sang again. This time he sounded with his sandals.[18] Thus his singing sounded even better. He was dressed in the finest of Huichol man's [men's] finery.[19] As he was finishing his singing, he prepared for a trip as far as his nealíka could reach (that is, "see").

On this trip he found the small tracks of a deer. These tracks were peyotes.[20] He ate one, and it went to his heart. From the tips of the horns [antlers] and from the tail he took another peyote.[21] In the spittle of the deer he found something like a little grub.[22] This was like an arrow. Eating all of this made him very drunk.

Then Kauymáli found a very large peyote. With the deer's spittle, which was of all colors, he painted his face with the designs of the peyote-dancers.[23]

While he was drunk from having eaten the peyote, he sang and waved his shaman's plumes. As he sang, he listened for anything the gods might say in reply. The gods heard his singing.[24]

The next day, when he was over his drunk, he wondered what he had done. He saw the great gods of the sea as many people in the form of snakes.[25] It was very cloudy and foggy. He had to wait until the following morning before he could see clearly.

The next morning Kauymáli found the ceremonial equipment. It was placed around the stone six feet high. This stone was Pálikata. Then to know where they were, he looked on all sides. He found that he was at the rock at the point of the sea where the Sun had been born. The paraphernalia was that of the Sun.

Nearby was a swamp.[26] In it grew many plants of *armá* (*matareal*, Sp.). This swamp was so deep that it could be crossed only by swimming. A candle for the Sun had to be placed in the middle of this snake-filled swamp. Kauymáli hoped for good luck on his mission. He jumped into the swamp with his clothes on. Tied to his head were his offerings of bread, chocolate, and candles. He dared not drink any of the water as he swam. Soon he arrived at the middle of the deep swamp. There he left the offering to the Sun.

When he returned to the bank, he told the Sun that he had fulfilled his commands. The Sun then told him to make him a teapáli painted with green deer. For this the Sun promised to continue to help him. This was done. Offerings were then made to the four points.

From these offerings four cliffs sprang into existence. On one of these cliffs a flower full of water was thrown. This grew in the middle of the rocky cliff,[27] and a spring of water came forth. Other sacred spots and rocks were dedicated at various places. These were for the use of the singers, both near and far, in asking favors of the gods.[28] Kauymáli did all this at the orders of the great gods of the sea during his dreams while drunk with peyote.

One of the sacred spots was in the peyote country near Real Catorce. Here was placed a rock. The rock was called a nealíka, the "vista"—that is, sight—

of which might reach as far as the sea. Others were placed in the caves of Santa Catarina, the Mesa of Nayarit, and elsewhere.[29] At all these sacred places power was granted to those who wished to become singers and curers.[30]

Having done these things for the Sun, Kauymáli talked to a deer. The deer was standing at the place near the sea where the Sun had been born. He talked of making votive-bowls for Pálikata. Finding ten of his animals (deer), Kauymáli sent them to the four points, since the first one was in the middle region.

In these ancient times *haikote* and other grasses were used for arrows.[31] These were brought. In the end of each arrow a small stone point was placed[32] and fastened there with sinew.[33]

The deer in the middle world-region were really people making the sounds of deer. When a large deer came out, Kauymáli prepared to shoot it with his bow and stone-tipped arrows. The arrow went completely through the deer. The stone point, however, was left in it.

"Bloody Hands," MataSúli, took the dead deer to the gods. He had to be very careful not to touch himself with his bloody hands. The gods did not like the stone point in the deer. They asked that other deer be caught, and this time in deer-traps.

But before this could be done, a beautiful [mountain] lion approached one of the deer on the plain. The [mountain] lion was ready to pounce upon the deer. The deer, however, ran away so fast that he dropped his horns [antlers], skin, and body and became the person, Muutáme Tatúapa. He did not know what animal had frightened him so.

Kauymáli told him that it was a [mountain] lion. This had been revealed to Kauymáli by Komatéame, who had said, "Now you will see whether or not I win. I will take away the votive-paraphernalia of the deer-hunters to get blood to bathe my sacred things."

At dawn the [mountain] lion went to where the other great gods of the sea were working. He caught a live deer with his bare hands. This was before the outcome of the struggle for supremacy between the Sun and the rain-gods was settled in the singer's mind.

The Sun said, "How is it that some of the rain-gods get ahead of me?"

The [mountain] lion cooked the body of the deer in the earth-oven. But he did not make any ceremony or other preparation. None of the great gods of the sea knew who did this. However, Kauymáli knew. The great gods went to the Sun. He told them who had killed the deer and where it was being cooked. The deer belonged to the Sun.[34] So Kauymáli was ordered to go and get the horns [antlers], which had not been harmed by the [mountain] lion.

Then began another contest to see whether the Sun or the great gods of the

sea would kill the first deer so that they might bathe their ceremonial paraphernalia in its blood. All put up nets to catch deer. Kauymáli also went.

By the Sun's command deer would be caught at dawn. Tatevalí said that he
would give a deer at three in the morning.[35]

Thus it was, and for this reason Kauymáli could not take away the horns
[antlers], for these belonged to Father Sun. The hunters left behind them an
old man. He was appointed to cook the deer after all the blood had been taken
for anointing the paraphernalia. Thus all would come out well and not badly
as [it had] with the Lion, who had cooked the deer without preparation.

Lion had cooked the meat without any preparation, intestines and all. He ate
the meat alone, and did not offer the blood. His name was Otótawe. For this
neglect[,] Lion remained a [mountain] lion and not a person, even though he
could catch deer very easily.[36]

The Sun ordered Kauymáli and Pálikata to search for the deer and follow
the orders of the shaman. The gods began to bet on the outcome. Kauymáli
was told by Pálikata to search in the gorges and find maguey plants in order to
secure *ixtle* fiber for deer-lassos. This fiber was found and prepared and made
into thirty lassos.[37] The lassos were colored black by ashes from grass.[38]

After working on the lassos[,] Kauymáli then made ceremonial paraphernalia. He made prayer-arrows hung with toy [miniature] lassos.[39] These had to be
offered to Pálikata by singing all during the night. Thus Pálikata would bless
the large lassos so that they would catch many deer.[40] A large and beautiful altar
had to be set up as well. This had to be arranged with offerings of tiny tamales
for the deer to eat[41] when he was killed.

Kauymáli then put up lassos [rope traps] on five little mesas. At night the
singer prayed to the fire, asking that deer might fall into the [rope] trap.

But that night no deer were caught, even though there were many deer and
the dogs [were] close to them. This was because the singing had not been done
well.

So the people called Tatevalí (Grandfather Fire), the greatest of all the singers.
They asked him to sing to find out what the trouble was. The Sun, Pálikata,
Wákuli (the owner of the deer), and other gods told Tatevalí that fifty deer
would be given if the preparations were made properly. Married people must
cease committing adultery, or no deer would fall into the traps. The people,
further, would have to confess their sins.

Kauymáli confessed that the Moon-woman had tempted him, causing him
to dream of intercourse with her.[42] He was cleansed with grass. The grass was
then burned. A woman followed Kauymáli's example, and with much shame
confessed adultery. After confessing five sins, she was cleansed in the same way.

Her husband also confessed to the fire (Grandfather Fire). He said that he had sinned with a young virgin.[43]

Thus all of the five deer-hunters had to confess their sins. One even confessed intercourse with female burros and sheep because he did not have a woman to serve his purpose. A woman confessed incest with her father. One man admitted intercourse with his sister-in-law, a virgin. His wife confessed incest with her brother. The fifth hunter, however, was still true. He had not tried either people or animals. He had married a woman according to the wishes of his father.

When all the five hunters and their wives had confessed their sins, the singing was continued throughout the night. The people prayed to the ceremonial paraphernalia of all the gods. Then it was revealed to the singer that by dawn[,] deer would fall into the traps by pairs until five pairs were caught.

Thus the prophecy of the shaman was fulfilled with great certainty. Within five days all the deer had fallen into the traps. Thus the Sun won by being first to gain blood for the anointing of his ceremonial paraphernalia. The Lion [mountain lion] of the rain-gods was defeated and was worth nothing.

Then the lassos were taken down. The spouses were angry at one another for the things they had confessed to the fire. There were recriminations and blows[,] which ended in a big fight. Only the last married pair had been true to each other. They did not have to fight. They had remained true, even if the others had not.[44]

Pàlikata told the people that they could sell the hides of the deer and buy candles to offer with prayer-arrows hung with tiny deer-traps. Then the people began to prepare their fields. They had to be very careful that any deer-hairs which [that] fell on their clothes should be dusted off on to their corn-fields. Thus would the earth give good crops.[45]

By thus following these customs established by the gods in the first times, the Huichols were assured long life and plenteousness [abundance]. They must marry if they wish to have great success in life and in the deer-hunt.

Kauymáli, the Wolf-Man, Is Outsmarted but Gets Revenge

1. Sub-story: Kauymáli is Outsmarted by the Moon

The Moon came out of his place in the mountains[,] where he had five holes in the ground. While working, Kauymáli found the Moon, who would emerge from the holes and go into the forest. The Moon was "measuring" (fixing or determining) various trees. He continued to measure things until he arrived at the sea. Here he remained for some time.

Kauymáli knew this place of the Moon very well and the many things to be found there. Arriving there one day he encountered the Moon, who was working to prepare his fields. He told the Moon that he would assist him in his work (in order to find out the things that Moon had). But he said, "I have no way to support myself. Will you pay me for my work?"

The Moon offered Kauymáli five pesos a day in money for his work. He gave Kauymáli a planting-stick and some excellent seed-corn. Then he left Kauymáli working, and went to see his things. He did not return for some time, and then he played a trick on Kauymáli. He changed himself into a planting-stick, and grasped Kauymáli by the arm. He also changed Kauymáli's money into potsherds.

This angered Kauymáli. He followed Moon and saw that he was digging sweet-potatos [sic], iéli [iéle]. He approached and said, "Why are you making a fool of me?"

Moon answered, "I am not trying to make a fool of you. I am very busy, brother, so help me and soon we shall have good food."

Thus beguiled, Kauymáli began to help Moon dig sweet-potatos. When five sweet-potatos were dug up, Moon said, "You continue working, as I have something else to do. Go ahead until you fill your sack."

So Moon left Kauymáli working. But soon the sweet-potatos turned into mere pieces of wood.

Kauymáli was angry. He followed Moon to punish him. He found him chopping wood, and addressed him angrily. But Moon replied, "Do not be angry. We are brothers. Help me fell this tree in which there is plenty of honey."

When the tree was felled, Moon told Kauymáli to strain the honey while he went to get a bottle. Moon did not come back, and the honey turned into stones and black water (which comes out of hollow trees in the rainy season). His steel ax was turned into a steel ax of the same form.[1]

"This Moon is a devil and not a real man," reflected Kauymáli. "When I find him this time, I will kill him without fail." He went to look for Moon and found him milking a cow. "Why did you tell me lies?" he asked Moon.

"Pardon me," Moon replied. "I forgot to tell you that I was going to milk. Help me so that we shall have something to drink."

Shortly after Moon had left, however, the milk and the gourd-bowl containing it were changed into a large stick. The cow turned into a large stone.

Kauymáli followed Moon once more, until he arrived at the sea. He said to Moon, "Why did you fool me back there in the mountains?"

Moon answered, "O, I just forgot to tell you that I was called to cure a woman in child-birth. Stay here, because the child is coming out." He showed Kauymáli the woman's belly, which seemed filled with children. Moon told her that she would have ten children. Then he went off, leaving Kauymáli there until the woman was delivered. Those born, however, were not children but toads.

In anger Kauymáli went once more after Moon, whom he found digging again. Moon said, "Here there is salty earth. I am digging salt."[2] He asked Kauymáli to find a stick and help him dig. Soon Moon went off. The piles of white salt were turned into black earth like charcoal, but very bitter.

Again Kauymáli thought what a devil Moon was. He followed him to where he was bathing. Moon said, "I am here in the water, trying to save a large cheese from the bottom of the water. Please undress and help me."

So Kauymáli undressed and helped the Moon raise the cheese. Moon left him holding the cheese, and went off. When he had disappeared, the cheese turned into a large white stone.

Kauymáli followed Moon and said, "Why do you tell lies to me? That was not cheese but a large white stone."

"Well, never mind," Moon answered. "Undress, and help me catch this large fish."

Kauymáli forgot his anger and complied. It was not a fish, however, but a large broken pot.

So Kauymáli followed Moon again in great anger. He found him uncovering something from a large box. Moon asked Kauymáli's help in saving the valuable contents of the box. So Kauymáli opened the box. But it contained only grasshoppers. Meanwhile Moon had departed, saying, "I am going after another box that contains animals which are good to eat."

Grasshopper, who had come out of the box, asked Kauymáli, Elder-brother Wolf, how many brothers he had. Wolf replied that he had fifty. So Grasshopper told him to call his brothers. Elder-brother Wolf called his brothers. They all came and sat in a line.

Wolf asked Grasshopper how many brothers he had.[3] Grasshopper sat down alone, but every time he made a sound[,] a new grasshopper jumped forth. The new grasshoppers were large[,] with great teeth and claws. They filled the whole patio. They attacked the wolves and ate their clothes and drove them off, crying from pain and fear of the grasshoppers.

Elder-brother Wolf, Kauymáli, knew that their enemies had all come from one grasshopper. So he bravely decided to attack this one, even if he should be killed. But when he sprang on the grasshopper, only its dried shell remained.

Tatevalí (Grandfather Fire) commended Kauymáli (Wolf) on his bravery. He said that henceforth Wolf should belong to him as his own animal.

The Grasshopper's name was *tawikone*.

Moon was in the water when the great gods of the sea told him that he would have to leave his home in the five holes in the earth and go to the sky to shine at night. His holes were to be protected. If any children open them, they become sick, and blood gushes from their bodies.[4] Moon also causes men to have nocturnal dreams about women.[5]

When Moon reached the sky, he defecated. The following stars came from his feces: *suláwiñána* ([blank space] *tray grande*, Sp.); the morning star, *túciáita* (*lucero*, Sp.); *halakútcici* ([blank space] *carro*, Sp.); *tcimamaci* ([blank space] *cabrillos*, Sp.).

The following animals also emerged: *túpina* (humming-bird, *chupa rosa*, Sp.); *yawi* ([blank space] coyote, Sp.); bees, *tciúli* (*coloména [colmena?]*, *[abejas]* Sp.); a bug, *ignáme* ([blank space] *chakokwano*, Mex.-Sp.); *waweami* (the queen bee, *el gordo*, Sp.); and *meata* ([blank space] [raccoon] *mapachi [mapache]*, Sp.).[6]

The great gods of the sea put Moon in charge of all these stars and animals. They fixed [it so] that the moon should change every month. The Sun allowed Moon only a little light to see everything. Moon was not allowed to see clearly, however, because he was even more half-bad than Kauymáli. For this reason, further, Moon was not allowed to talk. Thus, though the people may look at him, they cannot communicate with him.[7]

When the moon was full, Kauymáli remembered everything Moon had [done] while on earth. Since the moonlight was good, Kauymáli decided to go and find all of Moon's belongings and steal them. This, he thought[,] would be excellent revenge for the way Moon had deceived him. Moon could neither talk nor communicate with the great gods of the sea of Kauymáli's mischief because of the command of the gods. Most of Moon's things were animals.

Then Kauymáli stabbed the cattle belonging to Moon. They had been left in [the] charge of a rich Huichol, *harící tiama*. The cattle were butchered[,] and the meat was hung in a tree.

Four days later the Huichol who had been put in charge of Moon's cattle followed the tracks, even though they were covered and smudged by dragging a limb over them. But he lost the trail, and did not find the meat hanging in a tree.

Kauymáli took the meat to a natural corral "on this side." This place is called *hokowálika [hokowaiwelíka]*. Here they left someone to watch the meat stolen by Kauymáli to revenge himself on the Moon for his tricks. The man got rich from selling the meat.

2. Sub-story: Kauymáli Is Outsmarted by Hortimán, the Wind-devil

Hortimán (wind), the devil of the wind, was walking about.[8] He owned coyotes, and had also a burro, a mule, horses, cattle, a dog, hens, and roosters. From his ten hens he gathered a load of eggs. These he loaded on the burro.

Kauymáli decided to go after Hortimán. On meeting Hortimán he asked, "How well do your hens lay? You have hardly to work at all, since all you need to do is sell your eggs. Will you sell me your ten hens?"

Hortimán was willing to sell his hens for five dollars. So they caught the hens and Kauymáli took them home. He made pens for them, and gave them corn in the patio. He believed that they would lay many eggs for him, and thus he would not have to work. But when he had finished feeding them, they flew off into the sky. As they flew away, they hit him in the eye with their droppings.

Kauymáli was very angry. He knew that he had been deceived. He decided to go to Hortimán and get his money back.

But when Kauymáli confronted him, Hortimán pretended to remember nothing of their transaction.

Hortimán called his coyotes, which came to him from his field. He gave them food. There were five dozen of them, and each was as large as a burro. Hortimán told them what he needed. Meanwhile Kauymáli sat nearby, observing what was going on.

Hortimán tied water-gourds on the backs of his coyotes and sent them for water. They soon trotted back with the gourds full of water. Finished with their work[,] the coyotes, half-tired, lay down to rest.

Kauymáli said to Hortimán, "You are lucky to have such good animals to work for you."

"Yes," answered Hortimán. "It does not matter how far I send them. They come back quickly."

This interested Kauymáli, who had been sent so often by the gods. So he bought the coyotes from Hortimán for six pesos each. Then he took them home with him.

The next day before breakfast[,] Kauymáli sent the coyotes out for him, fastening water-gourds on their shoulders. The coyotes, however, acted wildly. They bit and tore at the water-gourds until the gourds were broken off. Then they ran away, taking one of Kauymáli's chickens with them. The chicken was carried to a mesa a great distance away. There the coyotes made a meal of it. Kauymáli was very sad at having been fooled again by the Air-devil.

Kauymáli was in his house when he decided to see Hortimán again and try to get his money back. But when he finally saw him, the Air-devil spoke so pleasantly and with such gestures of friendship that Kauymáli forgot all about his anger.

Hortimán was laying out a blanket that had four quirts upon it. The blanket was spread on a large box. This was like an altar, and around the blanket Kauymáli saw him place ten gourd-bowls. A burro began to eat out of these.

Kauymáli wondered why the burro was eating air out of the gourd-bowls, and how he could live when he ate nothing at all. He wondered if the burro could work. He decided to stay until noon to see what would happen.

Hortimán took five more blankets from his god-house and laid them side by side. When the burro had eaten all the air from the ten gourds placed around these five blankets, it lay down and bore another burro as large as it was. Then Hortimán took one of the quirts. He lashed the burro five times. The burro wheeled around to avoid the blows. Hortimán ceased. The burro stopped right in the middle of the center blanket. Hortimán beat it with five more blows.

At the fifth blow the burro passed pure silver money from its bowels. The money was new and shining. Hortimán then took the burro aside and allowed it to rest. Then he opened the fifteen large boxes and counted the money into one of them.

Kauymáli marvelled at the sight of so many boxes completely filled with new shining money.

Hortimán put money in each of the fifteen boxes to correspond to the fifteen blows he had given the burro. He would not allow Kauymáli to help him with this work, because the money was still very "delicate."[9]

When this work was finished, they began to talk. Kauymáli wished eagerly to buy this wonderful animal that could pass silver instead of manure. Hortimán, the Air-devil, was willing to sell the burro, because all his money boxes were full of money. He also had the other burro that had been born before the money was passed. So Kauymáli was able to buy the burro for fifteen pesos. He listened very carefully to the instructions of Hortimán.

When he arrived home, he explained to his wife what a wonderful burro he had bought. At dawn the next day he extended his blankets and placed the fifteen gourd-bowls side by side exactly as the previous owner had done. His wife watched his proceedings with much interest.

Then Kauymáli beat the burro fifteen times. The burro jumped around all over the blankets. He stopped still in the middle of the center blanket, but did nothing. So Kauymáli beat the animal forty-five times until the burro looked as bloated as it had been before. Now Kauymáli was confident of success. He raised the burro's tail in order to see the money come out. For his trouble, however, he had his face filled with manure and his new blankets soiled. The burro then ran off, and Kauymáli was left alone.

Kauymáli's wife refused to wash the soiled blankets because of his folly in spending his good money for such a purpose. So Kauymáli had to wash his own blankets. He was very angry. He decided to go and complain to the singer about Hortimán.

On his way he passed Hortimán, who was among his many animals. As Hortimán came back, he met Kauymáli, but excused himself to eat his own breakfast. The Air-devil was cooking food without fire, merely using rocks. On these rocks Hortimán was able to roast meat, as well as if the meat had been placed on burning coals. When he was ready to eat, Hortimán asked Kauymáli to join him. But Kauymáli was afraid to eat. He thought that the food might be "delicate"[10] since it was not cooked with fire.

When he had finished, Hortimán put up his utensils. Then he offered tobacco to Kauymáli. As Kauymáli smoked, he was tempted to buy the wonderful pot that would cook food and use only stones for fuel. Such a pot, he reflected, would save him a great deal of work.

The Air-devil told Kauymáli that the pot was a gift from Father Sun. He had been given the pot, he said, so that he would not have to work. But, he remarked, he would be willing to sell the magic pot for five pesos and the three magic rocks for fifteen pesos.

Kauymáli was anxious to buy these things, as well as some magic water. So he gave Hortimán the price that had been placed on these articles.

Kauymáli then placed the pot and the rocks carefully in his blanket. He walked cautiously with his burden so that he would not fall and break the pot. His wife was angry that he had spent more of his money on these things. So to show her how wonderful his purchase was[,] Kauymáli gathered green corn and green beans and put them in the pot along with the Air-devil's magic water. After this he put the magic stones under the pot. Then he called his wife to come and witness the wonder that was about to happen.

Nothing, however, happened. By noon[,] hunger finally forced Kauymáli to get wood for the fire.

The woman ridiculed Kauymáli for spending his money so foolishly. This made him violently angry. He lighted a fire under the pot. The pot got hot and blew up, throwing the magic water and the magic stones in all directions.

Kauymáli again went to Hortimán. He found him saddling his horses. Alone and unguided[,] the animals ran out to gather the cattle, and reported where they were. Kauymáli['s] wrath was dispelled at the sight of this. He bought one of these wonderful horses for twenty pesos. He bought the saddle also for a like amount.

The following day Kauymáli saddled the horse he had bought. The animal, however, ran off bucking until it had broken the saddle to pieces. But worse than this, while Kauymáli was saddling the horse[,] it bucked, injuring Kauymáli's foot so badly that it had to be cut off. Further, it blinded him in one eye.[11]

Then at last did Kauymáli take account of all he had spent on Hortimán's false things.

When Nakawé heard of all these proceedings, she called Kauymáli to her. She told him that he had been childishly foolish to spend all his money on the bad Air-devil. She punished him for his folly by leaving him with only one foot and one good eye.[12] His children, furthermore, were ordered to have the same defects.

Kauymáli, the lamed Wolf,[13] asked Nakawé's permission to go and revenge [avenge] himself on the Air-devil, Hortimán. As soon as he was able, Kauymáli,[14] the Wolf, went to the Wind-devil to see if he would recognize him. Hortimán, however, did not recognize Kauymáli, who asked him for work among his five shepherds with his many sheep. He was given the work.

So Kauymáli began to work for Hortimán. All the while[,] he considered how he might get his revenge.

Each of the shepherds lived in one of the five high caves.

Kauymáli borrowed a guitar with which to sing and amuse himself while alone with the sheep. He told Hortimán that thus he would not fall asleep and would be able to guard his charges better. Then he took his sheep to pasture, as did the other herders.

But as soon as he was alone, Kauymáli shut his sheep inside a large cave. He planned to starve them to death. In the twenty-two days that the sheep were shut up, they were reduced to eating earth. This killed them of [due to a] compacted stomach. While the animals were starving to death, Kauymáli amused himself by singing and dancing.

At the end of the twenty-two days Kauymáli cut the throats of the dying animals. Then he poured the blood down their gullets to make them look fat. Thus he deceived Hortimán into thinking that the sheep had not died due to any neglect on his part. The remains of the sheep were changed into white rocks.

Only one of the sheep was saved by Otuanáka.[15] This she took to the middle of the sea. She ordered people to bring her votive-paraphernalia in return for the gift of the sheep she made them.

Thus Kauymáli got his revenge by taking away all the wealth of Hortimán.

Hortimán had to take shelter in one of the five rocks. From this he comes out only as whirlwinds. Further, Nakawé cursed him and commanded that he always remain a devil. Thus the Huichols believe that whirlwinds cause sickness and death.[16]

Hortimán was commanded to wander restlessly over the world. He can only live in the five holes, in the rocks, or in the earth. From these holes warm air comes out.[17]

Youth Changes His Affiliations from the Sea-Goddesses to the Sun-Father and Makes a Vow to the Wolf[-]People in Order to Catch Deer

A boy, Mekási, lived in the sea where he worked hard among the people there. He killed many deers for the others, putting his deer-traps everywhere. Then the others put out their traps and killed many, while he killed none. He wondered how they killed so many while he didn't kill any, despite his great efforts.

In his dreams he heard Kauymáli say, "You do not fit here among the people of the sea. You are of the other people. Your family is far away. It does not work well with your traps because the great gods of the sea do not give you deer. Take down your nets and talk to your father, the Sun.

So he took down his deer-traps and wrapped them up carefully. He fasted from drinking water or [and] eating salt, so that Tata Sun would hear him.[1] He went to where Tatevalí was and said, "I have a father and brother working[,] but they do not kill deer. Will you help us?"

Tatevalí said, "Yes[,] I will help you catch many deer. I will tell you how, so that you will know. You go there where there is a cave. Go into the hole, which is the entrance of the cave. Then you will not have to struggle so much to catch deer."

His wife did not go, so he went there alone, without her. It took him five days to get there. He climbed up the five cliffs leading to the cave. He entered the house, which was very big. There he found the Elder Wolf, and his children.

The Elder Wolf gave him a chair and he sat down. Then Elder Wolf asked him why he came. He replied, "I have worked very hard trying to catch deer, but the people of the sea do not allow me to catch any. I was sent here to talk to you by someone who said you knew a better way."

Elder Wolf replied that he could not do the work of helping him in a better way to hunt. But he could sit in his chair and direct the younger Wolves as soon as they returned. He said, "Let us wait and see what they do."

But the youth said, "No, I am in a hurry."

Elder Wolf then said, "Well then go to the sierra and meet them. They will not hurt you. Look for arrows and a bow of brazil-wood. Have your wife make votive[-]bowls and offer candles to me. This is the payment of [for] the deer. I am "delicate[,]" and if this command is not carried out, you will die."

So the youth went to his wife and said, "If you can take a vow to wait for five years without having intercourse with a man, we can catch a deer. We must be continent for this long [a] time." The woman said it was not too long a time if they could catch deer in that way.

Then the man went to the sea and got brazil-wood, asking the permission of the great gods of the sea. They gave him permission to take some, if he would leave a lighted candle. In this way the tree would not die.

Then he made a beautiful bow and arrows, as Elder Wolf had told him to do. He had told him, "Do noy [not] be afraid[,] even if we change into wolves."

So the youth walked through the sierra. He had been told to "clean" his body by wiping it with dry grass. Thus he left all his "filth" in the grass, which he burned. He went back to Elder Wolf[,] who told him to set up an altar and for him and his wife to sit by the fire and arrange their votive offerings of bow and arrows.

He asked Elder Wolf if this was a satisfactory offering. Elder Wolf was pleased and introduced him to one of the younger Wolves. They shook hands since Wolf was glad that the man had brought so many beautiful offerings. There were fifty young Wolves who were listening to this conversation.

Elder Wolf told the younger ones to help the poor man who was struggling so hard for the deer. He assigned one of the younger Wolves to take care of the man, another to help him catch deer[,] etc. They were told to do this within five day[s]. The youth was told to put up his lasso-trap with offerings at a certain place. Elder Wolf gave him small votive[-]bowls, pots, and bowls of clay, etc. to put up on the platform of the deer-hunter's shrine. But the day after this[,] the lassos were arranged with the altar nearby.

At dawn on the fifth day, the Wolves met the man near his traps. Here they waited until the man approached. There were fifty Wolf-people waiting to help him. They already had a dead deer[,] which they had run down. They ate this raw, because they were hungry. But they told the man that he did not have orders to eat deer-meat in this way. When they had finished eating, they changed from wolves to people.

Then they divided into two parties of fifteen each. They went in opposite directions. They ran rapidly in a large circle while the man was ordered to stand still, even if the deer came close. This was the command of Elder Wolf.

Very soon the Wolves ran two male deer out of the forest. These [t]hey pulled down. Then their [they] continued crying and made a great din to frighten the deer. Two more came out[,] which were pulled down. The ceremonial paraphernalia were anointed with blood from these deer. Then they took them to their cave-house and prepared to eat meat. The youth cooked the meat in an earth-oven. The Wolf-people could not eat cooked meat. The youth could not eat it with salt, which was included in his vow.

The next day it was the same, and the wolves killed a large buck with three points. Soon they had killed five deer again. These were cooked as before. The following day they could not kill any more as this was not ordered. They went back to the caves and prepared to bake the old meat. But the fourth day the Wolf-people were able to kill five more deer. Some of these they eat [ate] and other[s] they changed into the form of people.

The fifth day they awaited the orders of Elder Wolf, who had asked the man if he wished more deer. He wanted five deer for the next five days. Elder Wolf ordered that he should be brought the hearts, the horns [antlers], the tail, and the hooves of the slain deer. They should be offered to him together with ceremonial paraphernalia. The man and his wife had to bring and offer all of these things.

So he went home and told his wife to prepare all of these things[,] since the Wolf-people were helping him. She was glad to arrange these new things, for the success of the second period of the deer-hunt. Of the deers they had killed she had saved these parts as well as the scapula to be used for a rasping stick after the meat was dried.

When all was done and deer had finally fallen into his traps[,] the youth could make the ceremony of parched corn for clearing his fields for corn. In the meantime they could not eat tortillas, but they could drink water.

Elder Wolf told his people not to bother the youth[,] since he was struggling so hard to catch deer. He gave his people money to buy some cattle from a neighboring ranchería rather than stealing them. So they went to buy a bull, but there were no animals there. The wolves went back to Elder Wolf and reported that the man had no cattle because he was so poor. They had just thought that he had cattle.

But they decided to go and see if the man was telling them the truth. They went at night and found that he had a corral filled with fifty calves. This angered the Wolf-people, so they broke into the corral and killed ten of the calves, and injured many others. They left only five unharmed. The owner, Taowáimi, was very sad.

Meanwhile the youth, Mekási, was finishing his work and had *tesgüino* [corn beer] made for his feast of parched corn. When this beer was already strained[,] fifteen people came, knowing that there was going to be a ceremony and feast. They looked like good people, but that night the youth dreamed that they were bad, because he dreamed that the next day he would fall down and be sick. They owned the cattle killed by the Wolf-people.

The next day was the last day of the ceremony, and in the feast which [that] followed[,] the guests ate all the food and drank all the tesgüino. But fortunately the man, warned by his dream, drank nothing. The fifteen people got drunk and abused him for having so much meat of deer. Their lassos would not catch deer. They went and broke his votive[-]bowls and the magic bow of brazil-wood, which they knew caused his success.

The Elder Wolf was angered by this, since these things had been offered to him. At dawn the next day the feast was over, so the people left. The bad people divided into parties and waited at a break in the cliff. Here also the Wolves waited for the bad people. As they approached[,] fifteen of the Wolves throttled the people who [had] desecrated the offerings of Elder Wolf. They tore out their entrails and ate them. The Wolves said, "You thought that you could fool us. But we have punished your sacrilege to our ceremonial paraphernalia. This was the end of the five years[,] so the youth was finishing his vow to Elder Wolf. As soon as he had given this ceremony[,] he could eat salt. Then he would no longer be "delicate."

Elder Wolf said to him, "You were the only one who could use the magic lasso deer-net traps. If I dream well, I will send one of my boys. When you finish your fast[,] you will be able to kill a deer each day to prepare for your last feast."

Thus it was easy for the youth to kill the deers necessary for his ceremony. He carried the horns [antlers] as an offering to Elder Wolf. The fourth day an evil-doer (sorcerer) approached and laughingly ate some of the meat, and hid the rest. Thus the next day the young man could not find his deer-meat. The sorcerer also found his deer-traps and cut them up.

Elder Wolf knew who did this and sent one of his boys to find out and follow the evil-doer. He lived at "Corral Prieto" (Mexican[-]named place) and his name was Tukauwi. So they waited until night and then went here and killed him by biting him to death.

Elder Wolf knew where the dried deer-meat had been hidden by the bad Tukauwi. Also the last day the youth killed his last two deer. Another man came to the youth, attracted to him because he killed deer so easily. He wished to be like the youth. He told the new-comer [*sic*] how it was done, and what to do in order to gain the favor of the Wolf-people, *uraúwi tewíali*. He told him that they lived in a certain cave. He said, "You can go there, but I can't take you there."

He went and the Wolf-people saw him coming. Elder Wolf knew that he was not coming for good. So he ordered him killed before he got there.

The youth continued his work. The Sun-[F]ather told him that another man knew of his vow to the Wolf-people; and told him also what had happened to the previous man who has [had] learned of it. The people of the man were coming to revenge themselves of [upon] the youth. The Sun-[F]ather told him in advance that they were gathering [and were] prepared to kill him. Sun-[F]ather said, "Go in good time so that they do not catch and kill you." So he went and hid himself.

Fifty people came, who he did not know. They encircled his hiding place. But the Wolves attacked them and killed [them] all. They told the youth and his wife where to hid[e] their many cattle for five days. They went there and did this. The Wolf-people wished to see whether the youth or his enemies would win. The Wolves helped the youth, taking care of his cattle, as though they were dogs. And every night they went and killed some of the animals of his enemies. This happened to an enemy in each of the five world directions.

This left only one of his enemies with any animals. They wondered what could be the matter. They said, "Who knows about this?" But on [no] one knew what could be the matter. But the last enemy, who had animals, knew what was the matter. He gathered these people together.

Together with the others[,] he armed himself to protect the remaining animals. Then they gathered around the water-hole, where the Wolves were preparing to kill the remaining animals. Among the people there came a boy well prepared to shoot. He asked for a truce to talk and said, "I come on an errand. Do all of you take care of animals? Are you brave?"

The people replied, "Yes and we will shoot all of your Wolf-people, as you deserve for killing all of our cattle. We know that it is you who is doing this."

Elder Wolf came up and said, "You here wish to kill us. But you will not succeed. You do not understand how these things are. Here you must sleep, to dream what will happen."

They dreamed to wait here [that they should wait there] for five days. They must also offer a bull to the Wolf-people, because they had not fasted as the youth had done. The leader tried to ask the reason of [asked for an explanation from] Elder Wolf, before they offered it. But he gave it so that the Wolf-people would not kill all of the animals. So they tied the bull where the wolves could kill and eat it. Fifty Wolves came up to the people.

The Wolf-people said, "You are not brave, you are afraid."

The bad people ran in all directions at these words, but they could not find the speaker of the words. In a little cleared valley they waited to see what would come out. Here they waited[,] although they heard nor saw neither animals nor anything. The next day they would go to see what happened. When they got there[,] a large deer ran out. They surrounded it and killed it easily. Their leader went to another part of the valley[,] where another deer ran out and was killed. Thus they killed deer in all parts of the world including the middle.

Then they went to the far points of the valley to see what could be seen and heard. They called five times and the owner of the remaining cattle said, "Let us see what our father says when we sleep." So they went back to their houses since they did not wish to continue this work because they were having such bad luck. They were afraid of the animals that they might meet the next day. The owner said, "Nothing will happen if we fulfill out [*sic*] [abide by our] contract with Elder Wolf."

So they went and found Elder Wolf. The people hid, while the owner approached and said, "Do you like out [our] work?"

Elder Wolf replied, "My father said that you must have ceremonial paraphernalia or we will have to continue harming you. Make five votive[-]bowls decorated [with] cattle, so that the animals would [will] not be killed, also make prayer arrows. Our final payment will be five cows and fifteen pesos. Take these to the door of the cave, but do not try to come in."

So the owner took these things[,] although there seemed to be no people in the cave, nor any sign of them. He left them in belief [believing] that the Wolf-people would come. He prayed that they would be satisfied and would not molest his cattle further. Elder Wolf found the offering to be satisfactory, and all was paid in full. So he ordered his children not to harm the cattle any more.

The cattle-owner went to visit the youth to tell him that he and his people had made it up with the Wolf-people[,] who would no longer molest his cattle. The offering of money could not be touched or it would burn. So the cattle owner told him to go get the money[,] which should be given to some poor man.

When the sun was going down[,] the cattle-owner heard the cries of the Wolves. There were fifteen wolves waiting who took off the clothes of the youth. They changed him into a Wolf-youth. He easily killed five and then ten deer and could eat the meat raw.

Two of the deer were carried to his house and left whole. His family hung up the deer. People armed themselves and found the meat. They wished to buy it, but the Wolf-youth gave it to them. Other people molested him asking for deer-meat. It would not harm him as a Wolf-youth to sell the meat, but he gave it to them. Daily deer-meat was not lacking at his ranchería.

[The] Wolf-youth had a beautiful wife who had kept her vow of continence for nine years. Thus it was almost complete. Once in a feast[,] another man approached her while she was asleep. Wolf-youth dreamed that this was happening and came up to see what was happening. She denied that she had been approached.

For five days the Wolf-youth blamed her. Then the other man approached her again; but she told him to wait until her vow was completed. But finally they had intercourse notwithstanding her vow. When the Wolf-youth found this out[,] he was beside himself with anger.

He said, "Now I don't care for you at all. Get out. I will go live with my brother." He bit her in the head and sent her away to the man who had slept with her. Then he changed back into a wolf and ran away. He had bit her eye out.

One-eyed, the woman went to her lover[,] who was pulling up deer-traps. She was well dressed. Her name was matírlalai. She said, "I know how to dream. You will kill fifteen deer."

Her lover, whose name was *kupéme[,]* caught this numbed [number] of deer. But when he got back[,] he could not wait for five days for intercourse with her. But she did not wish it until she had fulfilled this second vow.

After finishing the vow and the sacrifices for catching deer[,] she would be willing, she said. At the end of four days she told him to go to an arroyo to see what he would find in the little plain there. He went ther[e] and found four little deer-traps, with a fifth at the end of the valley.

He wore a plume in his hair and carried his wart-gourd tobacco containers. He wore his best clothes. So he sat down by the traps to see what would happen. As he waited, his mistress came form [from] the house. She said she had followed to meet him. She added, "We have finished the five[-]day vow. So here in this field we can have each other."

The man thought, "You didn't want me in the house, and now you come here where I am very busy." She caught hold of him and played with him; but he said that he was going. She would not release him. As the sun went down she told him not to be afraid as she could accommodate him. She said, "I will not let you go until we lay together."

He said he was so inclined and asked her to release him so that he could put up his festal paraphernalia. But she would not [wait], so attired as he was, he mounted her. The woman [was] soon satisfied and was going. She told him to remain there until she had disappeared.

Then he was instructed to go on to see what would appear. There he saw a deer come out[,] and the man looked at it. The woman had turned into a deer as she was crossing the creek, out of his sight. It was she, and she bounded away into the sierra. The man was greatly frightened for having been intimate with a deer-woman. He got fever and was ill. He thought, "This woman won over me. She came to tell me that I shall die."

He staggered home and found his real lover, whose form the deer-woman had taken. The woman knew what had happened and told him that he would die before the morning came. At dawn he was crazy and cried and yelled. At noon he was serious and moody. At sunset he had died as was ordered. They wrapped him in his blanket and left the body in the house while they prepared for the burial ceremony.

When they re-entered the house, his wrappings were there; but he was gone. He had gone to join the deer-woman, so that they could live together happily in the mountains. It was for this that she had taken the form of the woman he had loved. So she changed him into a male deer.

She said, "Now I have orders that you live here with me. Eat tortillas of deer-horn [antler,] which will make you drunk (peyote). They went off together to the mountains. Arriving there[,] they made [the] acquaintance of the other dee[r]-people. Then they met the Sun-[F]ather[,] who said to the man, "Now you have changed into a deer-man. I will make your penis long so that you can father deer-childre[n]. Every October you will have a rutting season. Thus you will have a family, st [so] that the people cannot end your race."

This was ordered to happed [happen] when they had intercourse on the ground. The deer-woman took the semen in her mouth (*maSa teiea*[, (H.),] "deer mouth"). The Sun-[F]ather gave them the middle world region for their pasture. He told them to eat a little colored earth[,] which is very "sacred"[2] and is called *maSa kuikuáipa*. This is colored black, yellow, white, etc. By their eating this[,] the people would not kill them.

The Wet Season Cycle of the Mythology

Keamukáme Establishes the Corn Ceremonies and Feasts

Keamukáme is a goddess of water, clouds, rain, and sea. She aids in the growth of corn. Nakawé is her mother.

Keamukáme was a snake. She was born near the waters of the Pacific. Nakawé looked at her daughter, and this is how she was born. Keamukáme first entered the sea green in color, but came out very white behind. She entered a second time, and came out looking at Nakawé. Then she jumped into the middle (of the sea?) with thunder and storm. She came out again, still very small, and thus she was born.[1]

Keamukáme said, "I am going to (measure, examine, mark, proportion). But what will Nakawé, the Sun, and Tatotsí say? I myself will say nothing until I talk to them." Nakawé, the Sun, and Tatotsí were called.

For five days Keamukáme played in the water and grew and grew. Then she came out as a snake.[2] She climbed to the sky and caused a rain. Then she fell to the ground and stopped at the sea.

The Sun said, "You must make a *teapáli* (god-disc), arrows, bread, candles, chocolate, a house, and other things. But what are you called?"

Nakawé said, "I will call you a woman. But I will have to dream for five days to find you a name." Nakawé then dreamed for four nights, but fruitlessly. On the fifth night, however, she dreamed that her daughter was to be called Keamukáme.

Then Nakawé got ceremonial paraphernalia. When the Sun came out, she prayed, even as the Huichols do. She took water from the sea, which is the most sacred water, and baptized Keamukáme.[3] Next Nakawé gave her daughter a stool, a house, and everything that she would need. This Nakawé did so that Keamukáme would aid her.

Now in these ancient times there was also a man. The woman looked at him. But Keamukáme was shut up after this and not allowed to look at men.

Nakawé talked to the Sun, and remarked that the man had not been baptized with sacred water and had no name.

The man left Keamukáme with Nakawé another day and said, "I am not baptized. No one will talk to me."

Nakawé answered, "You may come and meet her some other day."

Keamukáme came out beautifully dressed. Nakawé said to her, "Do you wish to marry this man after fifteen days when he is baptized and has a name?"

The Sun dreamed for five days and worked to find out what the man should be called. Then Sun went down to the sea and learned that the man was to be named Pálikata. The man was then baptized in Huichol fashion.[4]

Now he was allowed to enter the house with Keamukáme. The two talked while Nakawé listened.

Pálikata said, "I need a house."

"If you wish to marry," answered Nakawé, "we will make you a house and whatever else you need in your marriage."

After they had talked for a long time, Pálikata said, "I want a house, gourds, arrows, and all the other necessary things."

So they went, and soon they were there beside the gods near the sea. Thus, married and living together, Pálikata and Keamukáme were happy.

Nakawé said to Keamukáme, "Say and command what you need. You must have Pálikata make a field. I will give you food for seed." She continued, "Keamukáme, you should not work so hard. You should find another woman to work for Pálikata." Thus Nakawé searched and found another wife for Pálikata.[5]

When Pálikata returned from his work clearing the field, Keamukáme brought gourds the size of acorns, and tortillas the size of a small coin.[6] Pálikata was given of these to eat. A tiny bit only was necessary to satisfy him.[7] The following day Pálikata worked according to Nakawé's instructions. This he had to do for five days. Then he could plant his seed-corn.

The rains came, and the drying period passed. Pálikata said, "We must burn the brush." He asked the god of fire, Tatevalí, for fire. Tatevalí, however, refused to give it. Pálikata said to him, "I need fire."

Tatevalí was burning brightly. He replied, "I cannot go to burn your field." But he gave Pálikata a flower in a shaman's basket, saying, "I will take out my plumes. I myself cannot go. I would burn up your world, because I am very 'delicate.'" Taking out one green and one red feather he continued, "Carry these to your fields. They will serve as dried grass (kindling). In the center of your field put your teapáli (god-disc), place these feathers under it, and pray as I pray."[8]

Pálikata took the feathers, pondering over what Tatevalí had said.

In the field Pálikata arranged his teapáli and the plumes as he had been instructed. When he prayed, the feathers took [caught] fire. Thus was the large field burned of all its brush. In this great fire all the bad people (animal pests) were destroyed. The smoke, blown by the wind, was changed into clouds.[9] When the entire field had been burned, it was allowed to cool for five days. Then the field was baptized with sacred water to prevent it from burning. Keamukáme provided the sacred water.[10]

The other wife worked also. After five days, when the field had finally cooled,

Keamukáme told Pálikata to prepare the paraphernalia for a ceremony. All was arranged with a special votive-bowl with rays to the four points and a candle in the middle. They prayed all night, and the next day Pálikata planted. He planted for five days, using five little pouches of corn[,] which were replenished magically by Nakawé. In five days the corn was sprouted, and cried like a little deer.[11] Soon it could talk like a small child. In five more days the corn said, "I am hungry. My parents have brought me nothing to eat."

The plants then left the field and went to Nakawé. They entered her house and saw a pretty altar. On the altar was food, which they ate.

Keamukáme was asleep, and dreamed that the corn-children had come to eat. When she awakened, she could see nothing except that all the food had been taken from the altar.[12]

She slept another day, and the corn-children came again and ate. The Sun asked Keamukáme who was taking the food from her altar. Keamukáme replied, "I will dream." That night she dreamed that the corn-children said to her, "Since we have nothing to eat, you must come to the corn-field. Bring us the ceremonial paraphernalia of your altar here. In the middle of the field make a little house, and there place the teapáli (god-disc). Then make a small corral for the teapáli where a lighted candle may be put."

In the field, food offerings were made. When this was done, the Sun came out. The corn-children ate at the altar. Then they played all around the field.[13]

For five nights Keamukáme dreamed to put a votive-bowl in the midst of the corn. The votive-bowl disappeared into the ground, and the ears came out, from two to three on every stalk. It was a very good field. There were beans and squashes as well.[14]

Keamukáme then said to Pálikata, "I should like to eat the ears. We cannot, however. But I will tell you what we must dream." So she dreamed[15] what they must do. In five nights she dreamed[16] that Pálikata should make five lasso net-traps for deer. He was then to put them up in order to catch deer. "Let us see if we can catch deer," she said, "so that we may offer the blood to the corn."[17]

So Pálikata made the trap-nets. Then he went without eating salt and without having intercourse with his wife, sleeping on the other side of the fire. He went to sleep, and tried to dream whether he would kill a deer.[18] But neither he nor Keamukáme was able to dream.

Then Keamukáme and Pálikata prayed to Tatevalí. Pálikata asked, "Why do you not give me deer, Tatevalí?" At midnight Keamukáme saw in her dreams that they should hunt for the trapped deer. A shaman's plume had fallen as a sign that they would kill a deer.[19]

As the Sun was coming up, a deer ran out and fell into the trap. It was killed. Then Pálikata came home, bringing this deer[,] which was of two points. Keamukáme ran out with a handful of grass to greet him. They met near the god-house with its altar where the ceremonial paraphernalia was kept. The paraphernalia was placed on the beautiful deer. Keamukáme said to the dead animal, "Now, deer, you have your house, your altar, and your paraphernalia." To Pálikata she said, "Now do not eat either the deer or the blood until we have offered some to Tatevalí. Then we shall be able to kill more deer." When this was done, they bathed (anointed) all the ceremonial paraphernalia. Then Keamukáme said, "Now go and anoint the paraphernalia in the field."

Pálikata did not dare to get his hands bloody. They told mataSúli ("bloody hands") to butcher the deer. Then Pálikata offered the blood to the four points and to the middle (of the corn-field?) where the altar was set. This fed the corn.

The next day a female deer was killed, and the same ceremony [was] repeated.

In five days the green corn was ready to eat. Keamukáme, however, said, "We cannot eat meat or corn until we give a feast [ceremony] for the corn.

So for twenty-two days they slept apart and did not eat salt. Then Keamukáme said to Pálikata, "You must now take down your deer-traps, tie them up, and put them in the god-house so they can rest." This was done, but first the traps were well cleaned so that none of the hair would fall on the cleared ground (dancing patio or floor).[20]

Then they worked for five days, preparing for the fiesta. The women cooked, and prepared *tesgüino* [corn-beer], all according to the word of the green corn *(elotes)*. Beer was made, and when it was ready to strain[,] they were ready for the feast.[21] Then Keamukáme asked Tatevalí to come with his shaman's plumes, his tobacco-pouch (a wart-gourd), and the like. They communicated by pounding on the ground with their sandals in a dance.[22]

Tatevalí came and talked to Keamukáme. Keamukáme said, "I asked you to come because I am getting ready to harvest the corn. I wish you, Tatevalí, to sing, since we have everything ready. Sing for us all night."

Tatevalí replied, "Very well. I will sit here. You prepare blood in an intestine of the deer, and array the altar in the usual fashion. Also, cook the deer." He then sang all night.[23]

At midnight the gods came, bathed in the sacred water, drank the fermenting tesgüino,[24] and ate the food and the blood.

Tatevalí said to Pálikata, "I have given you a good field because you have kept the fasts and have not eaten meat or salt."

Then they cut twenty-five ears of corn and put them in sets of five[, adorned] with beautiful flowers. They also took five tiny ears of corn and, anointing them with blood, dropped them into the fire for Tatevalí.

Pálikata danced five times with the roasting-ears, which were then offered to the fire. As the offertory elotes [ears of corn] were dropped in the fire, a cloud rose up. Tatevalí caught it. It was a five-centavo piece. This was placed in the center of the votive-bowl.[25] Then the food and drink, as well as the deer-stew, were consumed. The people feasted and were happy.

Lastly, Tatevalí took two *ollas* [ceramic cooking pots] of deer-stew and twenty-five machetes[,] which he gave [to] the guests for working. The people then went to the field and prayed and drank the deer-stew. Then they started to work. As they were working, Keamukáme came with twenty-five gourds of elotes for them. These were set down by Tatevalí. Keamukáme also brought tesgüino for the workers as they were returning from the field. A basket *(itáli)* of tamales was then brought from the god-house for the workers. From the basket Tatevalí took out five tamales. These were distributed by running boys with plumes in their hair. Thus they made a pile of tamales.

Then tiny tamales, made for the fire-god, were given to all. Led by Tatevalí they encircled the fire and offered their food to it.[26] As they put the food in the fire, they said, "We are giving you tamales to still your belly-hunger."

Then Tatevalí blessed the four points with offerings of sacred water, and the people broke their fast of water. Similarly[,] salt was used for the first time since the ceremonies began. The boys with plumes in their hair arranged the plates and bowls for tamales and deer-soup.

Tatevalí said, "Thus have I taught you how to observe the harvest ceremony."[27]

Corn was still [unharvested] in the corn-field. In five days the corn dried. The teapáli was also still in the middle of the field. When the first corn was open, a votive-bowl was placed on the teapáli. To it were brought five of the ripe ears *(teyaya)*, tied together with many beautiful things.

Finally the people harvested, making five great piles of the corn. The corn was then taken to five store-houses to dry.

Keamukáme then said, "You must clear for five days more while I dream what we should do. I will make a votive-bowl. You, Pálikata, make ceremonial arrows. Put them in the mountains as an offering before setting up deer traps."

The arrows were thus left for ten days because it was cold and wet. During this time[,] twenty-five deer were caught. Their horns [antlers] and skins were brought to the house.

Tatevalí sang in the mountains to bring the deer together. No salt was eaten during the ten days. Then the deer-traps were brought in with all the meat. The meat was cut up and dried. The skins were prepared. The lassos were put away carefully in the god-house.

Then Tatevalí ordered a deer-dance. Twenty-five of the people danced in deer-skins with horns [antlers] to the five points of the patio.[28] Tatevalí next sent the dancers to the mountains. Here they prayed and anointed the paraphernalia with deer-blood. Pálikata meanwhile carried what horns [antlers] and paraphernalia were necessary to a teapáli in the mountains.[29]

The following year, after the fiesta of parched corn, the people again cleared the field of brush, and in twenty-five days [they] planted corn.[30]

When all the preparations were made for this feast, Tatevalí came again and placed the [clay] griddle *(comal)* ceremoniously on the fire. Then, when sufficient corn had been parched, he put five differently colored kernels of corn on the griddle. The tesgüino and parched corn were then given to the people.[31]

B The Water-and-Corn Goddess, Kacíwali, and the Ant-People

A goddess was born in the sea according to the orders of Nakawé. Nakawé said, "I will name you Kacíwali, of corn and of water. You shall live apart, and you had better stay for a little time where I shall send you. There I have fixed a mountain for you."

Kacíwali replied, "Wherever you order, there I will go, if you arrange everything for me."

Nakawé answered, "Yes, there I have prepared you a field and a house. In the house are five shaman's chairs, and all the other things that you need. You can sit and rest there as well as here. Thus, leave the ocean and see if you like it on that mountain-top where there is a small lake. The wind[1] will show you where it is."

Nakawé then caused a storm of lightning, thunder, and rain to take Kacíwali (a rain-goddess, presumably as a snake in the heart of a cloud) to the mountain. There Kacíwali descended into the little lake.

A man of the ant-people followed her. He arrived at the mountain-top, where all was as Nakawé had arranged. The man was contented and wished to remain. He said to Kacíwali, "Where do you come from? We should like to live near you, since it is very pleasant here. We are not bad people, but just."

Kacíwali answered, "Yes, you may stay. Make what fields and houses you need. I have corn which [that] increases rapidly, and this I can give you for seed."

So the man made himself round-houses and fields.[2]

When planting time came, the great gods of the sea saw that the ant-people had their houses and clearings. They needed only corn for seed, in the absence of which they were living on herbs and nuts.

When the first rains came, one of the ant-people appeared before Kacíwali with a votive-bowl and with candles. He asked of her seed for planting. This she could easily give, because she was "of corn."

So Kacíwali gave the ant-people five grains of corn of different colors. She gave the ant-people sacred paraphernalia. All this enabled the ant-people to gather and pray. Kacíwali then told them not to eat the seed-corn, one ear of which was placed in each votive-bowl. The votive-bowls were then placed on the altar.

At dawn, just when the ant-people were going to plant the corn, rain came and softened the ground. During the night the five kernels had increased to a whole bowl-full. Then the ant-people began to plant. In five days the corn had grown about fifteen inches high. In fifteen more days there were roasting-ears from this magic seed.[3]

Nakawé, however, told the ant-people that they could not eat any of the corn until a deer had been killed.[4] But the ant-people could not catch deer. For one thing, they had no deer-traps. For another, they did not even know what deer were. Because of this, Nakawé permitted the ant-people to pile their corn and then sing all night.

The ant-people had five singers. After the singing[,] the goddess, Kacíwali, took the first ear, giving the people only the stalks.

Then the ant-people gathered the corn. They worked five days, arranging a feast. But they had a difficult time persuading some one [*sic*] to sing. All were afraid. Finally one agreed.

In the morning the god-houses were full of corn-ears. The singer began his song, but sang badly.

When the ant-people had finished the harvest, one of their singers became sick. No one knew the cause of his illness. They tried to cure him, but without success. His brother then went to the great gods of the sea and told them that his brother was sick, and that neither the other singers nor himself had been able to dream what was the matter.[5]

The great gods told him, "You must bring us a large candle. If you do this, your brother will get well in five days and give a feast at your home.[6]

Elated, the ant-man returned to his people. He told them what the great gods had said to him. He ordered that corn be sprouted for *tesgüino* [corn-beer]. Then he carried a candle to the cave of the gods. Within four days the tesgüino was ready. The sick man became better.

When the tesgüino was strained,[7] the singer began his song. He sang badly, however, because he did not know how to sing well. Thus the gods did not hear him. Furthermore, the ignorant ant-people drank the tesgüino before the singing was finished and before the [corn-]beer had been offered to the gods all night. They did not even invite their neighbor-woman, Kacíwali.

Kacíwali was, of course, slighted. She said to herself, "I am going to change myself. I shall close my door and go to the feast to see if they know who I am and where I come from."

She then changed herself into a very small, poorly dressed girl. She took her gourd-bowl with her to see if she would be offered meat-broth. At dawn she went, but, as she approached the feast, [she] found that the people were too drunk to hear her greeting. She sat down to see if the ant-people would invite her in and offer her food and drink. The ant-people were inside the dancing-house, dancing and playing the violin and the guitar.

One said, "Who is this miserable, little girl? Where did she come from? We will not give her anything, and then she will not return to see us."

Kacíwali said to herself, "I did not come here to participate but to observe."

Two of the ant-people noticed her, but did not speak to her. Finally, in the late afternoon when the chocolate (which had been offered to the gods) and the soup were distributed, she became tired of sitting there all alone and neglected. So without having touched the feast, she left.[8] In five steps she arrived at the house of her mother (presumably Nakawé).

The mother asked, "Did the ant-people give you anything?"

Kacíwali replied, "No, they paid no attention to me whatsoever. I come [came] home hungry."

The mother gave her food, pondering on the inhospitality of the ant-people. She thought, "What shall we do to punish them?"

Kacíwali's mother left at midnight, after communicating with the other great gods of the sea by means of her votive-bowls.[9] Then she took away almost all of the ant-people's corn, leaving only enough for seed.

Thus at the beginning of the dry season the ant-people had no corn. The great gods, who sent a message by the wind,[10] approved of this. They had learned how badly the ant-people had treated their neighbor, Kacíwali, especially after she had given them seed. The great gods said, "Do now as you wish. We understand. We will go back to the point of the sea [seashore]. We must talk to our father, the Sun."

The Sun said, "Leave them without corn until they kill deer."

Meanwhile the ant-people had planted the corn left them by the mother of Kacíwali. But within fifteen days, when the corn was only half grown, the water failed. The rain fell on the fields of Kacíwali but missed the fields of the ant-people.

The ant-people now began to cry from hunger. In ten more days the women and children were ill from not having eaten, because the fields had dried up completely. At midnight they prayed in their houses, saying that in future they would make better ceremonies.

One of them then said, "Let us sing and see what will happen. Look! We are dying. All will be finished. We are hungry and sad."

So one of the singers of the ant-people began to sing. He continued all night. But at dawn, despite the efforts of the singer and the hopes of the ant-people, it still did not rain. The rain, however, fell on their neighbor's fields. Now the singer realized that he did not know how to sing well, since the ant-people needed water even for drinking.

Another sang all night, and, at dawn, affirmed that it would rain at noon. But the rain still fell only on the fields of their neighbor, Kacíwali.

The cousin of the last singer was asked to sing. He admitted that he was a poor singer, but said that he was losing his crops[,] too. So he sang, and the next morning said that it would rain at eight o'clock in the evening. But the rain fell only on the fields of their neighbor.

At last they realized that they were being punished. They said, "Let us remain awake and sing, while we try to think of whom we are being punished by."

Among them was a child whose fields had not dried up completely. The ant-people said to him, "We are in very bad straits. Please sing for us. You have fields that are still growing. Why is that? Sing, and tell us who is punishing us."

The child agreed to help them, and sang until dawn. The ant-people asked him what the gods had said about the person who was punishing them.

The boy answered, "Yes, I heard a little. Did you have a harvest feast of green corn? The Sun and the great gods of the sea told me that when the Sun came up, a little girl who was poorly dressed appeared here. This child is punishing us."

The ant-people replied, "We did not know this. We were all drunk at the time."

Two women, however, remembered the child, and recalled that no one had greeted her, while she sat alone and sad all day.

The singer reprimanded them severely for their fault. They became saddened and fearful. The singer said, "Now if this is true, it must be true also that someone is punishing us. The child must have told her mother. Her mother was the one that gave you the seed-corn. And how about that candle you gave her when she gave you the seed?"

All the ant-people were very sad because of the way they had treated the child. The men blamed the women. The women defended themselves by saying that because the men had not offered anything, they also had refrained.

The ant-people then decided that they must do something to [be] reconcile[d with] the one who was punishing them. They thought, "Now that we are weeping, maybe she will hear us. We will pray also, and perhaps she will think of us."

So the child-singer sang for five nights more to learn all he could from the gods. As he sang, he asked the gods of all five points what the trouble was. The people then took votive offerings to the caves of the gods of these directions. The child-singer dreamed that Kacíwali was happy at all the rain, and that she sounded her horn for joy.

The child-shaman sang the second night. He dreamed again, and told the ant-people what Kacíwali would wish them to do to satisfy her [atone] for their rudeness. In the first place they would have to go for five days without food and water. Also, they would have to make a small drum and well-decorated collars of reeds for rattles. Then on a small board would have to be painted a small parrot, a *catarina* parrot, and yellow, red, blue, green, and white snakes. Finally, they would have to make several beaded votive-bowls. All this would have to be done during the five-day fast from food and water.

The ant-people had to make also a *nealíka* of colored wool with the design of an eagle at the five points, together with pictures of oak-trees and five snakes in green paint. Furthermore, a cane of rattan-root, together with many shaman's plumes, would have to be offered to Grandmother Growth (Nakawé). Also they would have to make a small board[,] *etáli [itáli,]* bearing pictures of a double-headed royal eagle, painted in the middle, a jaguar at the wings of the eagle, and two [mountain] lions, one at each end.

The ant-people were willing to make these offerings. They realized that they were greatly at fault, and that only thus could Kacíwali be appeased. But they did not know how to make these sacred things. The child who had made fun of the visiting goddess in the form of a child was forced to make the required things. The ant-people were all willing to buy and make the materials for the sacred paraphernalia. When the five days were over and the things finished, they were all very tired.

On the fifth night the singer sang all night. In the morning he asked the ant-people, "Who has cattle that we may offer up blood?"

One ant-man had a cow that was dying of thirst. He killed it in order that the offerings might be bathed in blood. Others brought big candles. Another brought chocolate, and another paper for rosettes.

The singer was tired from so much singing. He could do nothing save continue, however. Kacíwali said to him, "Now that everything is finished, I will tell you when to bring the sacred objects, as soon as you sing again. If you do not find me there, come back in five days."

When the ant-people went to the house of Kacíwali, they heard nothing but the wind. Although they were weak from hunger, they had to carry the things back with them. The singer had to sing again, also, until it was revealed to him that Kacíwali was really there. When the ant-people went again to the mesa where Kacíwali lived, they saw an eagle, which flew away on the wind. Further, they found only the wind. The wind tried to greet them, but the ant-people did not understand its language.

The singer had to sing a third time. The ant-people went again to the house of Kacíwali. This time they saw only a little parrot, which flew away. The ant-people did not know it was Kacíwali.

The fourth day the ant-people were weeping for fear that Kacíwali would not accept their offerings because she was still angry.

The singer reassured them. "Be calm," he said. "I know that tomorrow, the fifth day, we will find Kacíwali. At midnight I dreamed that the reason you do not find her is that you do not know she is those birds you have seen. Tomorrow, exactly at noon, we will go to see what we shall find. We may find bad animals, because I dreamed badly."

So the following day they went to the house of Kacíwali just before noon. At exactly noon they entered the patio. When the singer entered the house of Kacíwali, he saw a large, glaring-eyed jaguar about to spring. The ant-people became drunk with fear. They were so terrified that they were almost petrified. All lost their memories. The singer dreamed that the jaguar blamed them for mistreating the child, who had really been corn.[11]

When the ant-people awakened, the jaguar was gone. In its place was a cornstalk with ears.[12] So they all prayed, and here they left their votive offerings. These were arranged in formal Huichol ceremonial fashion. When all the offerings were made, the ant-people could touch the corn and greet it. The corn listened to their greetings. When the ant-people had finished, the large corn-ear gushed water into one of the votive-bowls. With this water the ant-people bathed the ceremonial paraphernalia and baptized themselves.[13] This refreshed them after their long fast.

The shaman, from his dream, now learned that the *"tigre"* [jaguar] had said it would rain.[14] When the ant-people went outside, it was evident that it would rain. The sky was dark with clouds. Before they arrived home, the storm broke with thunder in all of the five directions. It was a great, fine rain, in truth. The houses were blown down, destroyed, and dashed away. And the ant-people were drowned.

All was finished, including the singer. His shaman's plumes only were carried to the Sun by a strong wind, because they belonged to the Sun.[15]

It continued to rain from the five directions all over the world. The five water-snakes, coming down from the clouds, were so tangled together that it couldn't stop raining.[16] All the arroyos were filled with water. There was plenty for Kacíwali.

The tangled snakes finally came down with lightning, and fell into a water-hole of the river (near Cartagena, between Colotlan [Colotlán] and Bolaños). They said, "Here we may play, since we were given permission by the great gods of the sea." And they played by a rock, *isulta*.

Although the water was very high, the snakes changed into fish.[17] The rock called to the Tepejuanes, asking them to catch the fish. The Tepejuanes took off their clothes and, swimming on balsa wood,[18] followed the fish-snakes.

The fish-snakes swam very slowly. But when the balsa-wood touched them, they always escaped. The Tepejuanes then asked five Mexicans to help them. The fish-snakes, however, always got away.

Now the mother of the fish-snakes, Kacíwali, protected the snakes because they were corn.[19] The fish-snakes came out of the water and flew to the sky. On coming to a mountain they rested in a small lake. Here they played for one day, because they were the children of Kacíwali. They were called *kaitsu [ketsu]*. Then they flew away again, and arrived at the edge of the sea. They came to their father and mother, and showed them the marks of the injuries they had received from the finger-nails of the Tepejuanes and the Mexicans.

The Sun was happy, because he was their father. He gave each one permission to go to one of the five directions. One remained with the mother, Kacíwali, and fell into her votive-bowl as corn.[20]

The end [demise] of the ant-people shows what will happen to the children of any people whose singers do not know how to sing so that the gods can hear. It shows also what becomes of people who do not carry the gods the things that they want. They shall be punished by floods and drough[t]. Those who observe the right customs, and bring Kacíwali things, will be granted favors of squash, corn, beans, and animals. Kacíwali will reward any poor man who presents himself filled with thoughts of the gods. If he will vow that for five years he will not eat salt, not have intercourse with any but his wife, and not drink tesgüino, Kacíwali will reward him with corn and animals.

But this is a very "delicate" (sacred) period. Only by asking favors and by keeping penitence for five years can people have children, animals, money, corn, and squash.[21]

Kacíwali has given orders for the shamans, also, in their guidance of the people. They must be very strict in observing rules.[22]

C Nakawé Punishes [the] (God)People Because the Sea Turtle Is Killed

There is a river HatoSámi near Tepic where there are five rocks[,] *kawí [káwi]*. On one side of the mountains the animal *"chachalote"* (Mex.-Sp.)[,] *tsimuaka[,]* H. [squirrel,] was born and grew. From the mountains it went and climbed on the kawí [káwi] rocks, jumping from one to another. It came to "this side" (one of the six regions) where there were many animals which [that] had been born in the sea (and therefore belonged to the wet season cycle).

The wolves wished to eat the "chachalote[,]" but they could not climb the rocks. In five days this animal grew to be very big so that it left large tracks. As it was trav[e]ling around near the river HatoSámi [Santiago River,] the chachalote saw large tracks of the sea turtle, which lay eggs near the sea. (My informant says he has seen these turtles and eggs.)

The turtle asked the chachalote if it could play with him. So [the] chachalote told it to climb the rocks, since he could not descend because animals were trying to kill him. So the turtle asked the great gods of the sea if he could play with [the] chachalote. It was necessary to ask because the great gods took care of their animal[,] the sea turtle.[1] The great gods said that it would be alright if[,] by holding on closely to the rocks, the turtle would take care not to fall. If he fell[,] the bad animals [wolves] would eat him from the broken shell.[2] So he went to play with [the] chachalote.

Chachalote told Turtle to take hold of his tail and not to let loose while they climbed the rock, which was very big. As [the] chachalote jumped very far at a bound, Turtle almost lost his hold. Chachalote said to Turtle, "Be careful, I thought you were going to lose your hold. You have to hold me well."

Thus he jumped again[,] and Turtle almost lost his hold. The third time he did lose [his] hold and fell down the high cliff directly in front of the wolves. Though he was crying, the wolves ate him all except his shell. Chachalote then said, "I will have to continue alone."

In these first times the world was situated around the large river[,] HatoSáme [HatoSámi]. Here lived all the animals that there were in the world. After five days, the world was getting dry. In five more days there was no water in the river. The people had nowhere to go to get water. The wolves and other animals died from thirst.

Kumúkame said, "Let us go to a spring which [that] never has dried up."[3]

So she sent her men for water[,] but the spring was dry and the earth parched into cracks. They dug into the ground but did not find water. They came back and reported [that there was] no[ ]water. They were sent to another spring, which was also dry. They went in another direction to look for water; but they found the water-holes all [were] dry. [B]y now even the (god)people were dying of thirst.

The Sun-[F]ather told them that he knew where there was a little water in the "middle world region." But it was drying up very fast. So they hurried there. Here they found a large cliff. In it lived Buzzard and his wife[,][4] the dead woman who had come from the sky-world.

The people asked them to lower some water from their cliff. The woman let down a large bowl of water.[5] But unfortunately it spilled so there was none to quench the thirst of the (god)people.

So the people began to wonder why it was that the water was all drying up, which had never happened to them before. The Sun-[F]ather and Kumúkame decided to try and dream[6] why it was that the world was drying up. The water-gods had hidden water so that the people would not die. But since the wolves had eaten her child, Turtle,[7] she had ordered her water to disappear.

The rock from which Turtle has [had] fallen[,] kawí téwali [tévali,] asked what had happened that Turtle had died. He also asked where the remains were. Chachalote told him how Turtle had fallen to his death and had been eaten by the wolves. It was the wolves' fault that the world was drying up.

Kumúkame asked Nakawé what the people could do [so] that there would be water. She said for them to get a singing-shaman to sing five nights so that she could hear and talk to him.[8] The people found a boy, Kauymáli[,] who could sing. He sang all night until dawn. In his singing it was revealed to him what was wrong and what to do about it.[9]

The people would have to get hooves of cattle,[10] votive[-]bowls, and green earth.[11] This last was the mother of Turtle[,] as had been commanded by Nakawé. A small bowl was filled with beads, a cow's hoof[,][12] and a small arrow. These were made to offer to the goddess of earth (including green-earth), Taté Iolianáka,[13] who was the mother of the turtle.

When this was done[,] Kauymáli sang [to] god another night. He dreamed that these offerings should be taken to the earth-mother of Turtle.[14] Also the people must find the broken shell of Turtle and offer a bit of it to the earth-mother.

So the people went to look for the shell. They asked the rock[,] kawí [káwi,] which helped them find it. They then gathered up the small pieces of the shell. The pieces they stuck together in their old form, as Nakawé had told them to do. Then they took all colors of yarn[,] which they used for the intestines of the Turtle. Earth-mother was put in as the head[,] and she came out as water.[15]

Thus they did everything that Nakawé had commanded because the people were dying with [of] thirst. Kauymáli sang again[,] asking where to put these offerings.

By this time, the only green thing in the world was a *"sausa"* (Mex.-Sp.)[16] tree. It was revealed that there the offerings of reconstructed Turtle were to be taken. They were offered in a hole dug at the roots of this tree.[17] When this was done, the singer sang again in a low voice. There he sang while the others listened. When he finished[,] he told the people what Nakawé had told him while he was singing. She had told him to dig there. This was done[,] and the earth was damp.

The next time it was wet. The third time it was more so. The fourth time water began to come out. The fifth time that he sang all night a stream of water gushed from the hole[,] which filled up the creeks of the world.[18] Turtle came to life and went to the sea, but the gushing spring of water remained.

Then the people had to set up altars on which were placed candles, and other paraphernalia. The people had to pray before they could drink the water, which was "delicate."[19] If they drank the water, they would die. However, the birds could drink, as could the animals.

But the people had to get a singing-shaman and pray. Then they had to toss water to the four points to bless it.[20] For sprinkling the water the flowers of *teauláh*[,] H. *(cardoniga)*[,] must be used (as a hyssop). The people also must be sprinkled.[21] When this was done[,] five votive[-]bowls of water could be placed before the singer. Then the people could (finally) drink. But the singer could not drink the water, because he must make a stricter penitence. Five days later he could drink[,] after the water had reached the sea. In the meantime he could only refreshen himself by anointing himself with the water at his feet.

One of the creeks from the gushing spring became a river and was filled with fish. One man took his wife to places where there were deep pools filled with fish. Its edges were grown with water rushes. Among the reeds they left their clothes while they hunted a water-hole full of fish. They made a torch of cat-tails, and thus got a net full of fish.

After midnight they were tired and said, "Let us lie down and rest awhile." The next day they were going to clean and dry their fish.

The next day they ate some of the previous day's catch. And that night when they lighted their candles, they noticed that there were many water-serpents in the water. But they caught many fish anyway. The next night they also fished and caught very many. Indeed they filled their baskets. There were more snakes in the water also this night.

The next night they found an animal that they did not know. This was a very bad animal which [that] was frightening away the fish. It was *hakúwi* (*"tigre del agua"* [water jaguar], the *axolotl?*).[22] Still they caught many fish.

So they said, "Now we are tired, let us go to sleep."

The next day there were many of these "tigre del agua."[23] And while they slept[,] the woman disappeared, and her husband could find nothing of her. He thought that she was answering a call of nature[,] so he went back to sleep. He dreamed[24] that his wife had been eaten up and was gone.

He waked up and called her, but he only heard a noise among the cat-tails along the river bank. Lighting a torch of these[,] he found the tracks of the animals which [that] had carried his wife away. As he went on, he heard the animals crunching her bones as they ate her. He took up his weapons[,] as he was terribly frightened. He climbed a rock while the "tigre del agua" collected below him and tried to jump up to where he was sitting. At dawn there was nothing but the tracks, so he went to his house and told the people.

Nakawé revealed to Kumúkame the [that] this had happened to the woman because the water, which belonged to Nakawé was still "tender" and could not be fished.[25] Nakawé ordered them to make torches in order to find any remains of the woman which [that] might be left. She told them not to be afraid of the animals because they were gone.

In the midst of the reeds they found a piece of the woman's foot, a bit of her finger, the top of her scalp with its hair, as well as the external genitalia. Not even bones or anything else remained.

Nakawé ordered that the remains be burned. So they built a fire of reeds and collected the parts. These were carried to the fire. To prevent all the reeds from burning,[26] they saved one tender shoot and saved it before burning the remains of the woman. This was used for sprinkling the water so that it would become "solid"[27] enough for the people to fish in. The people were also sprinkled.

The remains of the woman were changed into stone as they burned. Her head form[ed] rocks which [that] have a head-like form. They are still known to the Huichols, who call them *aitapáli*. From the finger came a green root called *maSakuili[,]* and from the foot the cactus[,] *tamukuli*. The genitalia remained painted on the rock.[28]

 The Corn Myth

1. [Sub-story:] The Creation of a Race through the Corn-People

A woman who lived at the edge of the sea was very rich and had ten houses. Nearby was another woman who was a widow and very poor. She did not have even corn, and she was hungry. She saw a little boy approach. He came up and embraced her, and asked if he might share the shade in which she was sitting. The boy, too, was hungry, but the poor widow could not give him any food.

In these times of the ancients the ants were people. The poor widow heard the ant-people grinding corn and making tortillas. She reflected, "Where do they get corn? I will go and ask them."

She gave the little boy a branch to play with. Then, since she had decided to trouble the ant-people by asking them for corn, she went to them and asked for food. She told the ant-people that she had nothing. She said, "Yesterday I found a little boy also in need of food. I cannot give him any, however, because I have none. Give me at least a handful of corn to make parched corn. Who has some corn for me?"

The ant-people replied, "We, too, are having a hard time getting corn. So we can give you only a gourdful for you and the little boy."

The widow thanked them, and asked, "What is your corn worth so that I can repay you sometime?"

The ant-people answered, "We buy it with oak[-]ash, and you need only a handful. This we trade for corn. Or, if you do not have any oak-ash, take a handful of grass. If you cannot take grass, take pitch-pine, or else a glowing branch of wood. Any of these we trade for corn."[1]

The poor widow arranged a bundle of grass on her back. Then she told the little boy to remain in the shade with the parched corn she had made for him. It was indeed very little. But it would last while she went with the ant-people to trade for corn. The pretty little boy was not the poor woman's son, but he obeyed her command. He remained in the shade while she was gone.

One hundred and twenty-five ant-people started out with bags, baskets, and the like to trade for corn. They did not carry grass. This they would get the next day. They were happy on their departure. When the dawn came, they lighted a fire and gave food to Grandfather Fire.

While the widow was asleep, the spirits of the ant-people got up and went away. Their bodies remained while their spirits sought corn. The spirits of the ant-people did not get back until the rooster was crowing.[2] They cut all the hair from the head of the widow, and tore up her clothes.

When the widow awoke, she found only the pile of her hair. The ant-people got in their bodies, and told the widow to go to sleep again. Then the ant-people went off to their homes, leaving the widow asleep and stripped even of her hair.

The widow awoke alone, and without corn. When the sun came up, she saw a high cliff. There she went with her bundle of grass, and sat down and wept because the others had deserted her.

The owner of the corn was far off at the side of the sea. His name was Komatéame. His wife was Otuanáka.[3] When the widow started to cry, the corn-owner and his wife heard her, even that far away. Komatéame said, "There is some woman crying alone in the mountains. What can be the trouble? She is very sad."

His wife looked and said, "Where could she come from?"

Komatéame said, "Let us go and ask her to come here." He had a dove which [that] lived in a zapote-tree near his house. So he tied a little red thread on the dove's foot, in order that the widow would know it had a master. Then he ordered the dove to go and bring the woman. He wished to know who had been stealing his corn.

Now the ant-people did not trade grass, lime, pitch-pine, or glowing branches for corn. They stole corn from the corn-owner, Komatéame. Komatéame, however, used these things to combat the ants (as the Huichols still do).[4] The ant-people merely said that they traded these things for corn. That is why they brought these things, which the corn-owner used to combat the ants.

When the widow saw the dove, she said, "Dove, since you wear a thread on your leg, you must have a master. It is too bad that you cannot talk. You could then tell me where your master lives."

The dove then spoke, "I come," he said, pointing, "from that way to tell you that my masters have seen you. They sent me to learn all about you, and to see what kind of person you are. We have houses where we are. You must join us."

The widow replied, "I am glad to go where there is corn, even though it must be with danger and difficulty." She was quite happy, thinking of corn and of her return to the little boy.

The dove then told her, "Get behind me. I will point the direction of the houses so that you can see where my master lives."

The widow did as she was requested. She saw not only five houses but five store-houses as well, each filled with corn. This made her very happy. She hoped to arrive soon, using as a guide the zapote-tree where the dove lived.

The widow had only to go fifty steps to where the corn-owner had placed dogs, and people with machetes to guard his corn. The corn-owner was quite angry because his corn was being stolen at night.

The dove said to the widow, "At night you must speak kindly to the dogs. In the daytime, however, you will be safe. I will fly ahead to guide you." The dove flew on ahead. Since it was dressed in white, it was easy to follow. On arriving, the dove told its master all that had happened.

When the widow saw the dove arrive, she took up her bundle and followed. The dogs ran up to bite her, but Komatéame sounded with his sandals, and the dogs were calmed.[5] This occurred five times, for the dogs were still angry. But the widow still came on, and the dogs did not hurt her. Finally she arrived at the edge of the patio of the *ranchería* of the corn-owner. Komatéame was seated in his chair, with an altar already prepared.

The corn-people[6] of Komatéame were boys and girls, all pretty and well-dressed. As the widow approached, they closed the corn-houses after the corn-people had gone in.

The widow spoke to Komatéame, saying, "I am very hungry. Hurry, and give me food and water."

Now the wife of Komatéame knew the thoughts of the widow, and knew, consequently, that the widow's heart was good.[7] So from the altar she took tiny *jicaras [jícaras]* (bowls), tortillas, and pots of water. These she brought from the altar *(itáli)*.

The widow ate of the god things. But she thought, "These little god things will not satisfy me at all. But let us see."

The wife then said, "Eat and drink."

So the widow ate and drank. The tiny plates and pots, however, did not become empty.[8] Similarly was the food replenished. Thus the widow was completely satisfied. When she had finished eating, she was told to take some food to her little boy. She thanked them, saying, "May the gods pay you."[9]

The wife, who knew the widow's thoughts, then said, "You thought that the tiny god bowls and plates would not hold enough to satisfy you. If you are still hungry and thirsty, continue eating."

The widow replied, "I myself am well filled. But I will take some for my little boy." Then, addressing the corn-owner, "The ant-people brought me here to trade this grass for corn. But by morning they deserted me. I was very sad until the dove came to invite me here. I came only to trade, and for nothing else. How much corn is it that you trade for grass, lye, pitch-pine, or glowing branches?"

The corn-owner answered, "But I have very little corn. I am poor and have many corn-children to rear. The ant-people are liars and thieves. They come here, and burrow into the ground to avoid my dogs and guard. Thus they get into my store-houses. My wife burns them with grass, lye, and glowing branches.[10] That is why they told you that I trade corn for such things. But it is not true. If your companions are thieves, tell me."

The widow replied, "No, they are not my people. I was born of others. I came out of the earth alone. I was with the ant-people, it is true. But they are not of me."

Komatéame looked at her hand and saw that the widow was telling the truth. Furthermore, had she been of the ant-people the dogs would undoubtedly have killed her. He said, "I am very sorry that I cannot trade you corn for grass. Carry it back where you got it. You may, however, take this magic tortilla. It will feed your boy for five days. At the end of that time come back, and I will talk to my people and see if I can give you some corn."

Now the widow was very much concerned about the little boy. So she hurried back. Passing the place where she had gathered the grass[,] she tossed it down, saying, "I bring back the grass to where it grew."

When the widow arrived back where she had left the boy, she found that he had but a little of the parched corn left. She gave him the magic tortilla, and he was very happy.

She left part of the magic tortilla with the boy. Then she returned to the house of the corn-owner, hoping to get some corn, which she needed very much. She had no difficulty in getting back. She knew the way, and she had with her a bit of the magic god-tortilla. When she arrived, she asked for another tortilla.

Komatéame said, "I have talked with certain of my people. As yet, however, I cannot arrange to sell any corn. Take this tortilla, and come back within five days."

This time the widow had returned without any difficulty. The dogs knew her by now, and did not attempt to harm her. She did as she was bid. On her return she approached Komatéame and asked, "Have you arranged yet to sell me three or four measures of corn?" The corn-owner replied, "I have not yet had time to talk to all of my family. Take this tortilla, and come back in five days."

So the widow went back again to the boy. She gave him food, on which he became well and healthy. In five more days she returned again to the corn-owner. "Have you finished the arrangements?" she asked. "Tell me if you can sell me corn."

"I still have the last of my family to talk to," the corn-owner answered. "But don't worry. Come back in five days, and by that time we will know."

So the widow departed again, taking another tortilla to her boy. Leaving the boy to live five days on this, she returned for the fifth time to the corn-owner. She thought to herself, "My, but I am having a difficult time getting this corn!"

Komatéame this time said to her, "I have now talked to all of my family. We can sell you some corn. But you must wait for twenty-five days more, while you build a house to protect the corn. Put a *teapalí*[11] in the gable in the front and back. Then make an altar *(newatále [neatáli])*, well arranged to receive the corn, together with plenty of ceremonial paraphernalia."[12]

Now the boy could hear them talking, even though he was far away. In the meantime he had grown large enough so that he could build the required house. When the widow finally got back, he had built a fine, big god-house in five days. The widow said to him, "You have built the house, just as they requested. How is that?"

The boy answered, "I could hear you talking. I bought candles and other ceremonial paraphernalia. The house should be finished in three more days. Then we will set up tiny god's bowls, candles, chocolates, and the like, which I have also bought."

On the fifth day the boy went with the widow to the corn-owner's. The boy was to take care of the corn.

Komatéame, the corn-owner, was dressed in the full festal array of the Huichols. His face made the poor widow drunk.[13] The corn-owner said to her, "It is all arranged. We can now give you corn."

They opened the corn-houses, and called to the corn-people inside, "Who wishes to go with this widow?"

From the first house the reply came back, "We are well here, and do not wish to go. We do not know how we shall be treated there."

This happened in four of the five corn-houses.

Coming to the fifth corn-house[,] Komatéame called, "I have talked to all of your family—your father, your mother, your cousins; and they said that you should go. So I command one of you to go."

The widow, however, said, "No. I don't want to take your people. I don't want a pretty little girl. She may be very well dressed, but she probably doesn't know how to grind corn."

The corn-girl on her part cried, "No, papa, you had better let me remain here." Weeping, she put her face in her large embroidered kerchief, like that [which] Huichol women wear.

But the corn-owner was inflexible. "Yes," he said, "I command you. Go, taking a candle and a votive-bowl. It is for the best. Go to where the widow lives, and if she does not abuse you, stay with her. She will maintain you as I have done. You will find a boy there who needs you."

The corn-girl then replied, "Since you command me, I will go. But if they abuse me, or if they reprimand me, I will come back in two or three days."

The brother of the corn-girl then cried, "Since I have lived here with my sister, I, too, will go."

But the corn-owner remonstrated. "No, you may not go. You can go at night, however, if you wish. But you must start at midnight, and be back here at dawn."

"Very well," answered the brother of the corn-girl. "I will go there at night and be back at dawn, after seeing how things are going."

The corn-owner now said to the widow, "I already know your heart. You came here for corn. You do not want a girl. But take her for five days, and let us see. Feed her and the boy who is going with you tonight. Since you have no corn, light your candles, arrange your altars, and pray. Then the next day you will find corn and other food. Since I know your heart, let us see how it results."

So the widow took the corn-girl to her home. There the widow's boy was waiting for them. He embraced the corn-girl, saying to himself, "Tonight I will try this girl." Then he painted his penis and his testes with several colors, for the girl was very pretty.[14]

Having met the corn-girl at the door and embraced her, the boy led her to the altar. He gave her food and water. The girl was pleased with the boy's attentions. She decided that she was better off here than at home with her brothers.

When the sun had set, even though there was no corn, the boy and the corn-girl slept with each other in the house. The widow slept by herself in the kitchen. This they had to do for five nights. And they had to treat the corn-girl well to see if she would stay with them forever, provided she liked it.

The first night there was the sound of falling corn. The widow heard this. The boy and the corn-girl, however, kept on talking. At dawn the sound ceased. The widow came out of the kitchen at dawn to light a candle at the altar of the god-house. She found the floor covered with corn. (This was due to a visit of the corn-girl's brother.) They all took some for food.

The second night the walls were piled half-way up with corn.

The third night the corn was higher.

The fourth night the god-house was almost full.

The fifth night the god-house was full to the top.

The widow in astonishment said, "This girl has brought us much corn. How does she do it?"

At the end of the fifth day the girl said to the boy, "This is what the widow wanted. Now I wish that you would work for five days and make a clearing so that we can plant some of this corn. Here, I have a machete, a hoe, and an axe for the work. Be strong for the work of clearing the field in five days. I myself cannot move or work.[15] The widow will have to cook. But even so, I will take care of you, so that you will be strong and not get sick."

To get helpers for the work the boy took people from his hands, feet, and back.[16] Machetes for them were procured in the same manner. They worked and made five clearings. Then they returned, and gave their tools back to the boy, who put them into his back again. Then the boy put the helpers back in his hands and feet, after they had ceremoniously partaken of the god-food and water.

That night the boy and the girl talked again to each other. "We love each other very much," the girl said. "We are getting used to each other. You continue working, and I will take care of you."

The second day the same thing happened. The helpers were brought forth from the boy's hands and feet. They worked all day, resting only at noon. Then the helpers again partook of the god-food, and again went back into the hands and feet of the boy.

The third day it was the same.

The fourth day dawned. Now the mother of the corn-girl knew what was going on, even though she was far away. It seemed to her that if the work was continued[,] all the animals would be robbed of shelter and would die. "I had better go and tell them to stop work, lest they kill all the vegetation," she said.

That night she came to the corn-girl. She told the girl to bid the boy not to work any more, so that he would not kill all the plants.

The widow asked the corn-girl, "Why did your mother come?"

The widow also had seen the boy's helpers working. She was angry thinking that she would have to work very hard preparing food for so many. She told the girl that she was lazy, and accused her of not helping to prepare food. "Why don't you help me," she cried. "You are lazy and worthless."

The girl was saddened by these words. So, although she was very ["]delicate,["] she took some corn and put it to cook. When she started to grind the corn, her hands became bloody and began to melt. The water of the pot was pure blood. This was because the corn-girl was [made] of corn.[17] The corn-paste (*masa[,]* Sp.), furthermore, was pure blood from the blood of her hands. She tried to work, holding the *mano* [grinding stone] in her kerchief.

When the boy returned, the girl told him what had happened. He was very angry. He blamed the widow, because the corn-owner had forbade them to put the girl to work. He gave the girl water, so that she might wash her injured hands.

The following morning, when the rooster crowed, the corn-girl told the boy that she was not happy and that she would have to leave. "I am going," she said, "since I am the corn-girl. Take my corn, even though I have to leave you in your house."

The boy had to give permission. The last thing the corn-girl told him was not to work any more but to watch his fields.

When the rooster crowed, the corn-girl left. She met her mother, who asked her why she was so bloody. The girl told her. The mother embraced her daughter. Then she put her to bed, and cured her of the injuries done to her hands.

At dawn the widow entered the corn-house. The boy was there alone. The widow knew that she had done wrong, and felt guilty. So, while the boy watched his fields, she followed the girl to try to get her to return.

The corn-owner said, "I told you not to make this girl work. You should have maintained her as I ordered you to."

The widow admitted this. "I know that it was my fault," she said. "I should not have put her to work. But please let her go with me again."

But the corn-owner refused. "No," he answered. "I love my children and take care of them. I do not want them abused. The girl is afraid of you. Your word is not worth anything. Now you can go without corn until you get a crop from the fields cleared by your boy."

The boy was still watching his fields when the widow returned. She promised to help feed him. But the boy was very angry for her fault in hurting his wife. He ordered her away to the place where she had come from on "that side" of the sea. He would prepare his own food. Then he hit her five times, knocking her down.

The widow went far away, jumping across the sea in five jumps. Here she remained, looking back toward her old home.

The corn-girl knew of this. She went to the boy at night, although she was still not cured completely of her injuries. But she could stay no longer than the first cry of the rooster. She said to the boy, "My father and mother do not wish me to come here. But I have brought you food. Papa says that after you have burned your clearings, I can help you plant your corn. I will give you five yellow ears, five black, five brown, five blue, and five red. I will also give you helpers, because you treated me well.

The seed was blessed in a ceremony by the girl and her mother at dawn. All the animal-people of the world had gathered to help the boy. There were crows (*kwatsa*), whose children were chief among the animals; the rat, *naika*; a large parrot, *iúwali*; a badger, *haitsu*; a solitary badger, *[s]uálu*; another rat, *hotsá*; a pack-rat, *maimáli*; a fox, *káoSai*; and another fox [skunk], *úpa tewíati*. All these came to help the boy at the orders of the corn-mother, Otuanáka, who promised to give them food while they worked.[18]

The workers found much corn already in the field. Planting sticks were prepared, and all went to work. By sunset, after working one day only, they had finished the great clearing. Then they followed the boy. The animal-people, however, gathered wood, and thus remained behind.

Now the boy made the grave mistake of going on ahead of the other workers. When he arrived at the house, the corn-mother asked, "Where are my family?" The boy was certain they would soon come. When they did not come, he returned. He found that the workers had all turned into animals and had dug up the field to get the corn-seed.

The corn-mother had dreamed this, and feared that this was what they had done. She went to see, in order not to shame the boy. At dawn she arrived. She saw that the ground was all dug up. She was very angry with the shameless ones, since she had not ordered this. She went to the middle of the field to find out if any of them would recognize her. Then she spoke to the sky-eagle. "Welíka [W]imali, do me the favor, please, to change me into a stick." The sky-eagle complied, and the colored snake, *wiáSu* (*malacoa[,]* Sp.), lent his color to the stick.[19]

When the sun arose, all the animals came out talking. Digging in the ground, they advanced gradually toward the center of the field. They arrived at the pole, but they did not know what it was. Then the corn-mother said, "I did not give you permission to do this bad thing. I intend to punish you for it." The animals, much frightened, scattered to all parts.

The corn-mother continued. "You were once people, but now I care for you no longer. So I will leave you in the form of animals." She then left the pole[20] in the center of the field to frighten them.

Then the eagle of the heavens was asked to take care of the fields and punish the animals. If rats or other animals disregarded the scare-crow, five hawks were commanded to punish them.[21]

No animals came out for five days. When they finally did, five hawks pounced down on them. They decided then to come out only at night. But the corn-mother ordered the fire to burn in the center of the field at night.[22]

In the field only the little parcels of seeded land not touched by the animals were left. In five days the corn was above the ground. The corn-mother went every day to see how the corn was growing. In five more days it was much greater. In another five days the corn was blossoming. The corn-mother decided to remain. She tied the flowers with fine hairs. Five days later the ears were forming.

The corn-mother now told the boy to bring several candles, some chocolate, some bread, and all the paraphernalia. The boy was pleased because the ears of corn were forming. The corn-mother told him that this was because the corn-girl was helping him. She said, "Your wife orders you to make new candles as well as votive-bowls. Then you must prepare the soil so that the pollen can fall. Also put up a deer-trap. The [sacred] paraphernalia has been bathed in water. Now everything needs to be bathed in blood to bless the fields."

So the boy put up his deer-nets, and killed both a male deer and a female deer. These were skinned. Then he bathed all the [sacred] paraphernalia and the *teapáli* in the fields with the blood. The blood ceremony was thus made.

In five days the roasting ears were cut. Five of them were tied with hair. These were anointed with deer blood and taken to the god-house of the corn-girl. He had worked very hard to grow the corn. Now he brought the corn-girl these ears to fulfill the orders of the corn-mother. For this reason also were the ears cut, because the new corn was "delicate." If the boy had not carried out the corn-mother's orders, but had eaten an ear without observing [performing] the first fruits ceremony, he would have died.[23]

The boy was now commanded to pray to the great gods — Tatotsí, Komatéame, MaSá KwáSi, and Tatevalí.

Tatevalí had told the boy how to kill the deer. Now he said, "You did not set up my votive-bowls and my arrows as payment to me."

Tsakaímuka demanded representation.

Nakawé asked also for arrows and votive-bowls. "I made the world, and I must have my part," she said.

Tatevalí said, "Before you harvest your corn, you must pray all day to us. Tomorrow put up a deer-trap to catch a deer so that you may bathe our votive-bowls in blood."

So the boy killed two more deer, a male and a female. For this he went five days without salt. Otherwise he would not have been able to kill any deer. Thus fasting, he killed ten deer. Then he took the skin of a dead deer, and dressed like a live deer.[24] After this[,] he bathed the votive-bowls and the ceremonial paraphernalia of all the gods, saying, "Now, gods, you eat the blood."

Finally, finishing in five days, they could cut the green corn. They took the most beautiful flowers of the fields. These were used to sprinkle the patio and the god-house with sacred water.

Then Tatevalí, the [Grandfather] Fire, ordered, "Cut five ears of corn, tie them together, and decorate them beautifully. Place them on the altar with a candle."

All this was done. In the field a keeper was placed at each of the four corners, with a fifth keeper in the middle. They searched for the best ears. When they arrived with these, the corn-girl met them at the door and bathed the ears with blood.

Tatevalí came to the patio in the evening to sing all night. He was to be paid by the blood placed on his jicaras [jícaras, gourd-bowls]. He said, "By singing, I will thus take away all the sickness, ill luck, and bad luck from the new corn."[25] Thus Tatevalí purified the new corn by washing the ears in sacred water, using his shaman's plumes.[26]

All the chief gods were pleased. The family entered the god-house, took the five new ears, and danced with them around the patio. While Tatevalí sang in the patio, all these beautiful ears were offered to the mother of each of the four points. This was to be the custom for all time, according to the command of Tatevalí.

When the sacred ears were offered to the goddess of the sky above, bowls of water were brought and placed on the fire. When these were burned, five deer hairs were taken by Tatevalí as a charm for the deer-lassos. The hairs were then stuck on a votive-bowl until they were to be used.

Then food was distributed, and the soup of the deer given out. The corn could now be harvested. Tatevalí then spoke to the boy, saying, "The old woman who took care of you will never have any more children. She is to take care of the animals who live on 'that side' of the sea. I am going to name her Ocianaka. Her children will be only animals."

Thus they began the harvest.

Now, since they had corn, the corn-girl wished five children by the boy. They continued to work hard.

The corn was allowed to ripen. The great gods then told them to make [complete] the harvest in five days.

The ear that was held by the five hairs ripened first. As the harvest advanced, the corn was brought to the corn-girl. Friends came to help with the harvest. They were given a share of the corn. But even the remainder still filled the corn-house.

Meanwhile they lived on roasting-ears and deer-soup. After they finished the harvest, they could eat tortillas. The girl, furthermore, could grind corn. This was commanded by her parents, since her husband now had corn of his own. Thus she passed out of her "delicate" condition.[27]

Thus the corn-girl watched over the corn and her husband, while he continued every year to work in the field. Their elders counselled them not to be unfaithful to each other.

When the rooster crowed, the girl finished sweeping the patio. This was done three times, but nothing happened. The fourth time, however, the Sun said, "I will leave flowers. These must be offered to her." So the Sun left flowers on the patio.

The fifth time, at midnight, as the girl was sweeping the patio, she found the flowers left by the Sun. She thought, "Who dropped these beautiful flowers in my patio? I will save them to show my mother. She will explain them." So she hid the flowers in her skirt.[28]

The Sun said, "She needs children to help her work."

At dawn the corn-girl went to her mother. When she looked for the flowers in her skirt, she could not find them.

The corn-girl continued to work for five days. In another five days she felt herself getting heavy. She noted this, but did not tell her husband. In another five days she discovered that she was pregnant. This was from the flowers of the Sun, as she dreamed that night.[29] Her mother asked her why she had not told her sooner. The girl said, "It must be from the flowers that I hunted for and could not find."

Five days later the girl was ready to bear [give birth]. But the Sun would not allow the child to come out. The corn-girl was in labor for five days. People came from the sea, but no one knew how to deliver the child.

There was, however, a child-shaman, Kauymáli, who tried to help. He thought that he could deliver the child, because he had no sin.[30]

Thus the child was born.[31] The girl did not know what had happened. The Sun then told her that her pregnancy was caused by the flowers she had found. Thus the corn-girl got over her sickness, cured by an innocent child, when ten adults had failed.

After five days more[,] the corn-girl washed, according to the child[-]birth ceremony of the Huichols. Arrows and jicaras [jícaras] were made for the great gods and placed on the altar.[32] The men went for deer to help the new mother.

As the Sun went down, the child-shaman, Kauymáli, who understood all these things, arranged for the bathing of mother and child [modeled] after the Huichol baptism ceremony. Kauymáli called the new mother to him. Then he said to the Sun, "I need strength for curing the mother and child who are still 'delicate.' I am but little good [only partially effective] in these ceremonies."

The Sun replied, "Do not eat tortillas during the ceremony. Then you will be good enough."

The child-shaman answered, "I will do as you say."

In the ceremony they gave tortillas, fish, and deer-meat to Tatevalí. But the child-shaman ate nothing himself, until he had first dreamed permission from the gods,[33] for otherwise the tortillas might have hurt him. Then he turned over the votive-bowls and other ceremonial paraphernalia.

In the next five days the corn-girl's child became sick. Kauymáli said, "How can we cure it?" He tried five times, and then spoke to the Sun. "I don't wish this baby to be sick," he said. "Help me to cure this baby by telling me how to cure it."

The Sun said, "Go to the lizard, *atákwe*. Get him to cure the child."

They walked with the child for five days toward the sea to see the Lizard. Arriving there with his food[,] Lizard asked, "Why have you come?" He knew well enough, however.

Lizard then asked, "Who are your father and mother? What do you want here?"

Kauymáli replied, "Here we have a sick child. Sun told me to come here and ask you to help us."

Now Lizard had five children, each of whom knew how to cure very well. He called one of them, saying, "If the first does not succeed, the others will try to cure the baby."

The first son of Lizard sucked, made cigarettes, and smoked [prayed over] the sick baby all night.[34] He said, "Dawn will tell whether I have succeeded." At dawn the baby was slightly better.

This was done for five days. But the baby did not get well, so the first son of Lizard knew that he had failed to cure.

Another son of Lizard came to try his skill on the sick baby. But he failed also.

The parents of the baby were very sad. They offered all their property for the cure of their child, thinking that they were not paying enough. The father brought five embroidered kerchiefs, five blankets, five *costales*, or pouches, and the like. Then he went to the Lizard, asking him to send the third son, since the others had failed.

The third son arrived. He cleaned the sick baby with his plumes. Then he went to sleep to dream what was hurting the child. He slept until midnight, and his dreaming was disturbed by snakes, birds, and so forth, which almost ate him. The next morning the baby was so weak that the third son could not cure it. He said, "My father ordered me here. But I am worthless. I have no force [power] to do anything. Ask the fourth son of my father. He knows more about this than I do."

The fourth son went to try to cure the baby. The father and the mother had eaten nothing for ten days, because of their grief. So they asked this curer to try. He agreed, although he doubted that he could do anything, since the others had failed.

So the fourth son of the Lizard smoked tobacco and prepared. The Sun and the Fire looked on. These gods knew what was the matter, but they were testing the sons of the Lizard. The fourth son failed to cure the sick baby.

On the fifth night, *atakakai* [atákwe], the Lizard himself, came to try to cure the baby. He slept, in order to dream. Five snakes came to him—the rattle-snake, the green-snake, the coral-snake, and two others. They even passed over him. This frightened him, and he ran away.

Dawn came sadly. The father and the mother now decided to go to the corn-father and the corn-mother, since all had failed to cure the child. When they arrived at the house of the baby's grandparents, the grandmother took the poor, thin, little thing.

Now the best curer was the child-shaman, Kauymáli. He knew all the time how to cure the child. He knew how to sing, dance, and perform cures.[35] The father and mother of the sick baby said to Kauymáli, "We have spent all our money and property on the Lizard curers. We have nothing to pay you. We are ashamed of ourselves, and afraid to ask you to cure our child, since we are so poor."[36]

The sick baby cried all night.

With the dawn, the father finally went to talk to Kauymáli. When he arrived, he said to Kauymáli, "I read in my heart that you know how to cure, even though you are not my child. I come, sad and ashamed, because my child is sick and I have no money. My parents-in-law sent me to you, since you are the greatest shaman-curer in the world."

Kauymáli replied, "You need not be ashamed. You can talk, and I can talk. It is good that we can speak our thoughts."

The father then said, "Even though it may not please you, I will talk frankly."

So they talked for five hours. The father admitted that his request might be futile, since he had no money. As the talk continued, the father began to cry. He wiped the tears from his eyes with his kerchief and said, "I am weeping for my sick child."

Kauymáli said, "I am indeed sorry. But don't let your tears fall on the ground or your child will die."[37] The father became silent. Kauymáli continued. "Do not be afraid. I will do all I can. Has no one told you what is the matter with your child?"

The father replied, "No. No one has told me."

"Well," Kauymáli said, "the others who tried to cure the child are all crazy. They should not attempt to cure, since they don't know their business. Do you know who is the father of the child?"

"I don't know," answered the man. "My wife told me nothing. I thought that it was I, since I slept with her."

Now the Sun was listening. He said, "Good! I must know all, whether it was you or another who fathered the child. Tell me, how did you plant your corn?"

The father told the Sun the whole story of the corn-crop.

"Right now," the Sun said, "I cannot go to see the child. But it will not die, because someone is holding it.[38] Who cured your wife when she was delivered?"

The father told the Sun that it was Kauymáli, who, indeed, had got thin and sickly-looking during the sickness of the child.[39]

The father then went home. He told his wife, the corn-girl, that the Sun could not come since he was busy. But, the father continued, the Sun still knew what was wrong with the child, since he had said that someone was holding it, and that it would not die. Thus they felt that the matter had been taken out of their hands.

The father then said, "Our *tata* (father) Sun will take care of the baby. I am very tired from so much walking. I am going to rest."

The child was dry and feverish and could not suckle. So they dropped milk in his mouth. The father thought of paying the Sun or the shaman with corn, so he went again to talk to the Sun. He was very sad.

Kauymáli, the child-shaman, asked, "Why are you so sad? I know in your thoughts that you are sad."

The father replied, "Our tata Sun sent me again to ask you to cure my sick child."

"Why did you go everywhere else first?" questioned Kauymáli.

The father answered, "No one has cured the child, although you are the sixth to try. The Sun sent me to you. I come at his command."

Kauymáli laughed and said, "Rest, and be quiet. I am going to talk to my companions.["]

Kauymáli ate a little, and then sat there, thinking how he could cure with his tobacco-gourds, his plumes, and his full festal array.[40] "Our tata is looking at me," he said to himself. "I will go alone, and leave all this finery behind." He believed that all the gods would be angry with him if the child died.

When he arrived at the side of the child, he saw how thin and feverish the child was. He quieted the mother. Then he began the work of curing. First he sat down and talked to the mother, trying to discover what was wrong with the child. He told her that he was sent by *tata dios* (the Sun).[41]

The mother informed Kauymáli that they were very poor, owing to the expenses incurred by the sick child.[42]

Kauymáli sat quietly and smoked, looking at the child. Then he commanded the mother to place an altar where she had found the flowers because the Sun would surely know. He ordered the father and the mother to stay at the altar with the child, facing the Sun, our tata.

The child, very ill, indeed almost dying, was brought out. Kauymáli listened to its joints.[43] He took out an arrow and sucked a grain of corn from the child's stomach, saying, "Did no one else do that?" He showed the grain of corn to the father and mother, and said, "This is what was hurting the child."

Then, from the child's foot he sucked out a live stone. This he also showed to the parents. He listened, and then from the top of the child's head sucked out bloody foam. From the breast he sucked a cactus spine. All these were taken out. Finally he cleaned the child with the light spitting that Huichol shamans use.[44] Then he said to the father, "Tomorrow, if you are not tired, come to my house without fail. The child will not die, unless it dies before midnight."

The parents discussed their going the next day to arrive at sunset. At the first cry of the rooster, they started out, without eating. The child was a little better, and barely able to suckle. It could also move a little. They got there at dawn.

Kauymáli asked, "Did you bring a blanket for an altar? If not, I will lend you one." So an altar was set up.

This time the shaman sucked from the child five tubes full of yellow, black, blue, red, and green blood.[45] He cleaned the child's stomach by spitting and blowing, as Huichol shamans still do. At noon he repeated the cure in order to prevent a new attack.

The Sun at its zenith heard and saw the child.

Kauymáli then took out a pointed bit of stone from the child's breast, as well as water from the child. At night he worked again on the child. He dreamed also what he must do to cure the child.[46] He decided that he would have to go for five days without drinking water or eating salt.[47]

The next night the spirit of *topína* (Humming-bird) arrived, and asked Kauymáli if he had observed the fast. Then topína disappeared, and, going to the Sun, reported[48] that the shaman was working well and had not broken any taboos.

The third day the child was a little better. The fourth night the spirit came again, and then went back to the sea,[49] after asking how the cure was going. Kauymáli awakened very frightened and disturbed. He said to his wives, "By no means eat any salt, lest we die. We are very 'delicate.'"[50] So the women could not eat salt either.

The fifth night the air came again, and talked with the sleeping shaman.[51] It told him that if he obeyed commands, he would win.

At dawn of the fifth day the baby could suckle. Soon it could move. The mother asked for her tiny god-bowls of water.[52] She called for some cotton also. Kauymáli placed the cotton on the water.[53] The cotton did not get wet. By this Kauymáli knew that the child would not die. He ordered all to pray to the great gods of the sea, to see if they could hear them.

The shaman then spoke to the Sun, telling him all that had happened. Then he said to the people, "Make five votive-bowls, each decorated with beads. Candles and chocolate must be bought also. Although I am not good, let us see. If the baby improves for five days more, we must take offertory votive-bowls to the caves of the gods of the four points.[54] This must be done after all the votive-bowls, arrows, bread, chocolate, and the like are prepared.[55]

These were taken to the caves of the gods, so that the child would not die. Then they entered the caves and prayed to the gods. They also offered to the Sun[56] strings of beads, five flowers, and so forth, all in votive-bowls, together with arrows made of many feathers. Then, in the middle of the earth, another offering was made.[57]

For fifteen days the child improved. Then it got worse. The shaman had forgotten to pay one of the gods. The Sun told him what was the matter. In five days all was made ready to clear a field for the forgotten god. This done, they gave salt to the fire. On the altar they placed more salt, which was blessed there all night. The shaman then told the people to pray to the fire, so that the child would get better and so that the parents would not become sick.[58]

On the fifth day the child was worse. The shaman cured it again, and asked which god had now been slighted. The Sun told him that it was Nakawé (Grandmother Growth). Nakawé was angry. Unless they appeased her, the child would die.

So the shaman ordered that they make five votive-bowls, decorated with beads in the form of snakes, with cotton[-]like clouds, and also small masks. These Nakawé wished. They were taken to her cave, from which sacred water was brought with which to save the child. This was done by the father and mother, who left the offerings and told Nakawé what they had done.

When they returned, the child got better. Soon it began to grow, until it became an adult.

Soon he began to desire intercourse with women. There were no women, however, save his sister. The great gods were asked if he might marry his sister, since there was no other woman for him. His need was urgent. The great gods asked, "Does your sister wish to?" But the sister had never menstruated.

The great gods decided to ask Nakawé, who had founded the world. They talked to her, requesting permission for the siblings to marry. Nakawé said, "Do not go before me, as they are watching me. Tell them to wait for five days. Then we shall know what can be done."

But in five days Nakawé was still undecided.

So they made a bed inside of the house. The boy asked what it was for. The shaman told him that Nakawé had said it was all right. When the Sun went down, the woman began to talk. She said that the gods had permitted it.

At dusk the boy was instructed to lie down. When he was asleep, the sister was ordered to go to bed beside him. "But do not do what you wish until the end of five days," they cautioned her. The two young people were ashamed of being brother and sister. But their parents commanded them.

In the morning they awoke together. The girl prepared food and other things, after the fashion of Huichol women. They were getting used to each other.

The second night it was the same.

The third night they were used to sleeping together.

The fourth night it was the same.

The fifth night the boy was ready. He got on top of his sister. But he could not enter her, since she was closed. So they worked awhile. The animal people heard the girl crying from the pain of the man's efforts. When he withdrew, streams of blood came from her. She cried, "Now we are married."[59] The blood fell on the floor.

The wolf-people smelled the blood and came close. They entered the house. The wolf, the [mountain] lion, and the tiger [jaguar]-people ate the blood. Thus these animals are bad, and are killed at any time (and without compunction by the Huichols). Nakawé had commanded them not to do this, lest they have no issue.

After fifteen days the brother and sister had a male child. The shaman, Kauymáli,[60] was asked to deliver the child. This he did. In five days the grandfather named the new child uSraíuli. He grew rapidly. Soon a girl-child was born from the same parents. These two grew up quickly and married. [Great-g]randfather Tatotsí was pleased with the increase of his family. As their [great-]grandfather, he baptized them.

2. [Sub-story:] The Struggle of the Sun and Nakawé (Dry and Wet Season) over Creation

a. Sun Saves One Boy from the Toothed Vaginas

The children of the brother and sister grew up and married. Their children were called *wawiakáme*, and their great-grandfather was Tatotsí. The grand-children of the brother and sister were called Na mutsúci. They married, and their children were called Ne eakai, who in their turn grew up and married. These had children, which were called Ne tułu. They grew up and married, having children called Ne a'aka. These in turn grew up, married, and had children[,] which were called *iteamauci*. By this time the old man had died, and could name no more children.

Among these there was no sickness, and sixty women and seventy men had families. The men always married their own sisters, according to the order of

Nakawé. Thus the people increased rapidly, extending themselves to the four corners of the earth. But because they were [living] so closely together, the women quarrelled.[61] At this time the rancherías of the families were next to one another, and there was very little room.

They asked Nakawé what they should do. Nakawé talked with the Sun. The Sun told Nakawé to order the people to move farther apart, and to live at greater distances from one another. Nakawé agreed that this was a good plan.

For five days the shaman, Kauymáli, listened to the conversation of the people. Their [*sic*] were innumerable children from their issue.

Kauymáli said, "Here I carry orders from the great gods that all is not well with you in living so close together. By fives, therefore[,] you are to take your ceremonial arrows, your *metates*, and your other effects. With these, each group is to go to one of the corners of the world, far away, in order to have room.[62] In the center the ranchería of the oldest parents is to remain, with all their ceremonial paraphernalia."

In five days this was done. The houses of the five families were finished and established in one of the corners of the world. Here they put all their utensils and implements. The first to marry was commanded by Kauymáli to maintain the old mother, who was quite helpless.[63]

Kauymáli said, "I hear all that is said by the gods of the sea and the sky. I am going to listen also to find out what you [must] do for the next five days." So he went to all the rancherías at the four corners of the world. He found the people happy, prosperous, and contented. All were observing the commands of the great gods, and all were in peace. In the center was the oldest brother with his old mother. Kauymáli told her that she would be fed and well-cared [*sic*] for.

The people increased. Kauymáli went to the sea where Nakawé lived, and told her that he had divided the people according to the wishes of the Sun. This Nakawé reported to the other gods of the sea. All were glad that the people were happy, healthy, and prosperous, since the first child had been cured with so much difficulty.

The great gods told Kauymáli that he might stay at the ranchería of the people at the center of the world.

But the brothers and sisters were still intermarrying. Soon the earth was crowded again, since the people increased so rapidly. Nakawé talked to the Sun about the great increase of the people.

The Sun said, "I will do this: in the vaginas of all the female descendants of the first child that was so sick, I will have Kauymáli put teeth." Thus, on the first morning, the women of the center ranchería had teeth in their vaginas.

The second night, this was done to the women of the ranchería of one world direction. While they were sleeping, five teeth were taken out of their mouths and put in their vaginas.

The third night the same thing happened to the women at the ranchería of another world direction.

The fourth night Kauymáli went to the next ranchería, and quickly put teeth in the women's vaginas. He had had a bad dream, and therefore hurried back to the ranchería in the center, which was his special charge. Nakawé was in her field below.

Kauymáli did not like this arrangement. He came to find out about it from the old lady who lived at the center ranchería. The old lady said, "If this business continues, I don't want it to happen to us. It must be a lie."

Her words made Kauymáli angry. He said, "If you think this is a lie, I will go. I have much to do, anyway, despite my special care of this center ranch."

Still angry because the old woman had called him a liar, he lit a cigarette, and then left for his own ranchería[,] where he could live very well. As he departed, he said to the old woman, "You will see in five days whether this is true."

The old woman wondered if the toothed-vagina business could be true. Meanwhile Nakawé looked on. She saw the Sun had picked a poor method to stop the increase of the people.

Nakawé asked Kauymáli, "What is happening to the people?" The wolf and the tiger [jaguar], who had touched the unclean blood before, were thinking. Kauymáli knew this.

Five days later Kauymáli learned that the women were at their rancherías. They wished their men to have intercourse with them. The men did not wish to lie with them, because they were afraid that when they made entrance[,] their members would be bitten off and would not grow out again. When each began intercourse with his wife, his member was bitten off. This continued until all the men were mutilated. Thus there were no more children. So all had cause for thought.

Within five days all the men were mutilated. "What shall we do?" they wondered, because they knew that now propagation must cease.

The Sun now ordered the men of the center ranchería to dress in full regalia, and have with them their bows and arrows. The Sun said, "I do not wish to harm you." The Sun held their lives in his hand.

But he saved one of the boys of the center ranchería. The Sun said, "I will take care that you are not injured. Hide behind a shaman's chair. Then go to Nakawé and the great gods of the sea."

On the other side of the sea was a large cave in which lived another tribe. The unmutilated boy was taken there for protection, and there he grew to manhood. He was changed into the form of these people.

That night one of the toothed-vagina women tempted Kauymáli. She said to him, "If you wish to come to me, I will stay awake for you tonight." So Kauymáli went to her. But upon making entrance, his penis was cut off.

Kauymáli, having stopped the increase of the people, and even his own, now decided to go to the great gods of the sea. To the great gods he said, "I come to tell you that there is only one of that race left. But he has been changed into another form. Only the Sun knows who this one is. But he will not tell who or where he is."

Since Kauymáli was brave, strong, and lively, the great gods said to him, "You need have no fear. But you had better talk to everyone."

"I will do it," replied Kauymáli, "even if it costs my life, although you, the great gods, cannot die. I will risk my life."[64]

The Sun then ordered all to present themselves.

Within five days Kauymáli had talked to everybody. Then he went to the center ranchería with the Sun, and said, "You put these houses into my charge. Now the people are finished. I brought you to see what will happen. You put me here. I was born from your sandal.[65] As I am brave, I am telling you all this."

The Sun answered, "Have you talked to Nakawé and the other great gods? You had better go and talk with them."

So Kauymáli went to the great gods. He said, "I think that now we should start a new race. The other, which was overrunning the world, was doing crazy things. Things are not yet right."

The great gods replied, "We are still pondering on what can be done. You wait until we decide. Perhaps we can do better than the Sun did with the toothed-vaginas."[66]

All the great gods of the sea then took their magic wands. Each listened to what the others were saying about the end of the increasing race of man. All were saying, "Let us make a better race." They asked Kauymáli to help them. They considered him brave, even though on one side he was fat, and on the other, withered.

Kauymáli was willing to go five times to sound with his sandals. Nakawé asked him, "Why do you hang your head? You go where the people with the women of wicked vaginas are waiting for you. They will not harm you. Go there, where you were born of the sandals of the Sun, and arrive within five days."

Kauymáli said, "I will go and talk to my father, the Sun, and ask him what to do." After five days of walking[,] he arrived at the place where he had been born. Here he sat down to think, holding his arms crossed.

The Sun said to him, "I wish to know what you are thinking of. But I must hurry now along my road. Come with me. If you do not talk to me, there will be neither people nor increase."

Kauymáli replied, "The great gods of the sea sent me here to talk to you."

"Have you weapons and regalia with which to defend yourself?" questioned the Sun.

"No," Kauymáli answered. "I have only ordinary clothes, and they are all worn out."[67]

The Sun then asked him, "Did you not see something when you lived there where the five rocks are?"

"I saw something shining," replied Kauymáli.

"Go there then, and ask its help," the Sun commanded. "That is my order for you to do your work."

So Kauymáli went there in the form of the wind.[68] He arrived, and said to Pálikata, "The Sun has sent me to get things with which to defend myself."

Pálikata had some deer-horns [antlers] that were strong and heavy. Kauymáli requested a hollow one, according to the command of the Sun. Pálikata asked why he wished this. Kauymáli said that the great gods of the sea had ordered it.

So Pálikata entered the house, where he had fifty deer-horns [antlers]. He gave one to Kauymáli, saying, "Do not break it, or it will not be worth anything. Now, there where you find the first people, at your house in the center of the world, you can make a bed and sleep. They are waiting for you. See if they have unmutilated organs [genitalia]."

Kauymáli waited for five days. His penis grew out again. It continued to grow, reaching finally such a great length that he had to wrap it around his waist and throw the rest over his shoulder into a basket that he carried on his back.[69]

The great gods said to him, "Do not approach women, but sleep one hundred meters from them." But Kauymáli's penis, when he uncoiled it, still reached to the women. Since he was half-bad, he had intercourse with them fifty times, although he was one hundred meters away.

During this trick[,] the women awoke, each unable to understand how she could have had intercourse by herself. They said, "Where does this come from?"

Nakawé used her magic staff to find out what Kauymáli had done. Then she said to the rock-people, "You rock-people, I can change you from rocks to people, since I established everything in the world.[70] I am as great as the Sun. I change you, therefore, to people. Come out of my cave as such." Thus Nakawé talked through her staff, in much the same manner as Mexicans use a telephone.[71]

Meanwhile Kauymáli had made his bed. "Now I have my bed," he said to himself. "If I whistle, a woman will come to me tonight." His bed was on top of a large rock.

So Kauymáli sent a dove five times to the woman. "Have you parents?" she asked. "I know that you have a mother, and that she is far away. Let us see what we can do."

Kauymáli replied, "I have a bed, and I am trying to begin a new race. Let us do it together."

The woman agreed, saying, "I will await you tonight. But you must not bring your deer-horn [antler]."

That night they were together on the high cliff. There they embraced, talked, laughed, and danced.

Now the Buzzard was in the middle of the sky, which is his cross. He heard all, and thus knew all that was said and done.[72]

The woman said to Kauymáli, "You do nothing but play. I had better go."

This made Kauymáli's penis angry, and he entered the woman half a yard.

The woman cried, "I want more, more!" She took more and more, squeezing it into herself. Soon she had taken all, even that which Kauymáli carried around in the basket. Then she said, "Embrace me. I want it all in."

So Kauymáli embraced the rock-woman. This made him very dizzy. He fell off the rock. At the same moment the woman changed back into a huge rock. Kauymáli's penis was held firmly in the solid rock. Thus was he caught and suspended in mid-air at Nakawé's orders. In this position he remained for days.

The great gods did not come to help Kauymáli for five days, although the Buzzard and Nakawé knew where he was hanging. Thus Kauymáli had to hang, head down, for five days, held by his gigantic penis that had been thrust into the woman who had changed into a huge rock.[73]

Then the Buzzard flew by Kauymáli and passed him five times, almost brushing him with his wings. "What are you doing there, hanging head-down?" Buzzard questioned.

Kauymáli replied, "I am very bad off. I found a woman who turned to stone."

Buzzard ridiculed him, saying, "You thought you were so good. But they have you. Here you will do very well."

Still defiant, Kauymáli replied, "Alright, it was my own free will. Come back to me tomorrow."

Buzzard promised to come back, provided he had a good dream about the matter. With his two wings he flew away to Nakawé to tell her all that had happened. Nakawé asked, "How is the family of Kauymáli?"

The great god, Komatéame, who had been born from the sandal of Nakawé,[74] said, "Why doesn't Kauymáli come home? Can the silly boy be saved? Who can climb to that rock to get him down? You, Buzzard, might fly there and get him loose."

Nakawé said, "Don't be afraid, Buzzard. I own that rock, since I made it. Because Kauymáli broke the command against intercourse, we will have to punish him for five days. He still has the magic deer-horn [antler], however, so we must save him.[75]

At the command of the great gods, Buzzard took Kauymáli food and water. Then he flew to all the points of the sea, telling the great gods what had happened. They were sad to see their plans for the increase of a new race go amiss. But Buzzard assured them that Nakawé would take care of the matter. Then Buzzard went to Pálikata, from whom Kauymáli had got the magic deer-horn [antler].

Buzzard told Pálikata that the two of them had been ordered by Nakawé to cut five cane plants.[76] With these the great gods would save Kauymáli.

The cane plants were blessed with sacred water. When this was done, Buzzard gave them to Nakawé.

Nakawé said, "Shall we place these on Kauymáli's hands, feet, and belt? Or shall we cut him loose with them?" Finally she smiled, and said, "We will have to fast from food and water for five days, so that Kauymáli will not die." This was done.

Then the great gods took their largest votive-bowl, and put a bit of squash inside.[77] Nakawé took the votive-bowl, and put it directly under the place where Kauymáli was hanging. He was crying for help by this time, after five days of punishment.

"It is good for him to be punished," thought Nakawé. She burned the bit of squash in the votive-bowl. The ash was wet by the sacred water within.

When all was ready, Nakawé asked, "Who is going to climb that rock to where Kauymáli is hanging?" She asked some to go, but the wind caused by Kauymáli was dangerous.[78] No one wished to go, so they left. Nakawé said, "You are all afraid. I am not afraid, however." Buzzard was finally requested to carry five people down the face of the huge rock, for even the great gods were afraid.

Now Buzzard was seated on his cross on high,[79] while Nakawé was under the rock, directly below Kauymáli. With her magic staff, which was made from cane, Nakawé calmed the wind.[80] It was noon.

Nakawé called to Buzzard, "Hurry, before the calm passes! All must be done quickly, or the Sun will win over us."

Buzzard took Nakawé to the hanging Kauymáli. She carried the reed with which to loosen him. Buzzard then hung in the air by beating his wings, and dug a hole in the rock with Nakawé's magic staff. Nakawé told him to work fast, but not to cut off all of the penis of Kauymáli.

Buzzard pried Kauymáli away from the rock five times, until Kauymáli's penis was five times [its] ordinary length.

In the meantime Nakawé was preparing to prevent Kauymáli's injuring himself by falling. So she sent up her staff to him.[81] Buzzard cut off the penis at one blow, and Kauymáli was carried slowly down to earth by the staff, landing in the votive-bowl.

The ash of the squash soon cured the wounded penis. Kauymáli was then taken to his house.[82]

On that same rock can still be seen a reddish-brown stain, which was left by the blood from the penis of Kauymáli.

At home, once Kauymáli recovered from the effects of the damp ashes of the squash, he sat down. Nakawé gave him some water to refresh him. She said to him, "We of the sea have won over the Sun, as I commanded. You were punished for five days at my orders because of your sin."

Kauymáli thanked her, saying, "Because of your favor, I did not die. I will embrace you. Now let us go where we live."

"Make your house as soon as you are well enough," replied Nakawé. "Ask of me all that you need, since I made everything within five days.[83] Where you are going, you will find those who look like people; they are, however, evil spirits."

b. Nakawé Destroys the Race and the World by Flood: The Huichol-Christian Flood Myth

So Kauymáli made his house near the sea, and here he lived alone. At the end of five days Nakawé found him. She left him a little pregnant bitch-dog. It was spotted black, white, yellow, red, and brown.

Every day, after Kauymáli had finished work clearing a field for crops, he found freshly-made [sic] tortillas ready for him. When he went to plant corn, the great gods of the sea were there in the field in the form of animals. Coming from work, he ate and drank of the food and water prepared for him, by whom he did not know.

But when he went back to work, he found that the clearing had grown up again overnight. This was because Nakawé had come to replenish the earth [restore the vegetation]. This happened three times, and Kauymáli was no nearer finished than when he had begun. So he sat down to see who would come.

An old woman with white hair came out and ruined his work. He was very angry, and thought of killing her with his machete. He called to her, "How [Who] are you, anyway? I am going to kill you."

The old, white-haired woman replied, "Calm yourself, my son. Do you not know who I am?

"No," Kauymáli answered. "I don't know you."

"I am Nakawé," the old woman said. "The Sun decided to rid the world of the bad breed of man. His efforts to make a new world, however, will come to naught, because I am going to bring the world to an end. All around the circle of the earth[84] the sea is full of serpents. They are angry, and are going to finish the earth and all of its animals. Then we can start over again. You do not, therefore, need to plant for five days, because the sea will break loose from its limits. Early tomorrow chop down the fig-tree[85] at the edge of the sea. I myself will collect all the animals in the world, so that they may not be lost. Neither you nor they will die, because I will help you.[86] Follow my instructions. Make a *canoa*."

So Kauymáli chopped down the fig-tree and hollowed out its trunk in the form of a great box. He worked fast, as time was pressing, and finished the box-like canoa in one day. Then, at Nakawé's instruction he took corn-seed of all colors, fire, squash, the bitch-dog, and beans. He put a teapáli in the ark, and on it placed his fire of squash-husks in order not to burn the canoa.[87]

At noon, when he had everything ready, Nakawé came back. She told him to forget everything, even his family, because he would never see them again. Then she had him get in the ark. He was able to sit up, since the canoa was so big.

By the end of five days all was ready. Nakawé closed the top of the ark. Inside, she had gathered all the animals that were to accompany Kauymáli: eagles, hawks, road-runners, quail, foxes, badgers, deer, crows, and parrots. They all sat on the limbs of the fig-tree.

Then the wind blew with tremendous strength (like chile) for four days.[88] Everything was changed by it. The people on the earth were changed into animals, and ate one another up. Thus the bad people were destroyed, and the land flooded over with blood.

Then the waters of the sea, which were like bull-snakes, burst from their limits and flooded the land. As the great floods of water rushed over the earth, the world broke up. In the middle region the waters picked up the fig-tree canoa. The canoa was raised up five times, until it reached the middle of the sky, which it struck with the sound of thunder.[89]

Here the canoa remained for five days, while the earth and the mountains were covered with water. Then it travelled straight off to the east.[90] Returning, it went straight to the west.[91] Then it journeyed to the north.[92] The next day it went to the south,[93] where it failed by five hours to arrive at the end of the sea. It was dark in the direction of south, because the Sun did not reach that far. Thus Nakawé measured the world.[94]

After this the canoe returned to the center of the sky, where the Sun was born. Here all remained. In five hours, however, they were lowered back to the earth.

The earth looked like a lake at this time. Nakawé said, "The world has been made anew." She opened the canoe, permitting Kauymáli to put his head out to see the new world. But all had to remain in the canoe for five days until the earth became solid.

The birds, however, flew from the branches of the fig-tree. The ducks got webbed feet from wading in the wet clay.[95]

Thus had they fallen down to the middle of the world that had been measured by Nakawé.[96] This was on top of a high mountain, near Santa Catarina. The canoe was moved by Nakawé to the exact center of the world. The world was remade and enlarged by Nakawé during the flood.[97]

At the end of five days the canoe was opened. Kauymáli, "the lame one," emerged to look on a new and tender world that was shining like a looking-glass.

Nakawé said, "In five days all shall be revivified and replaced with vegetation and animals." This came to pass.

Kauymáli emptied the canoe of the things he had put in it. Then Nakawé took the canoe back to the edge of the sea, leaving Kauymáli at the center of the world. Kauymáli was changed, and through him sprang a new race.[98]

Nakawé then told Kauymáli to take seeds from the bag at his waist. From these grew all the plants in the world. All the bad animals had been killed. The good animals, which had occupied the canoe, repopulated the earth. Thus Nakawé blessed the world with plants and animals.

Kauymáli took out the teapáli, with the fire of squash-husks still burning. He erected a temporary arbor in which to live. Since no other people remained in the world, he was alone, save for his bitch-dog.

Nakawé came in five days. She said, "I worked for the other people, and gained nothing. Now I have changed the world and made it over. You make your house and your bed, and put your things away. Within five days there will be deer in the mountains."

Kauymáli worked for five days, clearing the land for his fields. This was easy, because the plants were young and tender. He was happy to be at work again, but he missed other people. Nakawé promised him tortillas.

Now the little bitch-dog slept on a little bed of grass. While Kauymáli was away at work, Nakawé taught her to work and cook. Like all animals, the bitch was transformed. As soon as she heard Kauymáli working, the dog got up, made a ceremonial circuit,[99] and became a woman. With a tiny metate and pot[100] she prepared *nixtamal*[101] and made tiny tortillas. When she finished with the cooking, she made a counter-circuit and became a dog again,[102] returning to sleep on her little grass bed.

After finishing work, Kauymáli came back to the house. He put up his machete, saying, "I am hungry." When he found the tiny tortillas, he exclaimed, "Who could have prepared these?" He ate only three of them, but, although they were very small, [he] was well satisfied. Then he played with the little dog, who had helped him to find the tortillas by her thought.[103] This happened for four days.

On the fifth day he saw Nakawé entering the field. She announced herself by the sound of her sandals. Again she came as an old woman. Kauymáli said, "Here comes my mother. Perhaps she brings tortillas and water."

"How are you, my son?" Nakawé asked. "Who brings you food and water?"

Kauymáli said, "I find tortillas prepared every night for me and my dog, but I don't know who makes them. Who can it be?"

Nakawé said, "Do not work any more today. Go home and eat your tortillas. Hide behind a chair to see what happens. If you see a woman come out of your house to go to the river, you run to the dog's bed. Should you find a dog's skin, heat water rapidly, and cook some corn-meal dough (masa). Bathe the girl in this if she is burned."

Kauymáli decided to do this. As he approached, he saw smoke coming out of the house, and heard the grinding of corn. So he hid. A girl left the house to go to the river. Kauymáli ran into the house and found the dog's skin, which he threw into the fire. The skin burned. Then he took a handful of masa and stirred it in the water he had heated.

When the skin began to burn, the girl at the river started to cry, as though she were being burned. Kauymáli ran to her, and bathed her body in the water of the masa. She remained a woman.[104]

Kauymáli then said, "I have done just what mother Nakawé told me to do, so that you would remain a woman. Here are your metate, pots, comal, corn, and the like. Now you can cook. Here also are your gourds for water-carrying, so that you can bring water. I shall continue my work of clearing."

The woman was gentle, and soon got used to Kauymáli.

Nakawé had said that she would be back in five days. When she came, she was given food. The girl and Kauymáli were growing up. Nakawé said to them,

"Now you are people. You can cook, and the man will maintain you. I will tell you your names. You, Kauymáli, were half-bad, and must be named again. According to your dream of last night I was going to name you Kauymáli, but that will not do."

Nakawé dreamed another night that she would call him Kauimáli tsaolíkame.

The two worked hard, and prepared the many things they needed in their new life. They grew larger and larger. Finally the man wished the girl to lie with him. The girl also wished this. So Nakawé gave them permission to have a family. Knowing their desires, she stayed away from them.

During intercourse the girl cried from the pain. The wolf heard her. He came and entered the house, where he smelled the blood that was issuing from her at this time. Again he touched this blood. Nakawé said, "Wolf, you did this before. You will never learn. Go your way!"

So the wolf and the tiger [jaguar] who had touched the blood that came from the corn-girl could not be changed into people on that account.

In five days the girl was pregnant. Nakawé took the squash-ash[105] and the teapáli, and with these named all the female animal[-]people that were sitting on one side. Thus she blessed and tamed them. She did likewise with the male animal-people, and endowed all of them with life and fertility.[106]

Meanwhile the man worked with his wife. In five days he finished clearing in the four corners of the world, as well as his own place in the center of the world.

c. The Origin of the Mexicans

When the crops were ripe, deer were killed and the feast of first fruits given.

The people of Kauimáli [Kauymáli] increased very fast. Soon they plotted to enter the country of the people of TumuSawi [TumuSaúwi].[107] Tatevalí did not wish this; he wished them to plant their own fields apart from the others.

But in spite of Tatevalí[,] the people of Kauimáli, while the gods of the middle region were watching, entered the lands of the children of TumuSawi [TumuSaúwi][108] and stole food. They broke the taboo on first fruits, and ate this food without giving the ceremony.

Tatevalí was very angry. He ordered the children of Kauimáli to be called Mexicans.[109]

3. [Sub-story:] Nakawé Assigns the Gods and the Goddesses Their Homes

Nakawé then seated the great gods of the world around her, and blessed them in their order, men on one side and women on the other. Thus were the gods dedicated, as well as the arrows and votive-bowls belonging to each.

Then Nakawé said, "I wish to see whether this new world is not better than the old one made by the Sun.[110] I will fix and determine the work of all you gods."

To the male gods who had not been drowned in the flood she assigned the seas and waters. They passed through the sea to the other side. Nakawé saw that this was well. Then she assigned to each god the things that corresponded to him. She also caused the female gods to bathe in the sea. They went into the water and walked to the other side.

To another woman she said, "You were the water, but I shall change you into foam. You will be called Ereno (foam, H.)." Nakawé sent Ereno to the end of the sea where the Sun rises. Here Ereno sat like air (or wind).[111]

After five days[,] Ereno, the Huichol goddess of love,[112] became a beautiful woman. She sat on the topmost of five mesas. Nakawé made her fields, fixing them with her *bordón [bastón]* (staff).[113]

Nakawé then found a suitable cave for Ereno, to which Ereno could climb in five flights (jumps, literally).[114] Water in a spring, as well as implements, were also provided by Nakawé. Ereno was well content with the cave. Here she placed her arrows and votive-bowls.

Keamukáme, another goddess,[115] was also assigned a cave (near Jesus Maria, in the Cora country), because there were too many goddesses in the sea. It was a pretty place, and it pleased her.

Nakawé took Kokolúmali,[116] another goddess, to a cave near that of Keamukáme. Similarly Hautsikupúli[117] was given a cave nearby. Another, Úinu,[118] was likewise provided for not far from Hautsikupúli. Rapawíemi[119] chose a great rock, since she was very "delicate." Nakawé brought her some blessed (or sacred) water, so she became a spring of water.

Another goddess was placed at a second point of the sea where there is a cave. Aisulita[120] was sent to a cave in this quarter of the world. Noitcíkatci,[121] too, was given a cave. Here water was placed and blown through the air by Nakawé. The water fell on the floor of the cave, resulting in a beautiful round spring.

Then from her belt[,] Nakawé took the things needed by these goddesses. When they were thrown near the springs, beautiful flowers sprang up, each side showing flowers of different colors.[122]

a. Ereno's Child, Stuluwíakame [Huichol Goddess of Birth], Stolen and Rescued[123]

Ereno saw one of these decorated springs.[124] It pleased her, and she left beside it one of her children, Stuluwíakame. The child was stolen by Tukákame, a bad man who lived at Tukákame Mukuruli (red earth), a round corral of natural stone, which was about fifty meters high, and impassible, though pierced by five gates. The corral was filled with five houses.

Tukákame was a bad man whose animals were changed into skeletons.[125] He took Stuluwíakame and hid her head (blindfolded her?) until he thought she was tame. Stuluwíakame said, "I must answer a call of nature. You do not need to lock me up."

For five days Ereno searched for Stuluwíakame. She wished her daughter to live with her near the beautiful spring. She sent others to look for the child. But although they sought in all parts, they found nothing.

Then Ereno decided to fly everywhere, searching for her daughter. She came across the sandal tracks of the little girl, and also the unknown tracks of the man. Following these tracks for five days she arrived at the corral surrounded by the high cliffs.

A crow was sitting on a tree, saying, *"kwa, kwa."*

Ereno said, "Crow, it would be good if you could really talk and tell me where my daughter is."

The crow changed at once into a person, and said, "Why are you crying?"

Ereno replied, "I am crying because of my child for whom I have been looking everywhere."

"I know where she is," the crow said. "A bad man (*diabolo [diablo]*, or devil) has taken her, saying that you would not give her to him. I will show you where she is. She is there, in that corral. But you cannot get to her because of the high cliffs. Get on my back. I will take you down. But hurry, because he leaves at noon."

In a short time it was noon. The Sun said to Ereno, "Now you will see your child."

The girl came out of one of the houses to answer the call of nature. Ereno, from the top of the rock to which she had been taken by the crow, recognized her. The girl went back into the house, closing the door behind her.

Tukákame was asleep within. He would not come out to collect his skeleton-animals until the Sun got lower. Finally he came out, a big, well-made and well-dressed man.

Crow said, "There is the man who has your daughter. He is a bad man. He eats people and leaves only the skeletons."

Ereno asked Crow to fly to the girl with a message. She suggested that he might fly and sit on a tree and talk to the girl as she passed.

Crow agreed to follow [carry] out her proposal the next morning. The next morning he was in the corral sitting on a tree when the man came out to take his skeleton-animals to pasture. There were many chickens around. Crow went where they roosted, thinking that their noise would attract the girl's attention. She would think at first that a hawk was catching a chicken. So Crow did this. The man ordered the girl to see what was the matter.

Crow then said to the girl, "Your mother has been looking for you for ten days with much sacrifice and difficulty."

The girl began to cry. She asked where her mother was. Then she promised to have a message at noon the next day when Tukákame was asleep, as it was dangerous now.

Crow flew back to Ereno and told her what had been said.

The next day, when the man was asleep, the girl told Crow to inform her mother of all that had happened to her. Although she had become used to the man, she did not like to be shut up. The mother was to return in five days, bringing with her a lidded box with seats inside to sit on.

During this time[,] Ereno went to the Sun and asked for something with which to protect herself in case the bad man, Tukákame, followed them. The Sun gave her a box in which to hide, as well as weapons with which to defend herself.

In five days the box, with Ereno inside, was taken by Crow to the corral of Tukákame. Tukákame was asleep. The girl, Stuluwíakame, was ready to leave, taking with her none of the fine clothes that had been given to her by the bad man. She got in the box and put down the top, leaving only a small hole. A whirl-wind, colored black, white, yellow, red, and blue, lifted the box and carried it to where Ereno was waiting.

The noise of the wind awoke Tukákame. He took up his weapons and followed through the air. But he was knocked down with the machete given by the Sun, and the noise had been so great that it broke his ear-drums. So Tukákame was left behind[,] alone and deaf. The Sun, also, forbade him to follow them farther.

The box was carried in the air to the home of Ereno, which was called taté mateñeli (which is on the road to the peyote-country).[126] All was prepared here to receive the girl.

Ereno said, "Here you are to live. Here are your flowers, arrows, votive-bowls, house, water-spring, etc."

The spring, in the midst of which Stuluwíakame was to live, grew into five lakes. (This was exactly at the point where the ark fell.) Ereno asked what name should be given the girl.

Nakawé replied, "Stuluwíakame."

At the place, taté mateñeli, Stuluwíakame would live and have her family. So all the ceremonial paraphernalia was arranged for her. Ereno went back to her place at the point of the sea [seashore].

Stuluwíakame was changed into a swamp.[127] In the beginning of the rainy season (in May) she changed herself into a water-serpent (lightning). Then she and Na'aliwami [Na'aliwaemi] and another rain-goddess went abroad in a cloud of rain. They fell as snakes (lightning) in a great rain-storm on the ranch of Tukákame. As lightning-bolts[,] they destroyed his ranch, his five houses, and all his animals, according to the command of the Sun.

Tukákame was greatly frightened. He decided to leave his ranch for the sea. When he departed, he took with him only the bones of the people he had eaten.[128] Once he arrived at the sea, the lightning ceased and the rain stopped falling on the ruins of his ranch. Thus, having been driven from his ranch, he continued to live in the sea. His face was painted very ugly by Kauimáli, who had been ordered to do this by the Sun, so that people would know that Tukákame was bad and ate people. When people die, this mask warns them when they meet him.

Meanwhile Stuluwíakame went as lightning to the sea to talk to the great gods. Raining, she made a circuit, arriving back at the ruins of the ranch of Tukákame. Thus she watered the fields of the poor, according to the commands of the great gods of the sea.

Ereno told her daughter that it was better now, since there were many flowers[129] at her ranch. Stuluwíakame could give children[130] to the people who asked her favor and gave her payment in ceremonial paraphernalia. Her water, too, would be especially beneficent for children. The people would also have to give her good votive-bowls, itali [itáli] (beds [altars]), and other paraphernalia ornamented with flowers of all kinds, so she would be pleased with their fragrance.

(Myth continues with a list of dozens of flowers with which the paraphernalia of Stuluwíakame should be ornamented. Each of the four points should be decorated with colors — black, blue, white, yellow, and red. The center should show a small flower of the same kind.)

Stuluwíakame is also owner of the little parrot, whose feathers are a satisfactory offering. But her votive-bowls must have flower designs, and people who take her votive objects must have them decorated with flower designs.

Around the house of Stuluwíakame are rows of snakes of five colors. These are water, changed into snakes. Around her house also are [glass] beads, because the peyote-hunters in passing leave her beads. To step on one of these beads, however, means death to a child. The peyote-hunters, therefore, have to walk carefully near this swamp.[131] Furthermore, when they pass, they have to jump across the spring (or swamp) in five jumps. If they fail, this also means death to a child. They must reach the house of Stuluwíakame in five jumps. Her house is the swamp (ciénaga, Sp.), filled, in the middle, with many varieties of flowers that give the place a sweet odor.

If one falls into the swamp, he goes in to the neck. This is fatal to a pilgrim. If the pilgrims pass this place without mishap, and return finally to the Huichol country with peyote from Real [de] Catorce, which is beyond this place, they have to keep a vow of continence for five months. During this time, moreover, they cannot touch salt.

b. The Cave of Kacíwali

Kacíwali, the water-goddess, chose to live on a hill near Temastián.[132] Here she took her arrows, votive-bowls, and other things. Nakawé told Kacíwali that she wished these [to be] well arranged. Knowing how she was born and brought up in the sea, Kacíwali desired her votive-bowls to be decorated with beautiful blue beads. They were to be finished blue on one side and green on the other in the form of five snakes.[133] Her arrows are green and blue, with feathers of the same color. Her candles are thick, so that they will be strong. Nakawé provided these things.

Kacíwali then said to Nakawé, "Now I want my god's shaman's chairs to be green-blue.[134] My teapáli must have five circles of snakes: green, black, red, white, and yellow."

Using her magic staff made from the point of a cloud,[135] Nakawé caused these to be made. She then called this place escimakíta.

c. The Cave of Nakawé

For herself, Nakawé chose a place easier to reach. Here she brought her animals—the [mountain] lion, wolf, tiger [jaguar], and two others. Inside the cave Nakawé made a table and other things. By making five ceremonial circuits she made a rock which [that] was alive.[136] The transformed rock grew so big that it left only a path by which her children (the Huichols) could enter. Whenever Nakawé stopped in this cave she wanted her candles to be as thick as five candles and correspondingly heavy.

Then she ordered that her teapáli should have a small idol.[137] She wished also votive-bowls, arrows, and the like. She said, "Anyone who fasts from salt for five days and brings me gifts will receive my favor. Those who break the fast, however, will be killed by my animals. That is why it is so 'delicate' in my place."

Nakawé then commanded that feathers from her birds be brought to her in five shaman's baskets.

d. The Assignment of Rapawíemi

Nakawé then said, "I am going with Rapawíemi in another direction. So she took Rapawíemi to the Sun. She said to the Sun, "Here I can make an owner for my wolves, [mountain] lions, and tigers [jaguars], so that my belongings will be taken care of. They cannot hurt me, because I command them."

The Sun replied, "Very well."

So Nakawé went to the sea and ordered this.

e. The Continuation of Nakawé's Work in Dividing the World

Then Nakawé continued her work of dividing the world among the gods. All was fixed and determined. She said, "Let us see how it comes out."

In five days Nakawé commanded the clouds to come out of the sea and fall as water in the votive-bowls of the gods in their caves. The clouds complied, falling in those votive-bowls that were well decorated with colored beads.[138] (Well[-] decorated ceremonial arrows will also attract the clouds.[139] Five candles are also necessary.)

Nakawé planned to live in the middle of the world. Here she made fields and a table teapáli.[140] She ordered her family, haináli, to offer her the blood of the javelin ([javelina] peccary), five dogs, a tiger [jaguar], and several snakes.[141] These were to be used to anoint well-made model masks.

The clouds fell into the jicaras [jícaras]. But [votive] arrows and candles were lacking. Nakawé thereupon made arrows so that her children could shoot them in order to communicate with her. The arrows did this by going to the sky and then returning back to earth.[142]

When candles are lighted, all is good luck. But if a candle goes out, someone will die. When the first candles were made[,] the wind was so strong that one flew away. Even so, only two went out. This meant that two of the children of Nakawé were soon to die. Candles are Nakawé's hands. To them people pray for long life.[143]

If votive-bowls are laid out evenly, they will bring water from the sea.[144] Nakawé's children (the Huichols) can pray to these for water. One time the jicaras ([jícaras] votive-bowls) flew to the water and then came out "on this side." Votive-bowls must stand still. Those that move are "delicate."[145]

While the male and female gods were all around her, Nakawé took something from her belt. This she offered to the five points. Then she threw it into the sea, and asked one of the goddesses, "Do you know what this will produce in the water?" No one knew. Nakawé continued, "I did this so you would have water. When you have children, you can bathe them in the water to give them life and health."[146] Then she told them to remain still while she finished her work.

Nakawé took something else from her girdle and offered it to the five points. Neither the gods nor the goddesses knew what she was doing. When all was finished and well arranged and offered to the five points, Nakawé said that she would tell them what she had done at the end of five days. She said, "I cannot tell you now because it is growing. My animals are taking care of them."

At the end of five days she asked all the goddesses if they had dreamed what she was making. "Who dreamed the best?" she asked. "Who can win by telling me now?" But none of the great well-dressed gods could tell her anything.

So Nakawé told them to look at their feet. This they did. They saw that each had a teapáli,[147] and all the teapáli were lying in a long row.

The gods were pleased. They knew that now they would lack nothing.

Nakawé continued to take things out of her belt and offer them to the sea. She said, "Now look at what is in the water."

There they saw a large crocodile.[148] This was to protect Nakawé. They looked down again, and saw large beautiful fish[149] in the water. The gods were pleased that Nakawé was doing so well. They embraced her. They looked again in the water, and there they saw growing a large corn-field (milpa, Sp.).[150]

Nakawé now said, "Grasp your votive-bowls and catch what you see. Pray, baptize yourselves with it, and then taste it." So the gods looked again. This time it was salt.[151] Nakawé had thrown salt into the sea, and this had made the sea salty.

"I am making the things that you will need," Nakawé said. "Now you male gods look and see the five things that I make for you. See if you can dream what I am making."

She gestured them away. When they came back in five days, they did not know what she was making. So Nakawé said, "Look at your feet and see something to test your courage."

Looking at their feet by the margin [shore] of the sea they saw masses of snakes.[152] All had sufficient courage to disturb the snakes and not flee. Nakawé said, "These will defend you in [from] danger."

This was done a second time. They looked down from their shaman's chairs, and on the backs of their chairs saw a small eagle[153] seated. But they were not afraid, because they knew that the eagle would help them.

A third time they looked down. By each chair they saw a large tiger[154] [jaguar]. Although they were a little frightened, they did not run.

A fourth time they looked down. This time they saw that they had bows and arrows.[155]

The fifth time they saw a wart-gourd of tobacco and a small shining stone.[156] This they ate. It was the arrow of their heart.

4. [Sub-story:] The Story of Duck-boy, TumuSaúwi

a. The Origin of the Huichols by the Removal of Teeth from the Vaginas of the Women to be Married to TumuSaúwi

Nakawé then told the female gods to try to dream what she would be making in five days. At the end of this time they came back. None of them, however, had been able to dream what she had made. They saw a beautiful fish in the water.

This fish had to be caught by five people. But although the female gods tried five times, they were not successful. Nakawé then said, "Speak to the boy in the middle of the group. See if he can catch the fish." The boy had not had sexual intercourse. He, therefore, could catch the fish.

He took off his clothes, dove into the water, and came out as a duck. In his feet he held a big fish. He gave the fish to the owner of the votive-bowl in the center of the group. This pleased Nakawé.

Again he entered the water, and brought out even a larger fish, which he placed in the same votive-bowl. Each time he brought out a larger fish until he had caught five. Thus he worked for the votive-bowls of Nakawé, diving into the water many times until each votive-bowl of the male and female gods had five fish.

After five days[,] Tatevalí (Fire) said, "Now that we have our bowls full of fish, who knows the name of the fish? I myself will have to dream for five days to find out what to call it."

So for five days Tatevalí dreamed. At the end of this time he said to the Duck-boy, "Since you alone are innocent, you will have to kill the fish in the votive-bowls. We ourselves are not pure. Were we to do it, we should sully the paraphernalia. You must kill the fish in the votive-bowls to dedicate (consecrate) them. For this purpose open the fish, then take out a little blood *(sic)*. When the fish are killed and opened, throw them back into the water so that they will rot."[157]

This was done. Five days later Nakawé said, "Let us look in the water and see what we see."

All the great gods stood behind the boy and looked. There, under the water where the fish had rotted, they saw a beautiful corn-field.[158] Nakawé told all of the great gods to take the magic corn-ears from the garden for seed. Also, from the rotted fish were growing large and small candles.

The god people had to work for several days. After puzzling a day[,] Nakawé decided to call the Duck-boy. She said to him, "Stand here and watch these lighted candles. See that they do not go out. If they do not go out, you will be alright."

The candles did not go out. While the Duck-boy watched them [the candles], he heard Tatevalí (god of fire) telling the other gods that they should clear the fields, make houses, and set up an altar.

Five days later the votive-arrows were talking. In his dreams the Duck-boy heard them say, "Our mother is 'on the other side' (one of the world regions). Duck-boy should make twenty-five lassos for catching deer."[159]

He awakened, and thought, "I shall use bows and arrows, sandals, and wrist guards *(matsúwa)*."

Tatevalí said to the other gods, "Let us see whether he can do it. And let us not eat salt or touch our wives, for he is not married."

Meanwhile Duck-boy put up five deer net-traps (lassos), which were all he could find, at five breaks in the cliffs. Where the deer-traps were set, he put up an altar with many feathers. Here also he hung his tobacco-gourds.[160] Then he waited to see if deer would come.

When no deer came, he went to look at his deer-traps. But even had he found deer, he would not have known what to do with them. After much struggle, notwithstanding, he found no deer in his traps. He was sorry, and wondered if Tatevalí was fooling him. He went to all the traps of the four points, but still found nothing.

That night he dreamed that he was told, "Leave your deer-traps. They will not rot. Too many people are talking here."

So another day he said to his mother, Otuanáka (a corn-mother, like Nakawé), "Until they stop talking up there at my deer, I will not catch any."

After four days, at night, he dreamed that they should arrange a teapáli, well painted with pictures of animals. These were to be placed at the four points. Another was put in the middle region. He made them, consequently, to test his dream.

Another night he dreamed that he must make new arrows for all these five gods. These were to be placed immediately.

The third night he dreamed that he had made no arrow for Tatevalí. So he made an arrow. Then he went to see his luck at the deer-traps. He found bits of grass only, however, as a sign of deer.

The fourth night he dreamed that the grass said to him, "It is clear that you do not understand deer-hunting. You should have placed candles on the altar."

So, for luck, he went to the water-hole where the dead fish had rotted and got several beautiful candles. He came back and put these on the altars.

On the fifth day all was arranged. Yet he heard nothing save the whispering of the wind, and this he could not understand. He did not know what to do. After five days he had still caught nothing.

On the sixth day, when he was about to take down his nets, he felt sick and unequal to the work. He knew that the half-bad Kauymáli of the sea was listening. They could talk to him by means of his votive-bowl, while Kauymáli answered with his arrows. Kauymáli said he would come at noon.

Kauymáli came at noon. The sick Duck-boy asked if he would cure him. Kauymáli replied, "I do not know how to cure. I am as tender as a little boy. But let me see you." He approached five times to see the patient. Then he opened his shaman's-basket, and out of it took five beautiful plumes. With these he hoped to dream what was wrong with the boy.[161] He said, "If I dream well, you will get better and be up at midnight." He went away. But at midnight the Duck-boy was still unable to do his work.

The next day Kauymáli returned. He found his patient well again. He said, "Duck-boy, take care of this place and guard the fire. I have dreamed that you still lack offerings to the gods of fire. Until all the offerings are completed, you will kill no deer. Have you put chocolate and corn in the votive-bowls? Go to the sea and get them from the water-hole where the fish rotted."[162]

Now Kauymáli had three assistants. These communicated to him what the Duck-boy should do in order to be successful in getting deer. Duck-boy also lacked "chual"[163] (seed of *Amaranthus*, Sp.), which was to be ground up and offered to the gods. The gods also desired tiny god-bowls. Kauymáli told Duck-boy that he lacked all these things, as well as god's-sized [tiny] deer-traps and tiny arrows. Further, on five votive-bowls pictures of five deer were to be painted with beads in wax. If all these were given to the principal gods of the five world regions, deer would be brought to his traps, and then he could work. So Duck-boy hurried to finish these in five days.

When all this was done, the Duck-boy found many signs of deer: a rock freshly displaced; at another of the five points a small loose rock; at another a fresh deer track; in another many tracks; and in the middle region more tracks. But still there were no deer in his traps.

Four days later he dreamed that he should shoot an arrow at his trap. Then, Nakawé told him, he was to look for it. He shot an arrow at the trap from each of the five points, and each time found that the arrow was either displaced from where it had landed or broken. So he began to wonder who was disturbing his arrows.

That night, while he slept, the deer came to his altar, ate the food, and listened to the arrows. Then they went away. Kauymáli informed him of this. It enhanced his desire to kill both a male and a female deer. He went to his mother, Otuanáka, and told her all that Kauymáli had told him.

Kauymáli, who had dreamed, then told Duck-boy to shoot his fifth arrow. "Go very early," he said, "and if you see anything there, talk to it."

So Duck-boy went, and a beautifully dressed white mother waited at the middle region. Drawing near he saw people, and thought that they might be those who had broken his arrows. As he approached, the people disappeared. This happened four times.

The fourth time Kauymáli told him that he might talk to the people. "The gods of the sea," he said, "do not want you to kill deer just yet."

On the fifth day Duck-boy again approached the people. This time he sounded on his bow-string with an arrow. The intruders were really male and female deer, dressed as people and with their faces painted in peyote fashion.

He shot his arrow. It went close to the Deer-people, who picked it up. Duck-boy said, "Why do you pick up my arrow?" He motioned for them to come.

As they were giving him his arrow, they grasped him by the wrist, saying, "We will not give you your arrow until you listen to us. If you are willing to remain here for five days, will you do it?" Then they sat down in a circle, with the Duck-boy in the middle.

Duck-boy replied, "The great gods told me to catch deer. Thus for a long time I have been fasting and not eating salt."

The Deer-people answered, "Have no fear. What does Kauymáli say?"

"He said not to be afraid if I met anyone," the Duck-boy replied.

The Deer-people said, "You do not understand how these things are. If you do not stay, we will not give you your arrow back. Here, we have food." They offered Duck-boy an acorn-full of food.[164] But he did not like it. So they gave him a husk-tomato, but he didn't like this. Then they offered him cabbage of tender *amole*. He did not like this either. Then they tendered him deer-grass *(maSa rakéli)*. Duck-boy didn't like this, but he satisfied himself with some of it, although he ate very little.

Now, since he had remained, the Deer-people gave him his arrow, saying, "Have no fear, and do not cry. We have five rancherías with patios here, where we dance. Let us dance. Then you will get used to us."

So Duck-boy danced with the Deer-women and was very happy, and the Deer-men sang for him. Thus he was transformed into a Deer-man, and could not change back. The Deer-people told him, "You leave us all your ceremonial paraphernalia, and tonight go to your home."

So Duck-boy returned to his home. His finery was ruined by the rough treatment of the Deer-people, since they had struggled and wrestled while drunk with him. For five times he went back, and his mother did not know who he was. Kauymáli had said that he would be so changed that even his mother would not recognize him.

At dawn the next day the boy came back, sounding his sandals. The mother asked, "Who is coming?" She did not know him, for he was changed into a large male deer. She was weaving a basket. She said to herself, "It is too bad that my boy is not here to shoot this deer."

The deer entered the house, although his horns [antlers] barely got through the door. This broke the woman's loom, and she cried, "My son, my son, come home, come home. Here is a deer."

The deer smelled the altar. Then it dashed out of the house and ran away with great leaps.

Women from a neighboring ranchería ran up, and asked her if she had recognized her son. They explained the change in his appearance.

Meanwhile the Deer-boy had changed back into human form.

The woman said, "Where a deer is killed, it is not altogether dead, but is reborn."[165]

At the suggestion of the women[,] the boy went back to his mother. Thus, on the sixth day, he also came back in his human form. The mother was angry. "What is the matter?" she cried. "All your clothes are ruined. Who caught you? Bring your clothes here."

But the boy answered nothing. He sat down, rested, and ate. He said, finally, that some people had held him prisoner for five days.

This made the mother very angry. She said, "Now you are of no good [use] around here. I did not order you to do this."

Kauymáli, who wished meat, came up, and asked the boy if he had killed a deer. They boy told him all that had happened. Kauymáli said that both he and the boy's mother understood these things. "Go," he ordered, "and tell your mother. Then bring the Deer-woman here."

The boy agreed, saying, "Very well. I think that they are still there."

The mother rejoined, "That is good, because I cannot accept you under the present circumstances."

So the boy left. He found only the first woman, who had caught him. He wanted her to go with him, but she demurred, asking him to bring her food. Finally she "measured her steps" to ask her mother if she should go. Slowly, and with much protest, she was taken, because she had made him prisoner for five days, after taking his arrows. Although she cried a little, the boy took her. He said, "I did not cry when you took me. Do not be afraid. My mother will not hurt you." So she agreed to go with him, but only on the condition that he would release her as soon as they approached the house of his mother.

As they drew near, the boy's mother observed them very closely. She noticed that the boy was dressed once more in all of his finery. She had arranged an altar-blanket for the Deer-woman to sit on.

When they came into the patio, the mother embraced the Deer-woman, and said, "I will not hurt you. You have restored all of my boy's finery. Come in. Here is water and food. Sit down, and let us sleep and see how we dream."

At midnight the Deer-woman changed back into a deer and ran away, telling the boy to follow her tracks to where they led. She said, "Let us see if your mother can understand this." Then she went far away, and changed back into a woman.

At the sea, meanwhile, Tatevalí was saying, "What has happened to Duck-boy? Why doesn't he return with the deer that we wanted?"

Kauymáli told him all that had transpired.

Tatevalí continued, "Have her come and sit down again, then we can hear what they are saying. Have the boy take down his traps and go home."

When this was done, the boy was asked to tell Kauymáli what had happened. Tatevalí asked him if he would like to be changed into a Deer-boy. The boy replied that he would be pleased. Then he was asked about the Deer-woman, and whether she had herself changed back. The boy answered, "Yes, that is certain."

Tatevalí said, "Here all the singing has served for nothing. So wrap up your ceremonial paraphernalia and other things."

The boy did what he was told.

Then Tatevalí said, "Now that you are changed, your name will be Tumu-Saúwi Watakami."

Since the Deer-woman had been transformed also, Tatevalí changed her name to Takútsi. He told them that they must stay in their house "on this side," because they could not mix with the boy's mother. "It will come out alright," he said.

To Kauymáli, Tatevalí assigned the office of taking care of them. The boy was required to turn around five times. He was then changed into a tiny deer with very large horns [antlers]. In this form Tatevalí named him SuSuimáli, and ordered him to live in the mountains.

But in his new form[, the] boy had a difficult time. His horns [antlers] were too large for his body. So they took off his horns [antlers] and named him *tátSu* [rabbit]. Then from the horns [antlers] Tatevalí made other deer, which he called *kaukamali*. From the hoofs of tátSu he made another deer, so large that it could reach the branches of the trees. This one was very large. It ran away and ate from the branches of the trees of the five world regions. Tatevalí ordered him to stop at the votive-bowls of the great gods and lower his horns [antlers] over all the bowls. This deer was called *maSa* (deer). He always remained hidden among the five mountains, taking care of that region.

TumuSaúwi, however, seems to have taken his original form, for he was then sent to put up his deer-traps at one of the breaks in the cliffs. With him he took one who was a good shot at deer. He was also given a second name, tsaulískami.

At dawn the deer came out to the divide of the sierra. But the best shots were not near, and so the animals escaped to another sierra. They went after them, trying to overtake them by following their tracks. In the middle region they did not find the deer.

Tatevalí commissioned TumuSaúwi to catch the deer by driving them in circles into a little valley. But when TumuSaúwi arrived at the valley, the deer suddenly disappeared, as if into thin air. This puzzled him.

Tatevalí asked, "Did you have your offertory arrows? Was there fire in your house, and did the women pray for and take care of your success?"

This was done, and the women prayed all night. When all was ready and properly arranged, the gods asked Tatevalí to grant them deer. Tatevalí said, "You may be successful tomorrow."

That night they dreamed that the deer came in the form of people. At dawn the hunters left. Sun saw a medium-sized female deer with very small horns [antlers]. It was trembling, and was covered with foam. Green spume came from its mouth. TumuSaúwi told it to paint its face and heart with the peyote design, and then put on all its finery.[166] Thus he would have power to kill it.

A very small peyote, green on one side and red on the other, came out of the deer's mouth. Tatevalí told TumuSaúwi that if he used this he would become a curer.

The deer, robbed of its peyote, died, but from its horns [antlers] a new deer was born.[167]

The dead deer was brought into the ranchería by the people (gods). From the tips of its horns [antlers] five kernels of corn were taken. These were carefully guarded, so that all the people (gods) would be changed.

Then they spread out grass near the altar. On this they laid the deer, and arranged their ceremonial paraphernalia around it. Then the people prayed.

They were very happy, because, from the deer's horns [antlers], the deer were increasing rapidly.[168] But they did not dare touch the meat. They hung it on the altar until they had killed five more deer.

TumuSaúwi could not get blood on his hands or on himself because he was "delicate." Another was assigned to do this work. His name was *mataSuli [mata-Súli]* ("bloody hands").[169] He cooked the deer in the earth oven.

The next day another deer was killed. But this time TumuSaúwi was able to communicate with Tatevalí, who told him how to arrange an altar for anointing all paraphernalia with blood. Then the meat could be eaten and the fields planted.

After this[,] TumuSaúwi continued to fast without salt, because he was going to sing. He was helped by two chanters, *kuimeapúwa-mi* and *kaukamali*, who sat on either side of him, as Huichol singers and chanters do. There was also another assistant, *wipísuli*.

They sang all night amidst lighted candles, as at Huichol feasts. Then at dawn the deer-broth was put on the fire to burn [cook]. The men went to clear the fields. In the evening they returned to eat. TumuSaúwi, with a plume in his hand, took some sacred water. When he blessed it, it became salt for the deer-broth.

Thus they worked for five days, and the fields were all cleared. Then Tumu-Saúwi took the five grains of corn that had come from the magic deer-horn [antler].[170] These were placed in a votive-bowl on the altar in the center of the field. The corn increased to a whole jicara [jícara, bowl] full.

After the field was burned, the corn was planted. Soon the *elotes* [ears of corn] came. Then more deer were killed, and the feast of elotes [first fruits ritual was] given.

When the deer had been killed, Tatevalí said, "Now have all the paraphernalia bathed in blood and in sacred water, for another is to be born."

TumuSaúwi dreamed that his wife should be with children. They were told that in ten days the children would grow up to be Huichols. Then they would marry, and have three children themselves.

Having children, TumuSaúwi no longer had to work. He just dreamed. There being no others, the siblings had to marry among themselves. Tatevalí allowed this. All worked and followed the customs of TumuSaúwi according to the command of Tatevalí, with the consent of Nakawé.

Now the magic deer-horns [antlers] wanted teeth in the vaginas of the women, because the people were becoming too numerous to suit the deer.[171] But it was necessary to remove the teeth. Nakawé had the half-bad Kauymáli put a deer-horn [antler] over his penis, approach the women at night, and enter them. So that night, while the women were asleep, Kauymáli put a large deer-horn [antler] over his penis and thrust it into the women. Thus he ground the teeth out of their vaginas, although the process was very painful to them.[172] As he withdrew, Nakawé caught the magic deer-horns [antlers] before they touched the ground. Otherwise there would never have been any Huichols.

The women were crying from the pain; but they were without teeth in their vaginas. When the magic deer-horn [antler] was withdrawn, the loose teeth came out.

Now TumuSaúwi could have intercourse with the women. Soon they had five children by him. Then Kauymáli was told by TumuSaúwi to make votive-bowls for Tatevalí, Nakawé, and Otuanáka, on account of the new children. If this payment were not made, the children would die.[173] In five days this was done. The children were taken to the caves of these gods. There they were bathed, while the parents prayed.

Still, one of the children became sick and got as thin as a skeleton. By this time Kauymáli knew how to communicate with the gods. Thus he dreamed that deer should be killed. But they could not eat until all the [sacred] paraphernalia had first been anointed with blood. The horns [antlers] of the deer were then to be taken to the cave of Tatevalí.[174]

Then another child got sick. He became as thin as bones from the waist down. Kauymáli dreamed that this was because the lizards, playing on the limbs of the trees, had entered the waist of the child. He cured the child by sucking from it five small lizards. One of these had to be taken to the cave of Tatevalí.[175]

Another child became sick with fever, and could not eat. Kauymáli dreamed that he must have been playing in the fields and got a grain of corn into his abdomen. To prevent the corn's growing inside the child and killing it, Kauymáli sucked it [out] after the custom of the shaman-curer *(maSa kami)*. To be finally cured, the child had to be pledged [to pledge] that he would take fish from the river and offer the blood in the votive-bowls of Otuanáka.[176]

b. Kauymáli's Usual Sexual Weakness Brings Death to the Huichols

For five days TumuSaúwi was ill of small-pox. He dreamed that this disease was sent by Tatevalí (Grandfather Fire)[177] because he had not fulfilled his duties to that god. He was able to cure himself, however, by brushing off a handful of the pox, which he threw away. The pox affected a *culíakai*-tree,[178] which still shows the marks.

His children then got sick of [with] the disease. Grandfather Fire told him to anoint their bodies with the rubber-like sap of the culíakai, after it had been mixed with five ground kernels of corn. But it was to no avail. The first child died. It was ordered that the plague visit them for five years.[179]

After his first illness[,] TumuSaúwi continued to work clearing his fields. His wife was puzzled that apparently there were other people to help him. When TumuSaúwi came back from work and put up his machete, she said, "I notice that you have many people to help you. I thought they might be hungry, so I prepared food for twenty-five. But since you did not bring the others with you, you must eat it all, because you have made me foolish."

TumuSaúwi replied, "Those people are mine. I take them from my body. The great gods and tata (father) Sun gave them to me to come from my heart. You think you understand these things (of the gods, apparently), but you do not. Soon we shall have children to help us."

The woman did not believe this to be true. So TumuSaúwi continued, "Well, if you do not believe it, maybe it isn't true. Yet I tell you that I dreamed of the flowers of the gods. Until we have children to eat the food, my people cannot eat. So put up the food for another day."

Then he communicated to the gods of his wife's disbelief. All the great gods of the sea, as well as tata Sun and Grandfather Fire, the dry-season gods, told the woman that they had given TumuSaúwi the power of taking people out of his body. As for her, Nakawé and Otuanáka told her that she still lacked something. In five days they would send her something to make her complete. She was to wait and see what she found in her house.

When the five days had elapsed, the woman found, on the altar in her house, a beautiful wreath of flowers. She had forgotten what the goddesses had said to her. She thought, "How pretty these flowers are. I will put them in my clothing, and save them to show my husband when he awakens." But later when she looked for the flowers in her clothing, they were gone. Then she felt them in her womb.[180]

After a month she was far advanced in pregnancy. In twenty-two days more she had reached her term. Her husband said to her, "See, you did not believe me about those people I take from my body. Nor did you believe me when I said you would have a child."

For five days she was ill in delivery. Kauymáli was called to attempt to cure her. He came and sat on the shaman's chair and sucked her body. He also purified her with his hands (presumably by brushing) and with his shaman's plumes. After this treatment, she delivered the child. Much blood came from her. The child was taken and placed by the fire to warm, as well as given other care.

Then TumuSaúwi went back to work on his fields. He wished that all his stalks of corn had ears on them. So he took eagle feathers and tied them on the corn stalks. He did the same with green feathers from the parrot.[181] Then he addressed the eagle in the middle of the sky, the god of the sixth world region,, and asked him [her] to help by catching any animals that might enter his fields. With the help of the eagle the animals would not damage his fields.

After twenty-five days[,] the ears became full [ripe]. TumuSaúwi carried them to his god-house for the ceremony of first fruits. These offerings had to be watched all night, lest bad animals steal the sacred corn.[182] Kauymáli was assigned the task, because he was a singer-curer who could communicate with the gods. While he watched, a great harvest was continued. A great crop was gathered, and it filled all the store-houses of TumuSaúwi. But the bad people of Kauymáli (the Mexicans) stole some of the corn.[183] Kauymáli said that this was because the woman had not been careful to pick up all the grains of corn in making nixtamal.[184] He said to TumuSaúwi, "You had better get another woman to cook and help your wife, someone who will be more careful. You need *peónes* [hired hands] also to help you in your work."

But the wife of TumuSaúwi did not want another woman to help her. She said that the work was not hard. The children of Kauymáli knew this through him, and they knew also that if TumuSaúwi did not get more help[,] they would be able to steal more corn.

But TumuSaúwi did not get helpers, and the next year his corn produced almost nothing. He had barely sufficient corn from his good crop of the year before. So he prayed to the Sun.

The Sun told him, "You shall have no good corn again until you follow our orders. Since you have disobeyed us, for a punishment you cannot drink water all day while you are clearing your fields for corn. Furthermore, you must drink no *tesgüino* [corn-beer] nor *toache* (distilled tesgüino) [distilled drink similar to tequila]. Again, you shall be "delicate" for five years, and you and your wife may have intercourse only with each other."[185]

TumuSaúwi and his wife had to accept doing this penitance [penance], otherwise they would have no corn, and their children might die.

So they followed these commands. The man had a good crop of corn. The second year was equally good. The third year they had extra corn to trade for ribbons, little pouches, and various other articles of finery.

Then to the great gods of the sea they took sacrificed cattle, sheep, money, and the like, which they had collected during the first three years of their vow. TumuSaúwi's money-belt was so heavy that it made him hot carrying it. The woman, apparently, had a lot of money also, and attracted other men to her.

At a feast for building a house, one of these men bought the woman a bottle of mescal. She took it, and secreted it in one of the five waists [belts] she was rich enough to wear.

The hosts arranged the altar and baptized (bathed) everything with sacred water. Then the woman, and the man who was tempting her, sat down by the altar in the dancing-house to listen to the music of the violin and the guitar. Outside the singer sang (just as in [all] Huichol feasts).

The host had prepared much tesgüino and toache. When the music began, both inside and outside of the dancing-house, the masked clown directed the dancers within the house. In the dancing-house were fifteen men and a similar number of women.

There was plenty of toache, which was served to the guests in a very large wine-cup (*waso [vaso]*, H.-Sp.). All were given a like amount to warm them all equally, so that they would be lively all night, and yet not completely drunk. Those who were becoming too drunk were forced, by the [sacred] clown, to get up and dance. Thus they wore off the effects of the surplus liquor they had drunk.

While the others were dancing, the woman went out to buy more sotol [the plant used to distill toache]. When she was outside, the Mexican liquor sellers began to pinch and caress her. She bought another bottle of liquor and drank more, while the men continued to play with her. They said to each other, "We understand that the gods are helping her because of a vow of constancy she made. Let us try her, and see if she is true to her husband."

TumuSaúwi, her husband, however, heard her fall. He took her to a house, where he charged a woman to take care of her. But the other woman got drunk also, and when the men came[,] they found TumuSaúwi's wife alone. They undressed her, and laid with her. Having finished, they went off with her money. She was so drunk that she did not know what had happened.

The following morning she awoke, feeling badly. The host asked her to take more toache, but she did not want to. He said, "Last evening you drank plenty. Why don't you want any today?" And he made fun of her, as did the men who had slept with her.

When the feast was over, TumuSaúwi and his wife went home. The Sun told TumuSaúwi that his wife had done wrong, and that, therefore, she could not have any more children. This was revealed in TumuSaúwi's dream. When he got up, he accused his wife of having been intimate with the men. She denied his accusation. Then he asked to see whether all of her money was still in her money-belt. Thus he would know if she were innocent or guilty.

Ten pesos were missing.

Now all that she had bought was toache. TumuSaúwi asked if she had paid so much for one bottle of the liquor. Then he went back to the one who had sold her the stuff, and found that she had bought only six centavos worth. Thus he knew that she had been robbed.

Within five days[,] five of their children became sick, and weevils got into their corn. They gave remedies to the children, but that did no good. Two were dying, so they called Kauymáli to see if he could do anything.[186]

Kauymáli asked first why they were sick, so that he would know what [which] god to address. He slept in order to dream what was the trouble. In the evening he went to one side and laid down. At midnight it was revealed to him that all the children would die unless special efforts were made. TumuSaúwi and his wife, it was decided, would have to pay the gods the value of all the money she had wasted and that had been stolen from her. It was serious, because she had failed in the fourth year of her vow.[187]

This Kauymáli had to tell them, lest the same illness fall on them[,] too. At dawn he went to their house and informed them of what had been revealed to him in his dream. He said, "Your family is no longer in favor with the gods.[188] Your children, therefore, are not really yours. You will have to pray to the gods and confess all your faults. If this is not done, you will all surely die."

But Kauymáli blamed the woman more than the man, even though she had been so drunk as not to know she was doing wrong. The loss of her money made this seem clear. And breaking the vow meant that she was no longer "delicate."[189]

She said, "It was not wholly my fault, since I was drunk and asleep."

Then she cut grass, which Kauymáli used to brush off the contamination of the touch of the men who had taken advantage of her. The impure grass was then taken away and burned.[190] Thus was Kauymáli able to help the sick children. He told TumuSaúwi not to beat his wife, or it would go ill with their offspring. He left, saying that he would return the following day.

When Kauymáli was gone, TumuSaúwi began to think how his wife had betrayed him. She had ruined his good work of keeping his own vow for four years. He became very angry, and took up a quirt. Then he tore the clothes from his wife, grabbed her by the hair, and beat her naked body until she bled.

The sick children began to weep out of sympathy for their mother. She continued to deny any knowledge of her fault, asserting that she had been drunk. TumuSaúwi cried, "You are a mare, a burro, a *puta* (Sp., prostitute)."

The children, however, finally got the man to leave his wife alone. She had been badly beaten, and was so swollen that she could not make tortillas or suckle the children.[191]

TumuSaúwi now felt repentant. He remembered what Kauymáli had told him about not beating his wife. He had said that such an act would be bad, and that its penalty would be revealed in five days.

Kauymáli could not cure the sick children. In five days two boys and two girls were dead.[192] The dead children went to Mother Welika Uimali ([Welíka Uimáli,] the eagle-goddess of the sixth world region of above), the air- and cloud-goddess of the sky. The bodies of the children were buried, and the man was very sad.

The mother knew that TumuSaúwi was responsible for the death of her children, and did not wish to continue living. She blamed him, and was afraid that he might go on mistreating her. Thinking of her children, she wept constantly.

By this time there were plenty of other people in the world, so she decided to leave him.

Now Kauymáli wanted her himself. He assured her that he would take care of her if she left her husband. Embracing her he said, "I will not have relations with you immediately. I shall first bring you many of the rarest species of birds — parrots, parakeets, *güakamaiya* [*güakamaya*, macaw], and the like — so you can have their feathers."

Thus it was agreed. He would be gone five days getting these birds. Upon his return, they would have intercourse.

But while Kauymáli was gone, the woman died.

Kauymáli soon collected a large basket of birds of beautiful colors. On the way back, as he was passing a cleft in the cliffs, he stopped to sit down and rest from his load. He wished to be fresh for the woman he was going to have on his return. As he was lighting a cigarette, he heard the sound of sandals.

Now at this place two roads crossed at right angles. Along one road he saw a woman come running, as though flying. Kauymáli recognized her. He thought that she was coming to fulfill her part of their understanding. But when she drew near, he noticed that her face was very black. He wondered what had happened to her.

As she passed, he called, "Listen, where are you going? You are my wife. I am coming with these birds to fulfill my part of our agreement."

But the woman ignored him, and went by on the other road.

Kauymáli knew the road that she was following. He decided to run and overtake her. Leaving his birds, and even his cigarette[,] which was still inlighted, he pursued her. Following her tracks, even when they had passed all the ranches, he arrived finally at a large house in an immense corral. Here there were many people, because a feast was going on.

Since he did not know these people, he asked Ciwétome, the great goddess of the sea, to tell him if his promised wife was there. The goddess commanded him to sit on a rock nearby and watch. "Here is a bottle," she said, "which you must take to the sea-goddess, Nakawé. Nakawé has wool that she can give you."

So Kauymáli went to Nakawé and asked her for the bottle. This was a small, hollow reed that grew near her votive-bowls. It was given to him. Nakawé also gave him bits of wool of five different colors, as well as some large thorns from the sea. The wool was to stop the ends of the reed when he found the woman.

Then Kauymáli fulfilled the orders of the gods by sitting on a hill-top overlooking the corral. The people could not see him, but he could watch them from afar.

He had been warned by the great gods not to make a fool of himself. They knew his weakness, and were doubtful of the outcome. He was told to have no relations with the woman, because she was not now wholly alive.[193] He could touch the woman with the thorn, which would serve as a magic arrow. But under no conditions was he to touch her with his hands.

So he watched carefully the people in the corral (patio), and listened to what they were saying. Within the patio, which was at the point [shore] of the sea, many people were singing, dancing, and shouting, and following the orders of the clown. They made so much noise that Kauymáli could understand nothing.

So armed with the magic arrow, the reed, and the tufts of cotton, he approached and entered the patio. There were many dancers, and they went around him several times. He looked for the tracks of his promised wife, thinking she might be drunk or asleep. Finally he heard her whom he was seeking. She came out of the dancing-house drunk, and danced with men who embraced her.

The gods had told Kauymáli to shoot her in the heel with the magic arrow (the thorn from the sea) as soon as she was still. This he did. But at first she did not notice it. Then he shot her again. This time she felt the thorn, and called to one of the sober women, asking her help in removing it. As she stopped, Kauymáli ran up and seized the thorn.

By the thorn the woman was changed into a mosquito. Kauymáli shut her up in the little reed that he had been given. Then he sealed the ends with the wads of colored cotton from Grandmother Growth (Nakawé).

The woman said, "Why have you got me shut up? Let me out!"

But Kauymáli only closed the tube more tightly with the tufts of cotton, and then very carefully put it in his pouch. Then he ran away, followed for a short distance by the drunken people, who were angry at the loss of their companion. He soon regained his trail, and for five days journeyed back to the sierra where he had left his birds.

Now Kauymáli had been ordered not to heed the woman's complaints. By no means was he to open the tube until he got her back to the place where she had died (the land of the living). He had promised to follow the orders of the great gods of the sea, otherwise his efforts to save his promised bride would be of no avail. If the tube were opened along the road, she might escape. He would never be able to get her back.

The first night he gathered wood and built a fire. He put the magic reed near his head. Within the reed the woman talked to him, tempting his weakness for women.

The second night his captive made fun of his scruples.

The third night she said, "You are my husband, because we made an understanding (contract). I was very changed when you saw me at the patio, because I was dead. But now that you have saved me, let me out so that we may lie with each other."

But Kauymáli was not to be tempted.

The fourth night she begged him again to free her so that they could be intimate. Kauymáli was sorely tried, because his penis was hard with waiting. But he was afraid to do what she asked until they reached their destination. He said, "Wait until we get back to the sierra where our things are." He refused to let her out, promising, however, to free her the next day when his vow would be completed, even if they did wish to sleep together that night.[194]

She continued to trouble him, and he said, "I have several beautiful birds waiting, ready to give you. They are in the sierra where I met you when you were flying away from your old home. Tomorrow we shall be there, and then we can rest."

When they arrived, there was the basket of birds that Kauymáli had brought to populate the middle region of the world. He had brought also many kinds of the seeds that women need. Since he was tired, he sat down. He took up his pouch, which was well sewed across the mouth with five threads to prevent the loss of the tube. There he rested, still true to his vows to the great gods of the sea.

The woman begged him to let her out. She remarked that she was now tamed and would not make a fool out of him. She was willing, she said, to permit him to do all he wished with her.

Now that they had arrived at his cargo [basket of birds] and were near their final destination, Kauymáli began to believe her. So he opened his pouch and took out the little reed that held the mosquito. One by one, at her urging, he extracted the cotton wads with which the tube was closed. When he took out the last one, however, the mosquito-woman flew away,[195] leaving him with *penis erectus.*

He knew well that he had been made a fool of, and he followed her tracks, calling to her. Thus for the second time he had to leave his cargo of birds, while he ran as fast as he was able.

After about four hours he heard her laughing taunts. He came, finally, to the point [shore] of the sea. There were the great gods, who already knew how badly he had done. They reprimanded him. He could not catch the woman again as he had done before. Thus for all time[,] people when they die cannot return to their houses.

The gods relented, however, and asked him if he wished the woman. If Kauymáli had done right, the woman would not have died in fifteen days. She would have come back to the sea as a little girl in order to return to her house. But because of Kauymáli's laxity, this could be true no longer.

Then the goddesses asked Kauymáli if the woman did not have ollas, looms, pots, cotton, gourd-bowls, metates, and the like. These had remained in her house since her death.

So they established the first death ceremony. They ordered Kauymáli (the first singer) to sing all night of [about] the woman, how she had worked, the gods she knew, whether she had been faithful—in fact all about her. The clothes in which she had died were to be offered to the gods.

When she was buried, her heart remained standing by the side of the grave.

While the mourners wash, the soul climbs up the cross at the grave and goes to the sky. There it finds its mother, Welika Uimali [Welíka Uimáli], the eagle of the sixth world region of above.

When the woman had climbed up to the sky, her mother reprimanded her. There was an oak tree on which she had played as a child, breaking its limbs. Hanging from the tree like a swarm of bees was a huge bunch of lice. When the woman was alive she had eaten lice. Now the lice were ordered to bite her.

The oak tree then asked her for her hand, saying that it wished to play with her (as she had with it when [she was] a child). When she complied, the oak tree caught her hand painfully tightly and ran off with her, throwing her finally a great distance. She returned to her (dead) companions at the sea. They told her that she had died for having wasted corn. Then they took thorny branches and beat her until she bled.

Her body, furthermore, bore signs of her intercourse with the Mexicans.[196] It was exceedingly ugly, like that of a rattlesnake. For this reason, and because she had mingled with the Mexicans, she had to go back down the cross to her grave and enter a Catholic church. When she came out of the church, she went to a little mesa where there was a *"wishache"* (Sp.) tree [species of *Acacia*]. Here were the *vergonzozos* ("shamed ones"). They beat her with the branches of a *palonde [palo de] muerte.*[197]

When she returned to the region of above, she sounded her horn. It was like the cry of doves. Her dead relatives heard this, and gathered around a fig-tree.

An animal, which she had killed in a trap when it was alive, was watching the road. It seized her, and had intercourse with her.

At another place was a grub *(kuetáeme)*, watching the trail with dogs on either side. She had starved these dogs when she was alive. So they bit her for punishment.

A little further on was a dove cooking tortillas. She was hungry and asked the dove to give her some food. Nearby, however, was a crow. Once, when he had robbed her corn-field, she had insulted him about his long beak. So he told the dove to give her nothing.

Then she met a dead Mexican. He was collecting his animals in his corral. If she had not had intercourse with the Mexicans, she would have been able to pass by unmolested.[198] But she had to dance five times at the place where she was to remain all the rest of the time. This was according to the command of the great gods of the sea.

Finally she got to the ranch of her dead relatives. They were having a feast, and singing all night. Kauymáli, who had followed her through all of her adventures, arrived during the feast in the midst of the dance. He shot her in the foot again, and she was changed into a mosquito as before. Then he took her away in another tube wadded with cotton.

This time he took her to the peyote country. He appealed to the singers, because she talked like an owl, fox, metate[-]bird, dove, and other animals of death.[199] They said, "Let her out of the reed, and give her a drop of tesgüino." And they looked for the tesgüino.[200]

The singers then asked her why she had died. She could talk a little now, because her heart was warmed with the tesgüino. She told them that her husband had killed her by beating her. Since he wasn't even sorry, she had died. "Although I left my children," she said, "I cannot go back. I am very 'delicate.' My face is black. I might kill them."[201]

But the singers of the peyote country took her back to the house. They held her by the arms and forced her along, shaking their shaman's plumes on high.

When they arrived, her family and husband were weeping. She had come as a fly, but was changed into a rock crystal. She could still talk, however.

Her family bathed the stone with the blood of sacrificed animals. They saluted it by pressing it between their hands. They also fed it, giving it food and drink. Then the rock went away to the mountain, where it was to forget its family.[202]

After this[,] the survivors closed the road with thorns, nopales, and *tusú*,[203] so that she could not come back. Where she went were plenty of plants and fruits and everything that she would need in her new life. The plant, tusú, was then burned, and the face and feet of the corpse painted, so that the soul would not return.[204]

All these ceremonies were finished around the fire, which was very "delicate" and had to be put out at dawn. The ashes were carefully thrown far away.[205]

Then the property of the dead woman was divided among her children. The people then ate soup made from the animals that had been killed in order to anoint the little stone (soul) with blood. All the food had to be eaten, for any left over would be very "delicate."

Thus did the singers of the ancient times establish the mourning customs, so that the souls of the dead cannot come back to molest their survivors. The souls had to go to the sea [Pacific Ocean].

Kauymáli returned to the birds he had brought for his wife. They grew and prospered. Thus are there many birds in the sierra.

c. The Birth, Puberty (?), [and] First Fruits Ceremonies Established

TumuSaúwi's five corn-houses were full of corn when sickness again attacked his house. Two of his other children got small-pox. He himself had been cured with the rubber-like sap.

The children were of corn. The Sun revealed to the father that he should continue to work in his corn-fields, therefore. He should produce much corn and take good care of his children.

But his corn did not prosper, and all of his animals died. So he was poor again.

He looked about for some old woman to cook for him now that his wife was dead. He found one who was named *oka héwi*.[206] He told her that he was very poor and could pay her only ten cents a month. She, however, wanted twenty-five. They agreed on twelve and a half ("un real").[207]

Meanwhile, in the store-house, weevils had ruined the corn. But the new woman worked hard and did not waste any of it as her predecessor had done. She also took good care of the children.

Now TumuSaúwi had made a vow to the Sun of chastity for five years.[208] For four years he had remained true to this vow. As his "delicate" period was about finished, he asked the woman to lay with him. She said that while she was content to work, she was not sure of joining with him since she was of a different race. "The gods would not like it," she said.

The people of her race, for another thing, had their hands and their feet turned backward. She pointed this out to TumuSaúwi, and suggested that he marry one of his own race.

So TumuSaúwi went to a woman of his own race. He asked her to marry him at the end of his vow and at the termination of his contract with the old woman who was taking care of his corn and children. But this woman was afraid of him. Everyone knew that he had beaten his other wife to death.

So TumuSaúwi told the old woman that the woman of his own race did not wish to marry him. Thinking the matter over, he decided that he wanted this old woman, who was not of his race. He waited five days before he talked to her again. Then he told her that he had dreamed. "Here I have given you many clothes and everything for your work," he said.

The woman replied, "I am only a poor, ignorant woman. My parents (who were dogs) are dead. I have no one to advise me and arrange this marriage. If I had, my heart, possibly, would guide me to marry you."

An intermediary had taken TumuSaúwi's message to the woman of his own race. He was sent back for a reply. Only fifteen days remained of TumuSaúwi's vow. The intermediary advised him to go to the woman and sleep beside her, but not to touch her.

Late that evening the woman was sitting by her house, thinking of the man, and wondering if he would beat her. She heard a slight noise outside on the bed. It was TumuSaúwi. He said, "*Tecéamuka* (Good evening)."

She replied, "*Taméweli* (Come in). It must be cold where you are going."

He answered, "I came here only to see you."

She said, "Come in. I have bad dogs that might bite you if they smell you." Both were dressed in their best clothes. They continued to talk.

She said, "Your intermediary came to tell me that you wish to marry me. Is that true?"

TumuSaúwi replied, "Yes, I did send someone to ask you. Now I have come myself. If my cook were of my own race, I would marry her. But you are better. Besides, you are of my race."

She said, "You have a bad reputation because you killed your other wife. I am afraid of you. One blow from you might kill me."

He answered, "No, I am not bad. My other wife ruined me with her bad habits. But I have never beat[en] my cook."

Thus they talked all night until the rooster crowed. Then they laid down on the same bed. They continued to talk, however.

The woman said, "I will arrange my belongings and bring them where you can meet me. It should be on some hill where we can embrace."

The man awaited her at the appointed place. They sat down together, took hands, and greeted each other affectionately. At dark they left for his house. When they arrived, they opened her package. It contained bowls and kitchen utensils. She slept alone, while he slept in another house.

This was the last night that the héwi woman had contracted to work for TumuSaúwi. The next morning she left, taking with her all her things — leaving, however, beans, salt, and nixtamal (corn boiled in lye [lime]).

That night TumuSaúwi had intercourse with his wife. In twenty days she was advanced in pregnancy. In five days more a child was born.

After five days the mother and child could be bathed. Komatéame, an old woman, officiated at this ceremony.[209] First she filled five gourd-bowls with tamales. One was made in the form of a human head (a custom still followed by the Huichols). These were placed on the altar in the god-house. The father baptized the paraphernalia with the typical Huichol ceremonial spitting.

Then they brought the child, still covered with blood, as was the mother. Using a little tuft of cotton, Komatéame bathed the child lightly with sacred water. Then she "cleansed" the child's body with shaman's plumes. At dawn[,] water was heated. Then both mother and child were "cleansed." The Sun named the child *mowele teami* (feathers [beautiful prayer feathers]). Such a name lasts throughout life.

After this[,] the mother took the tamales from the god-house. Another child wished to eat them, but could not for it would die. Only the midwife and the grandmother *(teokále [taokari])* could eat of this special food.

The child grew very fast. But in fifteen days it became sick and vomited. This continued for five days. The father then went to the midwife. He told her to call her grandson (Kauymáli?) to come and see what was the matter. He came and studied the trouble. Finally he slept and dreamed that the great gods of the fifty temples of the sea wanted the child. Thus the child had to be presented to them.

"Therefore make arrows and votive-bowls," he said. "Buy candles, and take them to the caves of the great gods. Take them a painted board *(etáli)* with colored crewel. Tatevalí (Grandfather Fire) is angry. Take him the etáli, and also votive-bowls decorated with beads. This is why the child is sick."

The parents said, "We must take our child and present it there. Large black beans must be cooked. Five little heads made of tamale must be offered to Nakawé, as well as a wool [rubber] ball *(iouli uli)*. With it Nakawé will play with the gods to see whether the child will live."[210] They did not sleep, therefore, but went to the cave.

Komatéame, the midwife, went in first. Nakawé approached, and they tossed up the ball, which stuck to her hip-bone. She came up very close, holding the ball tightly so that the child would not die.

Nakawé then grasped the ball with one hand, while Komatéame held it with the other. The child was placed on the ball, and thus supported in their hands. They sang in the language of the great gods, offering the child to all of the great gods and those of the six directions. Being thus introduced, the child would be known by the gods, who would be gentle with it. Thus it would not be sick.

All this was done, and Nakawé and Komatéame both promised that the child would get well. These goddesses gave the child the name of tsikúli (god-eye), which has ever since had a special value for children.[211]

The mother became pregnant again. Another child was born. This was "bathed" in the same way.

When these two children grew up, they married and relieved their parents of much of the work, according to the commands of Nakawé and Komatéame. They in their turn had children. Soon there were many Huichols.

Now the old man, TumuSaúwi, gave them strict orders not to go to the feasts of other races. Otherwise they would be ruined (as he had been), and their women raped by the other men. Their women were not "opened." Neither were their boys developed. Since this was true, brothers married sisters.

When the first boy was mature, the father put up arrows by the fire to protect him against snake-bites and other dangers of the sierra.[212] Meanwhile the boy set lasso-traps for deer. If he was successful, he would have a long and successful life.[213]

The boy soon found fresh deer tracks. With his five dogs he chased a male deer into one trap and a female deer into another. Thus he was assured of a long life.[214]

Then, on a mountain far away, he saw a male and female eagle with beautiful feathers. He, in competition with several others, shot at them. In these times the arrows were old style: they had stone points. The arrow of the boy went through the hearts of both eagles in the same shot. He skinned the birds, leaving the tail and wing feathers intact. This was an additional sign of long life for him.[215] Then he stretched the eagle-skins inside the god-house, according to the command of the great gods.

All the ceremonial paraphernalia was anointed with the blood of the deer. The meat was roasted in the earth oven. Only the adults, however, could eat of it. The boy himself could not eat it. After the feast[,] his elders began to discuss whom he might marry. They set up five votive-bowls. At midnight the old woman awakened, shouting that she had dreamed well.

The next day they found twenty-five crotched sticks [poles with a forked end]. Taking these, the people made a ceremonial circuit of the world. On the fifth circuit they found five animal holes. They forced the stakes into the holes, until they heard the cries of animals from within. Soon they found what they were looking for.

"What animals have we here?" they asked.

They were lizards (*kacipáli [kácipli]*, H., iguanas, Sp.). The people pinned them down with the stakes [forked poles], and then dug them out. They broke their legs so they could not run, and also knocked out their teeth.

They hunted until they had captured fifty lizards. These were taken back to the ranchería, where they arrived about dusk. They travelled slowly, because their load was heavy.

When they arrived, they opened the first one and used its blood to bathe the blood [sacred paraphernalia] of Nakawé, and also the paraphernalia of the other gods. This was done by the women, and corresponded to the offering of deer's blood by the boy. Thus would the girl have a successful life also.[216]

The boy and girl could now marry. This they did. They also had children.

At one time all their children became sick. They called Kauymáli the curer. He told them to carry offerings of votive-bowls to the peyote country. If, however, they were unable to get there, they were to go to a cave near Santa Catarina, belonging to the goddess, Stuluwíakame. This had been revealed to Kauymáli by the Sun.

When this was done, they painted their faces with the peyote designs.

Now there was a nopal (cactus) and many other trees, including five pines, the owners of which were the great gods. By listening carefully, Kauymáli was able to get into communication with the great gods, using the sound of his drum. Thus it was revealed that the parents must sing to the music of the drum. This would please the gods, and the children would get well.[217]

Then Kauymáli took his shaman's plumes and went to the woods where there were many flowers. He came across a short, thick tree. This must have been hollowed out and left there by the gods, because the whirlwind had deposited here a teapáli on which to make a fire for heating the drum-head.[218]

At night, without even a light, they returned to the tree according to the command of the tree. They walked with the greatest care, since the tree was very "delicate."

Then they cut out the tree and let it down very carefully, holding it gently. They did not dare let it fall, as it would make a noise. They cut off a section about three feet long. This was wrapped carefully in blankets, and brought back by a boy. He was followed by the others. Just as the roosters were crowing, they arrived back at the ranchería. They placed the tree-section in the god-house before the Sun came up.

The next day they took off the bark, and then thinned the hollow tree into the form of the upright drum. The child by this time was a little better. The gods, however, revealed that more work was necessary.

So they had to go and set traps for five deer. That night they sang to aid the hunters. When the Sun came up the next day, two deer had been killed. The following day three more had fallen into the traps. Now the people could drink water again.

The deer were brought in. Kauymáli said, "This means life for the sick child."

They cooked the meat. The skin of the first deer was prepared to be used as the top of the drum.[219] The child got well.

It was September. Soon the feasts of elote [first fruits ritual] were to begin. The people prepared corn for tesgüino. Other deer were caught. All prepared rattles *(káitsa)* and other necessary paraphernalia.

The first night they gathered around the fire and told the sacred tribal myths.[220] At dawn the singer beat the new drum. The rooster soon crowed, and dawn came. The child was saved.

The children's faces were washed and then painted.[221] Then shaman's plumes and god-eyes were placed on ribbons on their heads. They were held by their mothers, who were seated in a circle between the altar and the drum, so that they might participate in the singing.

The shaman sang of all the gods, so that the children would learn and have long life. Then, in the afternoon, young men brought in five deer. When the singing was stopped, a stool was brought in for the killer of the deer. He was given fifty gourds of tesgüino. The tesgüino was sacred. Then the older men gathered about him in a circle, and told him that his success meant that he would have long life.

The boy's god-father[222] was there, well dressed. He was brought to the boy.

Only the boy could drink the sacred tesgüino. He also took the tamales. They were refilled [replaced], then others were brought, and they were refilled [replaced] also.

The boy filled his kerchief with tamales. He was given shaman's plumes, ribbons, and arrows. His wife was given beads, finery, and face-paint. All this was given as payment for killing the deer. Then the boy and the girl (his wife, no doubt) took seats to one side.[223]

All night the sacred myth was sung, explaining all of the Huichol customs. With this song the sick child was finally cured.

On the altar were squashes and ears of green corn. These had plumes stuck into them and, by means of flowers, were bathed with sacred water so that the new food would not make the people sick.[224] The first fruits were then danced in a ceremonial circuit around the patio all during the night (at intervals). At each of the six points they were presented in a different language, according to the word of the singers.[225]

This ceremony was given to take out the bad arrows that might be in the new fruits, which remained clear and pure.[226] A bit of food was offered to Grandfather Fire for him to eat.[227]

By dawn the new fruits were finally purified. Food now could be eaten. All throughout the rainy season the new fruits could not be eaten, along with deer, salt, and other "delicate" things.[228] Squash could now be eaten, as also deer-meat and salt.

Since in the peyote-country a grasshopper had lost his wings, the finery was taken off the children. The shaman's plumes represented the grasshopper's wings.[229]

Now the people could eat and drink their full [fill]. Tesgüino was drunk in great quantities, so that they might celebrate the breaking of their fast from deer-meat and salt during the rainy season. Squash, deer-soup, and salt were also consumed.

But Kauymáli said to the parents, "You may not have sexual intercourse for five days, until some clearing of a new field is done and deer killed.[230] If you have intercourse, your children will surely die."

The shaman, on [for] his part, had to work a whole month before he could even eat salt. Then he offered a whole handful to the fire.[231]

After five days, when deer had been killed, the green corn could be cut for this feast. The corn had to be blessed to remove any bad arrows.

As soon as the deer had been killed, they called the shaman and repeated the feast for the new corn.[232]

d. Pálikata (Elder Brother?) Saves TumuSaúwi's Abandoned Child, Which Becomes the Water-Goddess, Na'aliwaeme

Another child became sick. Fifteen people who were not singers wished to try and cure it. They were at a loss [about] what to do, because they did not know how to dream.[233] One tried for five days, but the child got worse. Then the others tried, but their efforts were futile. The parents paid all their money to these fakes.

Finally, when all [of them] had tried, Kauymáli asked "Were any of them able to help?"

The child meanwhile had become so sick that its parents could not sleep any more because of its crying and vomiting. Furthermore, they used up all their pitch-pine torches taking care of it at night. They began to give up hope. The mother thought it might be better to expose the child to death behind the house. So she stripped it, and left it naked, crying in the hot sunlight.

Pálikata and Ereno in the middle region of the world saw this.[234] They knew that the curers were no good. Indeed, Pálikata hoped that the parents would throw the child away. He considered the child a younger brother and was sorry for it.[235] Since he knew how to cure, at dawn, just as the rooster was crowing, he approached the dying child. He took it up and "cleaned" it without the mother's knowledge.[236] Then he carried it away.

In five days the father of the child wondered what had happened to his off-spring. He was angry when he was told what the mother had done. He ordered her to go and see whether the child were dead or alive. But the woman found nothing save tracks where it had struggled when sick, and the moisture of the perspiration it had left.

Pálikata had taken the child to another ranchería, Tsirai'atua. Here the people took care of it. They "cleaned" it of its sickness. Soon the child got well. It was then given a toy bow and toy arrows.

Then Pálikata and the child went on to *namatúr*. Here the child played, while Pálikata picked flowers for it. These flowers the child, Tsikuakame, strewed all along the road. Further, as he went with Pálikata, he shot arrows with the toy boy [bow]. Soon he had used up his last five arrows.

Along the road they found a small *petate* on which they could sit. This petate took away all the remaining fever of the boy.[237] Here the boy left a bunch of grass as a sign that they had passed that way.

Then they arrived at a damp place, and here the boy left signs made of mud. He was told to play in a spring. This left the water muddy. Thus they went on, leaving signs. They came to a cave. They entered very carefully so that the boy would not fall.

The cave floor was clean and level.

The child was growing up. Pálikata asked him if he wished to live in the cave. When he said yes, Pálikata changed him into a girl by taking away his bow and arrows.[238]

The girl spat in the center of the cave, and there was a teapáli. She spat again, and this time a snake appeared on the top of the teapáli.[239] Then she painted marks on the walls of the cave.

They continued on to another cave, *twokali*, where there is a rock named *kwaSa*. From there they went to *uulípa*. Then they went to *kuitapulista* (named place), where there is a round rock. Here the girl left an arrow. From there they went to *halakuna* (which is near Monte Escobedo). Then they came to *wipílita*, a green tree suggesting a [hair-]net *(wipí)*. They continued on to *muúmukaka* (*muu*, head, H.), so named because of a feature, near Monte Escobedo, that suggests a head. They arrived at *corral prieto* (Sp.), and from there went to (La Huerta, Sp.). Then they arrived at the oak, *tuaSámuieye*. They continued on to *kuka reveda* (Reveda, Sp.). Then they went on to *suláwimuyaka*. They arrived at *kuieyanalíla*. Here the girl left five little hills of earth. From there they went on to *hakumaíyewi*, and to Sawáapa (where there is a story of a sheep-horn). Then they arrived at *topína mayewí* (humming-bird). They continued on to *manoúami*, and then to Tsawílo, and then on to *kuiSu uwini*.

By this time they were drawing near where Father Sun was waiting for them at a place called *neatálisi*. Here the girl amused herself by picking flowers,[240] black, blue, white, yellow, and purple (or lavender). As she went on, she dropped these flowers. From them[,] beads of these colors sprang up.

Soon they drew near the door of the house of the girl's new mother. The new mother embraced the girl and played with her. Then they took her to see the things they were going to give her. They told her that her new brother and new father were waiting for her. So they went on. They made five efforts to arrive at her new father, but he was too far away. Finally they climbed a small hill. There was a large votive-bowl[,] which was filled magically with water. It held also a large candle. The girl was told to take this, dance with it, and not drop it, lest she die. So she danced.[241] Then they bathed her in the sea while the Sun looked on.

She was given a house and fields where she could stay. Thus she was dedicated to be a goddess of water,[242] being changed into this goddess.

Meanwhile the real mother had started out, following the signs her child had left. She did this because her husband blamed her for having abandoned the sick child. He had said to her, "You must find my child."

The first time she looked she found nothing save the marks of the child's writhings when it was sick, and also the water of its sweat. Later, however, she dreamed[243] where to go to look for the child's tracks. She then had to go to the gods to find this out. Arriving there she was met by the singer. The singer asked, "Why are you sad? What has happened to you?" She told him everything about the sick child. He told her to follow the tracks where she had dreamed of them.

But she did not know exactly where this was. Finally, after making five[244] circuits of the house, she found the tracks. She listened to them and found that they were of her child. They told her that a long time had elapsed since the child had passed that way. They said that Elder Brother (Pálikata) had gone by also, but without remarking where they were going.[245]

So the woman followed the tracks. She found the five colors of flowers left by the child, then more signs, and then the teapáli with the snake (painted) on it. The snake informed her of the passage of Pálikata and the child.

In five days she was able to arrive at last where her child was. But the child denied her mother, because the woman had abandoned her to die. She preferred her new mother. The mother then told the god-mother of the sufferings she had endured in the pursuit of her child. She begged for her child, who was now a water-goddess and as such in the bottom of a spring where she was well and could eat.[246] The god-mother, however, refused to surrender the water-goddess.

So the mother had to communicate with the sea (the greater water-goddesses), and ask them to have the child given up. She said to them "I have found my child, but the woman will not give her to me. She would not take her out of the water."

The gods told her that the child could not go back, but that she would return in the rains. They said, "You will have to make her a house with ceremonial paraphernalia and fields." The water-goddess child would need corn-fields. Thus whenever it rained, she would be not be [*sic*] able to come except as water.[247]

The water-goddess came as a green cloud[,][248] which rose from the spring and flew overhead until it approached her house. She was to fall as water. Within the cloud she had taken the form of a large snake of pure water. This cloud struck with other clouds, causing lightning and thunder.[249] If this sound did not frighten the parents of the water-goddess child, it would mean that they were really waiting for her.

The lightning fell. It knocked down a great pine in each of the five directions around the parent's house. This had been determined by Stuluwíakame, the foster-mother who ordered the corn to grow. A great storm of water passed five times over the house. In the house the people were very frightened by the falling lightning. The water-goddess was disappointed in her parents. She returned to her foster-mother.

On her return she arrived at the cave where she had spit the teapáli with the snake on it.[250] This cave is [N]a'aliwaeme kokalita, and is near Santa Catarina.

The painted snake became real again, and lived with the rain-goddess girl. She ordered the Huichols to bring them the first fruits of squashes of which they are the owners.[251] The people came with their offerings and prayed. They had to bring also their first ears of green corn, and votive-bowls anointed (bathed) with the blood of deer, sheep, and cattle. God-chairs also had to be brought as offerings.[252]

Then the goddess said to the Huichols, "When you harvest, sell the first of the crop and leave me one peso of the money gained from the sale. Here you can get water with which I will guard you. In your houses give feasts, killing animals bought with the money from the sale of my corn. Make five little god's shaman's-chairs so that I can communicate with the shamans when they sit in large ones singing."[253] Thus would the water-goddess tell the people why they and the animals get sick. She would protect the people.

In the cave the water-goddess had a large water-jar about twelve inches high.[254] It was painted with five snakes. This was left when water was taken from the cave. There were also smaller jars to hold the stone heart of the water-goddess. She ordered that money be offered in the large one. She commanded the people not to eat salt. Further, they were to have a ceremonial bath in the waters of the cave, pray, and take candles to her cave.[255]

e. Na'aliwaeme Gives Increase of Crops and Cattle for the Fulfillment of Special Vows

The water-goddess said, "When you enter the cave, go to the spring. As an offertory for the increase of cattle, save up offerings for five years. On approaching the water[,] you (the Huichols) must light candles."

When the first Huichols did as they were bid, they took out a small water-snake, *hakuiakáme*[256] (*salamacoa*, Sp.)[,] as they filled their gourds. The snake was very pretty. The women listened to what it said. Although it was very sacred, they carried it off wrapped up in their kerchiefs.[257] When the water is taken from the spring in the cave, a bull is apt to bellow, and then the water moves.[258] As they left, they saw a peso in the cave. This they took also, wrapped up like the snake.[259]

When they arrived home, they consulted a shaman. He told them to make a large box for these sacred things.

In five days the money had increased in the box. Also, the animals that had been bathed in the sacred water from the cave of the goddess increased.[260]

Almost at the end of five years the large box was about full of money. The snake, too, had given many cattle to be taken care of.[261]

Both the money and the animals were still "delicate" and might drive their owners crazy.

Among the cattle was a large bull. They listened to its horns. Then they dreamed that the water-jar said to cut off one of them.[262] It was so large it would hold a bushel; but it was cut off. It was well decorated and hidden in a pouch. Then the man went to a high hill and sounded his horn to call his many animals. At the sound the animals came together. Then the man went back to his house.

During all these five years the man was able to fulfill his vow of [sexual] continence. The woman, however, could not stand it. At a feast another man made love to her. He found out that she had money, and deceived her into thinking that the potsherds he carried were money also. So she surrendered, and he took her. Then she ate cheese, and this made her sick.

The shaman knew that he could not cure her. She had broken her vow of [sexual] continence that had been made in return for the increase of cattle and money.[263] He said to her, "You will not die, however. You may go to the mountains and see how it all comes out." The woman then confessed that she had been seduced and paid with false money, and also that she had eaten cheese. The shaman answered, "Your husband will sound his horn. Go to the mountains and see what the animals do to you. If they leave you unharmed, don't come back to your house."

So the husband sounded his horn. The bulls got angry, attacked the woman, and knocked her very far. The man did not attempt to save her because by this [sign] he knew of her guilt.

Within five days all the money and cattle were gone due to the woman's sin. The rain had taken them back to the cave. There the peso and the snake had been taken also. The man complained to the gods, for only thirty dollars and one bull were left.

Then the woman went crazy and wandered in the mountains. The mountain winds[264] (known as *haiwakame*) said to her, "I wonder where you will die."[265]

She went from ranch to ranch, asking for tortillas, but the wind scared her away from her food.[266] In her pouch she carried potsherds, thinking that they were cheese. She offered these in exchange for food. The water-gods of the sea said to her finally, "When the first rains come, you will die in a water-hole called *matiSasáwa*."[267]

Soon she died, coming out of the water-hole as pure air. This place is where Tukákame lives.

The man now told his family that he would vow to fast for five more years. "Let us ask for another favor from the *cantera* [volcanic stone used to make statues of gods] in the cave,"[268] he said, "and this time we must fast."

So he went and offered to serve for another five years. He took some more sacred water. Then he said to his family, "Do not act as my wife did, because I am very 'delicate.'"

f. Na'aliwaeme Aids the Survivor of Black Magic and Punishes the Unsuccessful Shamans

Five women were attracted by the man's new wealth. They approached him when he was sleeping, and offered themselves to him. But he would not take them. So they went to a wizard *(chapára tikiawaai)*, and asked him to curse the man and make him die.[269] The wizard, a well[-]dressed boy *hiwas*, came out of the sea this day. He said, "Let us see if he has strength enough to resist."

Then the wizard left thorns at his victim's door. If the man stepped on them when he awoke, he would die.

When the man awoke, he did step on the thorns. He had dreamed that five snakes would bite him. He scratched out the thorns, but it did no good. In five days he was very sick.[270]

So he called in five singers to cure him. They sucked thorns out of all parts of his body. Then they queried, "Who caused this?" The man did not know, so they set a watch [appointed a guard] to see what would happen. The chanter who was watching dreamed of snakes trying to kill the man.[271] He was so frightened that he climbed up on to the roof. That night he dreamed again, and this time of snakes that came and looked for him. They flew up and bit him, even though he was on the roof. This was a very bad omen.

Another night the shaman feared that his enemy would win unless he remained away from his wife and refrained from eating salt.[272] So he slept near the water, and allowed the snakes to bite the sick man.

The shaman finally dreamed who the five women were. He asked the man if they had not invited him to have intercourse with them. When the man admitted that they had, the *cantador* [singing shaman] knew that the patient was enchanted [bewitched]. Thus the shaman doubted whether he would be able to save the sick man.

The sick man now thought that his time had come to die. He called his children to him, and told them that he was enchanted [bewitched]. Within seven days he died, after telling his children to bury him wrapped up in five blankets along with five pesos. After he had barely touched their hands, he died.

So he was buried. This left only four of his family alive. But the enchantment [wizard's spell] followed his children, and one by one they died.[273]

Finally there remained only two. One of these was a woman. She took care of the few animals left by her father. The curers who had attempted to save her father asked her to pay them for their services, saying that such was her father's order. "You must pay for your brothers also, even if they all died," the curers said. But these were mere lies.

The woman retorted, "What kind of people are you, trying to collect from me? You say that my dead relatives said so, but they told me nothing. Wait a little until I consult my heart. I am confused at present. If my heart tells me to make this payment, I will pay. I must also talk to those things left by my family. So please wait for five days."

For five days she pondered. She disliked this claim, inasmuch as her family had told her of all their debts before they died. She went to the magic cantera in the cave of Na'aliwaeme and prayed to it.[274] The cantera [statue] told her that her father would have made it known to her if he owed any money. It said, "Your father and mother came to me and asked for increase of money and cattle. I helped them. I see how it will come out."

The woman said, "My father was very just in all his obligations. Now he is ruined. My brother and I are all alone and poor as well. Now they wish to ruin us[,] too. You helped my father and mother. Please guide me in this matter."

Na'aliwaeme, the owner of animals, replied to the woman in a dream.[275] "Go," she said, "and I will wait for you at noon tomorrow." At the appointed time she arrived in a breeze. She came to the one good house left by the dead father. When the door opened, the woman asked, "Who opened this door?" At the door were tracks, reversed heel-first. Thus the woman knew that it was the people who were enchanting [bewitching] her.

The Sun said to her in a dream,[276] "They came the day before, and they would leave nothing until all was arranged in some way." Then he promised to help her.

The woman then dreamed that the evil-doers came out shouting. Her problem now was to find out what they were saying. She greeted them, and all began to talk. She concealed the fact, however, that she suspected them because of their reversed footprints.

They said, "You must pay us certain animals and money. We have orders for this. Pay us now, for if we die[,] we will lose."

The woman replied, "I have not done anything, for I have not understood how these things are. But you will not lose, since there will be an owner even if all my family dies. You are certain to be paid. With the little money that I receive, all will be arranged. I will make an effort to get the money within five days." She talked in this fashion, because the Sun had told her to say to them what would please them most.

Continuing, she said, "I can, however, give you but one of my two animals within five days."

"We need it now," they replied. "Please favor us by giving it to us now. But if you cannot, we will have to wait."

The woman answered, "Although this is an inconvenience for you, I still have to follow the dictates of my heart. I am very sorry to delay you. But I will await you (at a certain spot) in five days."

Her heart told her to give them nothing. The cantera said the same thing.[277] The cantera said, "I am going to talk to the great gods. This is very unjust. I will be ready within five days."

So Na'aliwaeme shot an arrow. It went to the great gods of the sea. They asked, "Who shot this arrow? What words does it tell? You, the middle god, listen; and tell us what it says."[278]

So the middle god took up the arrow and listened to it. It told him all that had happened.[279] The gods were disturbed at this. They decided to answer, so that they might resist the demands of the wicked people.

The answer was conveyed by means of an arrow[,] which arrived while Na'aliwaeme was seated in her chair. She got the answer. Then she called for the girl.

The woman came and talked to the goddess. She did not dare to raise her face, nor could she approach very close.

Then she left, and went back to take care of her animals. She heard a second call, and went again. This time she was told not to be afraid[,] since the great gods were on her side.

Another day she came to talk, remaining at some distance. Na'aliwaeme ordered her to approach, but she stood still. Then she heard the sandals of the evil-doers who were bothering the animals. The goddess said, "Come over and get behind me." Then she left to watch her animals.

That night, as she was sleeping, she dreamed what the great gods had said.

They had said, "Do not be afraid. We will give you measure for courage. Wait, even if they take your animals."

Late, when the Sun was half-way up to the horizon, the evil-doers came. They made a wide circle of [around] Na'aliwaeme, who had hidden the girl behind her shaman's chair. The goddess read their thoughts, and knew that they were planning to steal the girl's cattle that very night. This staggered [alarmed] the girl, who had not been apprised of anything other than her ultimate victory.

The evil-doers said, "Now we will have to wait until another night."

Thus encouraged, the girl began to believe that she might win after all. So she waited patiently for what might come. Then she went to sleep, and was guarded by the magic water-jar [deity represented by the statue].

The fifth day, according to their word, the evil-doers returned and approached very close. The animals were ready. If the evil-doers took them, the girl would be able to see what they were doing.

Na'aliwaeme, however, knew everything that would happen. She said, "Let us talk to the god of fire [Grandfather Fire]. He will help us so that the curing-shamans will not finish this family completely."

The Fire told them to make an oven and build a fire. He gave Na'aliwaeme a magic arrow. Now they knew what to do. They made the oven. The Fire talked to them and to Father Sun by means of a breeze. Fire said to the Sun, "Look, I have news of what is happening to the girl."

The Sun replied, "I will help her too. I can do even more than Na'aliwaeme. I have knowledge now that will enable me to act."

The answer of the Sun in the form of an arrow fell to those about the fire. The animals were beginning to die, due to the efforts of the wizard. So they hurried to catch the evil-doers.

Then Na'aliwaeme requested the bad shamans to come near and talk. The gods came down as five whirlwinds from the sea.[280] These whirlwinds snatched up the evil-doers and carried them near the great gods. The great gods wished to learn whether they had children or companions. Then they tied them and held them head-down into the fire of the oven until they were roasted.[281]

E   The Snake-Man's Illicit Love for the Wife of a Huichol Begets the First Rain and Curing Singers of the Huichols

The Snake-people, Háiku, were born in the sea. They grew for twenty-five days until they became men. Near the sea was the *ranchería* where they had been children. Before they grew up, they wished to see if anyone knew them. So, accompanied by a man, they went to a spring. There they sat down on a large rock. The man said to them, "I will wait here for you." And there he waited for five days while the Snake-men went for water.

Huichol girls came to the spring. Something was left at the spring, and on the sixth day the girls found a little pile of sand as a sign. They wondered who had left the sign.

The next day they found a piece of driftwood which [that] had been cut. They wondered at this. The next day they found a beautiful green stone. The third day they found a little green onion. Thought they, "Who is leaving these things?" They took these signs in their hands and studied them closely.

The next day they came across a foot-print in the sand. The following day they found fresh spittle.

That night one of the girls had a dream.[1] This told her that on the following day she would meet someone at the spring. He would be the one who had left the signs. She dreamed[2] also that she would speak to him.

When she awoke, she told her husband that she had dreamed poorly. But she went to the spring anyway. There she encountered a man who was dressed in full Huichol finery.[3] He had a painting on one cheek; his wool shirt was blue; and the cord of his sandal reached halfway up his leg.

The man threw a rock into the water to attract her attention. She did not see him until he had thrown five pebbles in the water.

She was thinking, "Who are these people that I cannot see? Who is throwing stones into the water?"

The man spoke to her. "I threw the stones in the water. I live here. This is my house. I have been looking for you for a long time. I wish to talk to you about my thoughts."

"Hurry and finish talking," the girl said, "for I have much to do."

The Snake-man replied, "I left signs for you. These you have found. You surely must care for me, else you would never have looked at them so long. And you must have hidden these things so that your husband would not know about them."

"Yes," the girl answered, "I hid them. My husband would have hurt me."

The Snake-man then said, "From now on we shall meet here at the spring. I will always wait here for you."

"I will come back in five days," the girl promised.

She went back home. But at the end of the five days she returned to the spring. She was somewhat afraid of what might happen to her. She carried her water-gourd, as though coming for water, but she looked carefully on all sides as she approached.

The man was waiting for her. He bade her approach him. Then he took her hand, although she was half trembling from fear. They played together amorously for a while. Finally she sat in his lap. They caressed and interlocked legs. Then she went back to her house, saying that she would come back the next day.

The second time she was not so afraid, because she had been "gentled." She brought him a handful of salt for a present.[4] She told him to take it quickly, or her husband and family would know of her amorous tryst. Having "gentled" the girl, the man caressed her.

The next day the man brought her a little wild onion.[5] This she hid. But her husband smelled it and asked, "Who brought this wild onion into the house? No one has been here save us."

She replied, "Who knows? I am sure I don't."

The Snake-man knew that the husband had found the wild onion. He told the girl that he had heard all. He warned her that henceforth she would have to be more careful. This time he brought her nothing. But they continued their erotic play.

The husband, a Huichol of the first times, began to wonder why his wife spent so much time at the spring. She neither bathed herself nor washed clothes. Asked about it, she made a lame excuse. This made her husband more angry and suspicious. So he decided to go and watch.

But the Snake-man (Háiku) knew of the husband's approach. He hid himself. The woman came, got water, and went quickly away. Thus the suspicions of her husband were allayed. Her husband said to her, "I dreamed badly. I dreamed that you were false to me."[6]

His wife replied, "That is not true. Do not believe it. It is a mere dream."

The husband said, "Don't go to the spring again. I will send someone else for water for the next five or ten days. You stay here and work." So he sent others for water. But they found nothing, and came quickly back.

When the husband was asleep, Háiku approached the woman and quietly awakened her. He asked her why she no longer came to the spring. He begged her to come on the following day, saying that he longed for her.

The next day the woman asked her husband if she might go to the spring.

She offered to take her child with her. The husband told the child to go along and follow the mother. It was to watch all that happened. But the mother told the child to tell the father nothing. She ordered it to stay behind, saying that she had to go to the spring. But the child would not let her get away alone.

That night Háiku again approached. He asked her why she had not been at the spring the day before. She told him that her husband had refused to let her go unless she took the child. Háiku said that he would bribe the child.

The next day, when the woman left with her child, she said to the child, "I will pay you five pesos if you do not tell what happens."

The child replied, "Better that you do not pay me. I will not tell anyway. The money you give me might not turn out well."

So the child stayed at the spring. The woman went up the arroyo to where the Snake-man was waiting. Here the two remained a long time. The Snake-man had his way with the woman as much as he desired.

After a long time the husband began to call the woman. So the lovers arranged that Háiku should come to her house that night in hopes that the husband would be gone. Thus, when the husband dropped asleep, the Snake-man would be able to engage the woman in talk and intercourse.

That night the husband dreamed[7] that God,[8] Father Sun, told him that his parents knew all that was happening in the house. He related the dream to his wife. She said that it was not true. But the husband decided to sleep with his wife in his arms. Sleeping thus, he dreamed[9] that he saw some kind of animal. He asked his wife what kind of animal it was that would not let him sleep.

After thirty days the woman was pregnant both by her husband and by Háiku, the Snake-man, who had had intercourse with her. The husband suspected this. He accused her of "being full of another man."[10] The woman denied all this, protesting that she had been faithful to him.

Five days later she began to smell like a snake. "What have you anointed yourself with? Snake fat?" asked her husband.

"No," the woman replied. "I smell bad because I am dirty and have not bathed."

Father Sun told the husband in a dream what was happening.[11] He informed the man that his wife was having intercourse with an animal. Father Sun did not like it that a woman should be pregnant both by a man and a snake.[12] For this reason he had told the husband.

"I cannot, however, tell you which animal it was," said the Sun. "You must fast for five days in order to learn this. Do not drink water for five days, because this animal owns the water."[13]

So the husband fasted from water for five days. His wife often put water before him. But he would say that he was cold from anger and that he dared not drink water. He would touch only one tortilla. The woman wondered why he was so serious.

On the fifth day the husband went to a sacred hill. He told his wife that he would be back the next day. He went to this hill to try to learn who had approached his wife.[14] But although he sat there all day, nothing happened.

While the husband was away, Háiku, the Snake-man, came out of a pot in the house and sat in the kitchen. At midnight the husband came back unexpectedly. Háiku, however, heard the sound of the husband's sandals. So he hid himself again in the pot that was in the kitchen.[15]

The woman was weaving when her husband returned. He ate only a tortilla, and did not touch water.

Soon the husband fell asleep. He dreamed[16] that a snake fell on him. On awakening, however, he found nothing but the air. Thus he spent five more days upon the hill. By this time his wife smelled so strongly of snakes that he slept alone by a fire outside of the kitchen.

That night he dreamed that on the morrow he should refrain even from eating tortillas for five days if he wished to find out who was sharing his wife.

At the end of five days the husband heard Háiku talking. But the Snake-man was at such a great distance that he could not make out what kind of animal he was. So he decided to fast for five more days, even though his heart was burning with thirst.

Meanwhile the woman was approaching her hour of labor.

On the third day, when the husband came back from the sacred hill, he heard his wife talking with a man. He approached very quietly. But Snake-man heard his footfall and disappeared. So he found only the woman.

That night the husband dreamed that Father Sun told him that on the fifth day he would learn who was sharing his wife with him. So the next day he went to the sacred hill. At noon Snake-man left the husband's house to answer a call of nature. He was dressed in all the Huichol finery. The husband saw him, but remained very quiet. At last he knew the truth.

He waited for a short while. Then he put new points on his arrows and sharpened his machete. With his bow and arrows he approached the house very quietly. But the Snake-man heard him and changed into air.[17]

The husband asked his wife where the Snake-man was. She said that she was alone. The husband then accused her of intimacy with the man whom he had seen. But the woman protested [professed] her love for her husband and embraced him. This pacified him, and he asked for something to eat.

Surrounding their ranchería by the side of the sea were five other rancherías.

The husband went to one where there were twenty-five young men. He presented himself to the eldest, and asked for help from all of them. They promised to help him.

The husband said, "I have an enemy who is very strong. Therefore I need your help."

At the other four rancherías the husband asked for twenty more men to help him.

All these men were posted in this fashion: five at the door of the house; five behind the house; five at each of the cardinal points, etc. Here they were posted just to watch, which was not very hard work. They brought with them their lassos, bows, arrows, machetes, and knives. If Háiku came out, they were to kill him, even though he might kill the husband, who planned to go into the house.

When all was ready, the husband went bravely into the house. It was three in the morning. The woman realized that there were many men surrounding the house. In rushed the husband, and began to search through all her belongings. He knocked down that pot in which the Snake-man (Háiku) was hiding. Out rolled a huge snake.

The husband called aloud to the men as he shot five arrows into the snake. As Snake-man tried to escape, the men struck at him with their machetes and threw their lassos over him. Even so, Snake-man was not killed, but continued to run off. The people followed.

The snake ran off about fifty yards, even though filled with arrows. It arrived at an arroyo near the sea where there is a rock twenty-five meters high. Here it descended to its hole and got into the water.[18]

Soon it began to storm and thunder, so that the people could not follow to kill the Snake-man.[19]

Snake-man went down to the bottom of the water and told his relatives of his misfortunes. The water fairly boiled as hundreds of Háiku came out of the water.[20] They thought that Snake-man would die.

The same day the woman bore her child. The husband now knew who shared with him in its paternity.[21] He decided to go out and see if the snake was dead. He told his wife that she was not a Huichol, like he was, because of her intercourse with the Snake-man.[22]

"I don't love you anymore," he said. "You are a devil and an animal."

Then he shot arrows at her and killed her with his machete. When she was dead, he took her body to the arroyo for Háiku to find. The man, further, did not want the child because it was only half his.

Father Sun told the Huichols where the body of Háiku was hanging as a huge snake filled with arrows.

When it began to get dark, the many snakes of Háiku's family approached the ranch of the husband. They overflooded it with water.[23] This happened while the men were looking for the body of the Snake-man. The snakes had come also to see the child, which was their half-brother. But the child grew up into a Huichol rather than a snake.

Then the men were told where to bury the body of the woman. When they went to her grave again, they found a coil of snakes on it.[24] These were killed. But there was a great deal of water because the grave was gradually becoming a spring of water.[25]

Father Sun then ordered the husband to disinter the woman's body, no matter how decomposed it might be. So they took the remains back again to the arroyo, where they were re-buried. In five days the body had completely decomposed into water.[26] This water was blue in color. It could not be drunk lest the drinker turn into a wolf.

Father Sun then told the people to fast from water for ten days[27] while he went to talk to the sea-goddess, Otuanáka. "You are the creator of all,"[28] he said to Nakawé (Otuanáka). "What can be done with this water, now mixed up with the remains of the dead woman, so that the Huichols can drink of it?"

"Have them make me votive-bowls and bring them to the spring and place them there for me," Nakawé replied. "Thus the people will not become crazy from contamination with the Snake-people, as this woman was."[29]

This was done, and the water separated, white and blue. Nakawé then ordered them not to drink for five days until the water was "tamed."[30]

The child, kutómai, grew to manhood and married with "clean people" — that is, Huichols. But he was partially a Snake-man, as could be seen from his shining eyes and forked tongue. He grew up to be a sorcerer. He married and had a family. His children were all boys. They had long faces, which were very wide, and large eyes. They all became curers and singers.

The Sun said, "If nothing happens and they all live, let us see if they do not serve well some day, since they know how to cure and sing."

During the rainy season the people worked hard. The rain, however, stopped coming. The earth began to dry up. At this the Sun was sad. He wished for the grandchildren of Háiku to sing to see if they could make it rain.

For five nights each one sang after the other, but without results. The elder brother of the dead Snake-man was angry and would not send the water. This was revealed to his grand-nephew, who was singing.

The elder brother of the dead Snake-man had said to the grand-nephew, "Your people must fulfill all my commands or it will not rain. You must make five tiny models of houses, and five *teapáli* with pictures painted green in color, because that was the color of the dead Snake-man. Make also votive-bowls with designs in blue beads of Snake-man, coiled like Háiku. Also make arrows and hang from them feathers of a bird from the sea, *harámali*. Also make a little staff, pointed like a snake. Thus shall I be paid for granting the favor of rain."

The people did not altogether believe the singer, because he was half-snake. They were so sad, however, and they needed water so badly, that they decided to follow the commands.

Then one of the snake-singers sang again for the fifth time.

Just when the people needed rain the greatest in order to save their crops, the sky began to fill with clouds. As the singing continued, it began to thunder. Soon the rain storm swept across the world.[31] It rained for five days, until the world was thoroughly wet.

The Sun then blamed the people for having killed Háiku. He also blamed them for not having taken better care of the Snake-man's child, whose children were curers and singers who could bring rain.

The Sun then blessed all the Snake-man's grandchildren. Thus they are children of the Sun, as are the Huichols.

F "Mayor" Nasario,[1] the Orphan-boy, Saves His Brothers from the Ghoul, Tukákame, but Contaminated and Changed to Chipmunks (?), They Bring Insanity to the Huichols

Tukákame came out from the Sierra Morón and flew away to where he made his home. He sought a place where he would be unknown. There he built houses and cleared fields. He made five houses into a beautiful *ranchería* for his home. He had stools and chairs to offer passersby who might be hungry and stop at his ranchería. His ranchería was on top of a high mesa.

Below him dwelt a lonely little orphan-boy. He lived with his relatives, the great gods of the sea. The boy was sad as he went about his work.

Buzzard came to the boy and said, "Why are you so sad?"

The boy replied, "I am working here, but my efforts appear to be useless. I plant, but nothing grows from the seed."

Buzzard answered, "If you wish to better yourself, I will tell you of a certain place where you will help yourself by going."

"Please tell me," the boy begged.

"Well," said Buzzard, "don't stay here, so near Tukákame.[2] For success in planting you should move far away from him. Within five days build a house at the place about which I will tell you. Then go there to live. There in the sea are the great water-goddesses, Hakoóye Halióye. You are to ask favors of them. Cut some reeds and twist thread for making *náma* (back-shields).[3] Hang these on your arrows and present them to the water-goddesses. And tell them who sent you."

The boy followed these directions, and the goddesses took the arrows. They said, "Our country is very 'delicate.'[4] So you will have to remain apart at a considerable distance where you cannot see us."

The boy was instructed to toss the náma into the air. When it came down, it stuck into the earth.[5]

The goddesses said, "Now your offering of the náma has been made. At the bank of the river is a rock. Go there at sunset and set your votive-bowls on it. Then place a fish-line in the water, and see what happens.[6]

The orphan-boy did this. Immediately he caught five large fish.[7] He was instructed to carry them alive to his house. There he was to put them in a closed box for five days.

When he had done this, the goddess said, "Since you are an orphan, you need company and someone to work with you. Wait for five days and see what comes out of the box."

At the end of this time the boy opened the box. He saw that the fish had changed into children. These were to keep him company and help him work.[8] They were still "tender"[9] and had to be "tamed."[10] So the boy kept them for five more days until they grew into men.

At the end of this time the boy told his companions of a place in the sierra[,] which he had asked the gods for. He said, "If you wish, you may go there and clear the fields. Here are machetes and axes which [that] also came out of the box." But he bade them not to intrude into the fields of anyone else, for thus had the gods instructed him.

His companions were happy in their work. They sang and played as they labored. They burned the brush as soon as it had dried. When they needed sandals, the great gods of the sea revealed to them where such could be obtained. The great gods of the sea also told them where there were corrals stocked with horses and mules. This was so they would not have to walk the long distance to the sierra.

So they went to a cave, and there they found reatas. Then they followed the instructions of the gods until they finally arrived at the corrals. The corrals were filled with many horses, mules, and burros. So they lassoed some of the beautiful horses and mules for themselves and led them back to their houses.

All the while Orphan-boy, who had asked this favor from the gods, sat quietly by himself. By a similar request of Orphan-boy's, the people were provided with saddles, bridles, saddle-blankets, etc. They selected whatever they wanted. Then they mounted the animals and rode about, happy and singing.

The people, however, were naked. So Orphan-boy asked the great gods of the sea to provide them with clothes. The great gods revealed where there was a whole box of the finest clothes that the Huichols wear. The people followed instructions until they found the box and got all the clothes they needed.

Similarly, they were provided with cattle for meat, sacrifices, milk, and cheese. They had, furthermore, gardens of chile, sugar-cane[,] and fruit. These had grown up in fifteen days. Thus they were getting rich with very little effort. The Sierra Morón was a beautiful garden approached by a good trail.

Meanwhile the people of Tukákame on their parts were struggling to make a living. Theirs was the bad custom of not being very hospitable[11] to anyone who came to ask for a little food. They would excuse themselves by saying that they were having a hard time. Instead of giving food, the people of Tukákame would ask their guests to sit in their stools.[12] Here they would get stuck, and later on die. And then the bad people of the ghoul, Tukákame, would steal their animals.[13]

The fish-people saddled their horses and rode off in full regalia[,] shouting and sounding their cattle-horns. They went to see why the people were dying in the house of Tukákame. Tukákame's continued success would be an omen that all their easily-gained [*sic*] wealth would disappear.

The fish-people arrived at the ranchería about noon. The people of Tukákame were respectful and treated them well. They offered the fish-people food and rest, and gave food to their horses in the corral.

Then they brought forward stools. The fish-people, however, did not sit in them. Finally they did. They could not get up. It was as if they were nailed on to the stools. Thus they were made prisoners. The food, also, was changed into *"wishache"* [*Huisache* is the Spanish word for *Acacia pennatula*] thorns, filling their mouths and throats. There they remained for five days.

Meanwhile the gardens of the fish-people began to dry up.[14] This was an omen that the fish-people had lost against the people of Tukákame. Also, their bee-hives were filled with dead bees, and their animals were dying.

Orphan-boy said, "My brothers are dying. Tomorrow I must go where they are and help them. I will start at sunrise and follow their tracks. Thus I shall see what courage this Tukákame has."

At dawn Orphan-boy sounded his horn, happy that he had again requested a favor of the great goddesses of the sea. They had granted him a pistol filled with cartridges, a rifle, a saber, and a knife. Thus he was well armed, and, though alone, was not afraid. He had dreamed that his brothers were still alive,[15] although weeping in the face of almost certain death.

He had to follow their trail for five days. So he bade good-bye to the remainder of his family. Thus, well armed, he mounted his horse. He had bathed his horse in cold water to give it strength. He also carried water for his own use. The water was also to protect him against any fire with which Tukákame might seek to stop him.

Riding his horse[,] he climbed the Sierra Morón until he saw in the distance the ranchería of Tukákame. He soon arrived there on the trot, and was met by the people of Tukákame. He had his rifle ready. He talked to them, saying that his brothers had been lost. He was angry, and he wasted no words. He told them that the tracks of his brothers stopped at the ranchería.

Tukákame denied that the fish-people had come there. He offered Orphan-boy a stool and some food.

Orphan-boy replied, "No, I am here on my mule. I don't wish to change seats. Furthermore, I have food, and I don't wish to eat your food."

"Then let me put your mule in my corral for food and rest," said Tukákame. He took hold of the bridle of the animal.

But Orphan-boy made a thrust at him with his saber and shouted, "You have my brothers here, and I am going to find them. I will get good and mad if you don't give them up, together with their animals and other things."

Tukákame replied, "They are not here. If you are angry, come in and look for them."

So they arranged a contest with the bow and arrow to settle the matter. They put up a target two hundred meters away. This was Tukákame's hat. Orphan-boy hit it. Then they put up a small parrot. Orphan-boy knocked its head off with an arrow. Then they put up a parakeet. This was Tukákame's heart. If Orphan-boy could hit this mark, it would kill Tukákame.

Orphan-boy resisted all invitations to first sit on the stool and eat. Then he shot at and hit the parakeet, which was the heart of Tukákame.

Then they put up a woodpecker, another of Tukákame's birds. This was killed also, as were the other animals of this bad ghoul.

They placed an upright stick for a target. Orphan-boy knocked it down, split in two. Then they put up a pine stick. This was knocked down, as though struck by lightning. The third time another kind of stick of *uwé* was placed upright. This was split also. Then they put up a thick heavy log. Tukákame was sure that Orphan-boy would not be able to split this with an arrow. But the log was split as though by a ball [bolt] of lightning. Even a very heavy piece of wood was treated likewise. By this time Tukákame was very angry.

Then another contest was started by having Orphan-boy's mule climb five fences, each as high as a house. The mule jumped the first and went right through the second and conquered all the rest of the fences. Thus Tukákame knew that Orphan-boy had a good mule.

Then they wagered that Orphan-boy would not be able to enter the five gardens of Tukákame. These were to be fenced with tangled, thorny reeds. Orphan-boy got on his mule. Then with his saber he cut through the fences of thick cactus, "wishache" (*pá róva*, H.), and finally passed another thorny plant, *sulí*. Thus Orphan-boy won the wagers. He heard a distant thunder coming.

Within the garden were five big fires. These had to be conquered as well as other things. So Orphan-boy opened his bottle-gourd and bathed himself and his mule with the sacred water. The water made them very cold. This was the last test. Tukákame was certain that Orphan-boy would lose this time.

The mule went into the fire with the rider and put the fire out. Thus four of the fires were extinguished. The last fire was very hot from the blood of the many victims which [that] it had consumed. But Orphan-boy's mule took him bravely into the fire and put it out.

Orphan-boy had now won. He knew that Tukákame was completely bad. So he asked him to enter the fire with him. Of course Tukákame refused. But when he did so, Orphan-boy forced him into the fire with his saber, and held him there by a rope attached to his mule. Then he dragged Tukákame in a ceremonial circuit in the fire. The third time Tukákame caught fire. So Orphan-boy dragged Tukákame through the fire, which cooked him. The fourth time Tukákame was burned to water. The fifth time the mule pounded the water into the coals of the fire with its hooves.

Then Orphan-boy filled three gourds with the mixture of water and charcoal. He took the mixture to the family of Tukákame. They asked for their father. Orphan-boy replied, "He told me to bring you food to eat. Bring me some bowls." This was done. Orphan-boy filled the bowls, saying that the mixture was atole and that Tukákame had ordered them to eat it. Thus Tukákame's wife and children ate it, thinking that it was good. But no sooner had they eaten, than they jumped up painfully.

Then Orphan-boy told them to lead him to where they were keeping his brothers prisoners. They opened the door, and attempted to escape inside. Orphan-boy broke down the door. His brothers were prisoners inside.

Orphan-boy entered and detached the stools from his brothers. Then he put his brothers on his mule to save them. After this he burned the houses of Tukákame. In the flaming houses the remaining members of Tukákame's family were burned.

Then they looked for their horses. They found them eating "wishache" thorns because of extreme hunger. So they pulled the thorns out of the horses' mouths and bathed them with sacred water, thus curing them. After this they destroyed the corral of Tukákame.

Then Orphan-boy and his brothers mounted their horses and rode to where there was good pasturage for their animals. Here Orphan-boy's good mule was unsaddled. While the mule rested, it carefully watched Orphan-boy's weapons, lest any of Tukákame's family remained to molest them.

With the horses refreshed by rest and food, they continued on to a spring. There they got water and wild fruits for the men to eat. Since Orphan-boy had triumphed over Tukákame, all this land now belonged to him. So the brothers rode over the mesa to see if it was good.

Orphan-boy went one way, sounding his cow-horn. The blare of his horn restored the garden[,] which had withered while the brothers had been held prisoners by Tukákame.[16] The garden was not completely revived, however.

Orphan-boy had been so angry that his body was changed. He arrived home and greeted his family. His brothers remained behind. He told his family all that had happened, and how he had won over Tukákame. The brothers were also changed, due to their sufferings in the stools of Tukákame.

To get the brothers home it was necessary to take them fresh horses, since theirs were jaded. The bodies of the brothers were striped in color, and their families could not recognize them. When they drew near the house, it was seen that they were greatly changed. So they had to wait awhile. They were wiped with grass in an effort to remove the stripes from their bodies, and the grass was afterwards burned.[17] But this did not help.

The brothers could not continue to live with the others. They had to go back to their ranchería in the mountains. There they went and remained for five days. They tried to find out what they would be changed into because of the stripes on their bodies.

Their bodies fell off and went into holes[18] in the rocks. They came out as a strong whirlwind or tornado, *teaúka*. This is very bad.

Their hearts were changed into ugly chipmunks(?), *tcamóko*.[19] They had stripes on their backs, and their ears were very close to their heads.

Tcamóko are afraid of the great gods. Because of tcamóko there is insanity among the Huichols. If a Huichol follows or tries to kill a tcamóko, it is bad and he cannot go to church.

Tcamóko are bad. They cause men to abuse and beat their wives, as had been commanded by the great gods. Even good and handsome Huichol men or women can be made crazy by these animals. Especially is this so if they do not carry out their vows or get angry at their spouses.

These devil-animals cause men to throw chile at their wives. Crazy people are advised not to follow the ceremonies of the Huichols.

The gods love hard-working Huichol. But drunkards and abusive Huichols, however, they punish with insanity.[20]

Orphan-boy was changed from a Huichol into a Mexican after going to the sea (for purification?). He is known as an "elder," Mayor Nasario.[21]

G Death Comes to the Woman of the Mythical Pre-Huichol Race, Eáwali, Who Loved Bear and Buzzard [Origin of "Death-bird" Ghouls]

On a mesa on [in] front of La Caponeta the bears were born of their parents *hótsa kawi tewíali*. Here one of them grew up and in that sierra played from five days of age. It could not find enough food as a bear so it changed into a person. As a person he went into other mountains digging the roots with which he maintained himself. Thus it lived and grew. It killed deer and ate the meat and cracked the bones for their marrow. These he carried to his father, the bear, which pleased him.[1]

As he grew up, he passed throughout the sierra. He could climb like a lizard when he searched the rocks for honey. He had so much hair that the bees could not hurt him with their stings.

Now in these times previous to the appearance of the Huichols[,] there was another race of people called Eáwali. They found the tracks of Bear-man, so they followed it to its home.

Later one of the adolescent girls of this race was bringing water from the arroyo, while the men went for wood. The bear went and saw the men busy getting the wood. So he changed himself into a person and greeted the men.

He said to them, "What are you doing? I am just passing along this way." But the Bear-man had such a strong smell of bears that the men knew that he was not a person. The Bear-man realized this and did not wish to force things.

The girl passed Bear-man and smelled the same strong smell. At home she said, "I met someone who certainly was not human. He smelled like an animal. I don't want to go alone for water any more." So the next day she went with her brother. The Bear-man again approached and began to talk. The boy and girl hurried to finish their work and went home.

The next day Bear-man offered them *aguacate* fruit [avocados] from his garden. They talked this over and were tempted. So the next day they went to the garden of alligator-pears [avocados]. The boy and girl sent two men to see if it was alright, before they dared to go in.

The tree was full of aguacates. When they had climbed up[,] the Bear-man came out acting very angry. The man shot arrows at him[,] but this did not stop him. He knocked them down and beat them until he had almost killed them. They went back and reported this.

The next day another man brought a sharply sharpened machete and went fearlessly to the bear's garden. When the Bear-man approached (apparently as a bear), the man could not stop him with his machete. The bear hurt him very badly and chewed off his penis. When he went back and reported this[,] it frightened the boy and girl very much.

The brother of the boy and girl went, but he was also injured. Bear-man told him that he wanted the girl to come. But she was afraid to go.

Since she would not come to his garden, Bear-man decided to go to her *ranchería* and see her. When she went to the arroyo to get water, Bear-man was waiting for her. There they met while she was filling her *olla* [clay pot]. Bear-man said, "I have been looking for you. I have come to take you away."

So he grasped her and ran away with her to the sierra. They did not stop until they came to his cave, which was very far away. There was no one to help her and she was crying. After five days of her crying[,] Bear-man changed himself into a bear in order to bring her food. Slowly the girl was getting used to him, except when he played with her amorously and tickled her with his long claws (nails).

When he brought the food, she told him that she could not eat meat raw as he could. She said, "I need fire, a *comal*, pots, and a metate. You can live without these things, bit [but] I cannot."

So Bear-man went away again and soon came back bringing the things that she needed. Then she asked the permission of Bear-man to go and get water from the arroyo and to answer a call of nature. But the Bear-man did not trust her too much and went for the water himself. When he got back she drank heavily of it, because she had not drunk for five days.

Since she needed fire, Bear-man went and stole a box of matches from the Mexicans (sia.) as well as pitch-pine. Then she built a fire and cooked her tortillas and meat, while Bear-man watched her closely. When he was hungry[,] he just went to the mountains and found roots with his long claws.

The girl told Bear-man, that she also needs [needed] salt. He went to find it. When he left[,] she began to shout in hopes that the people would hear her. But she remained with Bear-man for a whole year. He brought her beans and green corn from the fields of the people.

The bear tried to approach her sexually but his member was long and hard as bone, except at the point. Despite her painful protests he lay with her and she became pregnant. Then she acknowledged, "Now you are my husband."

Her children were two little bears[,] which scratched her breasts when they suckled. The woman made nests of grass for them to rest [upon] when they slept. When they were growing up[,] the [she] asked Buzzard to tell her parents that she was in the bear's cave in a high cliff. She had no way to get out and escape. He said that he would bring her an answer the next day.

Buzzard flew to the ranchería taking the girl's message to her parents. The parents asked the great gods of the sea to help them rescue the girl. They were given ten ropes to let themselves down the face of the cliff.

The people got to the cave by dawn when the Bear-man was not there. Her brothers let themselves down the face of the cliff with their ropes. When they arrived[,] the girl killed [the] little bear-children by throwing them down the cliff. She embraced her family[,] and they all escaped before Bear-man got back. They knew that he would be angry and would try to revenge himself.

When they arrived at their home[,] they feared for the bear's return, so they built a house with five strong doors to be passed in succession. They opened the doors and let the girl in. The house was very strong and the people were well armed to defend themselves.

When Bear-man got back to his cave[,] he found no wife, babies, nor even tracks. But he searched until he found their tracks in the mountains. Thus he followed them until he arrived at the house. He was so powerful that he was not afraid of the five people within. He broke down three of the doors notwithstanding the machetes and weapons of the people. With the fourth door broken, the people were greatly afraid.

Due to their fear they knocked down and tied the Bear-man before he broke down the last door. Well-tied, they all carried him back to the sierra. They told him, "You are bad, and are not even a person. We are taking you back to your mountains and cave. It was ordered by the great gods of the sea that you should stay here. If you come back[,] we will kill you next time."

The bear said, "Do not kill me this time." So they threw him behind a rock near his cliff. They painted his picture on a board. This came to life as a real bear[,] which could not change into [a] man. This board painting was called *itáli*.[2] Thus the bad bears were finished. Thus the bears stayed in their mountains and did not molest the people further.

To purify herself from the impurity of her contact of [with] the Bear-man, the girl had to go to the sea where there was a rock[,] *tekualípa*. Here she must sit for five days in order to remove the traces of the bear. Here she cried for four days because her family had left her all alone.

The fifth day Buzzard came along and found her weeping. He sat beside her, and she asked him where her brothers were. They were dead so Buzzard told her, "I know where they are, but I doubt if you will be able to climb there. They are not none [in any] of the four points[,] but in the upper world[,] and it is a five[-]day (year) journey. In the middle of the sky there is a rock where you will find a bed. You will arrive there after two years (days). There you can rest before you try the next three[-]years' (days['])' journey. At the end you will find another world[;] there your brothers are living."

The girl said, "Then I guess I cannot go, since I cannot fly to the sky. Would you take me?"

Buzzard replied, "Yes if you will sleep with me every night." She agreed, so he told her to fast so she would not be to[o] heavy for him to carry. So she fasted from food and water until Buzzard came back at the first flush of dawn. Meanwhile she was busy making pinole from five magic ears of corn.

Buzzard came as he had promised and asked if all was ready. They changed languages to *kulimíse mitáli* [undefined by Zingg]. Then she got on his back after several efforts. She firmly caught hold of his penis and[3] Buzzard flew off making wide circles as he climbed into the sky. It took five years before they arrived. First they stopped in the midway cave where there was a bed and things for preparing food as well. Here they rested for a year[,] living on her pinole from the magic corn.

That night as she prepared to sleep on the bed, Buzzard told her to guard herself from *katai apoaka tewíali*, a green lizard.[4] She undressed and slept naked. Buzzard slept in another place. She slept with her legs open because she dreamed this was commanded on [in] the new language in the words, *mitáli paliwela* ("open your legs"). After five times she answered, "Yes my legs are open."

When Buzzard had asked her if she was asleep and she did not answer, he stepped up to her, naked and exposed, to take his pay from her nice, fat body. He walked around her five times, and then entered and finished before she awakened. When she awoke she asked, "Did anything happen to me by that little green lizard? You said to be careful about them, but I think you did something to me while I was asleep."

Buzzard laughed and said nothing. The next day he told her he did it while she was asleep without even waking her to show her that he was not big and hard like the Bear-man. She liked Buzzard on this account and embraced him, offering herself to him again. Three times was the payment for the trip. She offered the third one as soon as they should arrive to her relatives.

So she caught hold of his penis again[,] and he flew to the top of the sierra of the sky.[5] There at the entrance of the sky she met Tate Welíka Uimáli (mother eagle girl), the owner of the sky. Buzzard told Mother Eagle that he was bringing the daughter of some people who were already there. Thus they were allowed to enter. There were three roads and Eagle Mother told them which one to take. When they had entered[,] the gates were closed.[6] They looked around the upper world region of the sky. Everywhere was the green, green, green of pure clouds.[7] Buzzard wanted the third payment for carrying her and this was agreeable.

One of the roads was of beautiful flowers. Another was lined with votive[-] bowls. The third road, leading to her family was fare [far away]. Buzzard could not take her farther after her [his] hard work in having brought her that far. He told her that she would arrive at her family in five hours. So they embraced and kissed and he told her, "Forget all that has happened as you are in a new world." Then he flew off and descended in a slow flight of spirals.

The girl crossed five creeks and came to houses with the doors closed. She waited because there were no people in evidence, and the doors of the five houses were closed. Finally she walked up to the door and knocked. Someone heard and said in the new language[,] which she needed for this journey, "Whoever in [is] knocking, just open the door." The door opened and air came out.[8] Although there were not visible people inside[,] yet talking emerger [emerged] from the air.[9] It was the air which [that] talked.

She sat down thinking, "I will have to remain here even without people.["] She was very hungry and thirst[y] from her long journey. In one corner there were five ollas of water. A voice of air said, "If you are hungry[,] there is *atole* [maize mush] and cooked mescal (a sweet from the heart of the maguey) in the olla."

At noon she opened the olla. It, as she found the others, was full of blood together with human parts of the body. They just said that it was filled with water and the sweet of the mescal. She said, "I cannot eat such food. I had better go where I was[.] There, at least, there was corn."

At night she saw that the house appeared to be filled with dead people.[10] They got up looking like bats and flew away.[11] She said, "My, how many animals there are here. If the great gods will help me at dawn[,] I am going to the Eagle Mother at the gates of the upper world region."

At midnight the bats came back and stuck themselves on the bodies of dead people swimming in the ollas of blood. They said to her, "Are you hungry? There is plenty to eat." The bats went to the blood and drank it. She heard and saw this but could not eat. They said to her, "Help us eat all the atole (mush) which we have." But she did not go.

At dawn there was nothing there but only pure air.[12] The air said to her, "Why don't you eat?" But she replied, "No, I cannot eat such food.["] They said, "Now that you are here you will have to work. Go to the arroyo and wash my blanket and all my dirty clothes."

She said, "I[t] would be better that I should go to my own country. But let me see this blanket?" Then she went around the house and found only five bunches of rotting entrails hanging from trees. These were the girdles and ribbons of the dead people.[13] She returned and said, "You say these are clothes, but I cannot wash such horrid things." They said, "Anyway you will have to take them to wash."

So she took a long stick on which she put the entrails and carried them to the creek. They had told her that she would find *amoles* at the river with which to wash the clothes. So she tossed the intestines into the water and looked for the amoles (*Yucca*, Sp.).

In a little cave where they had said there was amole, she found nothing but toads. She said, "These are very ugly, I cannot use them as [a]mole in washing. They would bite me anyway."[14] She left the toads and went back to the house.

They said to her, "Did you finish washing after finding the amole?"

She replied, "There was [were] only toads which wished to bite me."

Then she got a stick and hit the toads. Blood streamed from their hearts and heads. Then she was sick from nausea at such a disgustion [disgusting] sight. She sat down swooning and lost her memory. In a dream she thought, "Now you are going to remain here and be changed into the form which you find here." This she heard when she was sick from the blood of the toads.

As soon as she recovered from her nausea she went and washed the blood off herself. Then she hung up the vile "clothes" of the dead people. When she came up to the house[,] a whirlwind[15] took her up and changed her into air. The Sun-[F]ather saw this.

A bat came from her heart and ate blood from the *canteras* (ollas). The air said, "Now you are like a bat, *ateílito*. Let us go down to the world below and find sick ones to take their hearts." So they all flew down to earth. She took the form of the metate bird,[16] *matailuwi*, another the dove, and another the owl, *muikúli* ("devil of the sky"). They came to the earth from the sky where they live.

III   The Christian Myth Cycle

A   The Bee-Mother Gives Wax for Candles

When the bee-people were created, there was a large mother-bee (queen-bee)[,] *wawéme*. She had been created by the great gods of the sea because they had a large candle[1] that would not light. This happened, even though there was no wind or anything else to prevent its burning.[2] The singer said to leave it until the next day. Then, perhaps, they would know what was the matter. So they put the candle in the sun to dry. Then they went off to hunt its owner. Tatevalí (Grandfather Fire) said, "Doubtless the mother of the candle is angry. Let us get busy and look for her and see what is the matter."

They called two or three boys and said to them, "You must do something for us. Sit down and listen to what we have to tell you. The singer informs us that the candle will not light because its mother (or patroness) has not given us permission to use the candles. She must be mad at us. So for five days you must look for the queen-bee."

One of the youths said, "I cannot guarantee to find her. It would be very difficult, since I do not know where she lives. Let us go, however, and see if we can find her."

The bee-mother had been ordered to put her dwelling and fields far from the houses of the people. But Tatevalí (Grandfather Fire) told the youths that he knew where she lived. He said that he would help them. The youths then went off, according to the instructions of Tatevalí, in different directions along the great sierra where the bee-mother lived. They travelled a long ways. Finally they met, and each told the other that he had found nothing.

So they returned to their homes. But the people needed candles so much that Tatevalí ordered them to go off again. They obeyed, and sought far and wide. But they found nothing, despite Tatevalí's encouragement that the bee-mother was certainly there. They continued looking for the tracks of the bee-mother. It was very difficult, however, because she could change herself into other forms.

On the third day they heard a whistle, similar to that of the quail. They walked toward it to investigate, but found nothing. Then they heard the whistle behind them. When they turned toward it, they heard it in front of them. At last they were getting closer. They were anxious to find out what kind of people were whistling. But they found nothing, and were forced to return to their homes again.

When they arrived home, the singer said to them, "Go again tomorrow. I have the brothers of the bee-mother, so they must be near enough to bring her food. Go again, and this time do your best to discover what or who it was that was whistling. I have dreamed of what the bee-mother is doing.[3]

They went again for five days into the great sierra. First they heard the cry of a hawk that was weeping. It was on "this side" (one of the four points), so they followed it. When, however, it sounded again in the middle region, they could see nothing. They became discouraged and returned to their homes.

But, after Tatevalí had dreamed of the bee-mother, they were sent out again. He encouraged them, and told them to go to a little meadow in the mountains where there were many flowers. Here they were to remain and see whom they would meet.

One of the youths said to the other, "You have good eyes."

"No," answered the other, "I don't see very well. But anyway let us see who will be the first to locate the bee-mother."

Before arriving at the meadow of flowers they had to sleep one night in the sierra. This they did, and then went on until finally they reached their destination.

At dawn they saw a bee flying by with a beautiful buzzing sound. It stopped at a flower. When it had got all the honey, it flew on. Another bee flew to a nearby flower and took the honey from it. A third was seen to go in another direction.

So one of the youths followed the bees on their return with honey until they stopped at a tree. The other youth followed other bees, but, when they took him farther and farther away, finally lost them. Thus they continued to hunt for the bee-mother in order to finish the five[-]day period. Then they returned home and reported.

Tatevalí said that he had dreamed again of the bee-mother.[4] He was certain that the bees were there, and that the sounds they had heard, like the other bees, came from her. He dreamed that the bee-mother would come to a certain place in the form of a man.

So the youths went to this place to wait and see what would happen.

One of them said, "I will go there and see how it is."

The other said, "I will go too and see if we finally win."

They waited there five days, very alert to see what would happen. Now although the bee-mother had promised Tatevalí that she would appear, one of the youths got tired of waiting and left.

The younger boy remained. The bee-mother, who knew of this, liked him for staying. She had talked to the great gods of the sea, wishing to name the flowers with the help of the boy. As yet things or people had no names.

The bee-mother came to the boy and said, "Though I cannot go with you, I will put you and your wife with the flowers. And I will care for you by giving you five meadows of flowers. Now that the other boy is gone[,] you will have less trouble."

Then she gave him five empty gourd-containers and left them with him to be filled. She had changed him into a bee, and he could now fly from flower to flower eating pure honey. There was no hardship in his new life. Although there were hills and stones, they did not interfere with him.

Then she gave him a stool and a machete. She said, "Sit there on the stool and cut your knee with the machete."

The boy answered, "Since I am so ordered, I will do it, even if I get sick and die. Perhaps I can call [for] help." Then he cut himself below the knee. Streams of honey poured from the wound. The flowers that were looking on named him *tamata ítsika támai* (*ítsika*—a flower that blooms in October). He bound up his leg[,] and it became well almost immediately. The containers he filled with the honey. Then, covered with flowers, he went to his home as a honey-boy. He arrived there crying like an eagle.

His family knew that he was coming. They met him in the ceremonial Huichol fashion at the edge of the patio. He was taken into the dancing-house and given to eat of the honey.

Now the bee-mother had told the other youth that she wanted him to eat only honey, fish, and deer (all sacred foods).

The other youth said, "I will dream about the matter and try to get you some." So he went in one direction to an arroyo. Here he found a frog[,] *sukúa*. He thought to himself, "I will take the bee-mother one of these." He left some honey and took a pile of frogs.

The bee-mother did not like this. She took them from him and threw them back into the arroyo from which they had been taken. Then she told him to look again for honey for her to eat.

So he went again, and came this time to a water-hole. Here he found the animals *tapokáti ciúli*. These he carried to the bee-mother. But she did not like them and threw them away.

The boy went to bed. The next day he made a third trip to look for honey for the bee-mother. He found a pile of little snakes[,] *halaíku*[,] and these he took to her. She was nauseated and threw them back into the water-hole.

All this time the honey-boy was bringing honey to where the bee-mother lived.

On his fourth attempt the other boy came to a rock where there were five bees' nests. He knocked them down. This angered the bees so much that they stung him. But he did succeed in getting a little honey. It did not have a sweet taste, however, being mostly water. This he offered to the bee-mother, saying, "Look, bee-mother. Look at this that I have found."

But the honey was worthless since it was not sweet. The bee-mother took it and flung it from her, even breaking the gourd-container.

Now since honey-boy was regularly bringing good honey without any apparent trouble, the other boy asked him, "How is it that you bring good honey so easily that it appears that you do not even work? Our mother is angry because I bring only bad things."

The honey-boy said, "I will show you how I work, although it may appear that I do not work at all. Follow me and watch what happens. I have fields where we can go and walk around, and I will show you where to stay. If you see everything, it will be well. There are many flowers, but I can take you there even if it is a little "delicate.""[5]

So they went, and honey-boy showed the other youth a rock. He said, "You stay there. I cannot join you until tomorrow when I shall have finished my five days of looking for flowers. While you wait, here are my stool and other things."

When the honey-boy came back, he sat down on the stool. Then he cut himself with the machete. Streams of honey gushed out like blood from the wound. This surprised the other, who asked if he might do it. The honey-boy said no, but told him to come back later with empty gourds.

But the other boy went back to his house and got a gourd-container and a machete. He sat down on a stool and struck himself a powerful blow that almost cut off his leg. But instead of honey, streams of blood poured out. He thought to himself, "How badly honey-boy has fooled me in order to get me to cut myself like this.["] He bound up his leg and limped into the house. It was all he could do to get there. He did not tell his wife what he had done.

The bee-mother was angry. Since his leg was so swollen, he could not bring her food. It was ten days before he could move around.

He blamed his companion for telling him a lie, and was so angry that he would not talk to him. He planned to go to honey-boy's house, although he did not wish to kill him immediately. He thought, "I will make a hole for an earth oven, and bring wood for a huge fire." With this he would kill honey-boy for telling him to cut himself. He decided to do this upon the other's return from the flower-fields.

At sunset the honey-boy came back from the fields, his gourds full of honey. He was singing.

The other began to sharpen his machete. Then he approached the honey-boy, who was filling five gourds with honey.

Honey-boy was resting, suspecting nothing. The other came up, and began to blame honey-boy in a loud voice for causing him to wound himself. He struck honey-boy five times with his sharp machete.

When the bee-boy [honey-boy] died, air[6] came from his body and told his family that the boy was in bad straits. The bee-mother knew that something was wrong because the wind talked to her heart.

Then the other dragged his companion to the oven and built up the fire. But while he was doing this, a bee came out from the heart of the honey-boy. When the body was thrown into the fire, a drop of wax was formed from the burning blood.[7] This fell a short distance away. The other did not notice it. He watched the body intently until it was completely consumed.

The bee that came from the bee-boy's [honey-boy's] heart flew away to a certain spot in the sierra where there were five pine[-]trees. He had no body, since he was the heart of the honey-boy. So he bored into the pine-tree to be its heart, while the pine-tree was to be his body.

That night as the sun went down, the murderer approached his house (and that of the bee-mother). He was happy and singing, for he was carrying honey for the bee-mother at last. He had brought the dead honey-boy's honey with which to please her. She recognized the gourds, however, and asked him where he had got them.

He said, "I found them by the wood-pile. The honey-boy will be here soon." Then he went to bed.

While the bee-mother slept, she dreamed that the honey-boy was dead and burned up.[8] She and her children wept, because they all loved him very much. His wife also was very sad.

That night the murderer approached the honey-boy's wife and raped her. The next morning his neck had grown very long and hung over the bed.

The bee-mother knew this. She knew also that he had killed the honey-boy for the latter's wife. So she took the form of the sword-shaped battening-stick (*oparu*) and attacked his long neck, giving him three blows.

He ran out, and she followed. She ordered him to eat frogs, snakes, and toads. She said, "You will be named *kuáSu tewéałi* [tewíałi] (the heron)."

Thus he lived, wading in the water. He had a very hard time, eating only reptiles.

The people now dreamed of the heart of the honey-boy living in the pine-tree. So the bee-mother sent three of her children to look for the bee. The first day they found nothing. The second day they found nothing. The third day they heard the buzz of the honey-boy's heart. It sounded like the whistle of a quail. The fourth day they went again, and heard the cry of an eagle. When they heard this, they cried, "Oh brother, answer us. Where are you?"

In answer they heard the cry of the eagle: "on this side"; "on that side"; "above"; and "below."

Meanwhile the bee-mother dreamed that he was not well off, and loved him all the more. In her dream the honey-boy said, "There is the oven where he killed me. There also is a bit of wax. This you must take to your house."

They went and found the wax, and took it back to their house.

Finally the others arrived at the place of the five pine-trees. Here they found the bee. Looking up they saw his long white face. He said that he was their brother, but that he could not leave. He asked for the wax. This was tossed to him. With a bit of it they anointed the tree in spots, so that, by flying from spot to spot, they could climb to him. When they reached their brother, they decided to live with him. So they were named *ciclí*, a tiny bee (*campeche*, Sp.)

At night they took the rest of the wax to the bee-mother for making candles. She dreamed how to make the thread for the candles from *ixtle* [agave fiber].

That night the tiny bit of wax increased until there was enough for several candles. The bee-mother learned to light them near the sacred paraphernalia as a payment for the gods. The bee-people took Nakawé a large candle made of the wax of these tiny bees (campeche). Then the bee-mother dreamed how to get more wax by watching where the bees put their nests.[9]

Kauymáli was also watching the bees because he wished candles offered to him in the feasts (or possibly to offer in the feasts). So he changed himself into a man. He came to the bee-mother and changed her name to *hopáme*.

He greeted her and her male companion. The latter was named *kulúsi* (the cross).[10] He asked [for] tortillas to be made. She gave him a big one. When he bit into it, it turned into honey.

Now that he had eaten, he saw many firefly-like things in the air. He went after them and found that they were fireflies.[11] For five days he hunted and caught them, getting between twenty and thirty a day until he had quite a few.

On the sixth day Kauymáli went to a tree that was filled with wild bees. He cut it down and got the wax[,] which he took to town. Here he traded the wax of campeche for store candles. These are better for the great gods.

When he came back, Tatevalí said, "I wish for five candles."[12]

Tsakaimúka took ten candles.[13] All the other great gods took five or ten.

Nakawé said, "I wish my share to be beautifully arranged and decorated with beads.[14] You, Kauymáli, bring them to my mountain *utsípa* ("this side," but near the sea).

At "this side[,]" in the middle of the world[,] Kauymáli left the candles un-lighted for Nakawé. He went away after more. When he returned[,] no candles remained. There were only the holes in the ground in which they had been standing. He found the candles in another place nearer Nakawé.

Then he left, only to come back again. In place of the five candles were five bunches of sweet-potatoes, *íele*. He reported this to his family, and told them to dig there very carefully with a stick that he gave them. The earth was soft, being of sand (the beach?). Close to the plant the digging revealed a sweet-potato.[15]

Then they planted a slip from the plant itself in order not to end this new plant. Thus were candles changed into camotes (sweet-potatoes).[16] Then Kauymáli, having left the slips of the sweet-potato for Nakawé as a payment for her having given camotes to maintain his people, came with five of his people.

Nakawé said, "You can plant the camotes behind the god-chair. Like the corn, this is mine. I lend it to you for a famine food."

Candles were also taken to the gods of the five directions.[17] They took as many as five or ten to establish the custom of the children of Nakawé. All the gods received their candles.

Then Kauymáli asked that the money that was gained from the sale of the wax be counted. It was stuck together and attached to the handkerchief in which it was wrapped. He counted it as it was exposed to view. Then he ordered that part of the money be taken to the caves of the great gods of the five directions in order to establish the custom for his family.

1. Sub-story: The Domesticated Bees (*castil ítsic*, H.)

The fine domesticated bees, castil ítsic, belong to the Sun, Tau. Tau was dissatisfied because the wild bees were poor wax-givers. So the tame bees were commanded to come and sit on his chair, and then on his heart, since he was their father. Here they sat for five days, because they were "delicate" (sacred).[18] Then the Sun ordered them to fly to the five points. They came back laden with pollen, which they placed in a votive-bowl.

Nakawé heard the buzz of the bees. She wondered what was happening. So the tame bees were ordered to go and see who might talk to them. Again they went. This time they brought back a bit of flower as well as pollen. It was also left in the votive-bowl. Soon it grew to be a beautiful flower in the bowl. In five days the bowl was full of beautiful flowers.[19] They did not know where these flowers of all kinds were coming from.

The Sun then ordered the bees to wait for five days while he communicated by note-writing.[20] The half-bad Kauymáli put the note in his pouch.

Kauymáli then called all the people in order to tell them what the Sun had said. Since no one was able to read the note, they looked for the one behind the rock. It was Kauymáli. In order to fool them he had magically jumped out of sight behind the rock. Further, he had changed himself into a small boy.

He approached the people to read the Sun's note. He took it, and despite their hurry, began to act as though he were puzzling it out. Then he said, "Is there any dust [pollen?] in the votive-bowls that we know nothing of? Also, we do not understand the magic flowers. The message speaks of these. It says that all the people should eat of this."

The Sun requested Kauymáli to bring the message back. Kauymáli told the Sun that the people had eaten the flowers. As a result they all awoke drunk. They vomited, and from the bits of flowers in the vomit children emerged.[21] Before the bits of flowers were dry, Kauymáli put them in his clothes so that they would not remain exposed to the Sun.

In five days the people were well again. The Sun then told Kauymáli to get drunk [ecstatic] so that he could understand these things and tell the people. Thus when Kauymáli was half-drunk, the people questioned his thoughts.

He said, "The Sun sent us these flowers because we have no children. We vomited them from the flowers. Thus all of you have children, just as I have. That is all the message says."

The Sun told his children, the bees that were sitting nearby, to go around at dawn and listen to what was going on in the world. He said, "Who knows how to put [give] names? Eat from the flowers in the meadows."

Buzzing in a bee-line, the bees went among the people.

The people asked, "What is that buzzing? Who knows it?"

The Sun had told Kauymáli that he would inform him of what they were called. When a bee stopped, one of the people said, "It is a gnat (*raípon hóna*)." But this was wrong. Kauymáli then ordered the people to dream what it was they heard, since the Sun had sent it to be known. So everyone lighted candles to enable them to put [give] names.

Thereupon there was the buzzing of many bees. The people were afraid. Thus they could not dream the name of the bees. Kauymáli said, "No, you cannot dream the name of the bees. I will do it. The Sun is in a hurry for the bees to be named. Let us see whether they are not named castil ítsic. In my field I have a cross and much ceremonial paraphernalia. And I have much power (*fuerza*), so I can hear these things."

Now that they were named, the bees left. They swarmed to where there were others on a rock. But since the bees were not well[-protected] on the rock, the people were ordered to make them houses (*caion [cajón]*, Sp., *wakí*, H.).[22] According to the command of the Sun, the bees were too tender to live in rocks and trees as wild bees do. The tame bees looked for houses that were more suitable for themselves and their children. Some chose one house, and some another. Thus there were domesticated bees everywhere.

The Sun told them that if they did not like their new homes they were to tell him. The bees had been people. Now, however, all the human paraphernalia was taken from them by the Sun and changed into wax.[23]

In five days the wax increased. The Sun told Kauymáli to make candles for him and the other great gods.

The wax of the domesticated bees was better than that of the wild bees. When heated, it would come out white,[24] not yellow like the wax of the wild bees. Kauymáli was put in charge of this work.

B The Birth of the Saints

In the sea the water boiled and green foam came up. When it settled, the Sun went down into the sea (at sunset) and asked why the foam lay on the water like a mirror. He listened carefully to the foam. It said that it would have no name for five days, but that at the end of that time it would be Guadalupe (Ereno).[1]

At the end of the five days the foam came slowly to the edge of the water. It emerged as a small picture, *kuimuSáuwi*[2] (the picture of a Catholic saint).

Kauymáli went to see what this was, and he painted the image of the kuimu-Sáuwi. When he had copied it, he placed it on the wall, as the "santos" [icons] are placed in the church or the Casa Real. Then he painted a similar picture of San José.[3]

Thus were Guadalupe and San José created. They were ordered to be placed side by side (as they are always placed in Huichol churches or in the Casa Real, as at Tuxpan).

Kauymáli also wrote[4] down the custom for these gods; because he is powerful, even if half-bad.[5] He named the woman Santa Guadalupe, according to the command of the Sun, and told them what to do.

Kauymáli also found San Juan[6] and wrote[7] down the custom of this saint in his note-book. He ordered him to live "on that side." Another god was formed and placed on "this side." This was Santo Kaytano.[8]

Kauymáli found another saint who was given the name of San Miguel.[9] This saint had been an eagle that had plunged into the sea to the bottom where lay the cross of Cristo [Jesus Christ].

Another saint to be born was Santa Saulina[10] (Paulina?). Next from the sea, according to the command of the Sun, was born Santa Magdalena.[11]

The story of Santiago began when there was a feast in the sea. Among the rain-goddesses was one who had brought with her much sotol (liquor) [the plant from which *toache*, a distilled liquor, is made]. And included among the guests was a man who was very thin and emaciated. He was also very poorly and badly dressed. He sat with the others, who were well dressed. There was much drinking going on, and, despite his protests, he was offered a lot of wine [toache].

The woman who had brought the wine [toache] mixed flowers with it to make it more tasteful for him. She really wanted this man[,] even though he was very poor. She approached him and, speaking quietly, said, "Come and talk to me."

He heard her, but paid no attention.

Then she threw a pebble at him.

He said, "Don't throw things at me."

But she replied, "Sh! Don't talk so loud." Then she told him to meet her at a retired [secluded] place nearby.

So they met and talked. She offered him wine [toache]. He liked the smell of the flowers in the wine. Soon he was drinking, and in a short time his heart was warmed. After a while they began to talk of getting married.[12]

He, however, was afraid to go on. For one thing her father was very rich and he very poor. For another, she had ten brothers who would surely be offended by his poverty. But they embraced. Then they parted to await the dawn, and without having touched each other despite their desires.

A few days later they were intimate at a feast at another *ranchería*. They decided to get married. This made her brothers very angry. They said that he was poor, lazy, naked, and miserable, while they were all hard workers and very rich. But the woman defended the man she wanted and gave him courage.

The poor man and his wife went to a feast. Her ten brothers were there. They attacked the man, but he was saved by his wife.

This happened [again] at another feast, and he was badly hurt. He was cured of his injuries. Then the brothers pounded him again. But his wife cured him in fifteen days.

At a fifth feast this happened once more. The man had to flee in order to save his life.

The brothers then complained to the *gobernador* [governor]. The gobernador sent the *topiles* [police] to catch the poor man who had the love of the rich woman. But the woman still loved him, and they decided to go on together.

She told him that she knew of a remedy that would give him great courage and a cold heart. Her father had told her that the remedy that gave a cold heart was slow but terrible[,] to avenge insult.

Her father had once informed her of a special spring of water where the man should go for five days without eating salt. She, however, should accompany him, because the way was dangerous and difficult.

At the end of five days they arrived at the spring and sat on a stone by its bank. They had to pray and not be afraid, even though the water should rise.

The man sat on a rock in the water, while the woman who was helping him sat behind. The water was very cold.

The next night he sat deeper in the water. He continued going deeper into the water until on the fifth night it reached his neck.

This night the owner of the water was to show whether she was going to grant the favor they requested. The same night from the bottom of the spring a thundering sound was heard. It caused the water to rise above the man's head; but it soon came down. Then the owners of the spring came out as male and female ice-people (gods) *uwí tewíali*.[13] They were short and ugly in appearance.

The poor men [man] had to wrestle with them in the water to see if he could win over them. So they wrestled at the five points of the world. The last time, in the middle region of the world, the gods told the poor man to follow the ice-people into the frozen lake.

The ice-people broke a hole in the ice, and the poor man followed them into the water. He won over them. From the bottom of the lake they gave him a piece of ice. This he ate so that he would have a cold heart. Then they told him to come out of the lake because he had gained that [which] he had requested. He came out stiff with cold.[14]

His wife made a fire to warm him. She was aided by the Sun.[15] After two days[,] he had recovered from the cold and could walk. Then the ice-gods showed him the places where he was to demonstrate his strength.

At one place were five small pine-trees about six feet high. He had to pull these out by the roots, after taking a running start. This he did to all five of the pine-trees. He even pulled out the largest one, which was in the middle region.[16]

Then the gods told him that now he was so strong and solid that his brothers-in-law would not be able to hurt him. The woman was very pleased with her husband's strength.

The man and woman learned that a feast was to be given at the ranchería, *taSecípa*. So they dressed in their best clothes and went. The man's ten brothers-in-law approached him to attack him again. They did not know that he had gained tremendous strength. When he would not leave, they began to insult him. So without arising[,] he picked up stones and knocked them down. Since his heart was so cold, he punished them thus for a day and a night.

The ice-gods finally told him to be calm and see what would happen. The brothers could not hurt him nor do anything against him because of his great strength. It was as though they were playing with him. His solidity even turned away the blows of their machetes. He finally picked them up by their arms and their hair and threw them in a pile.

Having lost their contest with the man, the brothers then got up and went home to cure their hurts [wounds]. They complained to the gobernador.

The gobernador dreaded to have his topiles try to take the man's wife away by force. But if he succeeded, he would imprison the man for five years.

So the gobernador sent thirty topiles to seize the poor man and bring him in. They found him sleeping, so they tied him. He broke the rope, however, and threw them out of the house, knocking down the door as he did so. Then he took down his guitar and began to play contentedly. He refused to go to the Casa Real, because he knew that he had done no wrong.

The topiles had to return and report their failure. They were sent back again and again for five times.

The man finally decided to go and face his enemies. When he approached, many people caught him and tied him in the stocks. But although the stocks were securely fastened, he knocked them into pieces. Then he sent the gobernador sailing with a shove.

By this time the people had had enough. The gobernador, furthermore, decided that the man was not at fault, since his wife was willing to remain with him in spite of her brothers' disapproval.[17]

The brothers lived in a ranchería nearby. They were giving a feast. The man went, though he was uninvited. There he got drunk and began to beat his wife. She was almost beaten to death by her drunken husband. This was because she had refused to sell one of her mules to a Mexican who was trading at the feast.

The man finally stopped beating his wife and fell into a drunken sleep.

Then the ten brothers saddled the mule to test the man. They put four hundred pesos in silver on the back of the wild mule. If the man succeeded in riding the animal, he would win both it and the money.

The strong man, however, was not very anxious to ride the mule. He was still drunk from what he had taken at the feast. So twenty men took him in his drunken stupor when he had his eyes closed. He awakened slightly, but did not wish to ride.

But the people said that he would have to in order to show his real worth. If he did not ride, they would think he showed off his strength and power only before women.[18]

So he made ready to mount. The men held the mule firmly until he was well [seated] in the saddle. Then they uncovered the animal's eyes and loosed it. An old man hit it with a quirt. Then the mule bucked madly and threw the man from the saddle. Then it ran away.

The man lay still on the ground, and the old man retorted, "They said that he was strong, but he is strong only for women.[19] He is worth nothing." So all took sticks and they beat him, finally leaving him for dead.

But the following day he could move. His wife cared for him and cured him of his hurts [wounds].

Her parents then had the mule brought again for their son to ride. The boy carefully covered the eyes of the saddled mule. The relatives released the animal. It went off bucking, with the boy sitting solidly on its back.

The mule ran like the wind, but it did not throw the boy. It ran until it was exhausted. Before the afternoon was over[,] it was thoroughly broken.

Thus the boy won. His name was Santiago.[20]

The Sun told them all that they must move carefully because they were still "tender." After this they could be named (baptized) according to the command of their *tata*, the Sun.[21]

Near the sea-shore were large cliffs. Here the saints went to follow the command of the Sun. There they remained shining as though painted on the rocks just as "saints" are painted on canvas. They had no clothes.

San José wished [to have] a bow *(óatsa)* for his violin. Kauymáli made him one. In five days it turned into pure flowers and made beautiful music[,] which could be heard as far as a harp.[22] San José asked also for a plate of solid gold. This was to be his votive-bowl on which his money could be placed.[23] Kauymáli made it for him. San José wanted further a piece of his heart to be hung around his neck (the sacred heart?), and also a green-and-red kerchief[,] which was to be folded and placed on his plate.[24] After San José had been completely decorated in this fashion, Kauymáli placed him back a little from the other saints.

Then the Virgin of Guadalupe wished [for] her decoration. She asked Kauymáli to make her five votive-bowls. These were to be placed at her feet. So Kauymáli commanded this. The votive-bowls came out of the sea[25] and were taken to her table (altar?). Next she requested some candles. Kauymáli got them for her out of the sea. These were large candles and were placed on her votive-bowls. Then Kauymáli went and found a circle of five colored flowers. These were gathered and placed on the candles.[26]

Then the Virgin asked that a bunch of five flowers be hung upon her breast, as had been done for San José. These flowers went into their bodies and became their real hearts. Thus their hearts are no longer seen on the outside (as is the sacred heart of Jesus?). The flowers in the body of San José were to become children.[27] Those of the Virgin entered her womb and became children.[28] Then Kauymáli ordered the two saints to copulate. This they did, becoming engaged.

Nakawé told Father Sun that she was doing this, and the Sun was agreeable. The saints had to be true to each other; and since they were "delicate,"[29] they could not talk. Thus was Santo Cristo born.

1. Sub-story: Santo Cristo and the Julios (Jews)

When Kauymáli finished making the candles, he took the wax that remained and used it to make a painted board *(étali [itáli]*, H.). The people asked him to come and sing for them. But he bade them wait until he had finished his painting. So they decided to wait, because they were curious to know what he was painting.

Kauymáli was painting prayers that he wished granted by the great gods. With beads and colored wool placed in the wax on the board, he painted a snake, a rattle-snake, a fish, a coyote, and a skunk [raccoon] (*mapache*). He also painted the opossum *takuache* [*tlacuache*, Mex. Sp. for opossum] *(iáuSu)*, [mountain] lion, bear, deer, dog, horse, mule, burro, burras, stud-jacks (*manadera*, Sp.), male and female goats, male and female pigs (note the animals associated with the Mexicans), royal eagle (double-headed Hapsburg symbol), eagle, hawk, parrot, parrakeet [*sic*], *orakate* (a bird from the coast), *pitacoche* (Sp.-H., "a bird that eats tunas"), quail, tiger [jaguar], wolf, and a singer. All the animals, hens, turkeys, and everything else in all colors he painted. The colored rocks of the five points were represented in the painting.[30]

Then Kauymáli took out of his god-house a branding iron[31] and pressed it against the board. An impression of Jesus Christ was left in colors. Thus also did he make [the Virgin of] Guadalupe and all the other saints, five of each.[32] Finally he painted the Sun and the animals of the Sun—the tiger [jaguar] and the eagle.

After this he communicated with the great gods of the sea about what he was doing, since he did it at the command of the Sun. The Sun told him that the painting needed the picture of the owner, the one to take care of the animals. So he painted the boy and the girl who were in charge of the animals of the Sun,[33] and the *tcikuáki* (masked clown) who presides at all feasts. He painted also the picture of a violinist and one of a guitarist.

The Sun then said to him, "It is alright now if you wish to sing. Sing, and tell me what it is that you wish."

So Kauymáli told the people that he would sing for them that night, after they had prayed all afternoon. Then they placed the three shaman's chairs (as in [all] Huichol ceremonies) in order to sing all night. Although his assistants did not wish to sing, they had to take the chairs at the side of Kauymáli.

Inside the dancing-house a [sacred] clown took charge. He assigned the others to "guard" the paraphernalia and see that the candles did not go out.

They needed a good violinist to play inside the god-house so that he could communicate with the gods by means of the violin. Kauymáli told them to have a contest to see who was best among ten players. Various players competed, but none could play very well. The hour for commending [commencing] the singing outside was approaching. It was necessary to find a good player of the violin to make music within the dancing-house.

Kauymáli took his magic painted board and painted Ereno seated on a rock in her beautiful clothes. Thus was she chosen to judge who was the best player.[34] It was urgent that they find a player, because the gods wanted the preparations finished. Already those animals that were to be sacrificed were thrown and tied. Even the great gods of the five directions came to hear the final contest.

The last one to try was a little boy, Santo Cristo. His violin was only six inches long. He was so uncertain about his ability that he didn't dare go into the god-house, but played on the outside [instead].

When he touched his violin, the sound was beautiful. The great gods of the five directions heard it and were pleased.[35] As he played, his violin and bow were magically covered with flowers and dripped water.[36] The other players were envious, because with this beautiful music the people could now kill [sacrifice] the animals.[37] The ceremonial paraphernalia was bathed with the blood. As the animals were being killed, the candles were lighted.

The dancing began in the god-house to the beautiful music of the violin. Ereno and Father Sun danced, as did the people inside the dancing-house.[38] While dancing, the Sun shot an arrow to the great gods of the sea to ask them if they were pleased with the music, the feast, and the anointing of the paraphernalia with blood.[39] If so, they were to give the people good health, prosperity, and crops.

The dissatisfied losers of the violin contest were envious of Santo Cristo. They drew apart and plotted. Santo Cristo knew that they were plotting against him because they had their faces toward him. But he could do nothing, since the great gods were there.

The Sun then commanded Santo Cristo to carry out his orders. He ordered Santo Cristo to tell the discontented players to gather in the field again. Thus the best player would be determined a second time.

The winner of the first contest, Santo Cristo, asked Kauymáli to communicate with the great gods to protect him from the others. Kauymáli promised to do this, and said to have no fear. The Sun then told Santo Cristo to change himself before going so that the others would not know him. "I know that they are thinking evil against you," the Sun said, "but take your things for the contest."

After this[,] Jesus was willing to go. Thus he went to the contest prepared to play, even against the others who were still angry.

In the field were fifty contestants sitting in a line on boards. Following the instructions of the Sun[,] Kauymáli had the first contestant play five times. The first, however, was a poor player. Similarly the others followed. Each played five times, and each tried both the violin and the guitar. Some had very bad instruments. Some had strings only of *ixtle*. And in other ways they failed. Some became angry with their instruments when, defeated, they had to leave the line of contestants.

As before, Ereno was there to reward the winner with an embrace and a dance.[40]

Finally only the last one remained. The others were surprised not to see the boy who had won the other contest. This last one was an old man. He had placed lime in his hair to make it look white, and he walked as if he were lame. His violin, furthermore, was changed into an old, broken thing.

They called him to take his turn, and told him not to be afraid. He said, "I doubt if I can play." He repaired his violin and bow. Then he took his violin in his hands and his guitar in his feet and played them both at once.

He played so well that Ereno said, "This one knows my wishes and my orders." And she got up and danced with him. She said to the others, "You others are no good. But as for this good player, I care for him with all my heart. I wish to marry him." So saying she embraced him while he played, and then danced with him.[41]

The others were displeased at this. Ereno and the winner, who was Santo Cristo, danced all over the patio, except in the middle where there was an altar. They danced for an hour, and Ereno would not let Santo Cristo go. The others could only look on, because they were no good.

Then Ereno took Santo Cristo to the great gods of the sea. She told them of his fears of the bad losers. The gods said that they would defend him, and asked him to play so that they could hear. So Santo Cristo played, and the great gods danced.

The bad losers followed, but remained at a distance. Nakawé from the sea sounded with her sandal.[42] This caused thunder, advising the great gods that the losers were near. The losers were *jurilos* (*judios*, Sp., Jews), and were against Santo Cristo. But Santo Cristo was safe with his protectors, who were the Sun and the other great gods.

Then the great gods said to the winner, "Change your form and go to the place (in the sea?) where the sun was born. Go in the form of wind."[43]

So Santo Cristo went there to see what he would find. He entered the sea. After an hour there was the Sun, looking at him.

The Jews said, "What fell into the sea? Let us go there and find out."

The Jews went and looked in the water. There they saw something shining. As they looked on, the winner left the water. But according to the command of Nakawé, the Jews could not look clear to the bottom of the water where Santo Cristo was born. Leaving the sea five times[,] Santo Cristo came back and found a great cross shining in the bottom of the water.[44]

2. Sub-story: Santo Cristo Leaves to Establish the World and the Customs of the Mexicans

The winner came out of the sea as Jesus Christ.[45] The Jews asked a dog[,] which lived in the sea[,] what it was [that] they had not been able to see. They said they wanted to catch a bad woman. So the dog ran, and the Jews followed it. But when the dog approached, Santo Cristo entered the water. The dog followed, while the Jews waited on the bank [shore].

But the dog was unable to catch Santo Cristo, although he tried five times. The last time that he failed, Santo Cristo knew that he was saved, because the dog had turned from him to follow a fish. Thus the animal was forced to live on fish. His name was *halúka*[46] (the mink?) [otter].

The Jews now did not know what to do. They put on wings and flew off. They procured a larva *icpála*, a machete, a knife, and a pistol. With these they came back to catch Santo Cristo. But Santo Cristo jumped into the water and swam to the middle. Again the Jews had to remain on the bank [shore], for Santo Cristo was protected by the great gods of the sea.

Kauymáli told Santo Cristo how he had painted everything in the world on the magic board[47] (étali). The Sun said, "Be strong and have no fear. We will take care of you and protect you."

So Santo Cristo escaped in a strong wind that blew him to all of the five directions.[48] The Jews shot arrows at him. One arrow hit him in the breast, making a wound from which the blood flowed. But this did not kill him, for he recovered from it as if by magic. The Jews shot other arrows that wounded both his hands and his feet.[49] He escaped, however, through a door[,] which closed on the Jews.

Finally Santo Cristo arrived at a tree. Here he stopped to make his cross.

Nakawé said to the Sun, "Our poor son is wounded and naked, though shining and beautiful. I will send him some of my clothes." So she sent him a bit of cloth with which to cover himself and from which to make a pouch. The pouch grew into a blanket. *Calcones* [*Calzones*, Sp. for trousers][50] grew from the bit of cloth, because his privates were exposed.[51] Now he could go out into the world to inspect it.

Although the Jews were following him, Santo Cristo travelled for five days in each of the five directions.[52] He studied all the plants, animals, leaves, roots, birds, etc. The people, crossing themselves, gave him food. But, since he had to continue his fast, he could not eat. He was communicating with the great gods about the Jews who were still following him. At the same time he learned all the geographical features according to the command of Nakawé.

Finally he arrived at "this side." He said to himself, "I like it here. The animals are good." He then drew a picture to send to Nakawé. In each of the five directions he left a communication for her. Wherever he did this, a Mexican town appeared. Soon he had founded five towns.

In the middle he put the principal town, and in this town was a very large church with a tower. This was according to the orders of the great gods of the sea. The Sun commanded him to make a road between the towns, and also pasture, water, springs, and things for the Mexicans to eat.

Santo Cristo was then told to approach the Mexicans. But he was to let Kauymáli[53] see how it was. Kauymáli told him to go and find out how things were going.

Nakawé[54] said to Kauymáli, "We will give you the things for these people who are being born. You, Santo Cristo, wait here with tata Sun. Do not go. Kauymáli, do not let them know you."

But the half-bad Kauymáli did not obey Nakawé's last command. He wrote many letters[,] which he left in all the towns. The people were not as yet very well formed. They were half wild, and did not know how to read. They took the letters, wondering what they were all about.

Then Kauymáli told the ants to set pebbles into piles.

The people did not know how to plant.

Kauymáli had to make five trips.

When Kauymáli had left the letters everywhere, he came back and said to Santo Cristo, "Let us see how the Mexicans are using their lands, water, and animals. They have only grass. We must establish gardens among them. Tell them not to work with the grass. Tell them to be calm. I am not yet finished with the business on which I am sent."

So Santo Cristo was sent to give the Mexicans all the plants they needed. He told them how to irrigate their gardens, following the orders of Kauymáli, who had altered the commands of the great gods of the sea.

The Mexicans were trying to read the letters left by Kauymáli. While they were talking about the letters, Kauymáli came and read the papers he had left. The people became quiet so that they might hear him. He did this in all the towns. Everyone who heard him thought that what he read must be true. They thought that these must be the commands of the great gods of the sea.

Meanwhile the Sun told the great gods of the sea that the Jews were plotting behind the door of rock where they had been left. All the great gods were given messages to know what had been done. The Sun communicated with the gods of the five points (*aca, alla, medio,* "above," etc.[55]). The Sun told the great gods that the Mexicans were looking for someone to read their messages. Further, the Mexicans were trying to dream what the great gods said. One dreamed that they said the world was being founded.[56]

Since the Mexicans were looking for someone to read their messages, they called Kauymáli, who, because he was half-bad, had written them. Through such means could he defeat the great gods and get the Mexicans for himself.

When he went to read the messages, he refused to sit in the shaman's chair because it was "delicate."[57] He would only read the letters standing up.

He took the letters and read them to himself, pretending not to understand them. Then he gave them to their proper owners, saying, "Here, put them up. They may be useful some day. Save them for the gods of the five points."

The great gods remained very quiet. They could hear what he said.

Kauymáli was sweating from the task of handing out all the letters. He asked, "Who left these?"

The Mexicans did not know. Kauymáli then said that he would tell them what the letters conveyed. "These say," he began, "that Nakawé tells you that, alone, you cannot succeed in your work of founding the world. It lacks much grass, water, etc. This letter also says that someone has been born whom you may have seen. In the water he has left a cross, which you can see." The Mexicans looked and saw the cross, so they made the sign of the cross.[58]

Kauymáli continued pretending to read. "He has put many things in the world. See that it does not escape, because bad people are persecuting (following) him."

Santo Cristo then wrote a letter to Nakawé. In it he said, "For five days I am going to work. Thus you may not find me. I shall look over the world for the third time. I will see you at dawn tomorrow, so let us arrange where we shall meet. My father (the Sun, doubtless) says that my quest will be useless because I am new, clean, and shining. I will not touch a woman, so you see I am without pollution."[59]

Ereno heard his promise not to touch a woman. She went to the devils on the other side of the sea who are called chinos [Chinese].[60] She said to them, "Let us see who has the most power, you or Santo Cristo."

Ereno then met Santo Cristo in a house. They were alone. She said to him, "Lock the door and let us lay together."

But Santo Cristo withstood the temptation of the goddess who had danced with him and embraced him when he won the violin-playing contest.[61]

As Santo Cristo left[,] he met the Mexicans. They were planting with sticks, but nothing grew. He greeted them and talked with them. They had no names and were, therefore, still of the devil. They said, "If you know all this from our tata, the Sun (identified with God), bless this field so it will grow. Bless us also for our good health."

So Santo Cristo blessed the fields and the people with the sign of the cross.[62] He said, "I name this field the planting (*étsa enéma*, H.). Let us see what comes up here."

Santo Cristo continued on. He met a man with a yoke of oxen. They asked him to bless this, because the man was working to no purpose since nothing grew. The man asked Santo Cristo to bless the animals and the plow. If he was from tata Sun, he could make the sign of the cross in the same fashion as he had blessed the other people. Santo Cristo did this, and changed the names of the things from grass to oxen, plow, straps, yoke, etc. Then he gave the Mexican some corn-seed and told him to plant it.

He went on until he saw a Mexican wasting time by planting grass like squash-seed. After blessing the grass[,] he named it squash. Then he took something from the back of his neck. It grew into a beautiful plant. It was the onion, *iu-uli*, and it grew because it had been blessed by Santo Cristo.

Five steps farther on was a Mexican who was wasting his time also with grass. Santo Cristo blessed it and named it *jitomate Sayúki* (tomato); *tomate* (husked tomato); cactus nopal (*nakáli* [H.]); maguey (century plant, *mai*, H.); banana (*kálu* [H.])[63]; sugar-cane (*sa* [H.]); chile (*kukúli*); *chile bravo* (i.e., a small hot chile, *akukúli* [H.]); plums (*kuálupa* [H.]); *guaymuchil* (*Pithecolobrium dulce*); potatoes (*pápas*, Sp.-H.); coffee (*café*, Sp.-H.); *silandro* [cilantro] (Sp.-H.); irrigation ditch; distillery (*taverna*, Sp.); *uki* ([H.,] pulque, Sp.); machete and ax; upland clearing (milpa, Sp., *wáSa*, H.); *vino* (mescal, Sp.); *tsápo* (*zapote*, Sp.); pomegranates (*granada*, Sp.); mango (mango, Sp.-H.); *iáoko* ([H.,] *aguacate*, Sp.); peaches (*melacaton* [*melocotón*], Sp.-H.); radishes (*rabano* [*rábano*], Sp.); annones (*nóna*, Sp.-H.); an abode [adobe] house; sidewalk (*cimienta*, Sp.); *ollas* [pots]; and streets running to the five points.

Then Santo Cristo went to another point and made another town with the following: a church with a tower; a sidewalk; and a *palacio* (government building).

He established a third town with the same things.

After this he established a fourth town with the following: tables; stores; carpenter-shop; and a blacksmithshop [*sic*] (with hammer, hard pistol, saber, and iron-pot).

Then Santo Cristo established the fifth town.

3. Sub-story: The Virgin of Guadalupe and San José

Santo Cristo was still at work composing the world of the Mexicans. He had not touched a woman and was still a virgin.[64] The Jews were pursuing him. They could not overtake him, however. Thus he wrote to Guadalupe and San José.

San José, having many children in his heart, was strong and resisted temptation. He did this for fear that the Jews would trick him and get his children.[65] So the Virgin and San José went to the Sun to find out in which of the five world regions Santo Cristo was working. They were pure. This was shown by their clothes, which were clean.[66]

The pair followed the tracks of Santo Cristo to the margin of the sea. When they arrived there, they were still true to each other. The people there wished to have intercourse with the Virgin because she was very beautiful.[67] But she observed the command of the Sun, and only asked them where Santo Cristo was.

Those of the sea advised her to continue on farther where she would come across three ranches of *gachupines*,[68] Jews, *turcos* [Turks], and *changos* [monkeys].

These peoples asked her where she was going. She informed them that she was seeking a certain person without a name. They were dubious, so she showed them her heart, which was her permit from the Sun. This she always carried with her, because she was surrounded by bad people.

San José had gone in a different direction. He was in another region. He arrived at the first town made by Santo Cristo. Here he got a pistol, a rifle, and a machete[69] with which to defend himself from the bad people. As soon as he arrived at the sea where the bad people were, he asked for Santo Cristo.

The bad people asked San José what he wanted. He refused to tell them. They tried to catch him, but he resisted them with his pistol, rifle, and machete.

Then the Sun directed San José to another world region where Santo Cristo might be. Here, in the land where the Sun was born, the trails of San José and the Virgin [of] Guadalupe met. San José heard the brawl of a Huichol feast. He saw that the gachupines, turcos, etc., were abusing the Virgin and attacking her by force because she was not drunk.

San José went to the Sun. He told the Sun that he, San José, was pure and clean. The Virgin, on the other hand, had not been true (women are always weak). So he went off in another direction to a place where he was to sleep with the Virgin. (This place is Analco, at the confluence of two important rivers.)

So San José went there. He wrote the Virgin, asking her whether she had been true. The letter fell at the feet of the Virgin. She opened it and read it.

She knew that, while she had sinned, San José had been true. So by means of her thought[70] she wrote to San José, saying that she had not sinned either and that she would come to him. Then she went to the mesa of Analco[,] which had been made by Kauymáli.

Thus by writing with their hearts [only] no more[,][71] they communicated, arranging a rendezvous at the mesa in the event that the Virgin was still true. When the Virgin arrived, however, her clothes were dirty and torn from her sins and struggles with the gachupines and Jews.[72] San José was now doubly certain that the Virgin had been untrue to him.[73]

He ordered her to sleep apart, saying that he would not touch her.

The Virgin had escaped from the Jews by telling them that she had to make water. On this pretext she was able to get away, jump into a hole, and disappear. She had gone to the sea, from which she had come out changed. Thus had she escaped from the Jews. Since San José would have nothing to do with her, she slept at a (certain) red cliff near the sea.

Kauymáli was ordered by the Sun to leave the pictures he had made of the Virgin of Guadalupe and San José at all the Mexican towns, as well as all the Huichol churches.

The Sun changed the Virgin after she had been at the mesa of Analco. Here she left her torn and dirty clothes.[74] The Sun gave her beautiful new clothes. He commanded that she be elevated to be with him.[75]

Thus San José lost the Virgin because he had suspected her, whereas she had been forced [not realizing that she had been raped]. The Sun commanded her to be decorated with many beautiful flowers in her splendid clothes.

Kauymáli told San José how beautiful the Virgin was. So San José wrote a note to the Virgin. This was taken to her by Kauymáli. In the middle of the note was painted a small flower. This was to be placed by Kauymáli in the middle region where the Virgin was.

At midnight the Virgin dreamed.[76] She got up to sweep the dancing-patio as she had dreamed. She found the flower and secreted it in her clothes. Five days later she discovered that she was pregnant.[77] Grandmother Growth (Nakawé) asked her about the flower and told her the cause of her pregnancy.

The Virgin soon gave birth to the child. San José knew of this. He had followed her to the little town, Sáusa.

The Virgin, who had been told what to do by Ereno (Nakawé), had written San José to be there. Her letter told him further that he would have to pay for the blood of child-birth.[78]

The message came to San José while he was asleep. On awakening he found a piece of paper. He wondered who had left it. When he read that he was the father of a child, he knew that he must go and join the Virgin. He answered in a note[,] which Kauymáli caused to be taken to the Virgin in a whirlwind. He told her that he would be with her in five days. Then he assured the Sun and the great gods of the sea that he would pay the Virgin for the blood she had lost in child-birth.

The child was a Mexican. San José bought it a *reboso* (shawl), skirts, shoes, and the like, and also everything that Mexican women need. These things he brought to dress both the Virgin and the child as a payment for the blood of child-birth.[79] He also sent one hundred and fifty dollars, as well as sugar, bread, candles, and chocolate.[80] He wished to rejoin the Virgin, but he could not until he had found Santo Cristo.

In the middle region the Mexican child was taking advantage of these gifts. Soon it grew up, but it was not allowed to go about freely. It was really a Huichol masquerading as a Mexican.

A man of the pack-ant people (*arriero*, Sp., *tsału tewíałi*, H.) in that place decided to steal the child. He knew where the child lived near the sea. So he dug a hole (as ants do) and came out on the other side near the child. The ant-man told the child that he had come to ask a favor of him.

The mother heard the voices. She asked the child who was talking. The child answered that he was only speaking his thoughts.

The ant-man went back into his hole, and the mother was reassured. Then the ant-man returned and told the child to join him in five days. When he came back, he carried the child off in his jaws, as pack-ants carry things away. So that the child would leave no tracks by which he could be followed, the ant-man took him to a church.

Kauymáli copied five pictures of the child. These are the pictures of the saints in the churches of the Mexicans. This Kauymáli did in all five of the world regions. Then the ant-man, having arrived at Analco with the child, took it back unharmed when this was finished.

In the ten days that the child was gone[,] the mother looked for him. But he was returned pure, clean, and unharmed. He told his mother that it was the ant-man who had taken him away.

The ant-man escaped to the sea, and the people could not find him. They did, however, fill in the ant-holes so that the ant-people could not return.

C The Myth of Santo Cristo

1. Sub-story: Santo Cristo Establishes Metal and Money

Meanwhile[,] Santo Cristo, following the orders of the Sun, was busy composing everything for the Mexicans. But he had to stop his work because the Jews were drawing close to him. He climbed into the tower of a church. The Jews did not follow him.

The church-tower, however, lacked something to give off sound, and the people could not hear. The only sound there was came from the buzz of the dung-beetle, *teapúawi*. This insect sounded with his wings whenever anyone was born.[1]

One of these beetles sounded in the tower where Santo Cristo was hidden. Four others sounded in the other towers of the church. They had come from the sea where they had been able to sound loudly. As soon as they reached the tower of the church, they turned into metal (bronze), giving off a clear, strong sound.[2]

When the insects fell into pieces, Kauymáli found the bits of metal. These he saved to give [to] the officials of the government. At the Sun's command[,] half of the metal was hidden in a cave.[3] During a fire[,] which swept through the cave and melted the bodies of the insects into metal, it was not harmed.

Santo Cristo saw this, as did the Jews. The Mexicans placed a cross at the cave because, from the burned bodies of the insects, only pure silver was left. With the silver the cross was decorated. But Kauymáli took both the buried metal and the silver from the cross and put it in his pouch. Later he gave it to the government.[4]

The insects that were not burned flew away to the other towns to see if there was any money (metal) there. It was all well hidden and guarded. This pleased the Sun. Then they returned to the caves where the money was buried. They found it well concealed. Then, followed by Kauymáli, they went to the tower of the church where Santo Cristo was hidden. Here the Sun had commanded that a sign be left for them.

Kauymáli went to the governmental officials and gave them the metal (silver, tin?) for making things such as tin cans and the like according to the command of the Sun.[5] The Sun ordered Santo Cristo to continue with his work of establishing the things for the Mexicans.

When Santo Cristo arrived at the sea after fulfilling these orders, the great gods asked him if he was tired. "Yes," he replied, "for I have worked long and hard at your command."

Then Santo Cristo told Kauymáli to go where he had been and calculate how much money his work was worth. So Kauymáli went to the stores, churches, houses, etc., noting what had been done and what they were worth. He also observed the things that needed to be done. He did this in fifty towns, until he arrived at the City [capital] of Mexico. This is in the center of the republic. Here he had to work for fifteen days, since the place was large. He noted everything on paper, and then told the people that someone was coming who would arrange everything completely and properly.

Finally Kauymáli arrived in the town by the sea where Santo Cristo was. The Jews wondered at the appearance of Santo Cristo because he had changed so much. They did not want him to be successful in his task of composing the world. They followed him.

Santo Cristo went to a very thorny tree[,] which the Jews could not climb. Here Kauymáli met him and gave him the notes of the things he had still to make. Santo Cristo had to dig wells and make reservoirs (*tanques*, Sp.) in the places where there were no springs.

The Sun and Tatevalí enabled Santo Cristo to get help in making these things. The helpers were cliffs in human form.[6] To them Santo Cristo sent notes telling them to come and help him. Five of them, bringing picks, shovels, bars, grubbing hoes, etc., all of which had been made at the command of the Sun from the metal of the burned dung-beetles,[7] came to help Santo Cristo.

The Sun then ordered American people (*gente americano*, Sp.-H.) to work this metal. When they came, there was a great noise of dynamite in the middle region where the insects had burned. This was near Real [de] Catorce (San Luis Potosí).[8]

The Americans used dynamite. With this they blew holes in the cliffs[9] in order to extract the metal. At Santo Cristo's command they made machinery to work the metal.[10]

The Sun commanded the Americans to stamp the eagle (the Sun's bird) on the silver money.[11] In this way the money would be "very Huichol," and could be used to maintain the Sun's people (the Huichols). When much money had been made, Santo Cristo blessed the strangers and named them *americanos*.[12]

Santo Cristo knew that he could not live much longer, since the Jews were pressing him closely. He worked hard, and ordered the Americans to do likewise. Much money had to be made so that the Huichols and Mexicans could buy cloth and the many other things they needed, all of which had to be brought in ships.[13]

According to the order of Santo Cristo, who was in his tower, the money had to be left in the National Palace in Mexico City. So the Americans worked hard and made the fifty piles of silver. They did not take out their share until Santo Cristo's money was finished.

As soon as the work was finished, the Americans wrote Santo Cristo. He was glad of this, because the people were very poor. However, he told the people to be very patient, since the money was "scarcely born."[14]

Now all the towns were given the money. But, now that the work was going well, they needed someone to take charge of the money and distribute it among the people.

At the sea the work was to begin, since the great gods of the sea had their money. TumuSáuwi, the first Huichol (Duck-boy), was ordered by the Sun and the great gods of the sea to teach the people there how to plant seeds. These he took from his pouch. Then he taught the Mexicans how to plant [sugar]cane, watermelon, and the plants of the coastal region of Tepic. San[to] Iago was ordered by Santo Cristo to take charge of this work.

Thus the Huichols could now go to the coast and work at the harvests of the Mexicans to gain money through their wages.[15] There was never [any] lack of money in Santiago, since Santo Iago himself ordered that money be made by the Americans. This money was kept in the National Palace.

Santo Iago then ordered that there should be *mayordomos* among the Mexicans. These were to boss the peones [hired hands], both Mexican and Huichol, who worked in the field. Santo Cristo was commanded by the Sun to give the mayordomos watches so that they would know when it was noon and thus be able to cry, "Now rest." The mayordomos on [for] their parts were commanded to give the peones rest at noon and to feed them well.[16]

All this work of Santo Cristo pleased the Sun.

The merchants needed cloth and various other things with which to stock their stores. So Santo Cristo sent a note to Mexico City by Kauymáli, and the stores were soon stocked with the goods that Santo Cristo had already made. Boxes were made of boards of pine that belonged to Santo Cristo.[17] This was done in the carpenter-shops he had established.

Other carpenters made doors, tables, chairs, and the like, all at the command of the Sun. The carpenters, further, were ordered to earn wages.

Then the Sun commanded Santo Cristo to start a fire in the town, and to instruct blacksmiths how to make machetes, knives, horse-shoes, and similar things.

2. Sub-story: The Jews Are Punished by the Sun for Pursuing Santo Cristo

Meanwhile the Jews had found out where Santo Cristo was hidden. The white heron, *maraíka tewíali*, had betrayed Santo Cristo to them. So Santo Cristo had to flee again, for the Jews were preparing arrows with which to shoot him. He sought refuge far from the Huichol country in the Sierra Morón. Here he hid in a pine-tree.[18]

The Jews were angry at the white heron because they had failed to catch Santo Cristo. By means of a note they asked the Sun where Santo Cristo was hidden. They affirmed that he was not a real god but a devil and an animal, and that therefore they wished to kill him. The Sun replied that he knew of none such, and that they would have to continue their search.

The Jews now thought that the white heron had lied to them. They were going to kill him. He was frightened, and told them that Santo Cristo had gone to the Sierra Morón.

So the Jews hurried to the Sierra Morón, but they did not find Santo Cristo. They followed his tracks clear to the National Palace of Mexico City. They asked the people there to capture Santo Cristo if they could. The people, however, were unwilling. Finally, since they could not find Santo Cristo in Mexico City, they traced his tracks back to the Sierra Morón. Santo Cristo meanwhile had gone back to his tower.

Santo Cristo told his father, the Sun, that he didn't wish to be killed until he had finished his important work. The Sun said that he would communicate with the great gods of the sea when he went [descended] into the sea at sunset.

Now just at this time when the Sun was talking to the great gods of the sea, the heron was bathing in the sea. The Sun saw him. He ordered a snake to kill the heron for having betrayed to the Jews the hiding-place of Santo Cristo.[19]

So the heron was killed, and his wings and head [were] taken off as a warning to the Jews when they returned to seek more information. The Jews knew that this was a bad omen. They were very angry. But from the heart of the heron a new bird appeared.

The Jews, still angry, renewed their efforts to find out where Santo Cristo was. They went about making inquiries regarding him. For information as to Santo Cristo's whereabouts they offered fifty centavos or a peso. But although they went to all the towns of the five points, no one could tell them anything.

The Sun had assured Santo Cristo, who was in his tower, that he would continue to defend him whilst he kept busy. This was because there were not enough churches. So Santo Cristo was changed into an eagle, and flew away from the tower. He was anxious to finish his work before he should be given over to the Jews. He flew to the place of the Sun.

The Sun told Kauymáli to see what happened where the eagle lighted. At these places Kauymáli found statues of the saints in pure gold.[20]

Then the Sun sent a note to the Jews. He told them that perhaps the one they were looking for was at the point [shore] of the sea. Although Santo Cristo was changed into an eagle, he still used the same sandals. Through these the Jews hoped to track him. They went to the point of the sea where there were many corrals and cliffs. They arrived only after great difficulty. But they still found nothing.

Kauymáli then told them that, if they were not afraid, to go to the very point [edge] of the sea. There they went, unafraid. This was the place of the Sun, where his brilliance might hurt their eyes. But, even though the Jews knew this, they looked straight at the Sun and asked him about Santo Cristo. The Sun dazzled them with his brilliance[,] and this made them drunk.

While they were drunk, the Sun put their feet on backwards. Then he put one of their eyes in their foreheads and the other in their chins.[21] When they awoke, they did not know what had happened[,] because the Sun was again in the sky.

They heard Santo Cristo whistling like a Mexican, and they followed the sound to all the five world regions. But they were unable to find him, because their feet were reversed and their eyes out of place. Meanwhile Santo Cristo had been concluding his work with the world of the Mexicans, and instructing the Mexicans in the usage of their new crops.

3. Sub-story: Santo Cristo Makes Cattle from Wheat, etc.

The Sun had given five grains of wheat. With these[,] Santo Cristo taught the Mexicans how to plant. When the wheat was ripe, he showed them how to grind it and make bread from it.[22] At his orders a bakery was set up so that bread would be provided for offerings to the gods.

Now in these times the Mexicans walked without *guaraches* (sandals). So Santo Cristo sent Kauymáli to a church in which an ox was shut up. Kauymáli made a sacred picture of the ox,[23] and Santo Cristo taught the people how to make leather for their guaraches.

Then Kauymáli went to the wheat field to see what he would find. There he found a small group of wheat-animals. Nearby, Nakawé had a wide-mouthed *olla* [pot]. To it the wheat-animals were brought. Then for five days, after Kauy-máli had painted the lower part of his face black from the wheat, the wheat was kept tightly covered in the olla.

At midnight Kauymáli went to the olla. But he heard nothing. He went again and listened. This time he heard a slight noise. By the fourth night the sound was as loud as if a live animal were inside. Finally on the fifth night he went again and uncovered the olla as he had been commanded. From the olla of Nakawé came five calves. These had been born from the wheat.

Then Kauymáli went to the bakery and got five loaves of bread. With these the five ollas were anointed, after which they were closed.

The five calves grew, and soon became quite large. Kauymáli then sent the kerchief of Nakawé to the sea. Soon there appeared a large black cow with a large udder. The cow was taken by Kauymáli to suckle the calves from the ollas of Nakawé.[24]

Meanwhile[,] the leather from the ox of the church was tanned[,] and the Mexicans asked Santo Cristo to teach them how to make sandals and shoes. But even when these were made[,] they could not be sold until Santo Cristo had given permission. The Mexican women also wanted shoes.

So Santo Cristo ordered the establishment of a shoe-shop (factory). Then not only could the animal skins be tanned in the same way, but they could also be made into sandals and shoes.

Within fifteen days there were plenty of shoe-shops in all the towns, and shoes for men, women, and children.

While the shoes were being given out, the fifty Jews with the reversed feet arrived. They asked who had shown the Mexicans how to make shoes, and sug-gested that it was Santo Cristo. But the people said that it was the Sun who had taught them. The Jews, however, refused to believe this. They recognized in the shoes the handiwork of Santo Cristo.

The cattle, together with the papers corresponding to them, were delivered to a man in the center of the town. This man had a corral, and in it the cattle were shut up at night. In the daytime they were pastured by a boy.[25]

Within fifteen days the calves were large enough to be themselves with calves. Thus in one year plenty of cattle were raised for the Mexicans. Indeed, there were soon too many. So Santo Cristo ordered the Mexicans to take the cattle to the mountains of the Huichols. Here they were to be left with the Indians on shares. There was as yet no order either to buy or sell cattle, milk, cheese, or leather, and such had to be given away.

In the church from which the ox had been taken there were also horses. They were let out to feed on the fresh grass near the town. No one knew how to break [tame] these animals. Acting on orders from the Sun, Santo Cristo asked "Santo" Santiago (as informant said) and San Antonio to break the horses.

Santo Cristo also ordered one of them to make saddles, bridles, spurs, *reatta* [reata], and *tapajo*.²⁶ Fifty of each were ready within five days. These were distributed, for there was as yet no order to sell. The horses were soon broken, especially by Santiago.²⁷

The church also yielded male and female mules. These were similarly broken and given to all the towns. Thus Santo Cristo established what was necessary for the Mexicans to work with.

The baker needed large eggs for making pastry. Near the sea were chickens. These Kauymáli caught. He brought a pair to each town. Soon there were eggs.²⁸

Santo Cristo ordered Kauymáli to take fifty small pigs from the church. These were distributed among the Mexicans and fed on corn to fatten them. When they were large and fat, they were killed. The lard was rendered out. This was done in five days so that there could be bread.²⁹

Santo Cristo then ordered thread and *estambre* (crewel) to be made[,] as well as a loom for weaving cloth and blankets. He also ordered the Americans to make factories.³⁰ The Mexicans on [for] their part planted cotton. The factories made *manta* (muslin), *percala, flanela*, etc. Santo Cristo, furthermore, wished [for] silk for [to make] ribbons. The ribbons were to be hung from his wrists and from the canes of the governors.³¹

By this time the Mexicans had many children. Some of the children did not even have names. The towns, consequently, began to get overcrowded. Santo Cristo therefore ordered Kauymáli to survey lands for the Mexicans in other parts of their world.³² There ranches, haciendas, and fields could be established.

This was done. At the orders of the Sun[,] fields and pastures were set up for those who had had no room. This was repeated in all four of the world regions. The middle region of the world of the Mexicans had already been filled.

After this it was commanded by the Sun that the rich should pay the poor to take care of their animals.³³ Santo Cristo was in his tower by the sea. He had to write letters to the Sun, for he could do these things only at the Sun's command.³⁴ Thus the land was divided among the people, and there was room for all.

Kauymáli then went around listening to what the people had to say, and watching them clear, plow, and plant their fields. Soon there was plenty of corn and beans. But the Mexicans had no storehouses. So Santo Cristo had to show them how to make storehouses (*trojas*, Sp.).

When the first squash was ripe, the Mexicans cut the fruit. They ate it without telling Santo Cristo. But Kauymáli knew this. He told Santo Cristo that his people had not followed the custom of giving a ceremony of first fruits, as Santo Cristo had wished.

Thus the Mexicans lost the right of giving this ceremony,[35] and Santo Cristo set up a line separating the regions of the Mexicans from those of the Huichols. The Huichols were given a hard life of [performing] many ceremonies. The Mexicans were given an easy life with no ceremonies.[36] Had the Mexicans given a first fruits ceremony, there would have been no difference between them and the Huichols.

The crops were good and were divided equally among the people. Well-worked crosses were made and set up. These were decorated with paper flowers. The flowers were made by an old woman and a girl who sat in front of the stores.

Meanwhile the Jews were following close behind Santo Cristo. They were now offering fifteen pesos for information about him. Santo Cristo was new and beautiful, as though alive.[37] He knew that he would live to finish his work among the Mexicans.

4. Sub-story: The Sun Battles Nakawé to Save the World Made by Santo Cristo

There was an eclipse[38] ("Moon-joins-Sun-in"). For five hours it was very dark. The Sun and the Moon were talking. Then, five hours later, the Sun walked away and it became bright again. Five snakes in the form of clouds[39] came out of the sea. Each went to one of the five points. They sought to destroy the world by causing it to rain very hard. They flooded the world. This caused much suffering, because the wood got wet, preventing the making of fires. The people, however, did not starve because they had saved food. But the animals were killed in the swamps caused by the rain.

The Sun was covered with clouds and could not come out. He had to tell the great gods of the sea that he could do nothing because he was imprisoned. But he continued to walk, even though covered with clouds. Finally he arrived at the sea (at sunset).

Now the sea (water-goddesses) wished to end the world that had been made by Santo Cristo. But the Sun did not wish this end for the Mexican world and all the people.

Nakawé had ordered all the rain. The Sun, Santo Cristo, and Kauymáli requested her to calm herself a bit and stop flooding the world. Nakawé had her staff[40] (like that used by the clowns) with her, and with it she cut the clouds in the form of a cross.[41] Then the clouds went back, permitting the Sun to come out once more.

The Jews had talked to Nakawé. It was they who had induced her to cover the Sun and thus cause a flood to destroy the world. When all this became evident, Santo Cristo talked to the Sun, who told him that when he died nothing more could be established among the Mexicans. So a little boy made the image of Santo Cristo in the form of a crucifix.[42]

The Sun told Nakawé that, although she owned the clouds that had imprisoned and covered him, he owned the vast spread of stars[,][43] which could easily kill the snakes and still remain numerous. "The stars are my children," he said.

The Sun knew where the snakes sojourned, because high in the heavens where he lived everything could be seen. The worst snakes lived in a cliff near the sea.

Nakawé covered her face with her cloak and commanded lightning to break the rock of the cliff. The water-snakes came out. Then, at the Sun's command, a star fell blazing from the sky into the water. The snakes fought with it for an hour. Finally thunder announced the victory of the star. Then, while Nakawé kept her head covered, another star fell from the sky and pounced on three snakes with their tails twisted together. The other snakes watched the sky apprehensively. Two other stars fell on them and tore them to pieces. They rose to the sky as bits of clouds.[44]

Santo Cristo watched this struggle, and Kauymáli wrote it down in pictures and colors[45] to tell to the Mexicans. Thus Kauymáli gave the Mexicans information so that they could learn what they had to keep in mind. The Mexicans copied the picture of the snake[,] which they now use for a money belt.[46]

The stars of the Sun are the same as his animals, the eagles.[47] So at the Sun's command Santo Cristo ordered all the palaces of the Mexican government to carry the eagle of the Sun (the Mexican coat-of-arms). This is "very Huichol," and makes them feel that the palaces are theirs.[48] Thus the eagles of the Sun guard the palaces of the government.[49]

The Sun at this time ordered the Huichols to kill deer. But the mountain rattle-snakes of the Sun bit the hunters.[50] When they were bitten, the Huichols called a singer. He sang all night, trying to cure them by the power of Father Sun and Grandfather Fire.

While thus engaged, the singers discovered a little rock. It showed that the Sun was angry because he had not been given an offering. So they made beaded votive-bowls as well as an offertory-arrow. The latter had a thorn placed in the head to represent the fang of a rattle-snake.[51] Then the Sun relented and ordered his eagles to gather in groups and battle the rattle-snakes. The eagles folded their wings and swooped down on the snakes, unafraid of their fierce rattling, and carried them up to the Sun.

The Sun ordered the rattles to be taken off the snakes and used on shaman's plumes. Such plumes belong especially to the Sun.[52] The bodies of the snakes were given to the eagles to eat. Thus eagles do not eat corn but rattle-snakes, according to the command of the Sun.

Since the eagle is on the government palace, it is also put on silver money.[53] This is the best money. Copper money without the eagle is not worth very much.[54]

5. Sub-story: Santo Cristo Establishes Cattle Ceremonies among the Huichols

When the land of the four other world regions was given to the Mexicans, there was no order to pay for it (or anything else). On the streets of the towns in these regions, at the street corners, Kauymáli was ordered by Santo Cristo to put numbers.[55] Kauymáli would come to Santo Cristo in the wind[56] and keep him informed of the progress of the work.

Animals were being lost and stolen. So Santo Cristo showed Kauymáli how to make branding-irons. These were made in an hour. Their impressions corresponded to the "signatures" of the owners of the animals. The branding-irons were given to the owners, who asked how much they would cost. But as yet there was no order to pay for anything, since the world of the Mexicans was being made. It was ordered, however, to brand animals.[57]

The irons were bathed in water (tempered?), and then reheated with fire of cow-dung.[58] Then a saint was brought, because it is the saints who give cattle. This was ordered by Santo Cristo, who also ordered cattle to give increase (like having children). This is serious and "delicate."

Santo Cristo similarly ordered that children be named in the presence of the saints.[59]

Parents are ordered to find *compadres* (god-parents), who kneel before the candles. Compadres must always be friends and, whenever they meet, embrace (as Mexicans do). If they become angry with each other, the candles will go out and the people will die. Furthermore, parents must buy a bottle of wine to be drunk with the compadres.[60]

Only a cattle-owner's compadres can brand his animals. For this they are paid a bottle of wine. If a compadre does not brand the animals, the person who does becomes a "half-way" compadre. The same is true for the branding of mules, horses, and burros. Sheep, however, are not branded. With them a different custom is followed.[61]

When the branding is finished, five candles are bought. These are set up to God (same as the saints), so that the family and the cattle will not die.

Santo Cristo had ordered saints [icons] and crucifixes to be made. The Cathedral in Mexico was filled with them, just as the government palace was filled with money.[62]

By the time all these customs had been established, the Jews were arriving at a town nearby. The improvements they saw told them that Santo Cristo was still alive. They demanded to know who had ordered these improvements. The Mexicans, however, only replied that it was they. The Jews then told the Mexicans that they were looking for the young man who had issued the orders for improvement. The reason they asked, they said, was that they had lost him. They described Santo Cristo, saying that he had scars in his hands and feet where he had been shot.

Santo Cristo had already ordered the Mexicans to make pulque.[63] The Jews, armed as they were with pistols, rifles, and machetes, were given a sample. They liked the stuff and began to buy. Soon they were drunk. While they were drunk, Kauymáli took away not only their money but also their arms, leaving only a penknife.[64] Then, to save himself, Santo Cristo ordered that the road be closed with "wishache" (a very thorny branch). This grew up at his command, closing the road.[65] Thus Santo Cristo had time to finish his work.

Santo Cristo then taught the Mexicans how to play *kakaman* (a Mexican gambling game). In this game a shell is painted on the inside with the Sun's image; and by this a little stone is turned to money.[66]

In this way did the bad and lazy among the Mexicans make money, or gamble away their own piles of money. The Huichols, however, are not allowed to gamble, the custom not having been established among them by Santo Cristo. Other gambling games established by Santo Cristo for the Mexicans were *baraja* and *tintitetero* (lottery?).[67] All was noted by Kauymáli, who informed Santo Cristo how his orders were being carried out.

Santo Cristo then ordered mouth organs to be made for the people. These were to be played when he passed. He also ordered violins, base violins, guitars, and accordions. These were made in the carpenter-shops. They were put in the stores of the Mexican towns before they were given to the people to be played on the plaza and in front of the government buildings. Thus the world would not be too serious.

In front of the pulque-field where the Jews were getting over their drunkenness was a cantina (saloon). Here the Jews went and offered twenty dollars for information concerning the young man who had taught the Mexicans how to make all these things. The Mexicans denied having been taught. They affirmed that they had done all these things by themselves. They offered the Jews a generous sample of the vino from the cantina. With this[,] the Jews got drunk again and began to fight among themselves. They were angry with their chief. They were going to kill him, but he begged off.

Meanwhile the work in all the churches was finished. Thus now there were many churches in Mexico. But this did not turn out very well, since the Sun was displeased. So Santo Cristo ordered Kauymáli to go to the cave where the remains of the dung-beetle, *teapúawi* (*teapúa*, iron, H.) had been buried. Kauymáli took out five pieces of metal.

Since a bell was desired, these pieces were taken to someone who knew what to do with them. The metal sounded very well. It increased rapidly, and soon there was enough to make fifty bells. Thus there were enough bells for all the churches in Mexico. These were placed in all the towers, according to the instructions of Kauymáli. In very large towns two bells were put in one tower. This was done so that God, the saints, and the people could come to mass.[68] It was all well done, because the priests had blessed the bells.

6. Sub-story: Santo Cristo Establishes the Government as well as Carnival and Holy Week Ceremonies among the Huichols

When the bells were finished, Santo Cristo had to leave the church and go to another place. He knew that now the Jews were close behind him.

Aided by TumuSaúwi, Father Sun, Tatevalí, and Nakawé ordered Santo Cristo to go about the world to see if all had been well done. So Santo Cristo climbed to the top of the high mountain to survey the world. But he did not like to walk in the sierra and the barrancas to establish all this work. This is why the Huichols do not have everything the Mexicans have.

But Santo Cristo did make a short trip through the mountains of the Huichols, although he did not do very much. He stopped and instructed the Huichols, who built the church at San Sebastián. It was the first and most important of the Huichol churches.[69] He also taught the Huichols to cut down trees and shape them into vigas [beams] and into boards. The boards were then smoothed into planks for benches and seats. Planks were also cut for the bench of the *governadores* [civil officials].[70] This was by the command of Santo Cristo.

Santo Cristo also visited the Mesa [de] Nayar (Nayarit, Sp.) and taught the Cora Indians all of these things.

When this work was finished, Santo Cristo informed Father Sun of every-thing he had done. The Sun then ordered that Walupe (an image of the Virgin of Guadalupe) be placed in the Huichol town of Guadalupe Ocotán. A beautiful image of another saint, "santo de la mesa," was sent to the Mesa de Nayarit for the Coras. At San Andrés was ordered a saint of the same name, as was com-manded for Santa Catarina. Tuxpan was ordered to have Guadalupe and Santo Cristo.[71]

Six old men were now chosen to be *kawitéros*. They were to listen to the orders of Santo Cristo and tell the people his story. Furthermore, they were to be in charge of all the affairs relating to Santo Cristo. Also *topiles* were ordered to bring from the margin [shore] of the sea five little balls of clay. These were used to make censers, *pútsi*.

At the sea also was a fine, solid tree of brazil-wood. It was felled and cut up, and from its heart was made a *vara* [sacred staff].[72] Each of the officials was given one of these to wear in his belt. The officials were then taught how to punish the Huichols who would not follow their commands.

Santo Cristo ordered the kawitéros to secure topiles for the governors [civil officials]. Each topile had to be supported (as one's children) by the official he served. *Tenanches* as well as *priostes*[73] were instituted. Then the topiles were ordered to make stocks, *telpiliya tatotsí*.

Since the first church was at San Sebastián, here was made a pillory as well as stocks. The pillory was alive and ate the throat of its victim. Thus it sinned, so that now only stocks are used.

Santo Cristo then ordered the kawitéros to establish the punishment of the whipping-post. Offenders such as thieves and adulterers are put in the stocks for several days without food and water. Then they are tried, and their guilt or responsibility for the offense is determined.

The topiles carry ropes with which to bind the prisoner and also for tying him to the whipping-post. They count at each stroke of the whip. The *aguacil* [sheriff], however, was ordered by Santo Cristo to do the whipping. The whip-ping is called "hot mush." It is given when the offense cannot be satisfied by either fine or payment.

The kawitéros were ordered to dream who were to be the new officials as well as the topile for each. It was also ordered that girls, who were to be [called] tenanches, should take care of the church, Casa Real, and sweep the dancing-patio.

The topiles not only capture offenders but also bring flowers for the altar, god-houses, and hats of the people.

When the churches were all finished, the kawitéros were put in charge.

Santo Cristo and all the saints do not touch women. They are "delicate."[74]

Thus, according to the command of Santo Cristo, the staff of the governor, which was given to the kawitéros, is sacred. If one in charge of a cane [staff] commit[s] adultery, his cane [staff] will break. If the wife of an official sin[s], one of her children will die. If the tenanches commit adultery, their censers break.[75]

Santo Cristo next ordered the officials to plant corn so that feasts might be given to the people of the community. The officials have to give the carnival feast, in which is performed the "bull-dance." The bull is an animal of Nakawé.

In the first times *maSákoa [maSakóa]* (deer-snake), a sea-serpent of Nakawé, was changed into a bull.[76] Kauymáli took its horns and put them on the altar of the church at San Sebastián.

Similar horns are used by the boy who impersonates the bull in the dance. A month before the dance he must fast from salt, meat, and sex.[77] Otherwise he would die.[78] When the ceremony begins, he has to roar like a bull and enact the part of that animal in a dance with the topiles.

Another boy, *wakéro* (vaquero, Sp.), was appointed to watch the "bull" in this dance and carry a stick to guide him.[79] Besides topiles, other boys were ordered to help in the dance. They had to make a corral for the bull to dance in and also try to get out of. If he has been true to his fast, he can break out of the circle of the dancers.[80] If he has not been true, not only will he be unable to break out, but he will be unable to roar well.[81]

In this ceremony the kawitéros have to fast as well as the boy. If they fail, they, too, will die. The singing-kawitéro uses the crown of Santo Cristo, *motéału*. This is also left for the singers of the ceremony who aid the kawitéro.

When the real bull is sacrificed, the boy "bull" drinks some of the blood and anoints his face with it. He also has to stain his clothing in the bloody dirt at the place of sacrifice.

Then in the ceremony, after the sacrificial bull is killed, substitute officials are appointed so that the proper officials can parade from house to house. In this parade each official ties a bottle of liquor[82] with a ribbon. This is then offered to [icons of] the saints, who have been carried to the house of the official where the dancing is in progress. The official, his wife, and his smallest child enter the circle of dancers. This makes the child strong like a bull. The woman and child then go, and the man tosses the vino [liquor] in the air to be caught by the dancers. He who fails to catch it will die.[83]

The saints are then paraded, while the kawitéro sings this myth of Santo Cristo. In the first times the saints got tired from this walking, and it was commanded to rain in order that they might be refreshed. Hence in the ceremony[,] the saints are placed in the center of the packed circle of dancers[,] over the prostrate figure of the boy "bull." All are covered with blankets. Then the women encircle the group and toss pinole on the blankets.[84] This commemorates the first times when the saints walked to the National Palace of Mexico. They arrived very tired, and were refreshed by rain.

Since the Jews had bought vino [liquor], and Santo Cristo had been saved by their drunkenness, Kauymáli was able to make off with their pistols, machetes, rifles, and money. Their money was given to Santo Cristo. He put it in a sack and changed it into potsherds. The Jews, further, had had a boy carry their money. So Santo Cristo ordered that in the Huichol ceremony a boy should carry the sack of potsherds. This commemorates the money of the Jews.

Thus pistols, rifles, and machetes of the Jews are commemorated in the ceremony also. This is due to the command of Santo Cristo. In the ceremony there must be also *soldados* (Sp.[,] soldiers) to fight with the thieves (*tinawáya*, H.) who steal the money.

Now Santo Cristo had ordered Kauymáli to survey and divide the world of the Mexicans. This was to allow the Mexicans to expand into the four other regions of their world. So in the carnival ceremony it was commanded that this event should be remembered. Thus piles of stones are set up. The boy who carries the sack of money anoints these stone piles[85] with the blood of a dog or a chicken. This makes them solid.

In the ceremony it was established by Santo Cristo as a joke that the real officials should be "captured" and "hanged" to make them reveal where the money had been hidden. Also, when the bull sacrifice has been made, the horns are taken by the boy "bull." With these he tries to knock down the little boys who carry the flags. They must be guarded and assisted by strong men to prevent their being knocked down. This was so commanded by Santo Cristo.

Santo Cristo then set Lent aside as a season when the Huichols should fast every Wednesday and Friday until noon.[86] This is a very "delicate" (sacred) time.[87]

The Sun then ordered the death of Santo Cristo after seven Fridays. The Thursday of the seventh week is the day when the death of Santo Cristo is commemorated. This was commanded by him. This Thursday is a fast-day. The Santo Cristo (i.e., the crucifix in the church or the Casa Real) is wrapped in cloths and prepared for burial in a bed-like sepulchre (*sepulcro*, Sp.-H.). This sepulchre must be made by kawitéros. It may not be made by anyone else, nor may it be made by children.[88]

It was ordered that the kawitéros should watch all night by the sepulchre in the Casa Real. Thus, after midnight, the kawitéros lower the cross into the sepulchre. At this time everyone must be serious and silent, while many candles and much incense is burned. This is because Santo Cristo's heart is alive in "la gloria" (Glory, Sp.-H.), and is watching his children, the Huichols.[89]

It was ordered that, all during the night of Holy Thursday, no one should sleep. The ashes of the burning candles must be carefully watched and snipped off with scissors as they burn. These ashes are saved. If they fall to the ground, some member of the family of the watcher will surely die.[90]

When Santo Cristo died, a bow and arrows were placed on his sepulchre so that he could defend himself, even though dead. Therefore the Huichols place a bow and arrows on a tall staff. The staff is then pounded all night before the sepulchre made by the Huichols. This pounding of the kawitéros with the long staff aids Santo Cristo in his journey to "la gloria."[91]

During this "delicate" time[,] the canes [sacred staffs] of the officials are buried in the sepulchre. About nine o'clock on the morning of Good Friday, the *bartéro* (*vartéro*, Sp.), who is in charge of the canes [sacred staffs], takes his staff from the sepulchre.[92] During this time matches cannot be used. So he has a *labón [eslabón]* (Sp.-H., steel for flint in making fire) with which to light fires, candles, etc. Ordinary coals of oak-wood cannot be used in the censers. For this purpose, therefore, the topiles are required to make charcoal from fires lighted by the bartéro with flint and steel.

About nine o'clock a procession of the women follow the bartéro. He lights a sacred fire of charcoal with his flint and steel. From this fire are lighted the candles of the women. If the fire strikes easily, it is a good omen; if not, someone may die.[93]

During the previous night all the people have kept silent outside the (closed) door of the church (or the Casa Real). They could not sleep. When the fires are newly lighted, the women make a line in front of the door. This line extends back to the fire. Then the bartéro [keeper of the staffs and eslabón] advances several times along this line, whirling his cane end over end. He knocks on the sealed door. Each time he goes back to the fire and begins again, knocking on the door louder than before. Finally, on the last advance, he knocks open the door.

Then the people follow the bartéro and the women into the church (or Casa Real), because God is alive again. Bottles of sotol (distilled liquor) are put upon the altar, and the officials are given drinks. Rockets are shot off, and all the people are happy.

The ashes from the candle are dampened with holy water brought from the priests in the Mexican towns. Crosses of ashes are then put on the heads of the children. This gives them long life.[94] The *mestro*[95] [maestro] blesses the palm-leaves that have decorated the sepulchre, and a bit of palm-leaf is given to everyone. This is saved until the person dies. Then it is tied in his hands and buried with him.[96]

The leaves of laurel are taken home and put on the cross at the family altar so that lightning will not strike the house.[97] A bunch of the yellow flowers[98] used in decorating the sepulchre are given to everyone at the ceremony. These are taken home to be given to the animals to eat. Since they are "the life of Santo Cristo," the animals do not get sick.[99]

When Santo Cristo had instructed the Huichols [about] how to observe these ceremonies, he went on to other regions. Here he gave his orders in writing at the government buildings. He sent notes by Kauymáli, saying that the stores should be filled with the goods he had taught the Mexicans how to make. He also gave Kauymáli balances, scales, and measure-sticks. Then he ordered the price at which *manta* (Sp.-H., cotton muslin) should be sold. He wished everything well arranged, because his time was approaching.

Santo Cristo was very tired from all this work. He went again to the tower of the church, saying, "God, my *tata* (father), will take care of me. Let us see when the Jews will find me."

He had already sent notes to all the Mexican municipal presidents when he had first stopped to bless the fruits, crops, and products. The notes told the Mexicans not to betray him to the Jews until his work was finished.

7. Sub-story: Santo Cristo Prepares for Death

By noon Santo Cristo was very tired. He told the people to put a cross on the tower of the church where he had been hiding.[100] He was hungry. But, although the people brought him food, he asked only for a censer of hot coals. From his pouch he took out a pinch of copal (incense used by the Indians of Mexico). This he dropped five times on the glowing coals. Thus he satisfied his hunger by eating the incense.[101]

In the National Palace of Mexico Santo Cristo left a note with Santo Nacario in which he introduced himself to General Ramón Corona.[102] This note also told them not to betray him to the Jews, even though he passed close by and the Jews offered them money.

Then Santo Cristo leapt from his tower and caused an earthquake.[103] He went fifteen leagues to a town. In the plaza people all knelt at his entrance and made the sign of the cross.[104] Santo Cristo blessed them and named everything in the town. He heard music, and he saw that there was happiness in the world, for the people were dancing, drinking, and feasting. He himself could not eat until noon, however, since he was fasting.

When he arrived at another town, the same thing happened. Santo Cristo went to the Catholic priest and told him the right customs to be followed. He then blessed the priest. Since the Jews were following closely upon his path, he told the Mexicans not to betray him. They were to say that he had not been there for five years.

He escaped from this town and hurried on to the next. The Jews were easily able to track him because of the scars in his feet.[105] Here he told the people not to betray him.

The Jews had a large machete. This had grown from the small knife that had been left them the time they got drunk in the Mexican saloon.

Santo Cristo arrived at another town. Here corn and money were plentiful. He blessed everything, including the church. He told the Mexicans of this town not to betray him. They did not need to lie. They merely needed to say that they did not know if it was Santo Cristo or not.

When Santo Cristo arrived at the Mexican National Palace, he called five whirl[-]winds.[106] These took him to the top of the tower, from which he could see what the great capital looked like. The people recognized him, and all knelt. He blessed them. The women loved him because he was so clean and beautiful.[107] He told the people not to betray him.

Now the Sun was getting tired of Santo Cristo. He told him to hurry and finish his work. The Jews were following closely. They saw that Santo Cristo's tracks were fresh. To anyone who would betray Santo Cristo into their hands they offered a hundred pesos. They even saw Santo Cristo, but he flew away and hid in one of the five pine-trees[108] that were there in the middle region. Here Santo Cristo stayed and rested for five nights. The Jews tracked him to the pine-trees. But the trees were so high that none of their arrows could reach him. Further, he was well hidden in the heavy foliage.

On the fourth night ten buzzards[109] *(wiłúka tewíałi)* joined Santo Cristo. They knew him to be good, and different, therefore, from the Jews. They sat around on the tree and talked to him, offering to carry any messages he had.

Santo Cristo told them that he would have to remain where he was until the Jews left. This was because there was still much to be done. He had to go to the Huichol community of San Sebastián. There he had to see if all was well arranged and being followed according to his teachings. He said that while Nakawé had arranged the world, he had improved it.[110]

The buzzards were asked to wait for Santo Cristo at the edge of the sea. As soon as the Jews left, Santo Cristo flew away. The Jews heard, however, and followed. He went to a town and blessed pulque, vino, and mescal. This he did so that the Jews would stop and get drunk.

Santo Cristo went to Analco to bless this place and to calm the angry gods of the sea. The buzzards were there also. Santo Cristo asked them to go to a mountain and wait, because he had to go to the Palace for five days.

The Jews were drawing close to Santo Cristo. He flew to the Palace in Mexico City. Here he had to measure[111] everything, and quickly, for the Jews were coming at midnight.

Santo Cristo wrote to the kawitéros, saying that he was in the capital. He told them that he had left a government among the Huichol composed of a gobernador, a *juez* [judge], and an *alcalde*, similar to that [which] he had established for the Mexicans in the National Palace.[112] He gave orders for the surveying of the sierra of the Huichols.[113] He also commanded the Mexican government to give the Huichols titles to their own lands. Then he ordered the Huichols to go to the National Palace to arrange any business they had.

While he was giving these orders, the Jews arrived. He changed himself into a little child. Thus Santo Cristo escaped because he still had to measure the capital, establish jails, and punish thieves so that there would be order in Mexico City. The Jews passed right by him. They did not recognize him in his disguise as a child.

The next day Santo Cristo changed into a cripple. He went on with his work.

Meanwhile the Jews were spending much money, trying to get information as to Santo Cristo's whereabouts. Santo Nacario and General Ramón Corona were there, but they did not betray Santo Cristo.

The time came for the beginning of the first Lent in Mexico City. Santo Cristo was the kawitéro[114] this first time, and sang the myth of himself. This made the Jews suspicious. They asked if Santo Cristo, a man with scars in his hands and feet, were [was] there. They said that he was a thief whom they wished to catch.

Meanwhile the ceremony had lasted for five days. The fifth day Santo Cristo sang in front of the National Palace.

When the long singing was over, everyone ate because Santo Cristo offered them a well[-]cooked rooster seasoned with chile. The yaquis, *gachupines* [Spaniards], *turcos* [Turks], *chinos* [Chinese], and *julios* [Jews] still lacked salt in their food. In other parts of the world, however, there was good, well-tasting [delicious] food. These people were not yet blessed.[115] They were seated on a bench to one side.

Santo Cristo was now going to bless the food of all the people. He knelt, as did the people. Then he threw the discharge from his nose into the cooked rooster he had prepared for them. The Mexicans ate it, and thus their food was blessed.

Then Santo Cristo threw mucus in the air, and it became salt.[116] This, however, made the foreigners sick, and they could not eat. But the Christians ate the food and it was good. The others were left wild [unbaptized], and were sent to the other side of the sea.

Into one of the beaks of the cooked roosters, however, they put the salt that Santo Cristo had prepared. The dead bird came to life, and sprang up and crowed, "Cristo! Cristo! Cristo!" Thus roosters crow to this day.[117] When Santo Cristo died, all the roosters crowed for him at dawn, as they still do.[118]

The Jews had come up [arrived] at the time of the preparation of this feast. But they were nauseated, and could not eat the food. They did not recognize Santo Cristo, because he had changed himself into a one-armed man. At other times he changed into a dwarf, a fat man, and a cripple.[119] Then later, at various times, he changed himself into a man with a peg leg, a blind man, and a one-eyed man. He did this in order to escape the Jews.

The Sun by this time was tired of Santo Cristo. He sent an order to the Jews. They read the message. It informed them that the kawitéro was really Santo Cristo. The order, however, was that they were not to kill him. He was to be imprisoned.

Santo Cristo had finished the work of the Sun.[120]

The Jews rushed to the National Palace. They seized Santo Cristo and bound him. Then they took him to the jail and put him in the stocks.[121] There was poor Santo Cristo with his feet in the stocks. The door of the jail was tied shut, and he was watched carefully by the gatekeepers. But Santo Cristo took off his feet and thus escaped from the stocks. He got out of the jail.

Then Santo Nacario, at the command of the Sun, identified Santo Cristo. He said to the Jews, "It is Santo Cristo. But he is able to change into a child, a fat man, a lame man, and so forth. But you Jews must not kill him. The Sun has not commanded this."

So the Jews caught Santo Cristo again. They stripped him. Then they beat his naked body with a flat side of the large machete that had grown from the small knife Kauymáli had left them. Santo Cristo was brave. He did not cry at all.

But the Jews wished to kill Santo Cristo. They tempted Santo Nacario with a sum of money. Santo Nacario promised them that he would arrange everything with tata Sun. In the meantime the Jews had put Santo Cristo back in the stocks. They tied his hands securely.

But Santo Cristo got a little boy to take off his feet again. This boy was *moSá tewíałi* (sheep-boy).

When the Jews learned that the sheep-boy had helped Santo Cristo to escape, they beat him in the face. But he did not cry. The Jews beat him so brutally that his face swelled. Thus sheep still have long, puffed faces, because the swelling never did go down.[122]

Santo Cristo sent a note to the store for five nails.[123] These were to put in his table in "glory." He also bought a beautiful ribbon. He wished the ribbon to tie on his arm when he was to die.[124] These things did not cost money. He also ordered a carpenter to make a cross, and he got tin-foil so that the cross would shine.

On the fifth day Santo Cristo had everything that he needed. He wrote notes everywhere, telling the people that he was going to die. Many cried, and all were sad, because all the Mexicans loved him. His work was finished, and his world was perfect.

The Jews got thirty piles of silver money[125] from the National Palace of Mexico. This money they gave to Santo Nacario for permission to kill Santo Cristo. At four P.M. they took Santo Cristo to the center of the plaza to kill him. They put him on the cross and nailed him there by his hands and feet. Santo Cristo was still alive, however.[126]

The great gods of the sea could not bear to see Santo Cristo suffering. So they sent an old blind god to Mexico City. But before he arrived, Santo Cristo was nailed to the cross and hung on high. As the blind god came up, the people were all kneeling with covered faces. They could not bear to see their god die in such agony.

The Mexicans, therefore, gave the blind god a saber. He was instructed to place it just under the nipple of Santo Cristo. Following their instructions[,] he pushed the saber very hard, and thus killed Santo Cristo without knowing what he was doing. Everyone wept as the saber pierced the heart of Santo Cristo, who gasped with his last breath, "*Ay Dios* (Ah, God)."[127]

As Santo Cristo died, a gush of blood streamed from the eyes of the blind man. His eyes were opened and he was able to see. Thus, seeing for the first time, the man saw his god dead on the cross with his head on one side.

The heart of Santo Cristo left the body and flew to "Gloria." At the same time, the other saints died. Thus ended Santo Cristo after his work in the world was finished.[128]

[Postscript by Zingg:]

This ends *Huichol Mythology*.

This story is told with great feeling, especially toward the end. The informant said frankly that he felt like crying. Since thirty pesos were paid for the betrayal of Santo Cristo, I had to pay my informant this enormous sum for this story.

When the money was turned over, the informant said that Sebastián, the chief singer of Tuxpan, had found out that I was paying so much. The informant was half afraid that he would be made the victim of witchcraft.

About this time there was much trouble brewing. One shaman had died, causing another to be charged with witchcraft and creating so much scandal that he was forced to move to another *ranchería*. Furthermore, four relatives of the informant had just died from small-pox. This was attributed to witchcraft on the part of the dead father, who had "left out a magic arrow" in order to call his children and grandchildren to him.

I attempted to soothe my Huichol informant against his fears of witchcraft, but with little success. He said, "It is our custom."

Epilogue

Jay C. Fikes

Readers of *Huichol Mythology* may appreciate the following brief summary of what happened at Tuxpan and to Robert Zingg from 1934 until his death in 1957. Zingg never returned to Tuxpan. After finishing his monograph on the Huichols *(The Huichols: Primitive Artists)*, he began investigating cases of "feral man"—humans who are allegedly raised by animals (Zingg 1940, 1941). Pursuing that endeavor, in 1938 Zingg wrote to Reverend Singh, who claimed to have found two young girls that had been raised by a female wolf near the village of Godamuri, India.[1] Numerous people in addition to Reverend Singh (in whose orphanage the girls lived) observed that the girls' behavior resembled that of wolves more than humans (Maclean 1977: 296–97). Instead of attributing their wolflike behavior to autism, mental illness, or some other pathological cause, Zingg took Reverend Singh at his word. Zingg never personally observed these two girls. Instead he relied entirely on Singh's assertion that he had been an eyewitness to the capture of the two girls immediately after their she-wolf mother was killed. Zingg simply believed that Singh's was a credible report about two children nurtured by a wolf, rather than merely another feral-child myth. The result of Zingg's long-distance collaboration with Singh was a book, *Wolf-Children and Feral Man* (Singh and Zingg 1942), that evoked considerable criticism from anthropologists, among them Ashley Montagu. Montagu rightly noted that even if "we might be inclined to put our trust in Mr. Singh's word, no scientist can accept as true any statement . . . until it has been independently confirmed by others" (Montagu 1974: 22).

Maclean identified several motives for Zingg's dismissal from the University of Denver in August of 1942, but emphasized that "Zingg's work on the wolf children was regarded by many as too controversial and by some even as a subversive influence" (Maclean 1977: 280).[2] Zingg never taught again after leaving the anthropology department at the University of Denver.

While serving in the American Red Cross during World War II, Zingg was posted to India. In India he met Singh's widow and took photographs of the orphanage where the wolf-children had lived (Maclean 1977: 284–89). Unfortunately, Zingg left India before conducting the type of investigation that might have produced evidence essential to soften the criticisms of his book about the wolf-children. In 1975 Maclean completed a firsthand investigation in India, reopening the wolf-child controversy without resolving it.[3]

Upon returning to America in 1945, Zingg ended up in El Paso, Texas. There he remarried and held a variety of nonacademic jobs. His second wife, Emma, told me that the debate about the authenticity of the wolf-children continued to trouble him. His reputation was tarnished further by the widespread but totally false rumor that he had committed suicide. Zingg died of a massive heart attack in 1957 (personal communication with Emma Zingg, 1996). Having heard reputable anthropologists spread that false rumor and having read Furst and Myerhoff's unsubstantiated assertion that Zingg's Huichol work "is particularly deficient in the areas of religion and mythology" (1966: 4), I can only hope that publishing the complete version of these myths that Zingg collected at Tuxpan will help rescue his Huichol research from its undeserved oblivion. The comprehensiveness and overall accuracy of his research at Tuxpan has inspired me (as it should other anthropologists) to do fieldwork there.

I first visited Tuxpan in 1996 to deliver a videotape copy of approximately fifty minutes of unedited film footage that Robert Zingg shot there in 1934. Visiting Tuxpan enabled me to complete a documentary film based on Zingg's 1934 footage. Since finishing the film, "Huichol Indian Ceremonial Cycle" (Fikes 1997),[4] I have recorded interviews with three elderly men, one of whom, Jesús González, is a shaman whose power was bestowed on him by the spirit of a sacred plant, *kiéri*. Jesús reported how he was taught songs in a vision induced by eating honey that contained kiéri pollen and also was dictated a myth describing the origin of the first Huichol shaman (Fikes 2001). Jesús González's chronicle credits kiéri pollen with playing a primary role in creating the first shaman, a role paralleled by Jesús' explanation of how that primordial shaman taught him songs when he was seven years old, without his actively seeking shamanic power.[5]

As my fieldwork in Tuxpan proceeds, I will continue to experience the feeling that I am "following in the footsteps" of Robert Zingg. In October of 2001, I filmed a first fruits ritual in the same village where Zingg had filmed the same ritual. The elderly people I filmed told me that they were infants and children in 1934 when Zingg filmed them there. Of course much about Tuxpan has changed since he was there.

Today Tuxpan has several times more inhabitants than it did in 1934. It is now a small town of about 500 inhabitants, accessible by unpaved roads and a tiny dirt landing strip. Electricity brought by power lines is always available, even in the Casa Real, where both aboriginal Huichol and Catholic-inspired ceremonies are still performed. Tuxpan's political officers no longer need to meet in the Casa Real, as they did in 1934. They now meet in a modern building nearby. Soccer fields, radios, televisions, pickup trucks, and small stores stocked with a variety of Mexican goods represent and amplify the erosion of traditional Huichol culture. Reliance on modern medicine provided by Mexican-educated doctors and nurses as well as attendance at government schools (from primary through senior high) are contributing to the development of a bicultural identity.

Huichols in Tuxpan still forbid priests to reside permanently among them, but continue to perform Easter (Holy) Week ceremonies originally taught to them by Franciscans. Seventh-Day Adventists residing in Tuxpan are working cautiously to gain acceptance for themselves and their gospel. One of Jesús' sons was baptized several years ago at a Protestant church in Guadalajara and trained in 1998 in organic gardening in northern California by Seventh-Day Adventists. Religious identity is being transformed. Jesus Christ is being proclaimed as a personal savior by some younger Huichols, rather than merely another Huichol ancestor, as he was understood in 1934.

Like Zingg, my attitude toward the Huichol was decidedly romantic when I began my fieldwork in Santa Catarina in 1976. Having witnessed nearly thirty years of cultural change, I feel some responsibility to reveal something about the dangers Huichols — and those who visit them — are facing today. In addition to the alcoholism, murder, and witchcraft that plague urban Huichols (Fikes 1993a), Tuxpan, like so many other places in Mexico, has a serious problem with involvement in marijuana growing. A rapid population increase in Tuxpan has not been accompanied by a corresponding increase in agricultural productivity. Cattle grazing and production of arts and crafts items for sale outside the community have in recent years been supplemented by cultivation of marijuana. This lucrative but illegal business involves only certain Huichols but is extremely hazardous to them all.

When my plane from Guadalajara touched down at the Camotlán landing strip on October 6, 2001, I noticed a wrecked airplane lying nearby. Huichols who were there to take me to Tuxpan in their pickup truck said it crashed because it was overloaded with marijuana. The Mexican army was camping next to the landing strip and checking our luggage as we got off the airplane. Some Huichol friends have confided to me their suspicion that conflicts over marijuana profits often result in murders transpiring regularly among them. They have warned me not to go to certain places in their territory. The Mexican army routinely patrols the boundaries of Huichol territory, sometimes invading it.

A few Huichols I spoke with about the motive behind the presumed murder of the American journalist Philip True (in December of 1998) suggested that he could have been killed by marijuana growers fearful that he would expose them or the location of clandestine marijuana fields in Huichol territory.[6] I mention this danger to warn romantics, journalists, and seekers of shamans "comparable to Carlos Castaneda's don Juan" (Fikes 1999) not to venture anywhere in Huichol territory—unless they have a local guide or have been invited back to a particular place.[7]

Today a large group of traditional Huichols are still committed to perpetuating the ways of their ancestors. There is also an ever increasing number of modernists dedicated to the pursuit of economic self-interest, even when that means working as undocumented, unskilled laborers in the United States or growing marijuana. There is obviously an urgent need to develop practical economic alternatives to deter involvement in such illegal enterprises.

Casa Real with two *širiki*, taken in Tuxpan during Carnival.

Tuxpan officials seated on "the bench of the mighty." Note the wooden whipping post in the middle background.

New officials of Tuxpan. Zingg's informant, Juan Real, is seated at left holding the bow.

Sebastián decorates sacred canes with flowers during the Cambio de
las Varas (Changing of the Sacred Staffs) at Tuxpan. Note the ceramic
incensors in the foreground.

Cambio de las Varas festival at Tuxpan. Officials seated on bench at right await the display of sacred paraphernalia, hidden by cloth curtains.

Procession to official's house during the nine-day Carnival ceremony at Tuxpan.

Kawitéro with crown at Tuxpan's Carnival.

People gathered for the sacrifice of the bull during the Carnival ceremony at Tuxpan.

Beginning of the Bull Dance during the Carnival ceremony at Tuxpan.

"Bull" (extreme right) trying to escape from the dance circle during the Carnival ceremony at Tuxpan.

Tuxpan officials tie pinole "beads" in strings during the Carnival dance.

Captured official (man with rope around neck) to be "hanged." Carnival ceremony at Tuxpan.

Shower of pinole to commemorate rainstorm. Carnival ceremony at Tuxpan.

Casa Real in Tuxpan during Semana Santa (Holy Week).

Singing shaman at Ratontita picks up the comal to offer to the four cardinal directions in the Ceremony of Parched Corn. Note the large ollas with brewing tesgüino.

Singing shaman at Ratontita offers kernels of corn to gods of the four cardinal directions before he places them on a comal to be "baptized" by the two chanters at his side.

Peyote dancers in the Ceremony of Parched Corn at Ratontita. Note the Túki (temple) in the background.

Procession of peyote dancers at Ratontita.

Peyote dancers in the Ceremony of Parched Corn at Ratontita.

A procession of women at the Ceremony of Parched Corn at Ratontita.

A girl ceremonially parches corn while a Father (in background) baptizes all members of the family with sacred water from caves near Santa Catarina.

Arrangement of gourd bowls for atole and soup at the Ceremony of Parched Corn.

Offering to the sun from the altar of the Rain Ceremony of Juan Real. Note the crucifix and retablo.

The Virgin of Guadalupe, a central feature of the altar at the Rain Ceremony, Vallecitos. Note the crucifix at left.

Arrangement of altar at dawn for the Rain Ceremony. Note the portraits of the Virgin and saints covered by cloth.

Sacrifice of the bull at the Rain Ceremony. Note the violin and guitar players (far left).

The sacred clown gives gourds of tesgüino to his wood carriers during the Rain Ceremony.

A masked clown participates in the Rain Ceremony. Note the feline features of the mask.

Setting up the offering of tortillas at the Ceremony to Prepare the Soil for Seed at the kawitéro Sebastián's rancho.

The finished altar of tortillas and gourd bowls for fish and deer soup at the Ceremony to Prepare the Soil for Seed at Sebastián's rancho.

Dancing with the corn-goddesses at Sebastián's rancho. Grass bundles and thorn brooms are used in the Ceremony to Prepare the Soil for Seed.

Preparation of the altar for the temple at the Ceremony to Prepare the Soil for Seed. Note the corn-goddess behind the shaman's chair. Taken at Ratontita.

Guests pick out their gourds filled with food from the altar at the Ceremony to Prepare the Soil for Seed. Taken at Ratontita.

Corn-goddess effigy (left) at the first fruits ritual, Sebastián's rancho.

Santos, with his son by his side, shakes the gourd rattle. Taken during the first fruits ritual at Sebastián's rancho.

Robert Zingg at Tuxpan in 1934.

A woman stirs brewing tesgüino.

A barranca near Tuxpan.

Preparing a corpse for burial.
The widow is giving him water.

Huichol violinists and harpists earn as much money as singing shamans or
Mexican musicians.

A woman weaves a belt on a complex back-strap loom.

An altar in a širiki near Tuxpan.

Robert M. Zingg at high school graduation, 1918.

Robert M. Zingg in American Red Cross uniform during World War II.

Notes

Introduction

1. Our use of the word *Huichol* must not lead readers to overlook regional variations in language and culture. The linguist Joseph Grimes (1964: 13) recognized three major dialect divisions that correspond to natural barriers in the Chapalagana River region. Weigand (1981) and Negrín (1985: 13) have independently identified four major Huichol cultural zones. In addition to kinship and lineage, one's affiliation with a specific ceremonial center was presumably the standard indicator of "Huichol" social and political identity prior to the colonial era, at which time the comunidades indígenas were created. Although each ceremonial center had its own particular name, they may have shared a similar annual ceremonial cycle and an underlying social organization to sustain it. The myth dictated to Zingg (this volume) suggests that there were originally twenty-five or twenty-eight aboriginal temple officers at Tuxpan. Diguet's data implied that there were thirty-seven Huichol temple officers (Diguet 1992: 111).

2. The Spanish system of administration introduced to the Huichols in the late 1600s contains several unpaid political offices. The principal position is that of governor, followed in rank by the judge (who was called *alcalde* in Tuxpan and *juez* in San Sebastián), sheriff (alguacil), and captain (Fabila 1959: 105–15; Weigand 1978: 103–8; Zingg 1938: 18–21). These four top officials are served by topiles, men who function as messengers and police. Huichol political officers have two primary duties: to arbitrate in judicial proceedings involving disputes between Huichols residing within the community and to represent the community in its dealings with non-Huichols.

Kawitéros play a central role in selecting these officers (Fikes 1985: 75; Negrín 1975: 13; Weigand 1978: 108; Zingg 1938: 16–18). In addition to choosing the officers, kawitéros star in the Cambio de las Varas (Changing of the Sacred Staffs) festivities, in the Carnival ceremonies, and in Holy Week rituals. Kawitéros in Tuxpan were considered the successors of Christ (Zingg 1938: 12, 18). Our research confirms Zingg's observation and strongly suggests that kawitéros were an aboriginal institution. Their prestige or social status is derived primarily from the community service they furnish as aboriginal temple officers. While serving as temple officers, they are presumed to have learned how to heal and sing. The most distinguished singers become proficient at conducting rituals. The best of them are selected to become kawitéros. Kawitéros excel in reciting the *cahuito*, or sacred ritual text (Fikes 1985: 73–77, 330).

The military function originally associated with the Capitán de Guerra has vanished. The prestige and authority of kawitéros is declining, and a recently created Union of Huichol Indigenous Communities has started to supersede the power and authority of these colonial-era offices.

3. The mildness characteristic of the 1702 rebellion may be attributed to two factors: 1) Huichols and Tepecanos clearly comprehended how the colonial system was supposed to work, and 2) they had accepted their place in that system. The result of the

Mixton War of 1541–1542 (Weigand 1985: 147; Weigand and Foster 1985: 103, 434) and more particularly of the Tepehuano revolt of 1616 must have persuaded Huichols and Tepecanos that fighting for complete freedom from Spaniards would be futile. The Mixton War was basically a conflict to gain control over Caxcanes, the eastern neighbors of the Tepecano (Weigand and Weigand 1996b). The two years of killing unleashed in 1616 by the Tepehuan revolt amounted to "one of the three bloodiest and most destructive Indian attempts to throw off Spanish control in northwestern New Spain" (Spicer 1962: 28).

4. Some, but not all, of today's Tuxpan Huichols migrated from Ostoc. Jay Fikes's preliminary fieldwork in Tuxpan has revealed that some of Tuxpan's inhabitants trace their ancestry to Huichols who fled from Tenzompa after 1910 to escape the violence of the Mexican Revolution. He has heard about a canyon, located to the south of Tuxpan, that is named after the Tlaxcalans. Further research on Tuxpan's ethnic composition and postcontact history is clearly needed.

5. In 1783 Don José del Valle reported that Huichols still inhabited Ostoc (Velázquez 1961: 43). In 1782 the Huichols of San Sebastián defended the title to their land after a portion of it had been occupied, in 1780, by don Miguel Maximiliano de Santiago, the rich miner from Bolaños (Rojas 1993: 106). The Huichols of San Sebastián evicted don Miguel Maximiliano de Santiago from Ratontita, but he subsequently won a ruling from a Guadalajara judge, who granted him a large part of Tuxpan. Santiago's claim to Tuxpan, which had heretofore belonged to the comunidad indígena of San Sebastián, was not discarded until 1788 (Rojas 1992: 83–89). Santiago (or another colonist) must have intimidated the Huichols of Ostoc around 1788, perhaps after his claim to Tuxpan was rejected. Two Franciscan reports dating from 1853 mention a group of Huichols having fled from Ostoc to take refuge in the comunidad indígena of San Sebastián. The Franciscans suggested that the Ostoc Huichol lands were stolen. The colonial government had done nothing to protect them (Rojas 1992: 153, 165). A significant social division between San Sebastián and Tuxpan, dating to this period, seriously affected the unity of this comunidad indígena during the Cristero Rebellion, and remains important in current politics (Weigand 1992a).

6. The letter Tuxpan officials sent to the governor of Jalisco in March 1935 demonstrates that they were definitely against being annexed by Nayarit (Rojas 1992: 256). The boundary dispute between Jalisco and Nayarit has been exacerbated by cattlemen from Nayarit, who for decades have invaded Tuxpan's territory. By 1955, Mexican cattlemen owned 66 percent of all cattle grazing on communal lands owned by San Sebastián and Tuxpan. They controlled more than 60 percent of those communal lands where their cattle grazed (Fabila 1959: 39, 43–52, 113). Few of them paid rent for using Huichol pasturage. Many of these Mexican cattlemen also served as rural police. By 1959, the cattlemen's harassment and murder of Huichols had become intolerable. Armed only with bows and arrows and .22 caliber single-shot rifles, 152 Huichols confronted the cattlemen. For the first time ever, San Sebastián and Tuxpan Huichols were united, defending their lands against a common enemy (Rojas 1993: 191; Weigand 1979). Nevertheless, Wei-

gand is correct in stating that since the Cristero Rebellion, Tuxpan has never been fully reconciled with San Sebastián. In fact, Tuxpan has been "flirting with an *ejido* form of organization, which, aside from being illegal, would also involve cattlemen from outside the comunidad" (Weigand 1979: 174).

7. Further insight into orthodox Huichol cognition may be derived from Zingg's discussion (1938) of how deeply mystic participation permeated the thought and behavior of pious Huichols. Zingg's pioneering effort has been supplemented by Fikes's portrait of how Huichol singers and seekers of wisdom pursue the highest order of meaning, a domain where meaning becomes a state of being. According to Fikes (1985), two achievements highly valued by devout Huichols are transformation into wolf form and identification with their tutelary spirit, Kaoyomari/Iromari. Achieving this type of union or radical identification of self with other is deemed vital for effective healing and singing, is intensely emotional, and is illustrative of the highest order of meaning. Because such deeply experiential meaning is nontransferable, it transcends the realm of rational discourse wherein meaning is merely denotative (Fikes 1993c: 120).

8. Zingg acknowledged that Huichol singing shamans were religious specialists "who could almost be called a priestcraft" (1938: 203). One of Zingg's photographs indicates that Juan Real was an assistant singer. Huichols call such assistants *cuinepohuamete* and consider them more knowledgeable than laymen but less competent than full-fledged singers. Zingg's assertion that Juan Real was a layman (1938: li) underestimated his ability as an informant on mythology. Huichols from Tuxpan told Fikes that Juan Real eventually became a singing shaman. In 1935 Juan Real was one of the new officials at Tuxpan and was entrusted with leading the procession through the stations of the cross during Holy Week, a position that required knowing how to recite the Lord's Prayer in Spanish (1938: lii, 100–101). Although Juan Real was not a kawitéro, his knowledge of Huichol myth was impressive and derived from a specific comunidad indígena. In this context, it should be noted that Lumholtz probably overestimated the percentage and number of singing shamans within the Huichol homeland, setting a precedent that was followed by New Age "anthropologists."

9. Professor Don Bahr believes that Zingg wrote in English all the myths that Juan Real dictated in Spanish. Bahr bases his conclusion on Zingg's footnote: "it was boring and intensely fatiguing to me to write frantically for at least eight hours a day, keeping up with his (Real's) Spanish patols [*sic*] which I wrote directly in English" (1938: liii). Bahr suggests that *patols* derives from the French word *patois* and means, in this context, a nonstandard form of Spanish. We would agree that Zingg transcribed directly in English many slang phrases uttered in colloquial Spanish by Juan Real, but we continue to assume that these myths were mostly transcribed in Spanish. Whatever the case may have been, our own research among Huichols convinces us that Zingg and Real have produced an authentic corpus of myths derived from a specific comunidad indígena.

10. Principal female ancestors such as Tacutzi Nacahue and Tatei Na'arihuame were being merged with María Santíssima (the Virgin Mary), whom the Huichols of Tuxpan identified with the Virgin of Guadalupe (Zingg, this volume). The Huichols of Tuxpan

had converted Kaoyomari into a composite character, a personality who was confused or blended with several other ancestors. Juan Real's myths portray Kaoyomari in a contradictory or ambivalent manner. Kaoyomari is acclaimed as a hero and esteemed as Elder Brother Wolf but is also defined as "half-bad." His sexual misdeeds cause Tacutzi to give him a new name, Kauimali. His sacrilegious offspring are identified as modern Mexicans (Zingg, this volume). Fernando Benítez distinguished Nuipashikuri, the mythical Huichol sexual deviant, from the deformed Wolf-Man called Mautiwaki, noting that Mautiwaki's deformity was a punishment for a sexual transgression committed during his avowed period of sexual continence. As Benítez recognized (1968a: 446–51, 1968b: 222–23), Zingg's composite character known as Kauymáli/Kauimali combined attributes of Nuipashikuri and Mautiwaki and then merged them with Kaoyomari, the world-organizer and tutelary spirit of Huichol healers and singers. Other anomalies pertaining to Kaoyomari's character have been specified by Fikes (1985: 53).

11. Associated with the monumental circular architecture of the Teuchitlan tradition, from which the circular Huichol temples are derived, are pseudo-cloisonne vessels whose iconography reveals the esteem accorded to the ancestor allied with the wind. Weigand suggests that circular architecture is a marker of the wind deity, who may have been revered as the patron of the polity of Teuchitlan by 400 A.D. (1992b, 1992c, 1993). Huichol veneration of Eacá Tehuari (Grandfather Wind or Wind Person) is conspicuous at Santa Catarina (Fikes 1985, 1993a) and Las Guayabas (Benítez 1968b) but is absent from Tuxpan. We suspect that veneration of Eacá Tehuari was vanishing among the Huichols of Tuxpan. This may have increased the importance they placed on making the sign of the cross when whirlwinds were sighted, an observation that also applies to San Sebastián.

Part I.
A. The Birth of Tatevalí (Grandfather Fire) and the Contest of Fire and Water (Nakawé)

1. Zingg, R. M.: *The Huichols: Primitive Artists* [New York: G.E. Stechert, 1938,] p. 302, fn. 12.

2. The Huichols wear, like a relic around the neck, a small mirror about an inch and a half in diameter. [Zingg, R. M.: *The Huichols*], p. 702, fn. 14.

3. Ibid., p. 243 ff.

4. A disc of the gods, some eighteen inches in diameter.

5. [Zingg, R. M.: *The Huichols*], p. 302, fn. 13.

6. Ibid., p. 236, fn. 19; and p. 302, fn. 14.

7. [Ibid.,] p. 302, fn. 15.

8. A large parrot of the sierra. [Zingg, R. M.: *The Huichols*,] p. 588, fn. 33.

9. Ibid., p. 693, fn. 39.

10. Ibid., p. 240, fn. 58.

11. It is, apparently, in commemoration of this that in the "esquite," and other first fruit ceremonies involving Grandfather Fire, a little boy and girl are dressed in festal ar-

ray with shaman's plumes to lead the procession to the fire. [Zingg, R. M.: *The Huichols,*] p. 419, fn. 51.

12. Ibid., p. 303, fn. 17.

13. [Ibid.,] p. 639, fn. 101.

14. Ibid., p. 303, fn. 18; and p. 605, fn. 15; and p. 640, fn. 105.

15. Ibid., p. 303, fn. 20.

16. Ibid., p. 352, fn. 5.

17. [Ibid.,] p. 703, fn. 16.

18. Another instance of the struggle between the wet and dry seasons.

19. Lumholtz translates [this as] *aspect,* but it is the ordinary Huichol word for *face.* The term is applied to the carved, ceremonial, gable cap-stone, and also the woven disc of reeds in sunburst form woven with colored crewel. Obviously the first [meaning], *gable,* is meant here. [Zingg, R. M.: *The Huichols,*] p. 601, fn. 3.

20. Ibid., p. 303, fn. 21; and p. 634, fn. 80.

21. Ibid., p. 303, fn. 22.

22. [Ibid., p. 303, fn. 21; and p. 634, fn. 80.]

23. Ibid., p. 303, fn. 22.

24. In the corn myth sub-story, "Kauymáli brings death to the Huichols" [Zingg, R. M.: *The Huichols*], p. 68–111, the present Huichol custom of "guarding" *(cuidado [cuidando])* or "watching" the altar when the sacred paraphernalia is exposed, is accounted for as commanded of *TumuSáuwi,* who passed the task on to Kauymáli. But since Kauymáli is "half-bad," his bad people (the Mexicans) came in and stole some of the sacred corn. Zingg, R. M.[: *The Huichols*], p. 363, fn. 25.

25. Ibid., p. 303, fn. 23.

26. Ibid., p. 283, fn. 61.

27. [Ibid.,] p. 178, fn. 13.

28. [Ibid.,] p. 178, fn. 13.

B. The Sun Myth

1. Zingg, R. M.: [*The Huichols: Primitive Artists* (New York: G.E. Stechert, 1938),] p. 312, fn. 82. The *Taukukui* [taukukúi] is a small parrot which, like the rooster, sings at dawn.

2. [Ibid.,] p. 66, fn. 66. [In the original manuscript, Zingg does not include a note number in the text for this footnote. — Ed.]

3. [Ibid.,] p. 310, fn. 59.

4. Ibid., p. 310, fn. 58; and p. 595, fn. 50.

5. A bird of the sierra. It has a crest, and cries like a child.

6. Zingg, R. M.: *The Huichols: Primitive Artists,* p. 310, fn. 59.

7. Ibid., p. 313, fn. 87.

8. Ibid., p. 640, fn. 106.

9. Ibid., p. 313, fn. 87.

10. [Ibid.,] p. 234, fn. 11.

11. Ibid., p. 315, fn. 93.

12. [Ibid., p. 315, fn. 93.]

13. Ibid., p. 315, fn. 93.

14. [Ibid., p. 315, fn. 93.]

15. Ibid., p. 310, fn. 60.

16. The rattle-snake belongs to the Sun-father. [Zingg, R. M.: *The Huichols*,] p. 312, fn. 71.

17. Ibid., p. 310, fn. 60.

18. [Ibid.,] p. 310, fn. 64.

19. Ibid., p. 312, fn. 72; and p. 589, fn. 37.

20. [Ibid., p. 312, fn. 72; and p. 589, fn. 37.]

21. Ibid., p. 312, fn. 74; and p. 647, fn. 6.

22. Ibid., p. 312, fn. 71.

23. Ibid., p. 312, fn. 73.

24. Ibid., p. 313, fn. 86.

25. Ibid., p. 640, fn. 107.

26. Ibid., p. 311, fn. 65.

27. Ibid., p. 270, fn. 10; and p. 311, fn. 68.

28. [Ibid.,] p. 361, fn. 19.

29. Ibid., p. 312, fn. 83.

30. Parrots make an awful din every morning at dawn. [Zingg, R. M.: *The Huichols*,] p. 313, fn. 89.

31. Ibid., p. 313, fn. 89.

32. Ibid., p. 234, fn. 11.

33. Ibid., p. 249, fn. 103; and p. 311, fn. 66.

34. [Ibid.,] p. 239, fn. 53.

35. Ibid., p. 318, fn. 1.

36. [Ibid., p. 318, fn. 1.]

37. Ibid., p. 65, fn. 67.

38. [Ibid., p. 318, fn. 1.]

39. Naming is the final creation of anything.

40. *Tau* is Huichol for sun. Zingg, R. M.: *The Huichols: Primitive Artists*, p. 311, fn. 67.

41. Ibid., p. 234, fn. 11; and p. 252, fn. 110.

42. Ibid., p. 313, fn. 86.

43. The sun sets in the Pacific [Ocean, to the] west of the Huichol country.

44. Lumholtz, [Carl:] *Symbolic Art of the Huichol Indians*, p. 11, says a Huichol boy in full costume casts himself into the fire, and emerges burning to shine in the sky. See also: [Zingg, R. M.: *The Huichols*,] p. 702, fn. 13; and p. 309, fn. 52. [Zingg incorrectly cites the Lumholtz title. It should be *Symbolism of the Huichol Indians.*—Ed.]

45. Ibid., p. 312, fn. 75; and p. 606, fn. 22.

46. Ibid., p. 363, fn. 31.

47. Ibid., p. 312, fn. 77.

48. Here Grandmother Growth (Nakawé) is merged with the Virgin of Guadalupe. Zingg, R. M.: *The Huichols: Primitive Artists*, p. 60, fn. 19.

49. An odd Catholic touch added to the pagan myth.

50. [Zingg, R. M.: *The Huichols*,] p. 310, fn. 62.

51. Ibid., p. 312, fn. 78; and p. 638, fn. 95.

52. Ibid., p. 234, fn. 11.

53. Ibid., p. 309, fn. 52.

54. This story of the sun.

55. Zingg, R. M.: [*The Huichols*,] p. 647, fn. 9.

[Ibid.,] p. 304, fn. 27. [Zingg inserted a footnote numbered "o" at this point, but he did not indicate in the text what it referred to.—Ed.]

56. This is done in actual Huichol ceremony. [Zingg, R. M.: *The Huichols*,] p. 203, fn. 7.

57. Ibid., p. 647, fn. 5.

58. Ibid., p. 606–7.

59. The story-teller seems to have shifted the story from the great gods to the Huichols.

60. This was seen in one ceremony at the *ranchería* of a singer, Sebastián. [Zingg, R. M.: *The Huichols*,] p. 312, fn. 79.

61. Ibid., p. 312, fn. 81; and p. 661, fn. 59.

62. The Tarahumaras catch deer by running them to the point of exhaustion.

63. The boy, dressed in full ceremonial regalia, who kills the sacrificial bull in Huichol ceremonies. Zingg, R. M.: *[The Huichols,]* p. 271, fn. [The footnote number is missing in Zingg's ms.—Ed.]

64. Ibid., p. 308, fn. 49.

65. Ibid., p. 270, fn. 13; and p. 311, fn. 70.

66. [Ibid., p. 270, fn. 13; and p. 311, fn. 70.]

67. [Ibid.,] p. 508 ff.

68. Ibid., p. 596, fn. 53.

69. [Ibid.,] p. 596, fn. 52.

70. Ibid., p. 604, fn. 10.

71. Ibid., p. 117, fn. 13; and p. 325, fn. 29.

72. Ibid., p. 265, fn. 2; and p. 311, fn. 70.

73. Ibid., p. 235, fn. 13.

74. Ibid., p. 272, fn. 20.

75. Ibid., p. 195, fn. 75; and p. 690, fn. 31.

76. Ibid., p. 638, fn. 96.

77. Ibid., p. 661, fn. 58.

78. [Ibid.,] p. 363, fn. 30.

79. [Ibid.,] p. 212, fn. 36.

80. Ibid., p. 648, fn. 15.

81. [Ibid.,] p. 166, fn. 70; and p. 647, fn. 10; and p. 212, fn. 38.
82. Ibid., p. 237, fn. 31; and p. 716, fn. 38.
83. Ibid., p. 214, fn. 47; and p. 218, fn. 58.
84. [Ibid., p. 214, fn. 47; and p. 218, fn. 58.]
85. [Ibid., p. 214, fn. 47; and p. 218, fn. 58.]
86. Ibid., p. 218, fn. 59.
87. Ibid., p. 212, fn. 36.
88. [Ibid., p. 212, fn. 36.]
89. Ibid., p. 212, fn. 39; and p. 214, fn. 46.
90. [Ibid.,] p. 212, fn. 38.
91. [Ibid., p. 212, fn. 38.]
92. Drunkedness [*sic*] is sacred.
93. Zingg, R. M.: *The Huichols: Primitive Artists*, p. 234, fn. 7.
94. Ibid., p. 617, fn. 56.
95. Thus do the gods cooperate to stamp out black-magic.
96. [Zingg, R. M.: *The Huichols*,] p. 212, fn. 39.
97. [Ibid.,] p. 213, fn. 40. This is drift-wood, which the informant says he has seen.
98. [Zingg, R. M.: *The Huichols*,] p. 213, fn. 41.
99. Ibid., p. 213, fn. 42.
100. The *batea* is the vessel of wood used by the women to catch the ground corn-dough from the *metate*. [Zingg, R. M.: *The Huichols*,] p. 213, fn. 43.
101. [Ibid.,] p. 214, fn. 48.
102. Ibid., p. 213, fn. 44.
103. Ibid., p. 213, fn. 45.
104. Ibid., p. 213, fn. 42.
105. [Ibid., p. 213, fn. 42.]
106. Ibid., p. 200, fn. 3.
107. [Ibid.,] p. 208, fn. 21; and p. 363, fn. 28.
108. Ibid., p. 611 ff.
109. Ibid., p. 212, fn. 36.
110. The only reference of Kauymáli having a god-house.
111. [Zingg, R. M.: *The Huichols*,] p. 238, fn. 45.
112. Ibid., p. 428, fn. 64.
113. [Ibid., p. 428, fn. 64.]
114. [Ibid., p. 428, fn. 64.]
115. [Ibid.,] p. 258.
116. This dance, done three days without water, was seen at Ratontita. Thirst is a fitting penance to the Sun-god. [Zingg, R. M.: *The Huichols*,] p. 589, fn. 36; and p. 423, fn. 58.
117. Ibid., p. 652, fn. 28; and p. 243 ff. The peyote dance is done in four points of the dancing-patio.
118. [Zingg, R. M.: *The Huichols*,] p. 279 ff.

119. Ibid., p. 309, fn. 53.
120. Ibid., p. 701, fn. 8.
121. The Huichols have seen the sun set in the Pacific.
122. Zingg, R. M.: *The Huichols: Primitive Artists*, p. 309, fn. 55.
123. Volcanic rocks prove this incident.
124. The sun is sacred and thus dangerous.
125. [Zingg, R. M.: *The Huichols*,] p. 313, fn. 85; and p. 587, fn. 30.
126. Ibid., p. 235, fn. 12; and p. 310, fn. 63.
127. Ibid., p. 151, fn. 25; and p. 310, fn. 56.
128. [Ibid.,] p. 151, fn. 25 ff.
129. Ibid., p. 282, fn. 59.
130. [Ibid.,] p. 151, fn. 25 ff.
131. Ibid., p. 656, fn. 34.
132. Ibid., p. 152.
133. High payments to shamans are often mentioned. The shamans tell the myths.
134. Zingg, R. M.: *The Huichols: Primitive Artists*, p. 153, fn. 30.
135. Ibid., p. 235, fn. 16.
136. Ibid., p. 116, fn. 5; and p. 184, fn. 30.
137. This is the ceremony to prepare the soil for seed.
138. [Zingg, R. M.: *The Huichols*, p. 116, fn. 5; and p. 184, fn. 30.]
139. Ibid., p. 701, fn. 7.
140. Ibid., p. 309, fn. 54.
141. [Ibid.,] p. 313, fn. 88.
142. Ibid., p. 313, fn. 88.
143. So that they would not be burned.
144. Candles are the best offering to the Sun[F]ather.
145. These ceremonies are: 1. [the] parched corn; 2. [the] peyote; 3. the drum dance; 4. the killing of bulls. The altar set up in these ceremonies and the offering of lighted candles continue to tame the sun. See also [Zingg does not complete this reference.— Ed.]
146. [Zingg, R. M.: *The Huichols*,] p. 431, fn. 65.

C. First Peyote (Deer) Journey Brings the Sun to the Sky

1. Zingg, R. M.: *The Huichols: Primitive Artists* [New York: G.E. Stechert, 1938], p. 327, fn. 41.
2. Ibid., p. 327, fn. 41.
3. Ibid., p. 328, fn. 44; and p. 515, fn. 12.
4. Lumholtz says of this rain-goddess, "*[T]ate na'aliwami*, in the East—a red serpent because she appeared in the lightning. She is mainly a water and rain serpent, bringing rain from the East, and I shall call her Mother East Water. Her supposed dwelling, and consequently her principal place of worship, is in a deep gorge with caves, near Santa

Catarina, in the eastern part of the Huichol Country." — Carl Lumholtz, *Symbolism of the Huichol Indians*, p. 13.

5. Zingg, R. M.: *The Huichols: Primitive Artists*, p. 328, fn. 45.

6. Ibid., p. 514, fn. 7.

7. Tatotsí is one of the principal Huichol Gods. Lumholtz speaks of him as "Grandfather Deer-tail, the second god of fire and the chief god of deer. He is the singing shaman. . . ." — Carl Lumholtz, *Symbolism of the Huichol Indians*, pp. 10–11.

8. This is the expanded term for the above god, literally Deer-tail. The god is generally called Tatotsí MaSákwáSi, Grandfather (?) [Great-Grandfather] Deer-tail.

9. This is the Huichol goddess of birth, daughter of the goddess of love, Ereno (sea-foam). Suluwíakame is in turn the mother of Peyote (deer).

10. Zingg, R. M.: *[The Huichols,]* p. 348, fn. 132.

11. This impious dropping of a coal of sacred fire into its contrary element, water, precipitates the struggle between the water (rain) and fire (sun and dry-season) forces[,] which provides the structural framework for so many Huichol myths. From this struggle the peyote custom is accounted for by the Huichols.

12. Here the deer, Peyote, sends out clouds, which in other contexts are synonymous with corn, the growth of which they aid. This shows the ceremonial association of deer, peyote, and corn or rain.

13. Deer-peyote and cloud symbol. Zingg, R. M.: *The Huichols: Primitive Artists*, p. 250, fn. 107.

14. [Ibid.,] p. 364 ff.

15. [Ibid.,] p. 208, fn. 19; and p. 264, fn. 39.

16. It is interesting to note that this not unimportant animal hero of Huichol mythology is here personified by Huichol clothes, frightens away the insects [flies] with his hat, and then resumes his more proper scavenger nature by cleaning the carcass. [Zingg, R. M.: *The Huichols*,] p. 364, fn. 40.

17. [Ibid.,] p. 208, fn. 20.

18. Ibid., p. 334, fn. 69; and p. 337, fn. 85.

19. [Ibid.,] p. 167, fn. 72.

20. Ibid., p. 594.

21. Ibid., p. 316, fn. 95.

22. [Ibid.,] p. 609, fn. 33.

23. Ibid., p. 303, fn. 19; and p. 605, fn. 13.

24. [Ibid.,] p. 305, fn. 31; and p. 605, fn. 14.

25. Ibid., p. 305, fn. 32.

26. Ibid., p. 316, fn. 97; and p. 407, fn. 27.

27. She is also the mother of peyote.

28. [Zingg, R. M.: *The Huichols*,] p. 334, fn. 72.

29. Ibid., p. 686, fn. 23.

30. [Ibid.,] p. 276, fn. 36; and p. 334, fn. 73.

31. Ibid., p. 243, fn. 73.

32. Ibid., p. 305, fn. 33; and p. 306, fn. 37; and p. 595, fn. 27.

33. Ibid., p. 306, fn. 38.

34. Ibid., p. 305, fn. 34; and p. 404, fn. 5.

35. Ibid., p. 404, fn. 5.

36. Ibid., p. 334, fn. 68.

37. [Ibid.,] p. 585, fn. 23.

38. Ibid., p. 305, fn. 35.

39. Ibid., p. 207, fn. 13; and p. 305, fn. 36.

40. This is commemorated in the peyote feast of parched corn by dropping god-tamales in the fire; see p. [Zingg does not include a page number.—Ed.], also [see] Lumholtz, *Unknown Mexico*, II, 271; and Zingg, R. M.: *[The Huichols,]* p. 258, fn. 143; [and] p. 306, fn. 39.

41. In the peyote ceremony of parched corn, Huichols are baptized.

42. [Zingg, R. M.: *The Huichols,*] p. 306, fn. 41.

43. Ibid., p. 306, fn. 40.

44. [Ibid.,] p. 588, fn. 32.

45. [Ibid.,] p. 241, fn. 63; and p. 606, fn. 28.

46. Appeal to authority of the past.

47. [Zingg, R. M.: *The Huichols,*] p. 310, fn. 61.

48. [Ibid.,] p. 312, fn. 76.

49. Ibid., p. 307, fn. 46; and p. 401, fn. 16.

50. Ibid., p. 274, fn. 30; and p. 302, fn. 11.

51. Ibid., p. 706, fn. 26.

52. Ibid., p. 404, fn. 10; and p. 705, fn. 25.

53. [Ibid.,] p. 334, fn. 74.

54. Ibid., p. 334, fn. 75.

55. Ibid., p. 306, fn. 42.

56. Ibid., p. 306, fn. 43; and p. 608, fn. 30.

57. Ibid., p. 306, fn. 44.

58. [Ibid.,] p. 409, fn. 39.

59. Ibid., p. 236, fn. 21; and p. 408, fn. 38.

60. Carl Lumholtz, *Unknown Mexico*, II, [p.] 128. The Huichols on their journey walk one behind the other—a prescribed ritual order.

61. Carl Lumholtz, *Unknown Mexico*, II, [p.] 268 *et seq.*

62. Ibid., II, [pp.] 272–73. "A procession of men appeared on the scene, each with an armful of wood. They were led by the shaman, carrying in his palms a large piece of green wood scarcely half a yard long. This was the pillow (*molitali*) of Grandfather Fire, and was carried as carefully as a baby. On arriving at the fireplace of the temple, the bearer lifted the pillow toward the five regions, and, lastly, offered it to the sixth by placing it on the ground. His companions built a fire over it, arranging the pieces to point east and west."

63. Zingg, R. M.: *The Huichols: Primitive Artists*, p. 236, fn. 22.

64. Ibid., p. 258, fn. 140.
65. [Ibid.,] p. 401, fn. 17; and p. 585, fn. 22.
66. The Tarahumaras also use rattles in their peyote dance. *Cf.* W. C. Bennett and R. M. Zingg, *The Tarahumara*, p. 293.
67. [Zingg, R. M.: *The Huichols,*] p. 647, fn. 9–10.
68. Ibid., p. 276, fn. 37; and p. 417, fn. 49.
69. Ibid., p. 306, fn. 45; and p. 613, fn. 47.
70. Ibid., p. 404, fn. 8; and p. 594, fn. 48.
71. [Ibid.,] p. 426, fn. 62.
72. Ibid., p. 406, fn. 26.

D. Myth of the Huichol Temple (Túki)

1. Zingg, R. M.: *The Huichols: Primitive Artists* [New York: G.E. Stechert, 1938], p. 608, fn. 29.
2. Ibid., p. 398.
3. Ibid., p. 249, fn. 104; and p. 304, fn. 25.
4. Ibid., p. 208, fn. 17.
5. Ibid., p. 310, fn. 56.
6. [Ibid.,] p. 363, fn. 29; and p. 646, fn. 2.
7. The best gift for the dry-season gods.
8. The best gift for the goddesses of the wet-season.
9. [Zingg, R. M.: *The Huichols,*] p. 175, fn. 7.
10. Ibid., p. 237, fn. 28.
11. [Ibid., p. 237, fn. 28.]
12. Ibid., p. 280, fn. 53.
13. [Ibid.,] p. 209, fn. 25.
14. Ibid., p. 650, fn. 17.
15. Ibid., p. 326, fn. 39.
16. [Ibid.,] p. 175, fn. 8; and p. 188, fn. 41.
17. Ibid., p. 190, fn. 53; and p. 208, fn. 18.
18. The only time Kauymáli appears as a god.
19. [Zingg repeats footnote 18 here, but this appears to be an error.—Ed.]
20. A mystic motivation for art-expression.
21. [A mystic motivation for art-expression.]
22. [Zingg, R. M.: *The Huichols,*] p. 191, fn. 59; and p. 250, fn. 106.
23. [Ibid.,] p. 587, fn. 31.
24. Ibid., p. 303, fn. 16; and p. 646, fn. 3.
25. Ibid., p. 188, fn. 42.
26. Birds of the Sun[-F]ather.
27. [Zingg, R. M.: *The Huichols,*] p. 179, fn. 20.
28. Birds of the Sun-[F]ather.

29. These are the staffs used in the peyote and other dances.

30. See also [Zingg, R. M.: *The Huichols,*] p. 188, fn. 44.

31. Fasting from water is the best service to the Sun[-F]ather.

32. Carl Lumholtz: *Symbolism of the Huichol Indians,* p. 184; and Zingg, R. M.: *[The Huichols,]* p. 659, fn. 44; and p. 185, fn. 36.

33. This command of the Sun is commemorated in ceremony. See [Zingg, R. M.: *The Huichols,*] p. 189, fn. 45.

34. [Ibid.,] p. 659, fn. 45. Prof. Preuss told me that a gesture of coition is made. This is often done in Huichol ceremonies as a joke. See also [Zingg, R. M.: *The Huichols,*] p. 539, fn. 2.

35. Ibid., p. 270, fn. 12.

36. Ibid., p. 659, fn. 46.

37. A fall symbolizes the disease.

38. Sacred water [was] necessary even for offering to Sun[-F]ather.

39. This is the "feast of unhulled corn cakes," no longer given in Tuxpan. See Lumholtz, C.: *Unknown Mexico.* Vol. II, pp. 27–50. See also Zingg, R. M.: *[The Huichols,]* p. 658, fn. 41.

40. Zingg, R. M.: *The Huichols: Primitive Artists,* p. 239, fn. 48.

41. Ibid., p. 239, fn. 49.

42. In the myth is interpolated the following interesting data on the baptism ceremony:

> Three male and three female children were brought to the altar. They had to have a god-father (*"padrino[,]"* Sp.) to kneel before "Dios" (God) and ask for their lives. The saint told them to buy a bottle of *sotol.* Then the man who knows how to pray (in the Catholic fashion), *picikáli* (H.)[,] *"mestro"* [maestro] (Sp.), placed a crown on the heads of the children and ribbons on their wrists. The god-father had to sacrifice an ox to anoint ("bathe") the saint with blood. At dawn they went into the church for work.
>
> The god-mothers (*"madrina[,]"* Sp.-H.) held the children and knelt at the altar. The "mestro" [maestro] had to be given a peso[,] as he could not work for nothing. This was given[,] for his work was very important. The money was put near Santo Cristo where the "mestro" [maestro] could get it. He would pray for an hour if he had a bottle of sotol to warm his heart to his work. This was given and done. Thus the children were given names. The god-parents (*"padrinos[,]"* Sp.) gave each other the *"abrazo"* (Spanish embrace) and were told to do this whenever they met. Also they must be kind and friendly to each other. The "mestro" [maestro] drank the bottle of sotol, while the fathers of the children gave more to everybody.

[Zingg, R. M.: *The Huichols,*] p. 55, fn. 7.

43. Ibid., p. 250, fn. 105.

44. [Ibid.,] p. 250 ff., fn. 106.

45. Ibid., p. 638, fn. 99.

46. Ibid., p. 201, fn. 4.
47. Mystical motivation of art-expression.
48. [Zingg, R. M.: *The Huichols*,] p. 208, fn. 22.
49. Ibid., p. 210, fn. 27.
50. [Ibid.,] p. 658, [d]iscusses this ceremony.
51. Ibid., p. 345, fn. 121.
52. [Ibid., p. 345, fn. 121.]
53. Ibid., p. 346, fn. 124; and p. 629, fn. 71.
54. Ibid., p. 329, fn. 51.
55. [A s]acred hole is especially associated with Otuanáka. [See Zingg, R. M.: *The Huichols*,] p. 329 and p. 180.
56. [Ibid.,] p. 242, fn. 69; and p. 181[,] fn. 26.
57. [Ibid., p. 242, fn. 69; and p. 181, fn. 26.]
58. Ibid., p. 179, fn. 18.
59. Ibid., p. 179, fn. 16; and p. 617, fn. 55.
60. Ibid., p. 190, fn. 50.
61. Ibid., p. 190, fn. 51; and p. 238, fn. 44.
62. Ibid., p. 191, fn. 57.
63. Ibid., p. 190, fn. 52.
64. Ibid., p. 190, fn. 55; and p. 277, fn. 41.
65. [Ibid.,] p. 191, fn. 58.
66. Ibid., p. 202, fn. 6.
67. Ibid., p. 239, fn. 47.
68. [Ibid., p. 239, fn. 47.]
69. [Ibid., p. 239, fn. 47.]
70. Ibid., p. 190, fn. 56; and p. 237, fn. 30; and p. 277, fn. 42.
71. "Thus the Huichols have to do today[,]" says informant. See p. [Zingg does not complete this footnote.—Ed.]
72. Zingg, R. M.: *The Huichols: Primitive Artists*, p. 147, fn. 4.
73. Ibid., p. 147, fn. 4.
74. Ibid., p. 147, fn. 4; and p. 190, fn. 54; and p. 236, fn. 20.
75. [Ibid.,] p. 189, fn. 49.
76. [Ibid.,] p. 602, fn. 7.
77. Ibid., p. 605, fn. 20; and p. 606, fn. 21.
78. [Ibid., p. 605, fn. 20; and p. 606, fn. 21.]
79. Ibid., p. 239, fn. 54.
80. Ibid., p. 605, fn. 19.
81. Ibid., p. xxxvii, fn. 9; and p. 270, fn. 11.
82. [Ibid.,] p. 601.
83. Ibid., p. xxxvii, fn. 10.
84. Ibid., p. 336, fn. 82.
85. [Ibid., p. 336, fn. 82.]

86. Ibid., p. 609, fn. 36.

87. [Ibid.,] p. 338, fn. 90.

88. Corn-fields are often conventionally represented on votive-bowl[s].

89. She is especially the goddess of lightening [*sic*].

90. [Zingg, R. M.: *The Huichols*,] p. 166, fn. 69.

91. In telling this myth the informant often calls Na'aliwaemi ["]Mar[í]a Sant[í]s-sima.["]

92. [Corn-fields are often conventionally represented on votive-bowl[s].]

93. Very commonly the Huichols stand their candles in votive[-]bowls.

E. Kauymáli Helps the Sun Win Over the Rain-Goddesses in First Getting Deer's Blood for the Sacred Paraphernalia

1. Zingg, R. M.: *The Huichols: Primitive Artists* [New York: G.E. Stechert, 1938], p. 234, fn. 8; and p. 361, fn. 17.

2. Ibid., p. 704, fn. 20.

3. Ibid., p. 242, fn. 65; and p. 243, fn. 78.

4. [Ibid.,] p. 608, fn. 31.

5. Ibid., p. 234, fn. 9.

6. [Ibid.,] p. 242, fn. 71.

7. [Ibid.,] p. 236, fn. 23.

8. Ibid., p. 236, fn. 23; and p. 347, fn. 131.

9. Ibid., p. 236, fn. 24.

10. Ibid., p. 237, fn. 27.

11. Ibid., p. 237, fn. 25.

12. Ibid., p. 362, fn. 24.

13. [Ibid.,] p. 242, fn. 70; and p. 585, fn. 24.

14. Ibid., p. 237 ff.

15. Ibid., p. 240, fn. 60; and p. 514, fn. 11.

16. [Ibid.,] p. 248, fn. 102.

17. Keeping them "tamed" them, no doubt.

18. [Zingg, R. M.: *The Huichols*,] p. 613 ff.

19. Ibid., p. 583.

20. Ibid., p. 257, fn. 141.

21. Ibid., p. 258, fn. 144; and p. 594, fn. 47.

22. This is the yellow root, *kíeli* [kieli], that is used for face-paint by peyoteros.

23. Zingg, R. M.: *The Huichols: Primitive Artists*, p. 258, fn. 145; and p. 585, fn. 28.

24. Ibid., p. 207, fn. 12; and p. 363, fn. 32.

25. Snakes and water-people identified.

26. This swamp is near the lake halakona. Here, at a point near the sea, the Huichols carry offerings, since it is necessary that they follow the advantage [example] of Kauymáli.

27. This rock near Tepic, called túkamelíka, is "as high as a cathedral."
28. Zingg, R. M.: *[The Huichols,]* p. 352, fn. 1; and p. 601, fn. 5.
29. [Ibid., p. 352, fn. 1; and p. 601, fn. 5.]
30. Ibid., p. 208, fn. 14.
31. Ibid., p. 609, fn. 37; and p. 704, fn. 19.
32. Ibid., p. 704, fn. 19.
33. "For this reason the Huichols use sinew in their arrows." (Informant)
34. Zingg, R. M.: *[The Huichols,]* p. 265, fn. 2.
35. [Ibid.,] p. 265, fn. 3.
36. Interesting association not fu[r]ther developed.
37. [Zingg, R. M.: *The Huichols,*] p. 337, fn. 87.
38. [Ibid., p. 337, fn. 87.]
39. Ibid., p. 337, fn. 88.
40. [Ibid., p. 337, fn. 88.]
41. These are also offered to Grandfather Fire, who is also the special deer-god.
42. Zingg, R. M.: *The Huichols: Primitive Artists,* pp. 282–83.
43. [Zingg indicates a footnote here, but no footnote text is included. — Ed.]
44. Zingg, R. M.: *The Huichols: Primitive Artists,* p. 140, fn. 16.
45. Ibid., p. 258, fn. 138.

F. Kauymáli, the Wolf-Man, Is Outsmarted but Gets Revenge

1. Zingg, R. M.: [*The Huichols,* New York: G.E. Stechert, 1938], p. 680, fn. 9.
2. Ibid., p. 690, fn. 29.
3. [Ibid.,] p. 360, fn. 14.
4. [Ibid.,] p. 514, fn. 8.
5. Ibid., p. 514, fn. 11.
6. Ibid., p. 515, fn. 13.
7. [Ibid., p. 514, fn. 8.]
8. [Ibid.,] p. 367.
9. [Ibid.,] p. 234, fn. 5.
10. [Ibid.,] p. 234, fn. 6.
11. Ibid., p. 361.
12. [Ibid., p. 361.]
13. [Ibid.,] p. 362, fn. 24.
14. [Ibid., p. 362, fn. 24.]
15. Ibid., p. 329, fn. 51; and p. 721, fn. 52.
16. It is quite noticeable how afraid of whirlwinds the Huichols are. Whirlwinds are common in the Huichol country, and the people scurry away at their approach, making the sign of the cross. I cannot recall ever seeing any of them standing unconcernedly by at the approach of a whirlwind.
17. The Tarahumaras believe that the wind lives in holes and that whirlwinds are wicked beings. [See] Bennett, W. O., and Zingg, R. M., *The Tarahumara,* pp. 324–25.

G. Youth Changes His Affiliations from the Sea-Goddesses to the
Sun-Father and Makes a Vow to the Wolf[-]People in Order to Catch Deer

1. Zingg, R. M.: *The Huichols: Primitive Artists* [New York: G.E. Stechert, 1938], p. 507.
2. This notion of the deer eating colored earth is associated with the dyes for face-painting in the peyote round, which is associated with the deer. My informant said that when the Huichols find the deer with colored saliva, they will not touch the carcass.

Part II.
A. Keamukáme Establishes the Corn Ceremonies and Feasts

1. Zingg, R.M.: *The Huichols: Primitive Artists* [New York: G. E. Stechert, 1938], p. 253, fn. 122; and p. 343, fn. 106.
2. Ibid., p. 343, fn. 107.
3. Ibid., p. 276, fn. 35; and p. 343, fn. 108.
4. Ibid., p. 276, fn. 34.
5. Ibid., p. 136, fn. 8.
6. Ibid., p. 274, fn. 25; and p. 656, fn. 35.
7. Ibid., p. 274, fn. 28.
8. Ibid., p. 711, fn. 32.
9. Ibid., p. 251, fn. 108.
10. Wet-season goddes[ses] always provide sacred water.
11. Lumholtz notices the identification of deer, corn, and peyote. Also see Zingg, R. M.: *[The Huichols,]* p. 257, fn. 135.
12. [Ibid.,] p. 605, fn. 17.
13. Ibid., p. 257, fn. 137; and p. 343, fn. 110; and p. 605, fn. 18.
14. Ibid., p. 343, fn. 109; and p. 635, fn. 83.
15. Ibid., p. 239, fn. 55; and p. 241, fn. 62.
16. [Ibid., p. 239, fn. 55; and p. 241, fn. 62.]
17. Ibid., p. 337, fn. 86.
18. [Ibid.,] p. 266, fn. 5; and p. 280, fn. 52.
19. Ibid., p. 647, fn. 8.
20. [Ibid.,] pp. 257–58, fn. 138.
21. The Huichols determine the beginning of their feasts as, for example, when the beer is strained.
22. [Zingg, R. M.: *The Huichols,*] p. 613, fn. 46.
23. Lumholtz says that Tateváli is the particular god of the shamans. Carl Lumholtz, *Symbolism of the Huichol Indians,* p. 10.
24. The tesgüino [corn-beer] is always placed fermenting on the altar the night before it is drunk.
25. The Huichols themselves place money in the centers of their most sacred votive-bowls.
26. Zingg, R. M.: *[The Huichols,]* p. 275, fn. 31.

27. [Ibid.,] p. 302, fn. 10.
28. Ibid., p. 400, fn. 14.
29. This is one of the common Huichol hunting shrines.
30. See [The P]eyote [M]yth.
31. Zingg, R. M.: *[The Huichols,]* p. 307, fn. 47.

B. The Water-and-Corn Goddess, Kacíwali, and the Ant-People

1. Zingg, R. M.: *The Huichols: Primitive Artists* [New York: G. E. Stechert, 1938], p. 246, fn. 89.
2. Ibid., p. 676, fn. 7.
3. [Ibid.,] p. 482 ff.
4. Ibid., p. 258, fn. 139.
5. Ibid., p. 208, fn. 16; and p. 239, fn. 51.
6. Ibid., p. 637, fn. 94.
7. Huichols count the beginning of their feasts from the straining of the tesgüino.
8. Zingg, R. M.: *The Huichols: Primitive Artists*, pp. 344–45.
9. Ibid., p. 635, fn. 84.
10. Ibid., p. 245, fn. 85.
11. [Ibid.,] p. 240, fn. 57; and p. 344, fn. 114.
12. Ibid., p. 344, fn. 115.
13. Ibid., p. 344, fn. 116; and p. 635, fn. 82.
14. Ibid., p. 344, fn. 117.
15. Ibid., p. 647, fn. 7.
16. Ibid., p. 254, fn. 124.
17. [Ibid.,] p. 252, fn. 111.
18. *Erythrina*, Sp. A very light wood, somewhat like cork. It is used by the Indians and the Mexicans of Jalisco, as by the Tarahumaras of the *bar[r]ancas* of Chihuahua, to lie on when swimming in swift water.
19. [Zingg, R. M.: *The Huichols,*] p. 252, fn. 111; and p. 344, fn. 118.
20. Ibid., p. 344, fn. 119.
21. [Ibid.,] p. 278, fn. 46.
22. Ibid., p. 209, fn. 23; and p. 209, fn. 25.

C. Nakawé Punishes [the] (God)People Because the Sea Turtle Is Killed

1. Zingg, R. M.: [*The Huichols: Primitive Artists* (New York: G. E. Stechert, 1938),] p. 321, fn. 9.
2. The land variety of the turtle is treated cruelly enough. The Huichols catch them and throw them in the air to break their shells so that they can serve as food for their tame hawks. The latter are kept for their feathers to furnish sacred paraphernalia.

3. Zingg, R. M.: *The Huichols: Primitive Artists*, p. 348.

4. See also "Huichol Mythology," p. 289g. Zingg, R. N.: *[The Huichols,]* p. 265, fn. 44. [Zingg cites the incorrect page. It should be p. 365.—Ed.]

5. [Zingg, R. M.: *The Huichols,*] p. 265, fn. 44. [Zingg cites the incorrect page. It should be p. 365.—Ed.]

6. [Ibid.,] p. 238, fn. 40.

7. Ibid., p. 321, fn. 9.

8. Ibid., p. 363, fn. 26 ff.

9. [Ibid., p. 363, fn. 26 ff.]

10. Ibid., p. 330, fn. 54.

11. Ibid., p. 330, fn. 53.

12. [Ibid., p. 330, fn. 54.]

13. Ibid., p. 330, fn. 53.

14. Ibid., p. 330, fn. 55.

15. [Ibid.,] p. 330, fn. 57.

16. A Mexican tree that resists drought.

17. [Zingg, R. M.: *The Huichols,*] p. 330, fn. 56.

18. [Ibid., p. 330, fn. 56.]

19. Ibid., p. 321, fn. 10.

20. [Ibid.,] p. 275, fn. 31.

21. [Ibid., p. 275, fn. 31.]

22. [Ibid.,] p. 321, fn. 13.

23. [Ibid., p. 321, fn. 13.]

24. Ibid., p. 238, fn. 39.

25. Ibid., p. 321, fn. 11.

26. [Ibid.,] p. 321, fn. 9 ff.

27. Ibid., p. 275, fn. 32; and p. 321, fn. 12.

28. Lumholtz mentions paintings of female genitalia on rocks in the Huichol country, though he did not know the mythical explanation and the association of these parts with water, earth, growth, fertility, and increase through the rain-season goddesses. See also Zingg, R. M.: *[The Huichols,]* p. 322, fn. 14.

D. The Corn Myth

1. The species of ants concerned here are called *salusi* (*arrieras*, Sp.), and steal corn from Huichol store-houses. They are combatted with the articles mentioned here.

2. Zingg, R. M.: *The Huichols: Primitive Artists* [New York: G. E. Stechert, 1938], p. 167, fn. 73.

3. It is doubtful if this is the name of the corn-owner. Elsewhere Komatéame is an old woman. [Zingg, R. M.: *The Huichols,*] p. 328, fn. 46; and p. 346, fn. 125.

4. [Ibid.,] p. 347, fn. 129.

5. [Ibid.,] p. 613, fn. 45.

6. Ibid., pp. 255–56.

7. Knowing the thought revealed character.

8. [Zingg, R. M.: *The Huichols*,] p. 274, fn. 27; and p. 347, fn. 128.

9. The Huichols use an expression, *"Pampa Dios,"* derived from the Spanish *"que Dios se lo pague,"* may God pay you.

10. Thus the Huichols kill these ants.

11. Zingg, R. M.: *[The Huichols,]* p. 605, fn. 12.

12. Ibid., p. 602, fn. 8.

13. Ibid., p. 240, fn. 59.

14. [Ibid.,] p. 128, fn. 30.

15. [Ibid.,] p. 256, fn. 130.

16. [Ibid.,] p. 256, fn. 129.

17. [Ibid.,] p. 234, fn. 3; and p. 256, fn. 131.

18. [Ibid.,] p. 256, fn. 132.

19. [Ibid.,] p. 328, fn. 50; and p. 712, fn. 33.

20. [Ibid., p. 328, fn. 50; and p. 712, fn. 33.]

21. Ibid., p. 328, fn. 48; and p. 640, fn. 104.

22. Ibid., p. 328, fn. 49.

23. [Ibid.,] p. 233, fn. 2; and p. 489, fn. 10.

24. [Ibid.,] p. 400, fn. 15; and p. 490, fn. 12.

25. Ibid., p. 233, fn. 2.

26. Ibid., p. 489, fn. 10.

27. [Ibid.,] p. 234, fn. 4; and p. 256, fn. 133.

28. Ibid., p. 362, fn. 26; and p. 362.

29. Ibid., pp. 59–60, fn. 15.

30. Ibid., p. 362, fn. 26.

31. [Ibid.,] p. 362, fn. 26.

32. Votive[-]bowls serve as prayer[-]arrows.

33. [Zingg, R. M.: *The Huichols*,] p. 116, fn. 10; and p. 117, fn. 12.

34. [Ibid.,] p. 151, fn. 22.

35. [Ibid.,] p. 362, fn. 27.

36. Ibid., p. 153, fn. 29.

37. [Ibid.,] p. 152, fn. 28.

38. Here, apparently, is meant the soul of the child. [Zingg, R. M.: *The Huichols*,] p. 147, fn. 5.

39. Ibid., p. 148, fn. 8 and 10.

40. [Ibid.,] p. 151, fn. 23.

41. The Huichols commonly identify the Christian God, *Dios*, with the Sun, and all God is the Sun. *Tata Dios* is the "God father."

42. [Zingg, R. M.: *The Huichols*,] p. 153, fn. 29.

43. [Ibid.,] p. 148, fn. 16. [Zingg cites the incorrect page. It should be p. 149.—Ed.]

44. Ibid., pp. 150–51.

45. Ibid., p. 150, fn. 19.
46. Ibid., pp. 238–41.
47. Ibid., p. 149, fn. 11.
48. Pruess [Preuss] reports that among the Cora the humming-bird is the messenger of the Sun. *"Der Kolibri wird, wie wir sahen, mit ihm* (the Sun) *identifiert und ist auserdem sein Bote* (S. 194 f.) *der ihm über das Treiben der Menschen berichtet und ihnen, wenn er an der Tür einer Hütte zwitschert, den Tod ankündigt.* R. T. Pruess [Preuss], *Die Nayarit Expedition*, Band I, p. LVI.
49. Presumably where the Sun is at night. Since the Huichols have seen the sun setting in the Pacific to the west, they believe that the sun spends its nights in the sea.
50. Zingg, R. M.: *The Huichols: Primitive Artists*, p. 148, fn. 9.
51. Ibid., p. 149, fn. 14; and p. 245, fn. 86.
52. Ibid., p. 152, fn. 27.
53. [Ibid., p. 149, fn. 14; and p. 245, fn. 86.]
54. Ibid., p. 243, fn. 76.
55. Ibid., p. 243, fn. 77.
56. [Ibid., p. 243, fn. 77.]
57. [Ibid., p. 243, fn. 76.]
58. [Ibid.,] p. 148, fn. 7.
59. [Ibid.,] p. 132, fn. 2.
60. Kauymali is called, in Spanish, El Chueco, the "lame one." This was because one side was withered or dry, the other, normal. This was due to his being a god [who is] "half-bad," while the other half was of "good thought."
61. Zingg, R. M.: *The Huichols: Primitive Artists*, p. xxviii, fn. 6.
62. [Ibid.,] p. xxviii, fn. 6.
63. Ibid., p. xxxvi, fn. 7.
64. [Ibid.,] p. 360, fn. 13.
65. Ibid., p. 361, fn. 18; and p. 614, fn. 48.
66. Ibid., p. 360, fn. 15; and p. 362, fn. 25.
67. [Ibid.,] p. 701, fn. 10.
68. Ibid., p. 245, fn. 87.
69. [Ibid.,] p. 362, fn. 21.
70. Ibid., p. 324, fn. 26.
71. Ibid., p. 324, fn. 22.
72. [Ibid.,] p. 640, fn. 103.
73. Ibid., p. 362, fn. 22.
74. [Ibid.,] p. 346, fn. 127; and p. 614, fn. 49.
75. Ibid., p. 362, fn. 23.
76. A kind of reed-like bamboo.
77. [Zingg, R. M.: *The Huichols,*] p. 255, fn. 127.
78. [Ibid.,] p. 245, fn. 88.
79. Ibid., p. 364, fn. 42.

80. Ibid., p. 324, fn. 20.

81. Ibid., p. 324, fn. 23.

82. Ibid., p. 255, fn. 127.

83. [Ibid.,] p. 324, fn. 25.

84. Ibid., p. 513, fn. 5.

85. *Ficus, sp.* "Salate," Sp.

86. As Grandmother Growth, she saves life from her own flood.

87. Zingg, R. M.: *[The Huichols,]* p. 596, fn. 51; and p. 605, fn. 16.

88. Ibid., p. 245, fn. 85. (Lumholtz records this figure of speech for a strong wind.)

89. Zingg, R. M.: *The Huichols: Primitive Artists,* p. 243, fn. 74.

90. Ibid., p. 243, fn. 75.

91. [Ibid., p. 243, fn. 75.]

92. [Ibid., p. 243, fn. 75.]

93. [Ibid., p. 243, fn. 75.]

94. Ibid., p. 68, fn. 74; and p. 243, fn. 74.

95. Rare explanatory element in Huichol mythology.

96. [Zingg, R. M.: *The Huichols,*] p. 68, fn. 74; and p. 243, fn. 74.

97. [Ibid., p. 68, fn. 74; and p. 243, fn. 74.]

98. [Ibid.,] p. 363, fn. 33.

99. Ibid., p. 244, fn. 84.

100. Ibid., p. 274, fn. 29.

101. Corn boiled in lye [lime].

102. [Zingg, R. M.: *The Huichols,*] p. 244, fn. 84.

103. [Ibid.,] p. 241, fn. 64.

104. [Ibid.,] p. 687, fn. 25.

105. Ibid., p. 255, fn. 128.

106. [Ibid.,] p. 324, fn. 28.

107. In a following story, on page 55 [Refer to section II.D.4., The Story of Duck-Boy, TumuSaúwi, in this volume. — Ed.], is given an account of the creation of a new race, the Huichols, through the Duck-boy, renamed TumuSawi [TumuSaúwi].

108. [Zingg again refers to footnote 107. — Ed.]

109. This origin-myth concerning the Mexicans well reflects the Huichol conception of the Mexicans as invaders of their lands. Further, one of the most striking things about Mexicans in the Huichol mind is that the Mexicans eat of new fruits without giving a ceremony. The Huichols can not [*sic*] understand why the Mexicans do not suffer for this. I have seen them refuse Mexican offerings of elotes, until they (the Huichols) had given the corresponding first fruit ceremony. See also [Zingg, R. M.: *The Huichols,*] p. 363, fn. 35.

110. Zingg, R. M.: *The Huichols: Primitive Artists,* pp. 318–20.

111. Ibid., p. 332, fn. 59.

112. It is interesting to note that this goddess, like the Greek Aphrodite, derives her name from foam.

113. [Zingg, R. M.: *The Huichols*,] p. 332, fn. 60.

114. [Ibid.,] p. 332, fn. 61. "The physiography of the Huichol country presents many mountains with a series of jumps or flights, causing the mountains to rise like pyramids." This is here referred to.

115. [Zingg, R. M.: *The Huichols*,] pp. 342–43, gives a discussion of this goddess.

116. Ibid., p. 343, fn. 111.

117. Ibid., p. 348, mentions this god.

118. Unidentified.

119. [Zingg, R. M.: *The Huichols*,] p. 346, fn. 122.

120. Ibid., p. 348, lists this goddess.

121. Ibid., p. 349, lists this goddess.

122. Ibid., p. 247, fn. 95.

123. The same story was repeated word for word, months later, by the same informant.

124. Suggestion here of votive-bowl.

125. Zingg, R. M.: *[The Huichols,]* p. 365, fn. 48.

126. [Ibid.,] p. 334, fn. 70.

127. Ibid., p. 334, fn. 71.

128. Lumholtz calls this character "the god of death." This is not accurate, however, since Tukákame does not appear in the death myth, nor does he appear in the mythology even as a great god. Tukákame is a ghoulish conception which [that] arouses great fear in the Huichol mind, greater than that of the gods.

Lumholtz gives some interesting data on a figure of this ghoul, carved for him. The ears "have serrated edges, and each ear represents the notches [notched] bone on which the shaman runs the accompaniment to his song on the deer-hunt(?). Thus one of his attributes is the mystic power of incantation, so effective with a good shaman, so dreadful in the hands of a bad shaman. . . . The figure is covered all over with stripes and dots of ferruginous clay, indicative of the blood with which he is smutched [smudged]. Round the waist and over the back are white lines representing human bones attached to strings; other white stripes, lines, and dots on the face and ears are meant to show his uncouth appearance." *Symbolism of the Huichol Indians*, pp. 60–61. See also Zingg, R. M.: *[The Huichols,]* p. 365, fn. 47.

129. The place of Stuluwíakame, filled with water, swamp, and flowers, is called "the place where children are born" (see the symbolic Nama #87). This association of water and flowers with "the place where children are born" seems to be a characteristic of Cora and Aztec mythology. The Huichol place, however, has a concrete identity lacking in Cora mythology, if we follow Preuss, who says,

> In the Cora sings of Jesus Maria, they *lauten* (give) only the place at which the god of fertility, namely the evening-star, was created or appeared (i.e., was born), as is shown in the following:
>
> 1. A general characterization . . . also with the addition—"on that side, on that side of the world in the midst of the waters"—"the place of birth"; "the place of life."

2. The place of growth and of planting . . . "the place of plowing before sow-ing"; "the place of flower pollen"; "between the flower pollen"; "the place of trees."

3. "The place of wetness"; "between the clouds"; "at the place of rain"; "at the place of night, in the night, the place of birth"; "at the place of the rain-stones"; "at the place of the acorns (? Pruess) on the rain-stones."

"These places are told of with scarcely an allusion to their identity. . . ." (*Die Nayarit Expedition*, B and I, p. XL)

In Aztec mythology, if we follow Pruess [Preuss], the place where children were born was called Tamoanchan, "the house of those descending" (Ibid., p. XXXVIII), and is next to Xochitl icacan, "where the flowers stand." The place of birth as "the house of those descending" corresponds to a Huichol conception seen in the votive Nama #87, where unborn children are represented above the Huichol "place where children are born," while children already born as represented below, just as is seen in the Aztec glyph of the Aztec goddess, Teteoinan (Ibid., p. XL, illustration 14).

See also, Zingg, R. M.: *[The Huichols,]* p. 335, fn. 79.

130. Ibid., p. 335, fn. 78.

131. Informant says that peyote-hunters carry arrows, votive-bowls, and other para-phernalia to Stuluwíakame to ask her for increase, not only of their children, but of their animals as well. The offerings are always buried in the mud of the swamp. See also Zingg, [R. M.: *The Huichols*,] p. 335, fn. 80; and p. 408, fn. 36.

132. The Mexican-Catholic shrine against lightning. Suggestion here of aboriginal shrine [C]atholicized.

133. Zingg, R. M.: *The Huichols: Primitive Artists*, p. 244, fn. 80; and p. 345, fn. 120.

134. [Ibid., p. 244, fn. 80; and p. 345, fn. 120.]

135. Ibid., p. 324, fn. 24.

136. Ibid., p. 244, fn. 83; and p. 353, fn. 7.

137. Ibid., p. 322, fn. 18; and p. 604, fn. 11.

138. [Ibid.,] p. 325, fn. 30; and p. 635, fn. 81.

139. Ibid., p. 609, fn. 34.

140. Ibid., p. 243, fn. 74.

141. Ibid., p. 271, fn. 17; and p. 326, fn. 40.

142. [Ibid., p. 609, fn. 34.]

143. [Ibid.,] p. 326, fn. 36; and p. 637, fn. 92.

144. Ibid., p. 325, fn. 31.

145. [Ibid., p. 325, fn. 31.]

146. Ibid., p. 325, fn. 32.

147. Ibid., p. 325, fn. 33.

148. [Ibid.,] p. 325, fn. 34.

149. [Ibid., p. 325, fn. 34.]

150. [Ibid., p. 325, fn. 34.]

151. [Ibid., p. 325, fn. 34.]

152. [Ibid., p. 325, fn. 34.]
153. [Ibid., p. 325, fn. 34.]
154. [Ibid., p. 325, fn. 34.]
155. [Ibid., p. 325, fn. 34.]
156. Ibid., p. 165, fn. 65; and p. 325, fn. 35.
157. [Ibid.,] p. 326, fn. 38.
158. [Ibid.,] p. 272, fn. 18.
159. Ibid., p. 608, fn. 29.
160. Corn-deer-peyote symbolism.
161. Zingg, R. M.: *The Huichols: Primitive Artists*, p. 149, fn. 15.
162. Votive[-]bowls from rotted fish is a mystic participation indeed.
163. [Zingg, R. M.: *The Huichols*,] p. 272, fn. 19.
164. [Ibid.,] p. 274, fn. 24.
165. [Ibid.,] p. 265, fn. 4.
166. [Ibid.,] p. 266, fn. 7; and p. 585, fn. 25.
167. [Ibid.,] p. 257, fn. 136.
168. [Ibid., p. 257, fn. 136.]
169. Ibid., p. 269.
170. [Ibid.,] p. 257, fn. 136.
171. Ibid., p. 257, fn. 136.
172. Ibid., p. 362, fn. 20.
173. [Ibid.,] p. 116, fn. 5.
174. Huichol informants told me that this cave is full of deer-horns [antlers].
175. [Zingg, R. M.: *The Huichols*,] p. 150, fn. 20; and p. 304, fn. 26.
176. Ibid., p. 150, fn. 21.
177. See myth of Huichol temple. Zingg, R. M.: *[The Huichols,]* p. 147, fn. 2.
178. *Kuáchalalá*, Sp. Ibid., p. 149, fn. 17.
179. [See myth of Huichol temple. Zingg, R. M.: *The Huichols*, p. 147, fn. 2.]
180. [Ibid.,] p. 247, fn. 99.
181. Thus it is, says my informant, Juan Real, that roasting ears are green. See Zingg, R. M.: *[The Huichols,]* p. 640, fn. 108.
182. Ibid., p. 283, fn. 62.
183. See 186 herein [Refer to section II.D.2.c., The Origin of the Mexicans, in this volume. — Ed.]
184. Corn boiled in lye [lime], which is the prototype for the hominy the colonists borrowed from the Indians of the United States.
185. Zingg, R. M.: *[The Huichols,]* p. 277, fn. 39.
186. [Ibid.,] p. 362, fn. 26 ff.
187. Ibid., pp. 276–77. [Zingg cites the incorrect page range. It should be pp. 277–78. — Ed.]
188. Ibid., p. 147, fn. 3.
189. Ibid., p. 277, fn. 40.

190. In the feast to the underworld goddess to prepare the soil for seed, a layer of grass is used to take away any impurities from the food. The grass is later carried ceremoniously away and burned.

191. It was a striking coincidence that when my informant told me this part of the story, Pancho, on the adjacent ranch, got very angry with his wife. It seems that Pancho's wife was jealous because he had been meeting, adulterously, another Huichol's wife in the arroyo. She, consequently, refused to cook for him. When another Huichol chided Pancho for his wife's disobedience, he became angry. He took a machete and, using the flat side, gave her a beating while they were in the store-house within sight and hearing of my informant and me.

Although the beating was not unduly severe, the woman and her children cried about it, as described in this story.

The old grandmother, who lives at the ranch contiguous to Pancho's, ran up and made him stop, by reason of his respect for her age and kinship to him.

In a few days their smallest child became sick. Pascual, a singer, told Pancho that it was because he had beaten his wife. They put a new ribbon around the child's head in order to cure it. See Zingg, R. M.: *The Huichols: Primitive Artists*, p. 143.

192. This is the penalty for disobeying the shaman, see Zingg, R. M.: *The Huichols: Primitive Artists*, p. 209, fn. 24.

193. In other words "delicate," or sacred. Zingg, R. M.: *The Huichols: Primitive Artists*, p. 153, fn. 35. [Zingg cites the incorrect page. It should be p. 154.—Ed.]

194. The end of the story approaches, and the informant hesitates to finish this story about death until all the rest of the myth is told. It would be dangerous, he says, to go back and repeat parts that he had left out.

195. Zingg, R. M.: *The Huichols: Primitive Artists*, p. 154, fn. 36.

196. [Ibid.,] p. 139, fn. 14; and p. 281, fn. 56.

197. Sp., "stick of death"; *Zanthoxylum [f]agara* (L.) Sarg.

198. Zingg, R. M.: *The Huichols: Primitive Artists*, p. 139, fn. 15.

199. Ibid., p. 163, fn. 58.

200. Ibid., p. 691, fn. 32.

201. Ibid., p. 154.

202. [Ibid.,] p. 163 ff., fn. 59.

203. One of the *Compositae*.

204. [Zingg, R. M.: *The Huichols*,] pp. 153–54.

205. Ibid., p. 154, fn. 34.

206. For discussion of this mythical race see, Zingg, R. M.: *[The Huichols,]* p. 356, fn. 11.

207. Low wages.

208. See 68-IV. [Zingg is referring to the original manuscript. Refer to II.D.4.b., Kauymáli's Usual Sexual Weakness Brings Death to the Huichols, in this volume.—Ed.]

209. Zingg, R. M.: *The Huichols: Primitive Artists*, pp. 346–47.

210. [Ibid.,] pp. 283–84.

211. [Ibid.,] p. 616, fn. 53.

212. This seems quite typical of Huichol religion. The prayer-arrows carry messages to the gods, and the messages may often be given graphic form in the shape of embroidered pictures hung on the arrows. (See Lumholtz, *Symbolism of the Huichol Indians*, p. 149). Here a scorpion is embroidered on a bit of cloth hanging to an arrow. It represents a mother's prayer that the scorpions will not sting her children — a typical Huichol protection. The Huichols will not learn to draw a few drops of blood from the wound. See [Zingg, R. M.: *The Huichols*,] p. 609, fn. 35; and p. 356, fn. 10.

213. [Ibid.,] p. 125, fn. 27.

214. See Lumholtz, *Unknown Mexico*, II, 40–50.

215. Zingg, R. M.: *The Huichols: Primitive Artists*, p. 125, fn. 27.

216. [Ibid.,] pp. 125–26.

217. Ibid., p. 335, fn. 77; and p. 488, fn. 8; and p. 650, fn. 18.

218. Ibid., p. 246, fn. 92; and p. 650, fn. 19.

219. [Ibid.,] p. 651, fn. 20.

220. This myth specifically, says my informant.

221. [Zingg, R. M.: The Huichols,] p. 487, fn. 6.

222. *Ñe natáta* — informant says this relationship is like a "padrino."
This mythological account of the establishment of Huichol ceremonies in the first times I have seen re-enacted twice in actual ceremonies. It is exactly as described here, except that the successful hunter does drink the tesgüino.

223. See description of first fruits ceremony.

224. Zingg, R. M.: *[The Huichols,]* p. 233, fn. 2.

225. Ibid., p. 243, fn. 76; and p. 244, fn. 81.

226. [Ibid.,] p. 237, fn. 29.

227. As the peyote ceremony of parched corn in the dry-season.

228. [Zingg, R. M.: *The Huichols: Primitive Artists*, p. 237, fn. 29.]

229. Ibid., p. 489, fn. 9.

230. Ibid., p. 280, fn. 54.

231. [Ibid., p. 237, fn. 29.]

232. Informant says that the green corn feast is the same as that of green squash.

233. Zingg, R. M.: *The Huichols: Primitive Artists*, p. 239, fn. 50.

234. Ibid., pp. 336–37.

235. Ibid., p. 337, fn. 83.

236. Ibid., p. 147, fn. 6.

237. [Ibid.,] p. 682, fn. 11.

238. Ibid., p. 123, fn. 26; and p. 337, fn. 84.

239. Ibid., p. 338, fn. 90.

240. [Ibid.,] p. 247, fn. 94; and p. 339, fn. 92.

241. Ibid., p. 339, fn. 93; and p. 637, fn. 93.

242. Ibid., p. 339, fn. 94.

243. Ibid., p. 238, fn. 41; and p. 242, fn. 68.

244. [Ibid.,] p. 244, fn. 82.

245. Ibid., p. 336 ff.

246. Ibid., p. 339, fn. 95.
247. [Ibid.,] pp. 338–42.
248. Ibid., p. 254, fn. 126; and p. 339, fn. 96 and 97.
249. Grandmother Growth would be the one to order things to grow.
250. [Zingg, R. M.: *The Huichols,*] p. 253, fn. 123; and p. 339, fn. 98.
251. Ibid., p. 255, discusses other mystical contents of the squash.
252. [Zingg, R. M.: *The Huichols,*] p. 339, fn. 99.
253. [Ibid.,] pp. 606–7.
254. Ibid., p. 341, fn. 102.
255. Ibid., p[p]. [340,] 341, fn. 102.
256. [Ibid., pp. 340, 341, fn. 102.]
257. [Ibid., pp. 340, 341, fn. 102.]
258. Ibid., p. 341, fn. 105; and p. 717, fn. 41.
259. [Ibid., p. 252, fn. 114; and p. 341, fn. 104.]
260. Ibid., p. 278, fn. 47.
261. Ibid., p. 716, fn. 39.
262. [Ibid.,] p. 717, fn. 43.
263. Ibid., p. 278 ff., fn. 47.
264. [Ibid.,] p. 278, fn. 48; and p. 367, fn. 58.
265. [Ibid., p. 278, fn. 48; and p. 367, fn. 58.]
266. [Ibid., p. 278, fn. 48; and p. 367, fn. 58.]
267. [Ibid., p. 278, fn. 48; and p. 367, fn. 58.]
268. Ibid., p. 341, fn. 101.
269. Ibid., p. 217, fn. 56.
270. Wisdom's data says 8 days; see Zingg, R. M.: *[The Huichols,]* pp. 216–17.
271. [Zingg, R. M.: *The Huichols,*] p. 238, fn. 46.
272. Ibid., p. 209, fn. 26.
273. Ibid., p. 217, fn. 57.
274. [Ibid.,] p. 341, fn. 101.
275. Ibid., p. 241, fn. 61.
276. [Ibid., p. 241, fn. 61.]
277. [Ibid.,] p. 341, fn. 101.
278. [Ibid.,] p. 242, fn. 67; and p. 609, fn. 33.
279. [Ibid., p. 242, fn. 67; and p. 609, fn. 33.]
280. [Ibid.,] p. 367 discusses wind.
281. Ibid., p. 367, fn. 57.

E. The Snake-Man's Illicit Love for the Wife of a Huichol Begets the First Rain and Curing Singers of the Huichols

1. Zingg, R. M.: *The Huichols: Primitive Artists* [New York: G. E. Stechert, 1938], p. 238, fn. 34.
2. [Ibid., p. 238, fn. 34.]

3. Ibid., p. 583 discusses the magic of the man's costume.
4. Zingg, R. M.: *The Huichols: Primitive Artists*, p. 128, fn. 33.
5. [Ibid., p. 128, fn. 33.]
6. [Ibid.,] p. 238, fn. 35.
7. [Ibid.,] p. 238, fn. 35.
8. Here Father Sun and the Christian God are identified.
9. [Zingg, R. M.: *The Huichols*, p. 238, fn. 35.]
10. Ibid., p. 116, fn. 6; and p. 142, fn. 20.
11. Ibid., p. 279, fn. 49.
12. Here the Sun is seen as an enemy of Snake—that is, water! See Zingg, R. M.: *The Huichols: Primitive Artists*, p. 252, fn. 116. [Zingg cites the incorrect page. It should be p. 115.—Ed.]
13. [Zingg again refers to footnote 12.—Ed.]
14. [Zingg, R. M.: *The Huichols*,] p. 238, fn. 33; and p. 352, fn. 2.
15. Ibid., p. 252, fn. 117.
16. Ibid., p. 279, fn. 50.
17. [Ibid.,] p. 238, fn. 36.
18. [Ibid.,] p. 252, fn. 115.
19. [Ibid., p. 252, fn. 115.]
20. [Ibid., p. 252, fn. 115.]
21. Ibid., p. 142, fn. 20; and p. 116, fn. 6.
22. [Ibid., p. 142, fn. 20; and p. 116, fn. 6.]
23. [Ibid.,] p. 252, fn. 115.
24. Ibid., p. 253, fn. 118.
25. [Ibid., p. 253, fn. 118.]
26. [Ibid., p. 253, fn. 118.]
27. Ibid., p. 253, fn. 119.
28. Ibid., p. 324, fn. 27.
29. Ibid., p. 253, fn. 120.
30. [Ibid.,] p. 253, fn. 121.
31. During actual ceremonies[,] the frequent rains enable the illusion that the singing causes the rain.

F. *"Mayor" Nasario, the Orphan-boy, Saves His Brothers from the Ghoul, Tukákame, but Contaminated and Changed to Chipmunks (?), They Bring Insanity to the Huichols*

1. It is this tainted Nasario who betrays Santo Cristo to the *julios* ([Judios] Jews). See end of Christian Myth Cycle. This story is intermediate between the Wet Season Pagan Cycle and the Christian Myth Cycle, and contains many Mexican-Spanish elements—horses, mules, etc.—that are found only in the latter cycle.

Huichol children are told this story when they are disobedient or act "crazy." My informant adds that this is to warn them of what may happen to them because of *tcamóko*.

2. [Zingg, R. M.: *The Huichols: Primitive Artists* (New York: G. E. Stechert, 1938)], p. 365, fn. 45.

3. Ibid., p. 620, fn. 61.

4. Ibid., p. 234, fn. 10.

5. [Ibid.,] p. 620, fn. 61.

6. Fish are sacre[d] to Nakawé[,] from whence come the human beings.

7. [Zingg again refers to footnote 6.—Ed.]

8. [Zingg again refers to footnote 6.—Ed.]

9. [Zingg, R. M.: *The Huichols*,] p. 233, fn. 1.

10. [Ibid., p. 233, fn. 1.]

11. [Ibid.,] pp. 344–45 mentions mythical sanctions for hospitality.

12. Ibid., p. 366, fn. 50.

13. [Ibid., p. 366, fn. 50.]

14. [Ibid.,] pp. 366–67.

15. Ibid., p. 238, fn. 37.

16. [Ibid.,] p. 717, fn. 43.

17. Ibid., p. 276 ff.

18. [Ibid.,] p. 366, fn. 52.

19. The Tarahumara word for Chipmunk is *tcitci móko*.

20. [Zingg again refers to footnote 19.—Ed.]

21. It is this tainted Nasario who betrays Santo Cristo to the julios (Jews). See end of Christian Myth Cycle.

G. Death Comes to the Woman of the Mythical Pre-Huichol Race, Eáwali, Who Loved Bear and Buzzard [Origin of "Death-bird" Ghouls]

1. The bear is personified among the Tarahumara to the extent of being called grandfather. Bennett, W. C. and Zingg, R. M.: *The Tarahumara*, pp. 112–13.

2. Zingg, R. M.: [*The Huichols* (New York: G. E. Stechert, 1938),] p. 630, fn. 75.

3. [Zingg begins a new paragraph at this point.—Ed.]

4. Mexicans believe that lizards or *axolatls* inter [enter] women's genitalia.

5. Zingg, R. M.: *The Huichols: Primitive Artists*, p. 167, fn. 74.

6. Assemilation [Assimilation] of Christian ideas of heaven [are] indicated. Zingg, R. M.: *The Huichols: Primitive Artists*, p. 167, fn. 75.

7. Ibid., p. 168, fn. 76.

8. Ibid., p. 167, fn. 79.

9. [Ibid., p. 167, fn. 79.]

10. [Ibid.,] p. 168, fn. 78.

11. [Ibid., p. 168, fn. 78.]

12. In the curious reversed world of the Tarahumara dead, bats are thought of as souls of the departed. Bennett, W. C., and Zingg, R. M. [*The Tarahumara*,] p. 112.

13. [Zingg, R. M.: *The Huichols*,] p. 168, fn. 80.

14. The Tarahumaras consider the toad's [*sic*] fatally poisonous. Bennett, W. C., and Zingg, R. M.: *The Tarahumara*, p. 129.

15. Zingg, R. M.: *The Huichols: Primitive Artists*, p. 168, fn. 82; and p. 367, fn. 55.

16. These "death birds" are mentioned on [in] the death myth of the Huichols. The Huichols have a much less ghastly region of the upper world region for their dead, see the myth "Kaumali Brings Death to the Huichols," p. 221. [Zingg is referring to the original manuscript. Refer to Kauymáli's Usual Sexual Weakness Brings Death to the Huichols, section II.D.4.b., in this volume.—Ed.]

Part III.
A. The Bee-Mother Gives Wax for Candles

1. The association between the bee and the candle is clear enough. I have a clear impression that Huichols esteem bees more for the wax than the honey.

2. Huichols think that the blowing out of a candle means death.

3. Zingg, R. M.: [*The Huichols: Primitive Artists* (New York: G.E. Stechert, 1938),] p. 304, fn. 28.

4. [Ibid.,] p. 238, fn. 39.

5. [Ibid.,] p. 235, fn. 15.

6. [Ibid.,] p. 167, fn. 71; and p. 636, fn. 85.

7. Ibid., p. 636, fn. 85.

8. Ibid., p. 238, fn. 42.

9. [Ibid.,] p. 237 ff. [and p. 238] on dreams.

10. In the Christian myth this incongruous introduction of the cross is fitting here.

11. This association of fireflies and candles is obviously because both give light.

12. [Zingg, R. M.: *The Huichols*,] p. 304, fn. 30; and p. 638, fn. 97.

13. Ibid., p. 316, fn. 98; and p. 638, fn. 98.

14. [Ibid.,] p. 637, fn. 90.

15. Ibid., p. 326, fn. 37; and p. 637, fn. 91.

16. [Ibid., p. 326, fn. 37; and p. 637, fn. 91.]

17. Ibid., p. 243, fn. 79.

18. [Ibid.,] p. 235, fn. 14; and p. 636, fn. 88.

19. Ibid., p. 248, fn 100.

20. My Huichol informant thinks that my writing is some kind of magic with Mexicans.

21. Zingg, R. M.: *The Huichols: Primitive Artists*, p. 248, fn. 101.

22. The more Mexicanized Huichols, like Pancho, the quarter-Mexican grandson of Marcelo, have domesticated bees. The "house" of the bee is simply a log hollowed out with a sharp crow-bar. A number of these are set on a shelf-like structure supported by crotched [forked] sticks holding cross-pieces. They are covered with a roof of grass to protect the bees from the hot sun. The hives must be guarded constantly against the *arrieras* (carrying-ants)[,] which eat the grubs. [Zingg, R. M.: *The Huichols*,] p. 720, fn. 51.

23. [Ibid.,] p. 636, fn. 86; and p. 720, fn. 50.

24. This is a mythological reflection of the technology of candle-making among the more-Mexicanized Huichols. Instead of making fuse-like candles, these make real ones. (See notes on bees[.])

B. The Birth of the Saints

1. The Virgin of Guadalupe is sometimes identified with Ereno or Nakawé. Zingg, R. M.: *The Huichols: Primitive Artists* [New York: G.E. Stechert, 1938], p. 61, fn. 25.

2. Ibid., p. 65, fn. 59.

3. Ibid., p. 61, fn. 26; and p. 65, fn. 58.

4. Writing is potent magic to the Huichols. See p. [Zingg does not provide a page number, but see Zingg, R. M.: *The Huichols*, pp. 15–16. — Ed.]

5. Ibid., p. 61, fn. 27; and p. 361, fn. 16.

6. [Ibid., p. 61, fn. 26; and p. 65, fn. 58.]

7. [Zingg again refers to footnote 4. — Ed.]

8. [Zingg, R. M.: *The Huichols*, p. 61, fn. 26; and p. 65, fn. 58.]

9. [Ibid., p. 61, fn. 26; and p. 65, fn. 58.]

10. [Ibid., p. 61, fn. 26; and p. 65, fn. 58.]

11. [Ibid., p. 61, fn. 26; and p. 65, fn. 58.]

12. [Ibid.,] p. 128, fn. 52.

13. [Ibid.,] p. 64, fn. 50; and p. 251, fn. 109.

14. [Ibid.,] p. 64, fn. 51.

15. Natural association of Sun and Fire.

16. [Zingg, R. M.: *The Huichols*,] p. 64, fn. 52.

17. [Ibid.,] p. 64, fn. 53.

18. [Ibid.,] p. 145, fn. 24.

19. [Ibid., p. 145, fn. 24.]

20. Santiago, the patron saint of Spain, is given a prominence in Huichol mythology that reflects the Spanish missionary work among this tribe. He is always shown on horseback. Thus it would seem that this saint has become the patron of riding animals among the Huichols. See [Zingg, R. M.: *The Huichols*,] p. 64, fn. 54.

21. [Ibid.,] p. 61, fn. 26.

22. The Mexican harp has made an impression on Huichol culture.

23. The Huichols do this to raise funds for their ceremonies.

24. [Zingg again refers to note 23. — Ed.]

25. [Zingg, R. M.: *The Huichols*,] p. 636, fn. 87.

26. [Ibid.,] p. 636, fn. 87.

27. Ibid., p. 60, fn. 15; and p. 247, fn. 97.

28. [Ibid., p. 60, fn. 15; and p. 247, fn. 97.]

29. [Ibid.,] p. 235, fn. 18.

30. Ibid., p. 47; and p. 63, fn. 46; and p. 629, fn. 73.

31. It is significant, in this story of Mexican influence, that the impression of Christ and the saints was made with a branding-iron.

The branding-iron has entered Huichol ceremonies; and, in the ceremony for rain, the animals are branded in the presence of the saints (see notes on material culture and rain feast). In this rain feast, which also blesses the cattle, all the sacred paraphernalia — both pagan and Catholic — comes into use. In Tuzpan [*sic*] it is the only pagan ceremony in which the "santos" are used. It is at this time, further, in a striking ceremony that animals are branded. [Zingg, R. M.: *The Huichols*,] p. 630, fn. 74; and p. 718, fn. 47.

32. [Ibid., p. 47; and p. 63, fn. 46; and p. 629, fn. 73.]

33. [Ibid.,] p. 302, fn. 14 ff.

34. Ibid., p. 62, fn. 29; and p. 332, fn. 62.

35. In Huichol ceremonies animals are always sacrificed to the music of the foreign violin and guitar. These Mexican instruments are fitting in this story, betraying the systematic attempt of Huichol philosophy to account for all Mexican elements in Huichol culture.

36. Zingg, R. M.: *The Huichols: Primitive Artists*, p. 247, fn. 96.

37. [A footnote is indicated here, but no information is included. — Ed.]

38. In this myth is the origin of the Mexican[-]style round dance. [Zingg, R. M.: *The Huichols*,] p. 71, fn. 90; and p. 332, fn. 64.

39. Ibid., p. 608, fn. 32; and p. 652, fn. 29.

40. [Ibid.,] p. 71, fn. 91; and p. 332, fn. 63.

41. See footnote 4, p. 320 of this myth. [Zingg does not indicate a footnote 4 on page 320 of his original manuscript, but I found the reference on p. 332 in Zingg, R. M.: *The Huichols.* — Ed.] Zingg, R. M.: [*The Huichols*,] p. 62, fn. 305; and p. 332, fn. 65.

42. Ibid., p. 60, fn. 21; and p. 614, fn. 50.

43. Ibid., p. 66, fn. 68; and p. 246, fn. 90.

44. [Ibid.,] p. 65, fn. 57; and p. 66, fn. 69.

45. Santo Cristo's saving himself by entering the water is not strange, since he is protected by the great gods of the sea. Everything associated with the sea is sacred to the Huichols.

46. Zingg, R. M.: *The Huichols: Primitive Artists*, p. 63, fn. 44.

47. Ibid., p. 629, fn. 72.

48. Ibid., p. 243.

49. Ibid., p. 62, fn. 34.

50. The pajama-like trousers of the Mexican lower classes.

51. Zingg, R. M.: [*The Huichols*,] p. 60, fn. 20.

52. Ibid., p. 243.

53. This is consistent with the previous myth [asserting] that the Mexicans are children of Kauymáli.

54. This is consistent with Nakawé's role as [a] creator and giver of all.

55. Zingg, R. M.: [*The Huichols*,] p. 243, fn. 73.

56. Ibid., p. 16, fn. 17.

57. Because, no doubt, the great gods sitting in their god-chairs would learn of the trick. See also [Zingg, R. M.: *The Huichols*,] p. 648, fn. 14.

58. [Ibid.,] p. 66, fn. 70.

59. Ibid., p. 62, fn. 32.

60. Ibid., p. 62, fn. 31; and p. 70, fn. 89; and p. 332, fn. 66.

61. [Ibid., p. 62, fn. 31; and p. 70, fn. 89; and p. 332, fn. 66.]

62. [Ibid.,] p. 67, fn. 71.

63. Here, the informant says, the story becomes as involved as tripe.

64. Zingg, R. M.: *The Huichols: Primitive Artists*, pp. 61–62, fn. 28.

65. Jesus Christ was tricked into the hands of the julios [Jews].

66. [Zingg again refers to note 65.—Ed.]

67. [Zingg again refers to note 65.—Ed.]

68. Literally, Spaniards, a fantastic race in the Huichol mind.

69. Typical Mexican weapons.

70. Zingg, R. M.: [*The Huichols*,] p. 16, fn. 16; and p. 242, fn. 66.

71. [Ibid., p. 16, fn. 16; and p. 242, fn. 66.]

72. See footnote 1, next page. [This note refers to Zingg, R. M.: *The Huichols*:, p. 701, fn. 6.—Ed.]

73. [Zingg again refers to note 72.—Ed.]

74. Zingg, R. M.: *The Huichols: Primitive Artists*, p. 701, fn. 6.

75. Here the Sun is identified with the Christian God. The informant explains that the Sun, the Virgin, and the Santa Cruz (i.e., Santo Cristo) are the three chief *mayores* (elders) like the Huichol officials. [Zingg, R. M.: *The Huichols*,] p. 59, fn. 13.

76. Ibid., p. 238, fn. 43.

77. Ibid., p. 247, fn. 98.

78. Ibid., p. 141, fn. 19.

79. [Ibid.,] p. 141, fn. 19.

80. Ibid., p. 60, fn. 16.

C. The Myth of Santo Cristo

1. This insect has a glistening, metallic-like body.

2. Zingg, R. M.: *The Huichols: Primitive Artists* [New York: G. E. Stechert, 1938], p. 68, fn. 77.

3. Ibid., p. 68, fn. 78.

4. [Ibid.,] p. 69, fn. 79.

5. The Huichols do not distinguish between silver and tin.

6. Cliffs, since mines are made in cliffs.

7. Zingg, R. M.: [*The Huichols*,] p. 69, fn. 82; and p. 681, fn. 10.

8. On peyote trips [hunts] Huichols see Americans working mines. [Zingg, R. M.: *The Huichols*,] p. 69, fn. 81.

9. [Zingg again refers to note 6.—Ed.]

10. Zingg, R. M.: *[The Huichols,]* p. 69, fn. 82; and p. 681, fn. 10.

11. [Ibid., p. 69, fn. 82; and p. 681, fn. 10.]

12. [Zingg again refers to note 8.—Ed.]

13. [Zingg again refers to note 8.—Ed.]

14. Apparently like children, silver is "delicate" at birth.

15. The Huichols, after Holy Week, commonly go to the coast to work. This myth is most illustrative of the philosophic bent of Huichol mythology, which seeks to give a rationale for everything that the Huichols see or do. Their trips to San Luis Potosí bring them into contact with much that is included here under silver and Americans. Their trips to the coast likewise bring much to their attention; they are treated here similarly. [Zingg, R. M.: *The Huichols,*] p. 69, fn. 80.

16. [Ibid.,] p. 726, fn. 55.

17. Ibid., p. 63, fn. 45.

18. [Ibid., p. 63, fn. 45.]

19. [Ibid.,] p. 63, fn. 42.

20. Ibid., p. 65, fn. 60.

21. [Ibid.,] p. 70, fn. 88.

22. Ibid., p. 273, fn. 21.

23. [A footnote is indicated here, but no information is included.—Ed.]

24. [Ibid.,] p. 73, fn. 1.

25. This treatment of cattle differs considerably from the custom of the Huichols, and represents Huichol observation of everyday Mexican life as incorporated in the mythology.

26. The blind used over the eyes of wild horses and mules in saddling.

27. This patron saint of Spain is always modelled on horseback. Zingg, R. M.: *[The Huichols,]* p. 63, fn. 49.

28. [Ibid.,] p. 273, fn. 22; and p. 723, fn. 54.

29. [Ibid., p. 273, fn. 22; and p. 723, fn. 54.]

30. Ibid., p. 70, fn. 85.

31. Ibid., p. 15, fn. 14.

32. Ibid., p. 67 ff., discusses surveying in the Huichol conception.

33. The Huichols of Tuxpan, while exiled by revolution for years from the sierra, maintained themselves as peones [hired hands], herding for the Mexicans.

34. Zingg, R. M.: *[The Huichols,]* p. 60. Christ derives power from [the] Sun.

35. [Zingg, R. M.: *The Huichols,*] p. 363, fn. 36. The lack of this ceremony among Mexicans puzzles Huichols.

36. The Huichols even admit that their ceremonies are hard work.

37. Santo Cristo is thought of as a crucifix.

38. An eclipse frightens the Huichols, who fear that the Sun might disappear entirely and never come out again, Zingg, R. M.: *[The Huichols,]* p. 515, fn. 14.

39. Ibid., p. 254, fn. 125; and p. 319, fn. 2.

40. Ibid., p. 324, fn. 20.

41. Ibid., p. 67, fn. 73; and p. 324, fn. 21.

42. My informant says that the crucifix remains so that Santo Cristo could not be killed completely. He likens this to photographs of themselves that the Indians are always asking me to take, so that their families will remember them when they die.

43. Preuss, *[Die Religion der Cora] Die Nayarit Expedition, Band I*, S.XXVII–XXIX, gives a similar myth for the Cora involving a conflict between snakes and the (morning) star. His explanatory bias in favor of the night sky indicates paraphrasing his material considerably:

According to the Cora myth[,] far away in the west lives the water-serpent *kúku*, which in the morning is killed by an arrow shot by the morning-star and is then consumed by the eagle of the day-sky. If the morning-star came too late, all men would be destroyed in a flood. And if the morning-star missed his shot, the river would overflow his banks.

When the water-serpent arrived, the dwellers of the sea (night-sky, hence the stars, I think Preuss means) plunged themselves into the lake of Santa Teresa, which symbolizes the original sea. "It was the end of the world. The men who lived there all went under the ground. All concealed themselves down there and live there below." (Preuss, p. 282, abs. 10)

According to the myth[,] the overflooded men become the water-gods Tsakate, which means "the only living ones" who are viewed by the Cora as stars (compare for example B.III L3 S92 [Possibly a call number for a book?—Ed.]).

That the Tsakate are the stars of heaven, the Coras certainly do not say. They offer sacrifices to them in a sense [that is] wholly contradictory, offering the sun-god [Sun-Father] arrows with the feathers of the Arara, which, as we have seen, signify the Sun and the Fire.

In the flood myth of the Cora is it especially interesting to see how, as in other flood stories, the episode of the saving from the catastrophe is handled in a manner completely different from the usual one. The flood attacks the evening and morning stars, which are preferably played against each other, and play an important role in the mythology and religion of the Cora.

44. [Zingg repeats note 43.—Ed.]

45. Huichols think that in writing there is magic, for writing is like their symbolic art.

46. [Two sequential footnotes have the same number on this page of the original manuscript. I have combined them into one citation.—Ed.] [First footnote:] Zingg, R. M.: *The Huichols: Primitive Artists*, p. 320, fn. 3. [Second footnote:] It is of interest that this snake symbol swallows money that bears the imprint of the eagle, the opponent of the snake.

47. [Zingg repeats note 46.—Ed.]

48. Hence Huichol visitors are free to use Mexican government buildings. [Zingg, R. M.: *The Huichols*,], p. 320, fn. 5–6.

49. [Zingg repeats note 48.—Ed.]

50. The rattle-snake is feared by Huichol hunters. Offerings, therefore, are made in mountain shrines.

51. The Huichols do this.

52. [Zingg, R. M.: *The Huichols,*] p. 647, fn. 4.

53. Ibid., p. 320, fn. 7.

54. [Ibid.,] p. 320, fn. 8.

55. In Huichol land there are, of course, neither streets nor corners.

56. The wind is sometimes the messenger of the Sun-father [*sic*].

57. [Zingg, R. M.: *The Huichols,*] pp. 448–49 discusses Huichol branding of animals.

58. Wood would be more "delicate" than cow-dung.

59. Though children are not branded, adds my informant.

60. [Zingg, R. M.: *The Huichols,*] p. 718, fn. 46.

61. [Ibid.,] p. 718, fn. 45.

62. Ibid., p. 65, fn. 61.

63. Ibid., p. 71, fn. 92.

64. A foreign trait, associated in the Christian myth cycle.

65. Something like this is done in the Huichol death ceremony.

66. Naive Huichols.

67. Zingg, R. M.: *The Huichols: Primitive Artists*, p. 71, fn. 94 and 95.

68. [Ibid.,] p. 18, fn. 24.

69. [Ibid.,] p. 18, fn. 24.

70. Ibid., pp. 12–14, fn. 8.

71. [Ibid.,] p. 66, fn. 63.

72. Yard, Sp., meaning the cane [staff] of the officials.

73. The latter actually are *topiles*, but in Tuxpan the name is not used.

74. Zingg, R. M.: *[The Huichols,]* p. 62, fn. 28; and p. 63, fn. 48.

75. My informant, however, looks wise when I mention the obvious immorality of the relationship of the *tenanches* with the officials, which is an eloquent explanation of the difference between the theoretic ideal of the myth and the actuality of the situation of unattached women supported by the officials.

76. [Zingg, R. M.: *The Huichols,*] p. 74, fn. 2; and p. 271, fn. 16.

77. Ibid., p. 14, fn. 10.

78. Ibid., p. 278, fn. 44.

79. As the Mexicans do in plowing.

80. Zingg, R. M.: *[The Huichols,]* p. 278, fn. 45.

81. In one dance that was witnessed[,] a boy sprained his ankle, thus causing gossip. It was said that he had broken his vows for the necessary fast.

82. Sotol, Sp., a very crude but powerful drink made from Daslyrion, sp. [Sotol is the agave plant from which *toache* is distilled. — Ed.]

83. [Zingg, R. M.: *The Huichols,*] p. 284, fn. 64.

84. Rain symbolism expected, since the saints appear in the rain feast. Zingg, R. M.: *The Huichols: Primitive Artists*, p. 90, fn. 15.

85. The stone piles represent the boundary markers set up by surveyors.

86. Zingg, R. M.: *The Huichols: Primitive Artists*, p. 96.

87. Because if [of] Good Friday.

88. This is a task for the dignitaries of the Catholic community.

89. Christ was a Huichol, so later ones are his children.

90. [Zingg, R. M.: *The Huichols*,] p. 98, fn. 18; and p. 636, fn. 89.

91. Ibid., p. 98, fn. 17; and p. 99, fn. 17.

92. [Ibid.,] p. 102, fn. 19.

93. Ibid., p. 57, fn. 9; and p. 102, fn. 21.

94. Ibid., p. 103, fn. 22.

95. *Mestro* is a Spanish-Huichol word for the native lay-readers, who were prepared by the missionaries. As among the Tarahumaras, these native officials represent the Catholic priest; but here they are less prominent in native religion than they are among the Tarahumaras. [Zingg, R. M.: *The Huichols*,] p. 55, fn. 4.

96. [Ibid.,] p. 103, fn. 23.

97. Ibid., p. 103, fn. 25. A not inconsiderable danger. The saints are prayed to as well.

98. [Zingg, R. M.: *The Huichols*,] p. 103, fn. 24. The same yellow flowers are used in the first fruits ceremony.

99. [Zingg repeats note 98.—Ed.]

100. Ibid., p. 66, fn. 64.

101. Ibid., p. 63, fn. 47; and p. 273, fn. 23.

102. Corona was the Mexican general who defeated the Cora and Huichol Indians [fighting] under [Manuel] Lozada in the revolution against Maxmillan [Maximilian].

103. Zingg, R. M.: *The Huichols: Primitive Artists*, p. 62, fn. 35.

104. Ibid., p. 67, fn. 72.

105. Ibid., p. 62, fn. 36.

106. [Ibid.,] p. 246, fn. 91.

107. Ibid., p. 62, fn. 33.

108. The pine-tree is associated with Christ.

109. The buzzard is considered a kindly, friendly fellow.

110. [Zingg, R. M.: *The Huichols*,] p. 60, fn. 22.

111. [Two sequential footnotes have the same number on this page of the original manuscript. I have combined them into one citation.—Ed.] [First footnote:] Zingg, R. M.: *The Huichols: Primitive Artists*, p. 68, fn. 75. [Second footnote:] Surveying, or measuring, is thought to form and create things.

112. [Zingg, R. M.: *The Huichols*], p. 18, fn. 23.

113. [Zingg again refers to note 111.—Ed.]

114. Ibid., p. 62, fn. 37.

115. [Ibid.,] p. 62, fn. 38.

116. [Ibid.,] p. 62, fn. 38.

117. Ibid., p. 63, fn. 43.

118. [Ibid., p. 63, fn. 43.]

119. Informant seems surer of this than of anything else. He says he knows it since he has been in Guadalajara and has seen these types.

120. Zingg, R. M.: *The Huichols: Primitive Artists*, p. 60, fn. 17 and 18.

121. Ibid., p. 9, fn. 5; and p. 62, fn. 40.

122. Ibid., p. 721, fn. 53.

123. Ibid., p. 62, fn. 39.

124. Ibid., p. 15, fn. 14.

125. This is why everything now costs money. See [Zingg, R. M.: *The Huichols*,] p. 64, fn. 56.

126. Informant almost weeps at this point in the sad story.

127. [Zingg, R. M.: *The Huichols*,] p. 60, fn. 24.

128. Ibid., p. 62, fn. 41.

Epilogue

1. Details of the controversy surrounding the wolf-children, Amala and Kamala, can be found in Charles Maclean (1977). Maclean acknowledges that even if it is true that the girls were discovered in a white-ant mound used as a wolf's den, this does not prove that they were suckled or reared by wolves (1977: 291). Such an inference, that the two girls were raised by the same she-wolf that had been killed just prior to their being found, would be easier to accept were it not for some apparently contradictory claims made by Singh. In his diary, Reverend Singh claimed to have participated in the rescue of the girls. Although this claim is supported by certain elders interviewed by Maclean (see note 3 below), four other sources, among them a report Singh wrote, suggest that Singh did not take part in rescuing the girls. Maclean indicates there are reasons why Singh may have wanted to conceal his participation in the wolf hunt and rescue of the girls (Maclean 1977: 300–301).

2. In addition to the dispute about the wolf-children, other reasons that Zingg lost his position as a professor of anthropology include declining student enrollment caused by World War II, his "amiable eccentricity," and the attempted suicide of his first wife, Christina (Maclean 1977: 280).

3. In 1975 Charles Maclean, using a map drawn by Singh, found Godamuri, the village near the she-wolf's den where the two girls had been retrieved. Villagers there told him Godamuri had been renamed. It was now called Ghorabandha (Maclean 1977: 299). A few miles from Godamuri (Ghorabandha), at a Santal village named Denganalia, Maclean interviewed several elders. They remembered the wolf-children being captured. One of those elders who participated in hunting the she-wolf testified that Reverend Singh was present at the platform where the wolf was shot on the day that the wolf-children were captured, October 17, 1920 (Maclean 1977: 300). Locating Godamuri and obtaining information from the Santal elders enabled Maclean to refute some of the criticism of the wolf-children published by Ogburn and Bose (1959). Emphasizing Ogburn and Bose's claim that Godamuri did not exist, Montagu (1974) characterized Singh's report as unreliable. I concurred completely with Montagu's opinion about this matter (Fikes 1993: 166) before reading Maclean. Although today I do not know precisely

what actually happened in India, it seems clear that Zingg wanted to believe that Singh told the whole truth and nothing but the truth about his involvement with the wolf-children. At worst, Zingg is guilty of not having worked as diligently as did Maclean to check the veracity of Singh's account before publishing it.

4. The video "Huichol Indian Ceremonial Cycle" surveys the spectrum of rituals, aboriginal Huichol and Catholic, performed at Tuxpan and adjacent villages, and the Peyote Dance held at the aboriginal ceremonial center of Ratontita in 1934. Zingg filmed the most salient aspects of these Huichol ceremonies but never edited his footage. The documentary I produced with his footage is now available online at www.entheomedia.org and from the Penn State Media Sales Center at 800-770-2111.

5. The orthodox way to be recognized as a healer or singer (shaman) involves fulfilling obligations incumbent upon all aboriginal temple officers. Some twenty-five different ancestors representing essential elements in nature, such as Rain Mothers (Fikes 1985: 155), must be served and represented by Huichol temple officers. Huichols obliged to serve a specific ancestor (e.g., Great Grandmother Germination, Tacützi Yürameca, or Camóquime, the Father of the wolves) for five years as a temple officer have the opportunity to ingest peyote and make personal contact with ancestors during pilgrimages to sacred sites (among them, the desert where peyote is collected) and to perform temple rituals. Healers have acquired this ability during one term (five years) of service as a temple officer. Singers must have served as temple officers for two terms or ten years (Fikes 1985, 1993: 68–69). Jesús' acquisition of shamanic power illustrates an exception to this rule (Fikes 1993: 116). Further research in Tuxpan should clarify how his gift (i.e., ability as a healer and singer) became publicly validated.

6. The truth about the presumed murder of Phil True may never be known. Two Huichol men who had confessed, allegedly under torture, to strangling True in December 1998 were recently found guilty of "intentional homicide" by all three judges on a Jalisco Supreme Court tribunal (Hayward 2002). The two Huichols are appealing this verdict. True's field notes affirmed that he told a Huichol named Juan (Juan Chivarra is the name of one of the Huichols convicted of killing True) that he had obtained permission to be in the area from Tuxpan, the community where he began his tragic trek through Huichol territory a few days before being killed. Juan replied, "We are in San Sebastián and you must get the governor's permission. I am going to my ranch and I will send some guys to get your pack. They will take you back to San Sebastián and maybe put you in jail. You can't come on the Huichol land without permission" (Schiller 1999). I received similar threats in Santa Catarina, but by paying a "fine" I was permitted to stay (Fikes 1999). True also wrote: "It looks bad for a bit," and concluded by stating that he was following Juan to his ranch (Schiller 1999). Susana Hayward, a journalist at the *San Antonio Express News* (the newspaper where True worked), reported (2001) that Juan Chivarra has "been expelled from two Huichol villages, allegedly for stealing cows and fowl, and growing marijuana." There is no compelling evidence to support my suspicion that True was murdered by Huichols who were worried that he had discovered marijuana.

There are other possible explanations for his death. According to Phil C. Weigand (2002), True died as the result of an injury to his head caused by a fall. Weigand's research confirms findings of the second autopsy, which was conducted on January 5, 1999. He notes that the second autopsy was performed by "experienced professionals accompanied by impartial witnesses, among them an FBI medical observer" and concludes that: "True clearly was drunk [the blood alcohol level was very high] when he fell hitting his head. The type of alcohol in his body is the type one drinks, not the type produced by decomposition of the body, though this was present, too. . . . The fall directly led to his death, producing a serious head injury. He died from the complication of that injury, which produced vomiting and respiratory problems. . . . Having that reporter drunk and injuring himself, eventually fatally, was not what they [the San Antonio newspaper people] wanted to hear" (Weigand 2002). Before the tribunal found the two Huichols guilty in 2002, Weigand and the Mexican judge who acquitted the two Huichol suspects discounted the first autopsy (performed on December 17, 1998), which concluded that Phil True was strangled. Weigand and the judge believe that their confessions were fabrications obtained by torture. Whatever the truth may be, Weigand and I agree that visitors to Huichol territory should have a permit and should not travel alone to places where they are unknown.

7. The National Geographic journalist, Paul Salopek, told a chilling tale about what happened to him after he stumbled into a marijuana field in the mountains north of Huichol territory. Observing the three owners of the marijuana field deliberating about "whether to kill this ignorant foreigner," Salopek saved himself by speaking to them about his father. They sent him away with a stern warning (Salopek 2000: 62–63). He also alluded to opium poppies being cultivated in the Sierra Madre Occidental (2000: 76–77), the mountain chain in northwestern Mexico inhabited by Huichols, Coras, Tarahumaras, and other tribes.

Glossary

As Zingg hinted in a footnote, his use of the word *drunk* (probably translated from the Spanish word *borracho*) tends to disparage Huichol singers (shamans), who strive to achieve altered states of consciousness using corn beer, tobacco, peyote, and other substances. Peyote is ingested specifically to see and hear more clearly what the ancestors are communicating (Fikes 1993: 192–93). In fact, except when the drunken state is intended to disable (see "Santo Cristo Establishes Cattle Ceremonies among the Huichols," where Christ escapes because the Jews chasing him become drunk), it may be more accurate to translate *drunk* as an altered state of consciousness, following Michael Winkelman's (2000) perspective on shamanism.

a'itapáli: "headlike" rocks formed from the head of (a) woman

akastes: Mexican Indian crates

akce: silver Ottoman coinage

alcalde: (Sp.) mayor or judge

alguacil: (Sp.) sheriff

amole: a plant used to wash clothes (Yucca sp.)

ará: wild squash

arma: (Sp.) firearm

arrieras: carrying ants

arriero: pack-ant people (tsału tewíałi, H.)

atole: mush made of corn or wheat, sometimes used as an offering to the Sun Father

baraja: (Sp.) gambling game

batea: (Sp.) vessel of wood used by women to catch ground corn-dough from the metate

cajón [caion]: (Sp.) small wooden house for bees (wakí, H.)(see also Zingg 1938: 809)

camote: variety of non-domesticated tuber (sweet potato)

campeche: (Sp.) a tiny bee (ciclí, H.)

canoa: (Sp.) canoe; described also with Christian connotations for the word "ark"

cantador: (Sp.) singer

cántaro [cántara]: large wide-mouthed pitcher

cantera: (Sp.) soft volcanic stone used to make statues of the gods

capilla: (Sp.) chapel or small church

cardoniga: unidentified plant (teauláh, H.)

casa real: "Casa Real," a large building where, in 1934, Tuxpan Huichols conducted government business and performed ceremonies. (Should not be confused with a tukipa compound [ceremonial center]. The closest tukipa to Tuxpan is located at nearby Ratontita.)

castil ítsic: (H.) domesticated bee

casuela: (Sp.) pot

chango: (Sp.) monkey

chikalóta: (Sp.) an unidentified plant (tsikalótci, H.)

chual: (Sp.) Amaranthus sp. (wawé, H.)

cimarrón: (Sp.) pagan or wild

cireal: (Sp.) an unidentified species of bird (kokaimúeli, H.) (Fikes thinks it is possibly the Rufous Collared Robin *[Turdus rufitorques]* or the Slaty Antstrike *[Thamnophilus punctatus]*.)

comal: (Sp.) round ceramic griddle used to heat corn dough to make tortillas or toast seeds

costales: (Sp.) burlap bags for holding corn

cristeros: (Sp.) anticommunist, pro-Catholic Mexicans and Huichols who fought against the federal government

datura: see kiéri

delicado: (Sp.) sacred

diablo: (Sp.) bad man or devil

Dios: (Sp.) the Christian god

doctrina: (Sp.) mission established by Franciscans

dueños: (Sp.) owners or masters

ejido: (Sp.) Mexican legal entity whose intent is to insure that land cannot be bought or sold as a commodity

elote: ripe ear of corn

eslabón: (Sp., H.) steel used with flint to make fire

esquite: parched corn

estambre: (Sp.) woolen yarn (crewel)

estancia: (Sp.) mansion or house on a cattle ranch

etáli: painted board

franela: (Sp.) flannel

gauchupines: derogatory word for Spaniards

gente americano: (Sp.) citizens of the United States

güakamaya: (Sp.) large parrot of the sierra, probably a species of macaw

hacienda: (Sp.) large estate worked by peasants

haíci: bunch of feathers

haikotes: grass used for arrows

haítsi: bunch of green leaves hung from the gable of the Huichol family god-house

halaíku: pile of little snakes

hatúwe: "water jaguar," could also be an ocelot

hawime itáli: round boards

hiwas: (héwi?) wizard

hokó: (H.) pine tree

iáusu: opossum (tlacuache, Sp.)

icpála: a larva

iéle: wild sweet potato (camote, Sp.)

iguana: a lizard (kácipli, ketsé, H.)

imúmui: ladder

ipulí: a ball of wool and five balls of twigs

ipulí uli: a rubber ball, possibly associated with the Mesoamerican sacred ball game (Zingg 1938: 283, 808)

itáli: altar, sometimes a blanket on which sacred paraphernalia are laid

ítsika: a flower that blooms in October [Fikes believes this is a species of grasshopper.]

ixtle: (Sp.) fiber of agave (or maguey)

javelína: (Sp.) peccary

jícara [jicara]: (Sp.) votive-bowl

jitomate: a small type of tomato

jitomate sayuki: tomato

judios [julios]: (Sp.) Jews (Anti-Semitic allusions pervade the Christian myths dictated by Juan Real.)

kácipili: iguana

kaitsa: rattles

kaSatcíki vokaki kumukáme: notched deer bones (used in deer hunting and other rituals)

kawitéros: elders experienced in ritual

kíeli: the yellow peyote root, which is the "vista"—sight—of the singers

kiéri: a plant in the genus *Solandra* that is revered as an incarnation of a deity (Fikes 2001). (Although plants in the genus *Datura* [also called jimsonweed] may be called "kiéri" in Tuxpan, such plants are not confused with the sacred kiéri that typically grows on rocks. Zingg incorrectly identified kiéri as *Datura* [Fikes 1985, 1993a], probably because he never saw it [i.e., the sacred kiéri in the genus *Solandra*].)

kuyé: a small sacred disk painted for use as an offering (Fikes says "kuyé" means wood or tree.)

lápa: a tree in the genus *Ficus*, of the great gods of the sea (matareal or salate, Sp.)

lauten: give

maestro [mestro]: (Sp.) the man who knows how to pray (picikáli, H.)

maguey: fibrous plants of the genus *Agave* used to make deer lassos (see ixtle)

malacoa: colored snake (wias[g?]o, H.) (See Zingg 1938: 812, where he spells it "maSakóa.")

manadera: (Sp.) stud-jack

mapache: raccoon (meta, H.)

mara'ákame: (H.) singing shaman (also marakami)

masa: (Sp.) corn dough

maSa kuikuáipa: sacred colored earth

maSakuili: green root formed from the finger of (a) woman

maSa teiea: (H.) "deer-mouth" ("The deer-woman took the semen in her mouth ['deer-mouth']")

maSáwi: (H.) "deer grass" (also masa rakéli)

matareal: (Sp.) a tree of the great gods of the sea (see lápa)

matsúwa: (H.) wristguard

mayawápa: arrows having cruciform decoration

mayordomos [mayor-domos]: (Sp.) custodians of Catholic saints or managers of workers

mayores: elders

mescal: (Sp.) distilled beverage made from agave

metate: rectangular stone mortar used to grind corn

milpa: (Sp.) cornfield

movieli: ceremonial wands; feathers attached to pine or brazil wood

muu: (H.) head

náma: "back shields" — a votive mat (Fikes 1985: 342)

nealíka: (H.) face (Lumholtz translates this as "aspect," but it is the ordinary Huichol word for "face." The term is applied to the carved, ceremonial gable capstone and also to the woven disc of reeds in sunburst form woven with colored crewel [see also Fikes 1985: 343].)

neatáli: altars (see Zingg 1938: 815); also newatále

nixtamal: corn boiled in lime

nopal: (Sp.) prickly pear cactus

óatsa: (H.) bow for a violin

olla: (Sp.) clay cooking pot

oparu: (H.) battening-stick

orakate: (H.) bird from the Pacific Coast

otate: (Sp.) cane or stick made of carrizo (a bamboo-like reed)

palacio: (Sp.) government building

palo de muerte: (Sp.) "stick of death," *Zanthoxylum fagara*

percala: (Sp.) percale, a type of fabric

petate: a sleeping mat made of a variety of palm fibers

picikáli: (H.) the man who knows how to pray (in the Catholic fashion) (maestro, Sp.)

piliwáli: a very old word for a gourd or wooden bowl (According to Fikes, it is a very ancient wooden bowl associated with the sacred staffs.)

pinole: (Sp.) a fine powder made from corn

pitacoche: a bird that eats cactus fruit

presidio: (Sp.) fortress or garrison of soldiers

priostes: people who serve mayordomos, i.e., custodians of Catholic saints

pulque: (Sp.) fermented juice of the maguey plant

pútsi: a tripod ceramic incenser

raípon hóna: a gnat

reata: (Sp.) a lariat or harness; rope used to tie one horse or mule to another

reboso: (Sp.) shawl

salamacoa: water snake (hakulakáme); could be another name for haicu (Fikes 1985: 333)

salate: (Sp.) fig-tree (Ficus sp.)

salusi: species of ant that steals corn (arrieras, Sp.)

sausa: a drought-resistant tree, probably a *sauce* (Sp.), a species of willow

Semana Santa: Holy Week

sotol: a plant used to make hats, shaman's baskets, and toache

sulí: an unidentified thorny plant

súsi [sútsi]: a squash

taiopá ki [Tauopá]: a god-house for the Sun Father

takuátci: (H.) opossum (Fikes says *tlacuache* is Spanish for opossum.)

takuátei: oblong shaman's baskets made of sotol fibers

taméweli: "come in"

tamíuwale: a sacred, thick loaf of bread

tamukuli: cactus formed from the foot of (a) woman

tanque: (Sp.) reservoir

taokari: grandmother (see Fikes 1985: 349)

tapajo: (Sp.) blinders on a horse/mule bridle

tapokati ciúli: small unnamed animals (possibly fleas) found near a waterhole

TaSecipa: a village at an unidentified location

tatélepots: flowers that sing (lichen, probably)

tauli: (H.) amaranth balls ceremonially associated with the Sun Father

tcamóko: evil, ugly chipmunks; also tcitci móko

tciúli: bees (colména, Sp. [colmena means beehive])

teáka: a "very delicate" stone that makes people sick

teapáli: god-disc, heart of Tateváli

teapúa: (H.) iron

teaúka: whirlwind or tornado

tecéamuka: "good evening"

tecomate: (Sp.) a bowl (aikutzi, H.)

tekualipa: an unidentified cliff or rock on the Pacific Ocean

tenanches [tenaches]: women who take care of the Casa Real or Catholic Church

tesgüino: (Sp.) corn beer

tévali: rock-crystals

teyaya: ripe ears of corn (consecrated and used in ceremonies)

tigre del mar: (Sp.) "tiger of the sea," jaguar; also hatúwi, probably an ocelot or perhaps a shark

tintitetero: gambling game (lottery?)

tlacuache: (Mex.-Sp.) opossum

toache: distilled sotol cactus juice, similar to tequila

toikuáki [tsikuáki]: masked [sacred] clown

topiles: police or messengers; agents of the government

tsikalótci: a plant, the stems of which are put inside ceremonial wands (movieli) so that they sound like the Sun's animal, the rattlesnake (chikalóta, Sp.)

tuapúSa: acorns

túki: Huichol temple

tukipa: a ceremonial center surrounding the túki

turcos: (Sp.) Turks, or possibly Armenians who emigrated from the Ottoman Empire

tusú: an unidentified plant used in funeral ritual

ulú túweli: "arrow of sickness," which Huichol sorcerers make for use in black magic

uSra: dust from the heart of the deer, peyote paint. (Fikes notes that such identification with the deer's heart indicates a sacred origin of the yellow root used for ceremonial face painting.)

uwé: planting stick

vara: (Sp.) yard; also a sacred staff (ítsu, H.)

vartero: (Sp.) the person entrusted to keep the sacred staffs and eslabón

ventana: (Sp.) small break in a cliff (literally, window)

vergonzozos: (Sp.) shamed ones

vino: (Sp.) alcoholic beverage

vista: (Sp.) "view"; the teapáli is the vista (sight or view) of the gods

wakí: (H.) house for bees (cajón, Sp.)

waSirá wa: a little magic bead used for healing

wawé: (H.) Amaranthus sp. (chual, Sp.)

wipí: (H.) hair net [or fishing net]

wishache: a thorny plant that Fikes (1993c: 142) identified as *Acacia pennatula*; also "tree" (pá róya, H.)

yalí: a thick log of sea wood

zapote: a tree bearing an edible fruit

References and Further Reading

Bauml, James A., Gilbert Voss, and Peter Collings. 1990. "Short Communications," *Journal of Ethnobiology* 10(1): 99–102.

Beals, R. L. 1941. "Review of Zingg, *The Huichols: Primitive Artists*," *American Anthropologist* 43(1): 99–102.

Benítez, Fernando. 1968a. *Los Indios de México*, vol. 2. México: Biblioteca Era.

———. 1968b. *En la Tierra Mágica del Peyote*. México: Biblioteca Era.

Bennett, W. C., and Robert M. Zingg. [1935] 1976. *The Tarahumara: An Indian Tribe of Northern Mexico*. Chicago: University of Chicago Press. Reprinted 1976, Glorieta, N. Mex.: Rio Grande Press.

Berrin, Kathleen, editor. 1978. *Art of the Huichol Indians*. New York: Harry N. Abrams, Inc.

Diguet, León. 1992. *Por Tierras Occidentales*. México: Instituto Nacional Indigenista.

Dreben, Steve. 1986. *Huichole: People of the Peyote*. Film distributed by Perry/Dreben Productions, 1911 Hillcrest Road, Los Angeles, CA, 90068.

Fabila, Alfonso. 1959. *Los Huicholes de Jalisco*. Mexico City: Instituto Nacionál Indigenista.

Fikes, Jay C. 1985. *Huichol Indian Identity and Adaptation*. Unpublished dissertation, Department of Anthropology, University of Michigan, Ann Arbor.

———. 1993a. *Carlos Castaneda, Academic Opportunism, and the Psychedelic Sixties*. Victoria, B.C.: Millenia Press.

———. 1993b. "Anthropological Visualization of the Huichol in Ethnographic Film: A Discussion of the Problem of Contextualization," in *Anthropological Film and Video in the 1990s*, pp. 221–40. Edited by Jack R. Rollwagen. Brockport, N.Y.: The Institute Press, Inc.

———. 1993c. "To Be or Not To Be: Suicide and Sexuality in Huichol Indian Funeral Ritual Oratory," in *Native American Ritual Oratory*, pp. 120–48. Edited by Arnold Krupat. Washington, D.C.: Smithsonian Institution Press.

———. 1997. "Huichol Indian Ceremonial Cycle." Documentary film distributed by Pennsylvania State University Media Center (800-770-2111).

———. 1998. "Blood for the Ancestors: Huichol Indian Social Stratification and Intertribal Alliance." Paper presented at the annual meeting of the American Anthropological Association, Philadelphia, Pennsylvania, December 4, 1998.

———. 1999. "Examining Ethics, Benefits and Perils of Tours to Mexico," *International Conference on Heritage, Multicultural Attractions and Tourism, Conference Proceedings*, vol. 1, pp. 407–22. Edited by Meral Korzay et al. Istanbul: Bosphorus University.

———. 2001. "The Man Who Ate Honey: Kiéri and the Calling of a Huichol Shaman," *Entheos* 1(2): 38–42.

Franz, Allen R. 1977. "Huichol Ethnohistory." Paper presented at the annual meeting of the American Anthropological Association, Houston, Texas, December 1, 1977.

Furst, Peter T., and Barbara G. Meyerhoff. 1966. "Myth as History: The Jimson Weed Cycle of the Huichols of México," *Antropológica* 17: 3–39.

Grimes, Joseph E. 1964. *Huichol Syntax*. The Hague: Mouton.

Hayward, Susana. 2001. "Ex-suspects Deny Meeting *Express News* Writer." Posted August 8, 2001 <http://news.mysanantonio.com>

———. 2002. "Tribunal Issues Guilty Verdicts in True Case." Posted May 31, 2002 <http://news.mysanantonio.com>

Hers, Marie-Areti. 1977. "Los Coras en la Época de la Expulsión Jesuita," *Historia Mexicana* 27(1): 17–48. México, D.F.: El Colegio de México.

Klineberg, Otto. 1934. "Notes on the Huichol," *American Anthropologist*, n.s., 36: 446–60.

Leonard, Irving A. 1942. "Peyote and the Mexican Inquisition, 1620," *American Anthropologist*, n.s., 44: 324–26.

Lumholtz, Carl. 1900. *Symbolism of the Huichol Indians*. New York: American Museum of Natural History, Memoirs 1(2).

———. [1902] 1973. *Unknown Mexico*, vol. 2. Glorieta, N. Mex.: Rio Grande Press, 1973.

Maclean, Charles. 1977. *The Wolf Children*. New York: Hill and Wang.

Mata Torres, Ramón. 1972. *Peregrinación del Peyote*. Guadalajara: Edición de la Casa de las Artesanias del Gobierno de Jalisco.

McCarty, Kieran, and Dan S. Matson. 1975. "Franciscan Report on the Indians of Nayarit, 1673," *Ethnohistory* 22(3): 193–222.

Meyer, Jean. 1992. "La Revolución en Occidente. El Caso Especial de los Huicholes," in Rojas, Beatriz, *Los Huicholes: Documentos Históricos*. México, D.F.: Instituto Nacional Indigenista.

Montagu, Ashley. 1974. "Wolf Children," in *Culture and Human Development*. Englewood Cliffs, N.J.: Prentice-Hall, Inc.

Negrín, Juan. 1975. *The Huichol Creation of the World*. Sacramento: E. B. Crocker Art Gallery.

———. 1977. *El Arte Contemporáneo de los Huicholes*. Guadalajara: Universidad de Guadalajara.

———. 1985. *Acercamiento Histórico y Subjetivo al Huichol*. Guadalajara: Universidad de Guadalajara.

Ogburn, W. F., and N. K. Bose. 1959. "On the Trail of the Wolf-Children,"*Genetic Psychology Monographs*, 60: 117–93.

Ortega, José. [1754] 1944. *Conquista del Nayarit* (Apostólicos Afanes de la Companía de Jesús). México, D.F.: Editorial Layac.

Plan Lerma Asistencia Técnica. 1966. *Operación Huicot*. Guadalajara: Poder Ejecutivo Federal.

Powell, Philip W. 1975. *Soldiers, Indians and Silver: North America's First Frontier War*. Tempe: Arizona State University Press.

———. 1977. *Mexico's Miguel Caldera: The Taming of America's First Frontier, 1548–1597*. Tucson: University of Arizona Press.

Preuss, Konrad Theodor. 1909. "Un Viaje a la Sierra Madre Occidental de Mexico," *Boletín de la Sociedad Mexicana de Geografía y Estadística* 3(4): 187–214.

Rojas, Beatriz. 1992. *Los Huicholes: Documentos Históricos*. México, D.F.: Instituto Nacional Indigenista.

———. 1993. *Los Huicholes en la Historia*. Mexico, D.F.: Centro de Estudios Mexicanos y Centroamericanos.

Salopek, Paul. 2000. "Pilgrimage through the Sierra Madre," *National Geographic*, June 2000, pp. 56–81.

Schiller, Dane. 1999. "True's Diary Describes Confrontation," *San Antonio Express-News*, March 15, 1999, section 01 A.

Sheridan, Thomas E., and Thomas H. Naylor, editors. 1979. *Raramuri, A Tarahumara Colonial Chronicle, 1607–1791*. Flagstaff, Ariz.: Northland Press.

Singh, J.A.L., and Robert M. Zingg. 1942. *Wolf-Children and Feral Man*. Denver: University of Denver.

Spicer, Ed H. 1961. "Types of Contact and Processes of Change," in *Perspectives in American Indian Culture Change*. Chicago: University of Chicago Press.

———. 1962. *Cycles of Conquest*. Tucson: University of Arizona Press.

Taussig, Michael. 1977. "The Genesis of Capitalism Amongst a South American Peasantry: Devil's Labor and the Baptism of Money," *Comparative Studies in Society and History* 19(2): 130–55.

Valiñas, Leopoldo. 1994. "Transiciones Lingüistícas Mayores en el Occidente," in *Transformaciones Mayores en el Occidente de Mexico*, pp. 127–65. Guadalajara: University of Guadalajara.

Velázquez, María del Carmen. 1961. "Colotlán: Doble Frontera Contra los Bárbaros," *Cuadernos del Instituto de Historia, No. 3*. México, D.F.: Universidad Nacional Autónoma de México.

Weatherford, Jack. 1988. *Indian Givers*. New York: Fawcett Columbine.

Weigand, Phil C. 1969a. *Modern Huichol Ceramics*, Mesoamerican Studies No. 3. Carbondale: Southern Illinois University Museum.

———. 1969b. "The Role of an Indianized Mestizo in the 1950 Huichol Revolt," *Specialia* No. 1 (Inter-americana No. 1). Carbondale: Latin American Institute, Southern Illinois University.

———. 1972. *Co-operative Labor Groups in Subsistence Activities among the Huichol Indians*, Mesoamerican Studies No. 7. Carbondale: Southern Illinois University Museum.

———. 1975. "Possible References to La Quemada in Huichol Mythology," *Ethnohistory* 22(1): 15–20.

———. 1978. "Contemporary Social and Economic Structure," in *Art of the Huichol Indians*, pp. 101–15. Edited by K. Berrin and T. K. Seligman. New York: Harry N. Abrams, Inc.

———. 1979. "The Role of the Huichol Indians in the Revolutions of Western Mexico," *Proceedings of the Coast on Latin American Studies*, vol. 6: 167–76. Tempe: Arizona State University, Center for Latin American Studies.

———. 1981. "Differential Acculturation among the Huichol Indians," in *Themes of Indigenous Acculturation in Northwest Mexico*. Edited by P. C. Weigand and Thomas B. Hinton. Tucson: University of Arizona Press.

———. 1985. "Considerations on the Archaeology and Ethnohistory of the Mexicaneros, Tequales, Coras, Huicholes, and Caxcanes of Nayarit, Jalisco, and Zacatecas," in *Contributions to the Archaeology and Ethnohistory of Greater MesoAmerica*, pp. 126–87. Edited by William J. Folan. Carbondale: Southern Illinois University Press.

———. 1992a. *Ensayos sobre el Gran Nayar: Entre Huicholes, Coras y Tepehuanes*. El Colegio de Michoacán, INI, CEMCA.

———. 1992b. "Los Codices Prehispanicos de Teuchitlan," *El Occidental*, Guadalajara, May 31, 1992.

———. 1992c. "Ehécatl: ¿Primer Dios Supremo del Occidente?" in *Origen y desarrollo de la Civilización en el Occidente de México*, pp. 205–38. Edited by Brigitte Boehm de Lameiras and Phil C. Weigand. Zamora: El Colegio de Michoacán.

———. 1993. *Evolución de una Civilización Prehispanica: Arqueología de Jalisco, Nayarit y Zacatecas*. Zamora: El Colegio de Michoacán.

———. 2002. Personal communication, February 10, 2002.

Weigand, P. C., and M. S. Foster, editors. 1985. *The Archaeology of West and Northwest Mesoamerica*. Boulder: Westview Press.

Weigand, P. C., and Acelia Garcia de Weigand. 1996a. "Los Huicholes Antes de la Conquista Española." Paper presented at the meeting of the Mexican Society of Anthropology, Tepic, Nayarit, 1996.

———. 1996b. *Tenamaxtli and Guaxícar: Las Raíces Profundas de la Rebelión de Nueva Galicia*. Zamora and Guadalajara: El Colegio de Michoacán and La Secretaría de Cultura de Jalisco.

———. 2000. "Huichol Society before the Arrival of the Spanish," *Journal of the Southwest* 42(1): 13–36.

Winkelman, Michael. 2000. *Shamanism: The Neural Ecology of Consciousness and Healing*. Westport, Conn.: Bergin and Garvey.

Zingg, Emma. 1996. Personal communication, February 18, 1996.

Zingg, Robert M. n.d. *Huichol Mythology*. Original unpublished manuscript.

———. 1937. *A Reconstruction of Uto-Aztekan History*. Chicago: The University of Chicago Libraries (private edition of Zingg's Ph.D. dissertation of 1933).

———. 1938. *The Huichols: Primitive Artists*. New York: G. E. Stechert.

———. 1940. "Feral Man and Extreme Cases of Isolation," *American Journal of Psychology*, no. 53.

———. 1941. "India's Wolf-Children: Two Human Infants Reared by Wolves," *Scientific American* (March).

About the Author

Robert Zingg was born in Colorado in 1900 and died of a heart attack in 1957 in El Paso, Texas. After earning his doctorate in anthropology at the University of Chicago, he completed one year of ethnographic research with Huichols living in and around Tuxpan de Bolaños, Jalisco. His Huichol research in 1934 yielded a massive collection of artifacts, hundreds of still photographs, nearly fifty minutes of film footage of several ceremonies, and the corpus of Huichol myths, published here in their entirety for the first time in English. This is the most comprehensive collection of Huichol myths ever published. Zingg was the first American anthropologist to study the Huichol and the first anthropologist to film their ceremonies.

About the Editors

Jay C. Fikes has been researching and writing extensively about Huichol shamans, myths, rituals, and ethnohistory since 1976. He is presently recording myths and filming rituals in Tuxpan, the Huichol community where anthropologist Robert Zingg did fieldwork in 1934. He produced a documentary film, *Huichol Indian Ceremonial Cycle*, based on Zingg's filming of Huichol ceremonies.

His participation in Native American Church ceremonies (in which peyote is revered as a teacher and consumed as a sacrament) and lobbying for legislation to protect religious freedom resulted in a highly acclaimed book, *Reuben Snake, Your Humble Serpent* (Clear Light Publishers, 1996). He continues to research, write, and teach about American Indian political and religious issues.

After completing his doctorate at the University of Michigan in 1985, he taught at several universities. Since 1998, he has taught courses on shamanism, symbolism, and visual anthropology as a professor in the anthropology department at Yeditepe University in Istanbul. His achievements are listed in several reference books including *Who's Who in American Education* (6th edition).

Phil C. Weigand is a research professor at the Centro de Estudios Antropológicos of the Colegio de Michoacán and a member of Mexico's National Research System. Since completing his doctoral dissertation, an analysis of cooperative labor organization in the *comunidad indígena* of San Sebastián Teponhuaxtlán (Southern Illinois University, 1970), his work has expanded to embrace the archaeology and ethnohistory of western Mexico as a whole. He has published some 150 articles (of which 20 are currently in press) and 21 books.

Phil Weigand, along with Acelia García de Weigand, is currently excavating and restoring the large Late Formative and Early Classic precinct of concentric circular architecture at Teuchitlán, Jalisco. He was awarded the Premio Jalisco for scientific research in 2000.

Acelia García de Weigand obtained her MA in Art History from the State University of New York in 1985. She has essays in Phil Weigand's book *Estudios históricos y culturales sobre los Huicholes* (Universidad de Guadalajara, 2000). She is coauthor, along with Phil Weigand, of the book *Tenamaxtli y Guaxicar: Los raices profundos de la rebelión de Nueva Galicia* (Colegio de Michoacán and the Secretaría de Cultura del Estado de Jalisco, 1996). She has also authored and coauthored thirty-three articles and chapters concerning West Mexico's archaeology and ethnohistory.